VOLUME I

LATIN

AMERICAN

URBAN

RESEARCH

LATIN AMERICAN URBAN RESEARCH

Series Editors

FRANCINE F. RABINOVITZ, *University of California at Los Angeles*
FELICITY M. TRUEBLOOD, *University of Florida*

International Advisory Board

MARVIN ALISKY, *Arizona State University*
HARLEY L. BROWNING, *University of Texas*
JOHN FRIEDMANN, *University of California at Los Angeles*
JORGE HARDOY, *Centro de Estudios Urbanos y Regionales* (CEUR), *Buenos Aires*
YVES LELOUP, *Institut des Hautes Etudes de l'Amérique Latine, Paris*
DIOGO LORDELLO DE MELLO, *Instituto Brasileiro de Administração Municipal, Rio de Janeiro*
WILLIAM MANGIN, *Syracuse University*
RICHARD M. MORSE, *Yale University*
T. LYNN SMITH, *University of Florida*
FRANCIS VIOLICH, *University of California at Berkeley*

This series is published in cooperation with
The Center for Latin American Studies, University of Florida

Volume Editors

I (1970) Francine F. Rabinovitz and Felicity M. Trueblood
II (1971) Guillermo Geisse and Jorge E. Hardoy

Latin American Urban Research

VOLUME I

FRANCINE F. RABINOVITZ
and
FELICITY M. TRUEBLOOD
Editors

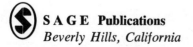

S A G E Publications
Beverly Hills, California

For information address
SAGE PUBLICATIONS, INC.
275 South Beverly Drive
Beverly Hills, California 90212

International Standard Book Number 0-8039-0062-7

Library of Congress Catalog Card No. 78-103483

FIRST PRINTING

ACKNOWLEDGMENTS

The editors gratefully acknowledge the contributions of the Center for Latin American Studies of the University of Florida, Gainesville, and its director, Dr. William E. Carter, to the publication of this series. Charles J. Savio participated actively in every stage of this volume, and J. Selwyn Hollingsworth aided in the preparation of the bibliography and other tasks. Roberta W. Solt was particularly helpful in assisting the editors.

Francine F. Rabinovitz
Felicity M. Trueblood

CONTENTS

**Part IV. POLICY PROBLEMS: THE CONSEQUENCES OF
              URBANIZATION**

**Appendix. URBAN STUDIES CENTERS IN
              LATIN AMERICA   *305***

VOLUME I

LATIN

AMERICAN

URBAN

RESEARCH

Chapter 1

INTRODUCTION: LATIN AMERICAN URBAN RESEARCH—1970

Francine F. Rabinovitz, Felicity M. Trueblood and Charles J. Savio

In recent years, there has been a vast increase in urban-oriented research related to the underlying social, economic and institutional forces shaping the urban environment of Latin America, the consequences of accelerated urbanization, and strategies for directing it. The existence of this publication is itself a reflection of this growth in concern. While it may be confidently said that urban development in Latin America is no longer a "lost" world to the social scientist, it may not be said with equal confidence that it is a well—or comprehensively—developed area of study. Therefore, rather than a synthesis of what has been done in the field, this inaugural volume of our annual series is a sampling of recent writing on selected aspects of Latin American urban development.

The studies in this volume were chosen to represent what we believe to be four major themes around which much of the significant current work on Latin American cities clusters. The areas of greatest current interest appear to be: (1) Urban migration and marginality: (2) Urban culture or values and norms; (3) Government institutions and decision-making in urban areas, formal and informal; and (4) Policy problems in Latin American urban areas, particularly those involving planning, housing, and the consequences of accelerated urbanization for national policy.

It is hoped that this volume will point up some of the major directions of existing studies and questions which recent research has opened for investigation. We shall then be better able to see what questions have already been answered, what gaps remain, and where the greatest potential for future research based on existing knowledge currently lies.

This introduction is an attempt to place the volume's contents in the context of current writing on Latin American urban development. In the interest of parsimony, we mention in this volume's bibliography (Chapter 2) primarily works not cited by contributing authors, and appearing in Latin American periodicals, or fugitive materials, available from January, 1968 to approximately August, 1969. Readers seeking syntheses of existing work prior to 1968 are urged to consult Richard M. Morse, "Recent Research on Latin American Urbanization: A Selective Survey with Commentary," *Latin American Research Review* (Autumn, 1965); Francine F. Rabinovitz, Felicity M. Trueblood and Charles J. Savio, *Latin American Political Systems in an Urban Setting: A Preliminary Bibliography* (Gainesville: Center for Latin American Studies, University of Florida, January, 1967); and Denton R. Vaughan, "Urbanization in Twentieth Century Latin America: A Working Bibliography" (Austin: Institute for Latin American Studies, Population Research Center, University of Texas, 1969). Several of the contributing authors also provide extensive citations to and comments on the literature in particular subject areas.

Any selection based on a choice of major themes is a presumptuous venture. The risk is run of omitting important research areas which for unexplained reasons manage to slip through the net established by editors and advisors. We apologize in advance for such omissions, and urge those whose area of interest has been slighted to make us aware of oversights by providing bibliographic citations, research notes, articles, and commentaries. Our greatest hope for this series is that it will, as part of the editorial process, become a communications network through which members of different disciplines interested in Latin American urban phenomena can become aware of each other's research and opinions.

CURRENT RESEARCH: FOUR MAJOR THEMES

(1) Urban Migration and Marginality

The most marked surge in the study of urban phenomena in Latin America appears to be investigation of the nature of the population which has migrated to the city. Pre-1965 research on Latin American urbanization was, on the whole, heavily weighted toward what has been labelled "the festering-sore-bleeding-heart" approach (Mangin, 1967) to the study of marginal settlement. Authors (Haar, 1963; Shulman, 1966; Burnett and Johnson, 1968: 519) suggested inhabitants were trapped in slums, that their growing frustration and alienation were manifested in popular support for aggressive radical movements which voiced mistrust of government and hatred for the dominant classes, that this would lead to political instability, and that a solution might revolve around eradication of blighted migrant settlements. Of course, there were some early efforts to juxtapose positive outcomes against negative by authors including Oscar Lewis (1952); John Turner (1966); Lauchlin Currie (1965); and Richard Morse (1965). In 1967, Latin Americanists were presented with two valuable works specifically aimed at correcting the negative view. The first is a collection of papers given at a conference at Cornell University of which the objective was to focus on the positive aspects of the city in the process of modernization (Beyer, 1967). The second was a review of the literature on marginal settlements in Latin America, which depicted squatter communities as involving a process of social reconstruction through popular initiative (Mangin, 1967).

In this volume, contributing authors explore four aspects of the migration process: patterns of rural-to-urban movement, intra-urban migration, the political and economic consequences of migration for the individual migrant, and the macroeconomic impact of migration. There is a surprising amount of congruence in these studies. All seem to continue in the "optimistic" tradition in that they suggest, in different ways, the inappropriateness of various mythologies which highlight the negative impact of migration.

Browning and Feindt, in their article, "The Social and Economic Context of Migration to Monterrey, Mexico" (Chapter 3), examine the process of migration to Monterrey, Mexico, substantiating with their findings the charge that many timeworn conceptions about factors influencing the decision to migrate, the composition of migratory groups and the kinds of contacts and forms of assistance used on arrival, no longer jibe with reality. Browning and Feindt argue that standard Western conceptions of "migrant man" are erroneous because they treat the migrant in isolation from his social group. The authors emphasize the importance of "split migration" as a cushioning mechanism. However, both they and Bruce Herrick, in his article, "Urbanization and Urban Migration in Latin America: An Economist's View" (Chapter 4), continue to be impressed with the degree to which economic factors explain migration, although the group structure itself influences the expression of economic relations.

William L. Flinn, in "Rural and Intra-Urban Migration in Colombia: Two Case Studies in Bogotá" (Chapter 5), traces both rural-urban and intra-urban movements in two *barrios* in Bogotá, and comments on the spatial pattern created by migration in the city. It is of interest that while Browning and Feindt discovered that more than half of those migrants to Monterrey whose origin was rural came in one direct move, Flinn finds similar results but notes that stepwise migration often takes place between generations.[1] This could be, as Wayne Cornelius notes in his article, only an indication that different types of migration processes do exist. But a comparison of the two articles points up one common methodological problem in making comparisons among studies of urban areas in Latin America. A series of assumptions must be made as to whether Bogotá and Monterrey themselves are likely or unlikely to have comparable migration patterns. We must also account for differences caused in findings by the fact that the operational definition of 'urban" is variable.

Flinn, for example, considers 2,000 inhabitants as the dividing line between rural and urban, and he is concerned with migration to a shantytown on the periphery of the city, not to the entire city itself. Many of the arguments about myths versus reality may well be confused by the use of a variety of different operational terms, or the study of cities or suburbs of essentially different types.[2]

A special type of migration not emphasized by contributing authors but receiving considerable comment in current literature is the invasion, in which, practically overnight, private or public land is taken over by the land hungry.[3] Several studies have noted recently that invaders are from the inner city, and stressed the desire "to get ahead" exhibited by these "consolidators."[4] Investigations of the behavior of the invasion leader or *poblador* are rare, although inventiveness and ingenuity have been attributed to them. However, findings on the relatively higher status of persons who decide to leave the center and stake a claim on land at the periphery, as well as comments attesting to the independent nature of these *paracaidistas,* provide a picture of mid-twentieth-century Latin American *invasores* which begins to sound like that of U.S. homesteaders in the nineteenth century. As Richard Morse has observed, current pictures of the *invasores* make them seem to be fulfilling, in a roundabout way, Alberdi's famous dictum, *gobernar es poblar.*

Another common focus, not pursued in detail by contributors, is that concerning the dynamics of *barrio* life itself. One of the most important additions to Latin American urban literature in the past year, Talton Ray's book, *The Politics of the Barrios of Venezuela,* describes in great detail the environment of *barrio* dwellers, as well as illustrating the character of land invasions, attempts at political organization and the role of *barrios* in national development. Many recent articles on this topic seem also to belong to what we have called the "optimistic" school of thought about migration and marginal settlement. The message transmitted is that the *favelados* are pioneers, and indeed, in some cases, almost flower children.[5] One is reminded of John Turner's emphasis on the freedoms available to squatters the world over: freedom of community selection, of budgeting one's own resources and of shaping one's own environment (Turner, 1968a,b). Writers have stressed the integrating role of social organizations within the *favela* as well, and have paid particular attention to the *puesto* or corner grocery store, and the *centro de macumba,* or spiritual medium's house (Valladares, 1968). The policy projection from such studies is not in the direction of support for *leyes de erradicación.* Authors tend to regard such projects as destroying genuine *participación de comunidad* which exists among *villeros,* and which cannot be restored through courses on the subect at relocation sites.[6]

A separate but related theme concerns the consequences of migration and settlement in marginal locales. Some authors have been concerned with the impact of migration on mental health (Mangin, 1968: 546–555; Rotondo, 1961: 249–257). Others have been concerned with the impact of migration on urban services, particularly on housing and sanitation (Turner, 1968a). In this volume, Wayne Cornelius (Chapter 6) undertakes a comprehensive review of findings about the consequences of migration for political behavior at the individual level. Cornelius tends to cast his lot with the "optimists," attributing the incongruity between prior expectations of alienation and radicalization and current research findings to an overreliance in part on urban theory developed without reference to Latin American phenomena. Cornelius also makes a methodological point: he argues for a combined anthropological-survey approach, rather than a strategy of "borrowing-and-testing" theories developed in more advanced areas of social science. One of the most striking findings in the literature he reviews is the indication that once the rudimentary needs of *barrio* dwellers are taken care of, their zeal for politics declines. Informal arrangements and associations of considerable strength remain, however. Pratt has recently interpreted this not as an indication of the low potential for organizing the bulk of *barrio* dwellers, whom he finds relatively sophisticated in trading votes with governments for legal recognition, services and police protection, but as attributable to their feeling that national politics has no relevance for them (Pratt, 1968).

An alternative focus in analyzing the consequences of the migration process has to do with the impact of migration on the city and the nation involved, as well as on the individual. In this volume, Bruce Herrick reviews in economic terms the causes of individual migration decisions and comments also on the possible consequences of migration for the urban and national economy. Herrick finds individual migration decisions rational under a "rate-of-return" hypothesis, but he also stresses that benefits to individuals may not be reproduced as positive results at the system level.

Other studies have investigated the social consequences of migration both for individuals and for national modernization.[7] To date, however, very few seem to look at the interaction of the nature of the city and the characteristics of the migrant or migration process. As Cornelius emphasizes, in the area of migration and marginal settler behavior, the interaction of migrants and migration attributes with city attributes is one of the fields that is least well explored.

(2) Urban Culture—Values and Norms

Richard Morse, in his comprehensive review of recent research on "São Paulo: Case Study of a Latin American Metropolis" (Chapter 7), continues the dialogue on the impact of migration by discussing the innovative responses urban settlers have made under the pressures of city life in the form of clientage and secessionist associations, and the national political role of the urban poor. Morse also adds, however, what we regard as a second important theme in current Latin American urban research and writing: an emphasis on the exploration of the value system or set of norms which a city may possess, and the role that city's cultural traditions play in relation to national or regional orientations.[8] In emphasizing the uniqueness of São Paulo, Morse also raises the larger issue of the extent to which cultural values are shared among industrial cities or are accompanied by stylistic differences sufficient to cause structural variations even in cities of this type.

In most cases, empirical work on urban culture, norms, and values in Latin America is just beginning, yet, there is a surprising amount of attention currently being given to the subjective orientations and complex of attitudes held by individuals and groups living in cities in Latin America. A common cultural theme concerns the opposing ways in which Anglos and Latin Americans view cities themselves (see, for example, Dallal, 1969; Morse, 1965; and Mangin, 1967). Another concerns the nature of rural or national values and their impact on action in an urban environment.[9] We are beginning also to obtain sample surveys which seek to tap the attitudinal structures of individual urban residents and elites (See D. Miller, 1968; Kahl, 1968; Cleaves, 1969; Karst and Schwartz, 1968; Goldrich *et al.*, 1967–1968). With the exception of studies linking values and the migration process, research seems currently to be emphasizing description of values and norms, with fewer studies specifically aimed at relating attitudinal variables to independent variables such as urban development levels.[10]

(3) Government Institutions and Decision-Making

Formal and Informal. A third major focus for Latin American urban-oriented research involves the forms and functioning of community and city political organizations and activities. Concerns today range from the basic effort to catalogue existing formal provisions for municipal government in Latin America, and studies of specific decisions or decision-making bodies in Latin American cities, to analyses of the distribution of power in areas or institutions.[11]

Roland Ebel, in his discussion, "The Decision-Making Process in San Salvador" (Chapter 8), approaches the subject from both the institutional and issue perspectives. His unit of analysis is the city itself. As Ebel points out, municipalities may have ambiguous juridical positions in Latin America and there is difficulty in disentangling local from national phenomena, especially when dealing with primate cities. Ebel chooses the municipal level, however, because he believes the entire political system bears down upon this stratum. But he conceives of the city's political system not as consisting merely of a municipal arena but also as being part of a "national municipal system." By implication, he is suggesting that cross-polity analysis is needed at the urban level, but at the same time saying that it cannot be done, in Latin America, without considerable reference to the larger political systems within which urban governments now operate.

Ebel's two case studies in San Salvador, one of municipal tax reform and the other of provision of city services, serve admirably to demonstrate the dynamics of decision-making in a Latin American city. That generalizations may not be easily made from this case (El Salvador, the nation, is small; San Salvador, the capital, is relatively large and the opposition party controls local political power) should not obscure the similarity to findings in studies of urban neighborhoods. For example, the discovery of the *ad hoc* nature of political organization at the neighborhood level is somewhat paralleled by Ebel's finding for the municipality that usually only immediate tangible ends arouse those whose function it is to articulate interests. Ebel also strengthens the evidence indicating the small number of persons actually involved in the decision-making process. Patronage is the name of the game, and with the small but growing exceptions provided by the press and radio, a personalistic route must be traveled to obtain want satisfaction.

Ebel looks at urban decision-making as a kind of intervening process between the national system and public policies. As Cornelius points out in his article in the present volume, one of the neglected areas of investigation in research on Latin American cities concerns the effect of different power distributions and political forms on differential responses to urban problems. Ebel's study reflects the fact that emphasis in political science has shifted from the way officeholders are supposed to carry out their responsibilities to the way party and official leaders actually do. We still have little to say, however, about how decision-making variations are related to the way problems are perceived or services provided.

(4) Policy Problems

Despite the hiatus in studies linking how decision-making processes operate to what kinds of decisions are reached, there is a rich and growing literature on urban policy problems in Latin American cities. John Friedmann suggests, in his article, "Urban-Regional Policies for National Development in Chile" (Chapter 9), the parameters of many of the compelling problems involved in the policy-oriented analysis of Latin American urbanization, listing eight issue areas to which he believes policy planners should now turn their attention. A prominent candidate is that of housing problems. Friedmann stresses that housing should not be considered a welfare expenditure, since not only is the worker's mental state improved when he is happily housed, but other benefits are possible:

the opportunity to carry on small industry at home and the chance to accumulate goods. Moreover, construction activity is stimulated and its beneficial effects circulate throughout the economy.

Many observers have recently examined the related question of what form housing should take when it can be made available. John C. Turner (1968b) for example, has criticized past efforts as being addressed only to the physical aspect of man's surroundings. Building standards should not be rigidly adhered to; even a shell would suffice which inhabitants could improve at their leisure. More importantly, attention should be paid to the location of the dwelling in relation to the occupant's place of work. Life in a *ranchito* near one's place of work is often regarded as more desirable than living in government housing across the city.

Many of the housing and land use planning problems which Friedmann (1968) stresses have been treated both by observers in the United States and Latin America (see, for example, Matos Mar, 1968: Part III; Oldman *et al.*, 1967; Uribe, 1966 and 1967; Ornelas, forthcoming; Dallal, 1969; Hardoy, 1968; Rodwin *et al.*, 1969). However, most of the social science literature which addresses itself to urbanization in Latin America from a national perspective deals with the impact of urban growth on national development,[12] rather than with national policies for meeting urban problems (see, however, de Mello, 1968, and Geisse, 1967). While debate over whether the rapid growth of cities is helping to "modernize" Latin American nations is far from settled, *cross*-national development investigations have proved rather difficult to interpret accurately in isolation from studies of within-nation relationships, as Wayne Cornelius emphasizes for the case of theories on the association of urbanization with participation.[13]

Friedmann's tack is not to correlate urban to national development but instead to advocate the solution of urban policy problems facing decision makers through linkage of national economic planning to a concrete spatial dimension, the "urban-regional frame." Elsewhere, Friedmann has argued that rapid urban growth is desirable because it speeds up modernization, but the burden of the argument here is on how to achieve advantageous urbanization patterns. Friedmann (1968) believes urbanization can come from opportunely placed "core regions" and "social development poles." The process is not without difficulties, but the "crisis of inclusion"—the troublesome discrepancy between urbanization and economic growth which ensues—can be handled through formation of a government strong enough to carry out reforms necessary for incorporating excluded sectors. Friedmann here indicates that in Chile regional development planning has now become sufficiently institutionalized to be an irreversible fact, but acceptance of the urban-regional strategy actually implies a major overhaul of public politics. It is important to recognize that national policy planning involves not only developing plans and programs, and a process of converting the plan into a series of steps which will make it a reality, but also a concrete idea of what the political preconditions of implementing the plan will be.[14]

FUTURE RESEARCH

The Need for Notions About Types of Cities

Each of the contributors to this volume sets out his own priorities for future research. It is striking that one of the most conspicuous themes in need of attention is an analysis of the types or kinds of national urbanization patterns, cities, and subunits, across which variations in other patterns—be they migration, norms, governmental decision-making or policy problems—may occur. Few authors currently state their rationale for study site selection, much less relate it to the purpose or findings of their investigation.

There are some fascinating hints at possible bases for typologizing urban experiences in the existing literature. Richard Morse (1964) has suggested the Weberian paradigm of the patrimonial society plus the Catholic way of life as a way to assign Latin American urban societies to a general family. Using national urbanization as the unit, Lowdon Wingo (1967) has provided a sophisticated analysis of types of population trends within Latin America. Leo Schnore (1965) has given us a summary of literature indicating spatial structure patterns within Latin American cities. Wagley and Harris (1965) provide us with a typology within cities of subcultures. Wayne Cornelius here notes the need to typologize kinds of marginal settlements. Other typologizing notions are contained in numerous works, ranging from those which deny the rural-urban dichotomy to those which use a specific characteristic to construe phenomena as urban.[15] For example, Luis Unikel, in this volume (Chapter 10) discusses the distribution and growth of the Mexican urban population and the process of urbanization in Mexico in comparison with other nations. Unikel identifies the structure of Mexican cities according to size and primacy principles, and the level of urbanization by an index geared to the percentage of population in localities in different size classes. He also describes the process of urbanization from the perspective of regional units. His urbanization index avoids the fallacy of seeing "urban" growth and changes in the percentage of population in cities as identical. But does a decrease in primacy in fact mean greater capabilities for serving regional needs, as Unikel hypothesizes? Does size in fact differentiate between cities in Mexico or other countries on other characteristics? Are there dimensions other than primacy which might make a more fruitful basis for typologizing Latin American cities? Is the level of urbanization a meaningful research statistic for analyses of national development, in view of the marked regional variations in its actual expression? At the moment we are seemingly unable to say. A firm foundation for future Latin American urban research clearly requires the development of more explicit notions of relevant types of cities, neighborhood or urbanization patterns on dimensions along which urban experiences can be classified for different purposes.

The Need to Investigate the Performance of Urban Jurisdictions

Charles Anderson (1967: 203) has noted that in studies of Latin American national affairs "although much has been written on what the state *must do* to stimulate development, very little has been said, except critically, about what the state *has done* in the name of stimulating economic and social change." This applies equally well to urban research. A large task remains in gathering and synthesizing basic data on who lives in urban areas and what their fertility, nutritional, mortality, employment, migrational and residential profiles are like. Even less is known about the patterns of policy emerging in the cities of Latin America and their relation to political and demographic conditions. Questions of what the city is and what functions it performs today in Latin America, and of whom or what it serves are unanswered both at the philosophical and the quantitative level. Those interested in the human resource potential of Latin American cities have argued that we know more about certain Andean villages than we do about Buenos Aires. Soon, one suspects, we will know more about the attitudes of urban residents and the process of decision-making in cities than about the actual operation of Latin American cities as instruments of modernization or traditionalism.

The Need for Collaborative Effort

Another great shortcoming of which the editors became painfully aware during the editorial process had to do not with substantive problems but with the difficulty of painting a picture of urban research circa 1970 which adequately reflects work being done in the United States, Europe and Latin America, largely from a base within the United States. Lloyd Rodwin *et al.* (1969) writing on collaborative planning in the context of the joint efforts of a U.S. and a Venezuelan group to plan a "new city" in Venezuela, has shown how subtle differences in values and frames of reference affected views of events, strategies and policies. Inevitably, perception of "major" research is colored by disciplinary training, nationality and distance from sites of major interest. In consequence, *Latin American Urban Research* (Volume II) will reflect not only the progression during the year, but will focus on Latin American and European perceptions of urban development, through the joint editorship of Guillermo Geisse, of the Centro Interdisciplinario de Desarrollo Urbano y Regional

(CIDU) in Chile and Jorge E. Hardoy, of the Centro de Estudios Urbanos y Regionales (CEUR) in Argentina. In view of the repeated warnings of our contributors about overreliance on North American models for explaining Latin American urban development, it is hoped the application of a Latin American or European viewpoint, based in different cultural traditions as well as on different experiences of disciplinary emphasis, will help us to move toward a more truly useful mode of analysis for comparative urban research on Latin America.

To repeat, if research efforts are to be at all meaningful, attempts must be made in the future to coordinate, evaluate and synthesize, hypothesize and test, and, yes, even speculate as to ultimate utility and application. In this, as in everything, one simply begins. This volume, therefore, is a modest attempt at so doing. And with the cooperation of readers and researchers, it can be much more.

NOTES

1. The Flinn and Browning and Feindt articles form part of a growing series of studies on the migration process and less commonly on spatial patterns. In addition to those items cited by contributing authors, see Balán (1969); Cardona-Gutiérrez (1969); and Unikel (1966). The small town and the intermediary sections of the migration process remain relatively unexplored, but see Casimir (1969) and Margulis (1968).

2. There are many discussions of the problems of delimiting an "urban" area. For recent examples, see McGranahan (1966); United Nations Bureau of Social Affairs (1966). The United Nations has at present declared itself unwilling to impose a standard. See U.N. Statistical Office (1967: 63, 298).

3. For descriptions of invasions see Flinn (1968); Mangin (1963); Powelson (1964).

4. In addition to articles cited by contributing authors, see Dietz (1969); Proyecto de Acuerdo presentado al Honorable Cabildo por el Consejal Germán Samper (1966: 132); Turner (1968b).

5. See, in addition to articles cited by contributors, Parisse (1969).

6. See, for example, Romano de Tobar (1968).

7. See, in particular, Matos Mar (1968).

8. Another extremely provocative essay which also discusses both marginal settlement patterns and differences in urban value systems is Leeds (1968).

9. See Seckinger (1968); D. Miller (1968) has applied the rating scales reported in this article to establish national norms in Buenos Aires and Lima as well as in cities in Spain, England and the United States. Also see Stoddard (1968: especially 7-14).

10. Some exceptions include J. Selwyn Hollingsworth, "Relationship between Value Orientations and Stages of Development in Three Colombian Cities," (forthcoming Ph.D. dissertation, University of Florida, Gainesville; Hollingsworth is attempting to test the hypothesis that the greater the social and economic development of a city, the more modern the value profiles of individuals who are there, by administering items from scales developed by Florence Kluckholn to *dirigentes* in Medellín, Cali, and Popayán, Colombia); Thomas Lutz," Political socialization and the developing political subcultures among urban squatters in Panama City, Guayaquil and Lima: Comparisons of attitudes in organized and unorganized squatter settlements," (forthcoming Ph.D. dissertation, Georgetown University, Washington,

D.C.; Lutz considers the relationships between political attitudes and the types of neighborhood organizations in squatter settlements; see T. Lutz, "Developing political subcultures among Panamian squatters," mimeo., 1967; "A Comparative View of Squatter Settlements in Three Latin American Cities," mimeo., 1968; "Some Aspects of Community Organization and Activity in the Squatter Settlements of Panama City," mimeo., 1968); Wayne Cornelius, "Political Correlates of Migrant Assimilation in Mexican Urban Environments," (forthcoming Ph.D. dissertation, Stanford University; Cornelius examines the interaction of attitudes and characteristics of settlement zones in areas in Mexico City and Monterrey. He is also concerned with migrant evaluations of governmental outputs at the local and national levels and the relationships between migrant attributes and government efforts at service provision in migrant zones).

11. For institutional views, see Alisky (1968); Ivan Richardson, "Municipal Finance in Brazil: A Comparative View," mimeo., 1968, and part of a larger study of Metropolitan Rio which examines Guanabara and the thirteen *municípios* in the Greater Rio area; Rabinovitz (1968) for a premature summary of power structure studies. Decision-making analyses are rarer. See those by Fried (forthcoming).

12. See in particular the reports of the Jahuel Seminar devoted to this theme in Miller and Gakenheimer (1969). Harley Browning has considered the impact of urban population redistribution and growth from the perspective of national demography in Beyer (1967: 71–116). See also Benjamin Higgins, "Urbanization, Industrialization and Economic Development" in Beyer (1967:117–155). Bruce Herrick has specifically examined the impact in Chile of urbanization on economic development (1965); Rabinovitz has looked at the relationship of urbanization to national political variables (1969). On these themes see also Horowitz (1967); Quijano (1968); Germani (1968); Hardoy (1966); Hurtado (1966); Quijano (1966 and 1967); Neira (1963); Ramírez (1965).

13. For example, a recent study combining survey data with aggregate information available for five nations, including Mexico, indicates that, contrary to most expectations based on aggregate studies, there is no relationship between urban residence and political participation. The tendency for urbanization and political participation to covary is not because city dwellers are more active than country dwellers but is due to an ecological correlation phenomenon. See Nie *et al.* (1969).

14. On the relationship of regional and national urban planning and institutional change, see Wingo (1969) and J. Miller (1968).

15. The most famous typologizing notion is Robert Redfield's folk-urban typology commented upon by Lewis and Hauser in their contributions to Hauser and Schnore (1965: 481–517). A recent ambitious typologizing effort, which uses a factor analytic technique similar to that developed by C. A. Mosher and Wolf Scott for British towns, is applied to Mexican cities by Alschuler (1967).

REFERENCES

ALISKY, M. (1968) "Provision for municipal government in Latin American constitutions." *Public Affairs Bulletin* (University of Arizona) 7, No. 1.

ALSCHULER, L. (1967) Political Participation and Urbanization in Mexico. Ph.D. dissertation, Northwestern University.

ANDERSON, C. W. (1967) *Politics and Economic Change in Latin America: The Governing of Restless Nations.* Princeton: D. Van Nostrand.

BALÁN, J. (1969) "Migrant native socioeconomic differences in Latin American cities: a structural analysis." *Latin American Research Review* 4, No. 1 (Spring): 3–51.

BEYER, G. H., ed. (1967) *The Urban Explosion in Latin America.* Ithaca: Cornell University Press.

BURNETT, B. and K. JOHNSON (1968) *Political Forces in Latin America: Dimensions of the Quest for Stability.* Belmont, Calif.: Wadsworth Publishing.

CARDONA-GUTIÉRREZ, R. (1969) "Migración, urbanización, y marginalidad." Pp. 63–87 in *Urbanización y Marginalidad.* Bogotá: Asociación Colombiana de Facultades de Medicina.

CASIMIR, J. (1967) "Duas cidades no nordeste do Brasil: sua estructura social e sua importância para a planificação regional." *América Latina* 10, No. 1 (January–March).

CLEAVES, P. S. (1969) *Factors Influencing the Chilean Municipal Councilman's Orientation Toward His Office.* Berkeley: University of California (mimeo.).

CURRIE, L. (1965) *Una política urbana para los países en desarrollo.* Bogotá: Tercer Mundo.

DALLAL, A. (1969) "Urbanismo y planificación." *Cuadernos Americanos* 28 (January–February): 107–118.

DIETZ, H. (1969) "Urban squatter settlements in Peru: a case history and analysis." *Journal of Inter-American Studies* 11 (July): 353–370.

FLINN, W. L. (1968) "The process of migration to a shantytown in Bogotá, Colombia." *Inter-American Economic Affairs* 22 (Autumn): 77–88.

FRIED, R. (forthcoming) "Mexico City." In W. Robson (ed.) *Great Cities of the World.* 3rd ed. London: Allen & Unwin.

FRIEDMANN, J. (1968) "The strategy of deliberate urbanization." *Journal of the American Institute of Planners* 34 (November): 364–373.

GEISSE, G. (1967) *Asentamientos urbanos e integración nacional.* Santiago: CIDU y PLANDES.

GERMANI, G. (1968) "¿Pertenece América Latina al tercer mundo?" *Aportes* 10 (October): 6–32.

GOLDRICH, D., R. PRATT and C. R. SHULLER (1967–1968) "The political integration of lower class urban settlement in Chile and Peru." *Studies in Comparative International Development* 3, No. 1: 3–22.

HAAR, C. M. (1963) "Latin America's troubled cities." *Foreign Affairs* 41 (April): 536–549.

HARDOY, J. (1968) *Urban Planning in Pre-Columbian America.* New York: Braziller.

———— (1966) "El rol de la ciudad en la modernización de América Latina." *Cuadernos* (Buenos Aires) No. 6.

HAUSER, P. and L. F. SCHNORE, eds. (1965) *The Study of Urbanization.* New York: John Wiley.

HERRICK, B. (1965) *Urban Migration and Economic Development in Chile.* Cambridge: M.I.T. Press.

HIGGINS, B. (1967) "Urbanization, industrialization and economic development." Pp. 117–155 in G. Beyer (ed.) *The Urban Explosion in Latin America.* Ithaca: Cornell University Press.

HOROWITZ, I. L. (1967) "Electoral politics, urbanization, and social development in Latin America." Pp. 215–254 in G. Beyer (ed.) *The Urban Explosion in Latin America.* Ithaca: Cornell University Press.

HURTADO, C. (1966) *Concentración de población y desarrollo económico: el caso chileno.* Instituto de Economía, Universidad de Chile.

KAHL, J. A. (1968) *The Measurement of Modernism: A Study of Values in Brazil and Mexico.* Austin: University of Texas Press.

KARST, K. and M. SCHWARTZ (1968) *The Internal Norms and Sanctions in Ten Barrios in Caracas.* Los Angeles: University of California (mimeo.).

LEEDS, A. (1968) "The anthropology of cities: some methodological issues." Pp. 31–47 in E. M. Eddy (ed.) *Urban Anthropology: Research Perspectives and Strategies.* Athens, Georgia: University of Georgia Press.

LEWIS, O. (1952) "Urbanization without breakdown: a case study." *Scientific Monthly* 75: 31–41.

MCGRANAHAN, D. (1966) "Social research in the U. N." In R. L. Merritt and S. Rokkan (eds.) *Comparing Nations: The Use of Quantitative Data in Cross National Research.* New Haven: Yale University Press.

MANGIN, W. (1967) "Latin American squatter settlements: a problem and a solution." *Latin American Research Review* 2, No. 3 (Summer).

———— (1965) "Mental health and migration to cities: a Peruvian case." Pp. 546–555 in D. B. Heath and N. Adams (eds.) *Contemporary Cultures and Societies of Latin America.* New York: Random House.

———— (1963) "Account of a Lima invasion." *Architectural Design* 33 (August): 368–369.

MARGULIS, M. (1968) *Migración y marginalidad en la sociedad Argentina.* Buenos Aires: Editorial Paidós.

MATOS MAR, J. (1968) *Urbanización y barriadas en América del Sur.* Lima: Instituto de Estudios Peruanos.

MELLO, D. L. DE (1968) "Institucionalização das áreas metropolitanas." *Revista de Administração Municipal* 86 (January-February): 5–25.

MILLER, D. (1968) "The measurement of international patterns and norms: a tool for comparative research." *Southwestern Social Sciences Quarterly* 48 (March).

MILLER, J. (1968) "La política y la planificación." *Boletín Informativo de PLANDES* 26 (March-April).

MILLER, J. and R. A. GAKENHEIMER (1969) "The social sciences and urban development in Latin America." *America Behavioral Scientist* 12, No. 5 (May-June).

MORSE, R. M. (1965) "Recent research on Latin American urbanization: a selective survey with commentary." *Latin American Research Review* 1, No. 1 (Autumn): 35–75.

———— (1964) "The heritage of Latin America." Pp. 151–177 in L. Hartz (ed.) *The Founding of New Societies.* New York: Harcourt, Brace & World.

NEIRA, E. A. (1963) "¿Son las ciudades una forma de cristalización social?" *Cuadernos de la Sociedad Venezolana de Planificación* 1, No. 2.

NIE, N. H., G. B. POWELL and K. PREWITT (1969) "Social structure and political participation: development relationships." *American Political Science Review* 62, No. 2 (June): 361–378.

OLDMAN, O. et al. (1967) *Financing Urban Development in Mexico City: A Case Study of Property Tax, Land Use, Housing and Urban Planning.* Cambridge: Harvard University Press.

ORNELAS, C. (forthcoming) Land Tenure, Sanctions and Politization in Mexico City. Ph.D. dissertation, University of California, Riverside, Department of Political Science.

PARISSE, L. (1969) "A favela carioca: um mundo a ser descoberto." *Cadernos Brasileiros* 51 (January-February): 35–46.

POWELSON, J. P. (1964) "The land grabbers of Cali." *The Reporter* (January 16): 30–31.

PRATT, R. B. (1968) "Urbanization and the crisis of inclusion in Latin America: toward the political integration of the urban lower class." Pp. 99–125 in *Acta Final*. New Orleans: Twelfth Congreso Interamericano de Municipios.

Proyecto de acuerdo presentado al Honorable Cabildo por el Consejal Germán Samper (1966). In *Urbanización y marginalidad*. Bogotá: Asociación Colombiana de Facultades de Medicina.

QUIJANO, A. (1968) "Dependencia, cambio social y urbanización en Latinoamérica." *Revista Mexicana de Sociología* 30, No. 3 (July-September): 525–570.

——— (1967) *Urbanización y tendencias de cambio en la investigación del desarrollo urbano*. Santiago: CIDU.

——— (1966) *El proceso de urbanización en Latinoamérica*. Santiago: CEPAL (mimeo.).

RABINOVITZ, F. F. (1969) "Urban and political development in Latin America." In R. Daland (ed.) *Comparative Urban Research*. Beverly Hills, Calif.: Sage Publications.

——— (1968) "A review of community power research in Latin America." *Urban Affairs Quarterly* (March).

RAMÍREZ, G. P. (1965) "La urbanización y el cambio social en Colombia." *Revista de Agencias Sociales* (Puerto Rico) 4, No. 2 (June): 203–220.

RODWIN, L. et al. (1969) *Planning Urban Growth and Regional Development: The Experience of the Guayana Program of Venezuela*. Cambridge: M.I.T. Press.

ROMANO DE TOBAR, M. (1968) "El Buenos Aires de los 'villeros'" *Mundo Nuevo* 29 (November): 28–34.

ROTONDO, H. (1961) "Psychological and mental health problems of urbanization based on case studies in Peru." Pp. 249–257 in P. M. Hauser (ed.) *Urbanization in Latin America*. New York: UNESCO.

SCHNORE, L. F. (1965) "On the spatial structure of cities in the two Americas." Pp. 347–398 in P. Hauser and L. F. Schnore (eds.) *The Study of Urbanization*. New York: John Wiley.

SECKINGER, R. L. (1968) "Cultural aspects of local government in Brazil." In *Latinamericanist* (Gainesville: University of Florida) December 15.

SHULMAN, S. (1966) "Latin American shantytown." *New York Times Magazine* (January 16).

STODDARD, E. R. (1968) "Comparative structures and attitudes along the United States-Mexican border." Paper presented at the Conference on Urbanization of the United States-Mexican Border, June 15, El Paso, Texas.

TURNER, J. C. (1968a) "The squatter settlement: architecture that works." *Architectural Design* (August): 355–360.

——— (1968b) "Housing priorities, settlement patterns and urban development in modernizing countries." *Journal of the American Institute of Planners* 34, No. 6 (November): 354–363.

—— (1966) "A selected bibliography: uncontrolled urban settlement—problems and policies." Paper prepared for U.N. Centre for Housing, Building, and Planning and presented at the Interregional Seminar on Development Policies and Planning in Relation to Urbanization, Pittsburgh.

UNIKEL, L. (1966) "La urbanización en la zona metropolitana de la Ciudad de México." *Comercio Exterior* 16, No. 11 (November): 839–849.

U.N. Bureau of Social Affairs, Population Division (1966) "World urbanization trends 1920–60." Paper presented at the Interregional Seminar on Development Policies and Planning in Relation to Urbanization, Pittsburgh.

U.N. Statistical Office (1967) *Principles and Recommendations for the 1970 Census.* Series M, No. 44. New York: U.N. Statistical Office.

URIBE, P. (1967) *Tendencias y perspectivas de la política de vivienda en América Latina.* Santiago: CEPAL (mimeo.).

—— (1966) "Los factores estructurales del desarrollo y el problema de la vivienda en América Latina." *Boletín Económico de América Latina* 11, No. 2 (October).

VALLADARES, L. (1968) "Una favela por dentro." *Mundo Nuevo* 29 (November).

WAGLEY, C. and M. HARRIS (1965) "A typology of Latin American sub-cultures." Pp. 42–69 in D. B. Heath and R. N. Adams (eds.) *Contemporary Cultures and Societies of Latin America.* New York: Random House.

WINGO, L. (1969) *Latin American Urbanization: Plan or Process?* Reprint no. 75. Washington, D.C.: Resources for the Future, Inc., January.

—— (1967) "Recent patterns of urbanization among Latin American countries." *Urban Affairs Quarterly* 2, No. 3 (March): 81–110.

Chapter 2

BIBLIOGRAPHY, 1968–1969

AGULLA, J. C. (1968) *Eclipse de una aristocracia: una investigación sobre las élites dirigentes de la ciudad de Córdoba.* Córdoba, Argentina: Ediciones Libera.

ALERS, J. O. and R. P. APPELBAUM (1968) "La migración en el Peru: un inventario de proposiciones." *Estudios de Población y Desarrollo* (Lima) 1, No. 4 (serie original No. 2).

ALISKY, M. (1968) "Provisions for municipal government in Latin American constitutions." *Public Affairs Bulletin* (University of Arizona). 7, No. 1.

ALSCHULER, L. (1967) Political Participation and Urbanization in Mexico. Ph.D. dissertation, Northwestern University.

ALZAMORA, P. (1968) "Estructura político administrativa para la planificación urbana en Chile: limitaciones y perspectivas." *Revista de Planificación* (Santiago de Chile) (March 5): 69–84.

AMATO, P. W. (1969) "Population densities, land values and socio-economic class in Bogotá, Colombia." *Land Economics* 45, No. 1 (February): 66–73.

ANDERSON, C. W. (1967) *Politics and Economic Change in Latin America: The Governing of Restless Nations.* Princeton: D. Van Nostrand.

ANDRADE L., G. (1968) *La situación urbana—El proceso de urbanización y sus implicaciones.* Santiago de Chile: Centro Interdisciplinario de Desarrollo Urbano y Regional.

ARANGO, R. (1968) "Caracas, ciudad progresista de América." *Universidad de Antioquia* 170 (July-September): 1041–1051.

Argentina. Poder Ejecutivo Nacional. Ministerio de Bienestar Social (1968) *Plan de erradicación de las villas de emergencia de la capital federal y del Gran Buenos Aires. Primer programa: Erradicación y alojamiento transitorio.* Buenos Aires.

EDITORS' NOTE: In a few instances, 1967 items have been included because of their importance and/or lack of availability until 1968 or later. References have been examined to approximately August, 1969, with the exception of non-U.S. publications, whose cut-off date is earlier in most cases. We are grateful to Denton R. Vaughan of the University of Texas, to the staff of the Centro Latino Americano de Pesquisas em Ciências Sociais, Rio de Janeiro, Brazil, and to its Director, Manuel Diégues, for assistance in compiling bibliographic materals.

ARRIAGA, E. E. (1968) "Components of city growth in selected Latin American countries." *Milbank Memorial Fund Quarterly* 46, No. 2, Part 1 (April): 237–252.

Asociación Colombiana de Facultades de Medicina, División de Estudios de Población (1969) *Seminario nacional sobre urbanización y marginalidad.* Bogotá: Tercer Mundo (March 28–31).

BALÁN, J. (1969) "Migrant-native socioeconomic differences in Latin American cities: a structural analysis." *Latin American Research Review* 4, No. 1 (Spring): 3–51.

——— (1968) "Are farmers' sons handicapped in the city?" *Rural Sociology* 33, No. 2 (June): 160–174.

BAMBERGER, M. (1969) "Un sistema político cerrado." *Aportes* (Paris) 22 (January): 77–88. Translation of following article.

——— (1968) "A problem of political integration in Latin America: the *barrios* of Venezuela." *International Affairs* 44, No. 4 (October): 709–719.

Banco do Nordeste do Brasil, S. A., Departamento de Estudos Econômicos do Nordeste (ETENE) (1968) O consumo alimentar no nordeste urbano. Fortaleza, Ceará, Brazil (June).

BARBOSA, N. M. (1968) *Quadro geral das locações urbanas.* Rio de Janeiro.

BERQUO, E. S. *et al.* (1968) "Levels and variations in fertility in São Paulo." *Milbank Memorial Fund Quarterly* 46: 167–185.

BEYER, G. H., ed. (1967) *The Urban Explosion in Latin America.* Ithaca, N. Y.: Cornell University Press.

BIRKHOLZ, L. B. (1968) "Planos diretores municipais no Estado de São Paulo e sua implantação." *Separatas da Revista DAE* (São Paulo).

BREESE, G., ed. (1969) *The City in Newly Developing Countries.* Englewood Cliffs: Prentice-Hall.

——— (1968) "Some dilemmas in poverty, power and public policy in cities of underdeveloped areas." Pp. 443–464 in W. Bloomberg, Jr. and H. J. Schmandt (eds.) *Power, Poverty and Urban Policy: Urban Affairs Annual Reviews.* Vol. 2. Beverly Hills, Calif.: Sage Publications.

BROWNING, H. L. and W. FEINDT (1968) "Diferencias entre la población nativa y la migrante en Monterrey." *Demografía y Economía* (Mexico) 2, No. 2: 183–204.

BRYCE-LAPORTE, R. S. (1968) "Family adaptations of relocated slum dwellers in Puerto Rico: implications for urban research and development." *Journal of Developing Areas* 2, No. 4 (July): 533–540.

BUECHLER, H. C. (1968) "The reorganization of counties in the Bolivian highlands: an analysis of rural-urban networks and hierarchies." Pp. 48–57 in E. M. Eddy (ed.) *Urban Anthropology: Research Perspectives and Strategies.* Athens, Georgia: University of Georgia Press.

BUGATTI, E. (1969) "La guerra contra las villas miserias." *Primera Plana* 7 (August): 55–58.

BURGGRAAFF, W. J. (1968) "Venezuelan regionalism and the rise of Táchira." *The Americas* 25, No. 2 (October): 160–173.

BURNETT, B. and K. JOHNSON (1968) *Political Forces in Latin America: Dimensions of the Quest for Stability.* Belmont, Calif.: Wadsworth Publishing.

BWY, D. P. (1968a) Political Instability in Latin America: A Comparative Study. Ph.D. dissertation, Northwestern University.

—— (1968b) "Dimensions of social conflict in Latin America." Pp. 201–236 in L. H. Masotti and D. R. Bowen (eds.) *Riots and Rebellion.* Beverly Hills, Calif.: Sage Publications.

CALCAGNO, A. E., P. SÁINZ and J. DE BARBIERI (1968) "El diagnóstico político en la planificación." *El Trimestre Económico* (Mexico) 35 (July-September): 389–422.

CAMARGO, J. F. DE (1968) *A cidade e o campo o êxodo rural no Brasil.* Universidade de São Paulo, Coleção Buriti No. 20 (Rio de Janeiro).

CARDONA GUTIÉRREZ, R. (1969) "Migración, urbanización, y marginalidad." Pp. 63–87 in *Urbanización y Marginalidad.* Bogotá: Asociación Colombiana de Facultades de Medicina.

—— (1968a) "Investigación nacional sobre marginalidad urbana en Colombia." *América Latina* (Rio de Janeiro) 11 (October-December): 128–134.

—— (1968b) "The urban marginal society: a product of the urbanization process." Pp. 59–86 in *Acta Final.* Twelfth Congreso Interamericano de Municipios, New Orleans.

CARDOZO, F. H. and J. L. REYNA (1968) "Industrialization, occupational structure, and social stratification in Latin America." Pp. 22–44 in C. Blasier (ed.) *Constructive Change in Latin America.* Pittsburgh: University of Pittsburgh Press.

CARRILLO-ARRONTE, R. (1968) *An Empirical Test on Interregional Planning: A Linear Programming Model for Mexico.* The Hague: Alfa.

CARVALHO, J. M. DE (1968–69) "Estudos do poder local no Brasil." *Revista Brasileira de Estudos Políticos* 25/26: 231–248.

CASIMIR, J. (1967) "Duas cidadaes do nordeste do Brasil: sua estructura social e sua importancia para a planificação regional." *América Latina* 10, No. 1 (January-March).

—— (1968) "A teoría dos pólos de desenvolvimento e sua aplicação aos países subdesenvolvidos." *América Latina* 11, No. 4 (October-December): 3–16.

Central Unica de Trabajadores de Chile (1968) *América Latina: Un mundo que ganar.* Santiago de Chile: Editorial Universitaria, S. A.

Centro Interdisciplinario de Desarrollo Urbano y Regional (CIDU) (1968) *Reconocimiento y bases para un programa de desarrollo urbano, Sector Manuel Rodríguez.* 5 vols. Santiago de Chile: CIDU.

—— (1968?) *Estrategia de desarrollo para el área intercommunal Santiago Oriente.* 3 vols. Santiago de Chile: CIDU.

Centro para el Desarrollo Económico y Social de América Latina (DESAL) (1968) *Encueste sobre la familia y la fecundidad en poblaciones marginales del Gran Santiago, Segunda Parte: Resultados globales de la muestra de mujeres.* Santiago de Chile: Sección de Impresión de DESAL.

DESAL (Centro para el Desarrollo Económico y Social de América Latina) (1967a) *(Documentos) La Situación demográfica, ecológica, cultural, económica y social de la provincia de Santiago.* Santiago de Chile (mimeo.).

—— (1967b) *Marginalidad en América Latina: Un Ensayo de diagnóstico.* Santiago de Chile.

CERISOLA, M. I. E. (1968) "Fecundidad diferencial en La República del Paraguay según condición de ruralidad y nivel de instrucción de la mujer." *Revista Paraguaya de Sociología* 5, No. 12: 34–52.

CHAPLIN, D. (1968) "Peruvian social mobility: revolutionary and development potential." *Journal of Inter-American Studies* 10, No. 4 (October): 547–570.

———— (1967–68) "Industrialization and the distribution of wealth in Peru." *Studies in Comparative International Development* 3, No. 3: 55–66.

CHEN, CHI-YI (1968) *Movimientos migratorios en Venezuela.* Caracas: Instituto de Investigaciones Económicas, Universidad Católica Andrés Bello.

CINTA G., R. (1968) "Un enfoque socioeconómico de la urbanización." *Demografía y Economía* (Mexico) 2, No. 1: 63–80.

CLEAVES, P. S. (1969) *Factors Influencing the Chilean Municipal Councilman's Orientation Toward His Office.* Berkeley: University of California (mimeo.).

Colombia. Dirección Departamental de Estadística. (1968) *Anuario Estadística de Antioquia: 1967.* Medellín.

Congreso Interamericano de Municipios (n.d.) *Acta Final.* Twelfth Reunion, New Orleans, December 8–12, 1968. New Orleans?: 1969?

Conjuntura Econômica (Rio de Janeiro) (1969a) "Metrô de São Paulo: Aspectos financeiros." Vol. 23, No. 5 (May): 83–96.

———— (1969b) "Guanabara—State of Rio—coming merger." Vol. 16, No. 1 (January): 131–139.

COPE, O. G. (1968) "The 1965 Congressional elections in Chile: an analysis." *Journal of Inter-American Studies* 10, No. 2: 256–276.

CORNELIUS, W. A. (1969) "Urbanization as an agent in Latin American political instability: the case of Mexico." *American Political Science Review* 63, No. 3 (September): 833–857.

COTLER, J. (1967–68) "The mechanics of internal domination and social change in Peru." *Studies in Comparative International Development* 3, No. 12: 229–246.

COSTA, J. M. M. DA (1968) "Planejamento regional e diversificação da economia." *Revista de Administração Municipal* (Rio de Janeiro) 15, No. 88 (May-June): 245–268.

CURRIE, L. (1965) *Una política urbana para los países en desarrollo.* Bogotá: Tercer Mundo.

DALAND, R. T. (1968) "Uma estratégia de pesquisa em administração urbana comparada." *Revista de Administração Municipal* 15, No. 89 (July-August): 365–386.

DALLAL, A. (1969) "Urbanismo y planificación." *Cuadernos Americanos* 28 (January-February): 107–118.

DELGADO, C. (1968a) "Tres planteamientos en torno a problemas de urbanización acelerada en áreas metropolitanas: El caso de Lima." *Cuadernos de Desarrollo Urbano y Regional.* (Santiago de Chile) 9 (December).

———— (1968b) *Notas sobre movilidad social en el Perú.* Santiago de Chile: Centro Interdisciplinario de Desarrollo Urbano y Regional.

———— (1968c) *Ejercicio sociológico sobre el arribismo en el Perú.* Santiago de Chile: Centro Interdisciplinario de Desarrollo Urbano y Regional.

DIETZ, H. (1969) "Urban squatter settlements in Peru: a case history and analysis." *Journal of Inter-American Studies* 11 (July): 353–370.

DI TELLA, T. S. (1968) "The working class in politics." Pp. 386–394 in C. Véliz (ed.) *Latin America and the Caribbean: A Handbook.* New York: Frederick A. Praeger.

DUCOFF, L. J. (1968) "La brecha entre el desarrollo rural y urbano: La experiencia de México." *Revista Mexicana de Sociología* 30, No. 2 (April-June): 201–216.

EBANKS, G. E. (1968) "Differential internal migration in Jamaica, 1943–1960." *Social and Economic Studies* (Mona, Jamaica) 17, No. 2: 197–214.

EDDY, E. M., ed. (1968) *Urban Anthropology: Research Perspectives and Strategies. Southern Anthropological Proceedings* No. 2. Athens, Georgia: University of Georgia Press.

ELLIOTT, S. M. (1968) *Financing Latin American Housing: Domestic Savings Mobilization and U. S. Assistance Policy.* New York: Frederick A. Praeger.

ERBSEN, C. (1969) "São Paulo: world's biggest city by 1980?" *Clipper* (Pan American World Airways, Inc.) 9, No. 4 (August-September): 6–11.

FÁBREGA, E. E. (1966) "La ciudad de Panamá y el problema de los municipios." *Presente* (Panama) 5 (January): 5–9.

FAÚNDES-LATHAM, A. G. RODRÍGUEZ-GALANT and O. AVENDAÑO-PORTIUS (1968) "Effects of a family planning program on the fertility of a marginal working-class community in Santiago." *Demography* 5, No. 2: 122–137.

FERREZ, G. (1968) "O que ensinam os antigos mapas e estampas do Rio de Janeiro." *Revista do Instituto Histórico e Geográfico Brasileiro* (Rio de Janeiro) 278 (January-March): 87–104. Illustrated; part IV of previously published work.

FISHER, J. (1969) "The intendent system and the cabildos of Peru, 1784–1810." *Hispanic American Historical Review* 69, No. 3 (August): 430–453.

FISHER, R. (1968) "Some observations on social organization among the urban unemployed in Belize, British Honduras." Pp. 14–18 in *Manpower and Unemployment Research in Africa.* McGill University.

FLINN, W. L. (1968) "The process of migration to a shantytown in Bogotá, Colombia." *Inter-American Economic Affairs* 22 (Autumn): 77–88.

FLINN, W. L. and A. CAMACHO (1969) "The correlates of voter participation in a shantytown barrio in Bogotá, Colombia." *Inter-American Economic Affairs* 22, No. 4 (Spring): 47–58.

FRIED, R. (forthcoming) "Mexico City." In W. Robson (ed.) *Great Cities of the World.* 3rd ed. London: Allen & Unwin.

FRIEDMANN, J. (forthcoming) "The future of urbanization in Latin America: the role of the periphery." *Studies in Comparative International Development.*

———— (1969) *Urban and Regional Development in Chile: A Case Study of Innovative Planning.* Santiago, Chile: Ford Foundation (mimeo.).

———— (1968a) "El papel de las ciudades en el desarrollo nacional." *Cuadernos de Desarrollo Urbano y Regional* 9 (December).

———— (1968b) "The strategy of deliberate urbanization." *Journal of the American Institute of Planners* 34, No. 6 (November): 364–373.

———— (1968c) "Política e planejamento do desenvolvimento regional." *Revista de Administração Municipal* 15 (September-October): 485–496.

GAKENHEIMER, R. A. and J. MILLER (1968) "Social science and urban development in Latin America [Jahuel Seminar]." *International Social Science Journal* (Paris) 20, No. 4: 706–708.

GARCÍA, A. (1968a) "Las clases medias en América Latina." *Cuadernos Americanos* 27 (September-October): 122–127.

———— (1968b) "Reflexiones sobre los cambios políticos en América Latina:

Las clases medias y el sistema de poder." *Revista Mexicana de Sociología* 30 (July-September): 593–602.

GARCÍA VÁSQUEZ, F. (1968) *Aspectos del planeamiento y de la vivienda en Cuba.* Buenos Aires: J. Alvarez.

GAUTHIER, H. L. (1968) "Transportation and the growth of the São Paulo economy." *Journal of Regional Science* 8, No. 1 (Summer): 77–94.

GEISSE, G. (1968a) *Problemas del desarrollo urbano regional en Chile.* Santiago de Chile: Centro Interdisciplinario de Desarrollo Urbano y Regional.

——— (1968b) "El caso de Chile [urbanización]." *Revista de la Sociedad Interamericana de Planificación* (Cali, Colombia) 2: 24–30.

——— (1967) *Asentamientos urbanos e integración nacional.* Santiago: CIDU y PLANDES.

GEORGE, P. (1968) "Problèmes urbains de la République Argentine." *Annales de Géographie* 77: 257–277.

GERMANI, G. (1968) "¿Pertenece América Latina al tercer mundo?" *Aportes* (Paris) 10 (October): 6–32.

——— (1967–1968) "Mass society, social class, and the emergence of fascism." *Studies in Comparative International Development* 3, No. 10: 189–199.

GIUSTI, J. (1968) "Rasgos organizativos en el poblador marginal urbano latinoamericano." *Revista Mexicana de Sociología* 30, No. 1: 53–77.

GOLDRICH, D., R. PRATT and C. R. SHULLER (1968) "The political integration of lower class urban settlement in Chile and Peru." *Studies in Comparative International Development* 3, No. 1: 3–22.

GROSS, B. (1967–1968) "The administration of economic development planning: principles and fallacies." *Studies in Comparative International Development* 3, No. 5: 89–110.

GUADAGNI, A. A. (1968) "Costos y tarifas en el suministro de electricidad del Gran Buenos Aires." *Desarrollo Económico* (Buenos Aires) 8, No. 29: 137–164.

Guia de pesquisa de habitação e urbanismo (1968) Preliminary ed. Rio de Janeiro: Coordenação de Documentação e Biblioteca.

HAAR, C. M. (1963) "Latin America's troubled cities." *Foreign Affairs* 41 (April): 536–549.

HANSON, R. C. *et al.* (1968) "Quantitative Analysis of the Urban Experiences of Spanish-American Migrants." Proceedings of the 1968 Annual Spring Meeting of the Ethnological Society: 65–83.

HARDOY, J. (1968) *Urban Planning in Pre-Columbian America.* New York: Braziller.

——— (1966) "El rol de la ciudad en la modernización de América Latina." *Cuadernos* (Buenos Aires) No. 6.

HARDOY, J. and R. P. SCHAEDEL, eds. (1969) *El proceso de urbanización en America desde sus orígenes hasta nuestra días.* Papers presented at the 37th Congreso de Americanistas. Buenos Aires: Editorial del Instituto Torcuato di Tella.

HARDOY, J. and C. TOBAR, eds. (1969) *La urbanización en América Latina.* Buenos Aires: Editorial del Instituto Torcuato di Tella.

HARDOY, J., R. O. BASALDÚA and O. A. MORENO (1968) *Política de la tierra urbana y mecanismos para su regulación en América del Sur.* Buenos Aires: Editorial del Instituto Torcuato di Tella.

HARDOY, J., A. ROFMAN, O. YUJNOVSKY and R. BASALDÚA (1968) "El caso de Argentina [urbanización]." *Revista de la Sociedad Interamericana de Planificación* 2, No. 5/6: 31–38.

HARRIS, R. N. S. and E. S. STEER (1968) "Demographic-resource push in rural migration." *Social and Economic Studies* 17, No. 4: 398–406.

HAUSER, P. and L. F. SCHNORE, eds. (1965) *The Study of Urbanization.* New York: John Wiley.

HERBERT, J. D. and A. P. VAN HUYCK (1968) *Urban Planning in the Developing Countries.* New York: Frederick A. Praeger.

HERRICK, B. (1965) *Urban Migration and Economic Development in Chile.* Cambridge: M.I.T. Press.

HIGGINS, B. (1967) "Urbanization, industrialization, and economic development." Pp. 117–155 in G. Beyer (ed.) *The Urban Explosion in Latin America.* Ithaca, N. Y.: Cornell University Press.

HOBSBAWM, E. J. (1969) "Los campesinos, las migraciones y la política." *Pensamiento Crítico* (Habana) 24 (January): 75–87.

HOROWITZ, I. L. (1967) "Electoral politics, urbanization, and social development in Latin America." Pp. 215–254 in G. Beyer (ed.) *The Urban Explosion in Latin America.* Ithaca, N. Y.: Cornell University Press.

HORWITZ, A. (1968) "Servicing the 'barrio pobre': the role of government, the social agencies, and the private sector." Pp. 131–138 in *Acta Final.* Twelfth Congreso Interamericano de Municipios, New Orleans.

HOSKIN, G. (1968) "Value patterns and politics in a Venezuelan city: the case of San Cristóbal." *Buffalo Studies* 4, No. 3 (August): 85–110.

HOUSTON, J. M. (1968) "The foundation of colonial towns in Hispanic America." Pp. 352–390 in R. P. Beckinsale and J. M. Houston (eds.) *Urbanization and Its Problems.* Oxford: Basil Blackwell.

HURTADO, C. (1966) *Concentración de población y desarrollo económico: el caso chileno.* Santiago: Instituto de Economía, Universidad de Chile.

Instituto Latinamericano de Planificación Económica y Social (1968) *Discusiones sobre planificación: Informe de un seminario* [Santiago de Chile, 6 a 14 de julio de 1965]. 2nd ed. Mexico, D. F.: Siglo XXI Editores, S. A.

Inter-American Development Bank (1969) *Socio-Economic Progress in Latin America.* Eighth Annual Report, 1968, Social Progress Trust Fund. Washington, D.C. Pages 331–380 devoted to urban development in Latin America.

International Migration Review (New York) (1968) "Annotated bibliography on Puerto Rico and Puerto Rican migration." Vol. 2, No. 2: 96ff.

JÁCOME, J. M. (1968) "O planejamento municipal no América Latina." *Revista de Administração Municipal* 15 (July-August): 423–446.

JAGUARIBE, H. (1967–1968) "Political strategies of national development in Brazil." *Studies in Comparative International Development* 3, No. 2: 27–50.

JARAMILLO GÓMEZ, M. (1968) "Medellín: a case of strong resistance to birth control." *Demography* 5, No. 2: 811–826.

JOHNSON, D. L. (1967–1968) "Industrialization, social mobility, and class formation in Chile." *Studies in Comparative International Development* 3, No. 7: 127–151.

JONES, G. W. (1968) "Underutilization of manpower and demographic trends in Latin America." *International Labor Review* 98, No. 5: 451–470.

KAHL, J. A. (1968) *The Measurement of Modernism: A Study of Values in Brazil and Mexico.* Austin: University of Texas Press.

KARST, K. and M. SCHWARTZ (1968) *The Internal Norms and Sanctions in Ten Barrios in Caracas.* Los Angeles: University of California (mimeo.).

KINSBRUNER, J. (1968) "Water for Valparaíso: a case of entrepreneurial frustration." *Journal of Inter-American Studies* 10, No. 4 (October): 653–661.

KNOWLTON, C. S. (1968) "The spatial and social mobility of the Syrian and Lebanese community of São Paulo, Brazil." *Proceedings of the Southwestern Sociological Association* 19: 39–43.

KRIKUS, R. J. (1968) Rapid Urbanization: A Challenge to Political Development. Ph.D. dissertation, Georgetown University.

LANDSBERGER, H. A. (1968) "Do ideological differences have personal correlates? A study of Chilean labor leaders at the local level." *Economic Development and Cultural Change* 16: 219–244.

LATTES, A. E. and R. POCZTER (1968) *Muestra del censo de población de la ciudad de Buenos Aires de 1855.* Buenos Aires: Editorial del Instituto Torcuato di Tella.

LEEDS, A. (1968) "The anthropology of cities: some methodological issues." Pp. 31–47 in E. M. Eddy (ed.) *Urban Anthropology.* Athens, Georgia: University of Georgia Press.

LEEDS, E. R. (1966) "Complementarity of favelas with the larger society of Rio de Janeiro." Paper presented at the 37th International Congress of Americanists, Mar del Plata, Argentina, September.

LEEMAN, A. (1968) "Arica und seine Verbindung mit dem bolivianischen Altiplano." *Geographica Helvetica* 23, No. 1: 15–24.

LEONARD, O. E. (1968) "Social and economic trends in modernization of Latin America." *Sociology and Social Research* 52, No. 2: 208–216.

LEWIS, O. (1968) *A Study of Slum Culture: Backgrounds for La Vida.* New York: Random House.

——— (1952) "Urbanization without breakdown: a case study." *Scientific Monthly* 75: 31–41.

LLERAS, A. (1969) "El monstruo de la urbanización." *Visión* 36, No. 8 (April 11).

LODI, C. (1968) "São Paulo, seu planejamento urbanístico." *Urbanização* (Lisbon) 1 (April): 7–24.

LÓPEZ, J. E. (1968) *Tendencies recientes de la población venezolana: Estudio geográfico de la población de un país subdesarrollado. Ediciones del Instituto de Geografía, Colección Humboldt, No. 1.* Mérida, Venezuela: Instituto de Geografía; Facultad de Ciencias Forestales, Universidad de los Andes.

MACDONALD, L. D. and J. S. MACDONALD (1968) "Motives and objectives of migration: selective migration and preferences toward rural and urban life." *Social and Economic Studies* 17, No. 4 (December): 417–434.

McDONALD, R. H. (1969) "National urban voting behavior: the politics of dissent in Latin America." *Inter-American Economic Affairs* 23, No. 1 (Summer): 3–20.

McGRANAHAN, D. (1966) "Social research in the U.N." In *Comparing Nations:*

The Use of Quantitative Data in Cross-National Research. New Haven: Yale University Press.

McGREEVEY, W. P. (1968) "Causas de la migración interna en Colombia." Pp. 211–221 in *Empleo y desempleo en Colombia.* Centro de Estudios Sobre Desarrollo Económico (CEDE). Bogotá: Ediciones Universidad de los Andes. Reprinted in Latin America Reprint Series, No. 301, Center for Latin American Studies, University of California, Berkeley.

MAGALHÃES, J. P. DE A. (1968) "Diretrizes para o desenvolvimento regional." *Revista de Administração Municipal* 15 (March-April): 125–150.

MANASTER, K. A. (1968) "The problem of urban squatters in developing countries: Peru." *Wisconsin Law Review* 23, No. 1: 23–61.

MANGIN, W. (1968) "Poverty and politics in cities of Latin America." Pp. 397–432 in W. Bloomberg, Jr. and H. J. Schmandt (eds.) *Power, Poverty and Urban Policy. Urban Affairs Annual Reviews.* Vol. 2. Beverly Hills, Calif.: Sage Publications.

——— (1967) "Latin American squatter settlements: a problem and a solution." *Latin American Research Review* 2, No. 3 (Summer).

——— (1965) "Mental health and migration to cities: a Peruvian case." Pp. 546–555 in D. B. Heath and N. Adams (eds.) *Contemporary Cultures and Societies of Latin America.* New York: Random House.

——— (1963) "Account of a Lima invasion." *Architectural Design* 33 (August): 368–369.

MANGIN, W. and J. C. TURNER (1968) "The barriada movement." *Progressive Architecture* 49, No. 5: 154–162.

MARCONDES, J. V. F. and O. PIMENTEL (1968) *São Paulo: Espírito. Povo. Instituições.* São Paulo.

MARGULIS, M. (1968) *Migración y marginalidad en la sociedad Argentina.* Biblioteca América Latina No. 10. Buenos Aires: Editorial Paidós.

MÁRMORA, L. (1968) *Migración al sur: Argentinos y chilenos en Comodoro Rivadavía.* Buenos Aires: Ediciones Lefera.

MARTÍNEZ, H. (1968) "Las migraciones internas en el Perú." *Aportes* 10 (October): 137–160.

MATOS MAR, J. (1968) *Urbanización y barriadas en América del Sur.* Lima: Instituto de Estudios Peruanos.

MELLO, D. LORDELLO DE (1968) "Institucionalização das áreas metropolitanas." *Revista de Administração Municipal* 15 (January-February): 5–25.

MENDOZA-BERRUETO, E. (1968) "Regional implications of Mexico's economic growth." Pp. 87–123 in *Weltwirtschaftliches Archiv* (Kiel), Band 101, No. 1. Reprinted in translation as "Implicaciones regionales del desarrollo económico de México." *Demografía y Economía* 3, No. 1.

MERCADER, A. and J. DE VERA (1969) *Tupamaros: Estratégia y acción.* Libros Populares Alfa No. 32. Montevideo: Editorial Alfa.

MERRILL, R. N. (1968?) "An evaluation of Chile's housing program: problems and prospects." Latin American Studies Program, Dissertation Series, No. 8. Ithaca, N. Y.: Cornell University.

MILLER, D. (1968) "The measurement of international patterns and norms: a tool for comparative research." *Southwestern Social Sciences Quarterly* 48 (March).

MILLER, J. (1968) "La política y la planificación." *Boletín Informativo de PLANDES* 26 (March-April).

MILLER, J. and R. A. GAKENHEIMER (1969) "The social sciences and urban development in Latin America." *American Behavioral Scientist* 12, No. 5 May-June). Comprises the entire issue.

MORCILLO, P. P. (1968) "Política de desarrollo urbano." *Revista de la Sociedad Interamericano de Planificación* 2, No. 5/6: 66–69.

MORSE, R. M. (1965) "Recent research on Latin American urbanization: a selective survey with commentary." *Latin American Research Review* 1, No. 1 (Fall): 35–75.

——— (1964) "The heritage of Latin America." Pp. 151–177 in L. Hartz (ed.) *The Founding of New Societies*. New York: Harcourt, Brace & World.

MOSSÉ, R. (1969) "Programação cultural do municípios." *Revista de Administração Municipal* 16 (January-February): 5–13.

MOUCHET, C. (1968) "Aspectos de las áreas metropolitanas." *Revista de la Sociedad Interamericana de Planificación* 2, No. 5/6: 61–65.

NASON, R. W. (1968) Urban Market Processes in Recife, Brazil. Ph. D. dissertation, Michigan State University.

NEGRÓN GARCÍA, L. F. and J. J. VALLAMIL (1968) "El caso de Puerto Rico [urbanización]." *Revista de la Sociedad Interamericano de Planificación* 2, No. 5/6: 11–17.

NEIRA, E. A. (1963) "¿Son las ciudades una forma de cristalización social?" *Cuadernos de la Sociedad Venezolana de Planificación* 1, No. 2.

NIE, N. H., G. B. POWELL and K. PREWITT (1969) "Social structure and political participation; development relationships." *American Political Science Review* 62, No. 2 (June): 361–378.

NUN, P., M. MURMIS and J. C. MARÍN (1968) *La marginalidad en América Latina: Informe preliminar*. Buenos Aires: Editorial del Instituto Torcuato di Tella.

OLDMAN, O. et al. (1967) *Financing Urban Development in Mexico City: A Case Study of Property Tax, Land Use, Housing, and Urban Planning.* Cambridge: Harvard University Press.

OLIEN, M. D. (1968) "Levels of urban relationships in a complex society: a Costa Rican case." Pp. 83–92 in E. M. Eddy (ed.) *Urban Anthropology*. Athens, Georgia: University of Georgia Press.

ORNELAS, C. (forthcoming) Land Tenure, Sanctions, and Politization in Mexico City. Ph.D. dissertation, University of California, Riverside, Political Science Department.

PARISSE, L. (1969) "A favela carioca: um mundo a ser descoberto." *Cadernos Brasileiros* 51 (January-February): 35–46.

PAYNE, L. (1969) "Lost cities of the Maya." *Today's Health* 47 (February): 56–59.

PEATTIE, L. R. (1968) *The View from the Barrio*. Ann Arbor, Mich.: University of Michigan Press.

PEDERSON, P. O. (1969) *Innovative Diffusion Within and Between National Urban Systems*. Copenhagen: Technical University of Denmark (mimeo.). Part I, the case of Chile; part II, the case of Latin America and international innovative diffusion.

Peñalosa, F. (forthcoming) "Ecological organization of the transitional city: some Mexican evidence." *Social Forces.*

Pineda Giraldo, R. (1968) "Una política sobre los tugurios." *Revista de la Sociedad Interamericana de Planificación* 2, No. 5/6: 70–71.

Plaza, G. (1968) "Needed: an urban policy for Latin American development." Pp. 23–28 in *Acta Final,* Twelfth Congreso Interamericano de Municipios, New Orleans.

Posada, R. (1968) "Los polos del desarrollo urbana en Colombia." *Revista de de la Sociedad Interamericana de Planificación* 2, No. 7: 28–34.

Powelson, J. P. (1964) "The land grabbers of Cali." *The Reporter* (January 16): 30–31.

Pratt, R. B. (1968a) "Urbanization and the crisis of inclusion in Latin America: toward the political integration of the urban lower class." Pp. 99–125 in *Acta Final.* Twelfth Congreso Interamericano de Municipios, New Orleans.

────── (1968b) Organizational Participation and Political Orientations: A Comparative Study of Political Consequences of Participation in Community Organizations for Residents of Lower-Class Urban Settlements in Chile and Peru. Ph.D. dissertation, University of Oregon.

Pratt, R. B., D. Goldrich and C. R. Schuller (1967–1968) "The political integration of lower-class urban settlements in Chile and Peru." *Studies in Comparative International Development* 3, No. 1: 3–22.

Preston, D. A. (1968) "Aspects of rural emigration in Andean America." *Northern Universities Geographical Journal* 9: 9–15.

Problemas Brasileiros (São Paulo) (1968) "Lei orgânica dos municípios." Vol. 59 (February): 39–52.

Puenta Leyva, J. (1969) *Distribución del ingreso en un área urbana: el caso de Monterrey.* México, D. F.

Pumarino Carte, G. (1968) "Desarrollo urbano: su relación con el desarrollo económico y social del país: Algunas consideraciones." *Economía* (Santiago de Chile) 26: 49–57.

Quatro Rodas (1969) "Rio: Edição especial de turismo." Vol. 9 (August).

Quijano, A. (1968) "Dependencia, cambio social y urbanización en Latinoamérica." *Revista Mexicana de Sociología* 30, No. 3 (July-September): 525–570.

────── (1967) "Urbanización y tendencias de cambio en la investigación del desarrollo urbano." Santiago: CIDU.

────── (1966) *El proceso de urbanización en Latinamérica.* Santiago: CEPAL (mimeo.).

Rabinovitz, F. F. (1969) "Urban and political development in Latin America." Pp. 88–123 in R. Daland (ed.) *Comparative Urban Research.* Beverly Hills, Calif.: Sage Publications.

────── (1968) "Sound and fury signifying nothing?—a review of community power research in Latin America." *Urban Affairs Quarterly* 3, No. 3 (March): 111–122.

Ramírez, G. P. (1965) "La urbanización y el cambio social en Colombia." *Revista de Agencias Sociales* (Puerto Rico) 4, No. 2 (June): 203–220.

Ramsey, R. W. (1968) The Bogotazo, Tentatively as History. [Occasional paper]. Gainesville. Center for Latin American Studies, University of Florida.

RATINOFF, L. A. (1966) "La urbanización en América Latina: el caso de Paraguay." *Revista Paraguaya de Sociología* (Asunción) 6 (May-August): 17–42.

RAY, T. F. (1969) *The Politics of the Barrios of Venezuela.* Berkeley: University of California Press.

Review of the River Plate, The (Buenos Aires) (1968a) "Planning of urban decentralization." Vol. 144 (December): 1019–1020.

———— (1968b) "Low cost housing: 2,300,000 units needed." Vol. 144 (October): 659–660.

Revista Brasileira de Estudos Políticos (Belo Horizonte, M. G., Brazil) (1968) Número especial sobre as eleições de 1966. No. 23/24 (July, 1967, January, 1968).

Revista de Administração Municipal (Rio de Janeiro) (1968) "Urbanização nos países subdesenvolvidos: Relatório de um Simpósio Internacional realizado em Noordwijk, Holanda, em dezembro de 1967." Vol. 15 (November-December): 665–680.

Revista de la Sociedad Interamericana de Planificación (Cali) (1968) "La urbanización y la planificación urbana en América Latina: casos, aspectos, conclusiones y recomendaciones." Vol. 2, No. 5/6 (March–June).

RIVAS, N. V. DE (1968) "Familia de clase urbana en transición y delincuencia juvenil." *Universidad* (Sante Fe, Argentina) 74 (January-March): 153–217.

ROBERTS, B. R. (1968a) "Protestant groups and coping with urban life in Guatemala City." *American Journal of Sociology* 73, No. 6 (May): 753–767.

———— (1968b) "Politics in a neighborhood of Guatemala City." *Sociology* (Oxford) 2, No. 2 (May): 185–203.

RODWIN, L. *et al.* (1969) *Planning Urban Growth and Regional Development: The Experience of the Guayana Program of Venezuela.* Cambridge: M.I.T. Press.

ROGLER, L. (1968) "The culture of the 'Barrio Pobre': barriers to the acculturation of the urban peasant to city life." Pp. 90–96 in *Acta Final.* Twelfth Congreso Interamericano de Municipios, New Orleans.

ROMANO YALOUR DE TOBAR, M. (1968) "El Buenos Aires de los 'villeros.' " *Mundo Nuevo* (Paris) 29 (November): 28–34.

ROMANO YALOUR DE TOBAR, M., M. M. CHIRICO and E. SOUBIE (1969) *Claseobrera y migraciónes: tres estudios.* 2nd ed. CEUR 9. Cuadernos del Centro de Estudios Urbanos y Regionales Asociado al Instituto Torcuato di Tella. Buenos Aires: Editorial del Instituto Torcuato di Tella.

ROMERO, J. L. (1968) "La ciudad hispanoamericana: la estructura socioeconómica originaria." *Cuadernos Americanos* 37 (September-October): 149–164.

ROPER, H. (1968) "A new city in Venezuela [Santa Teresa in Tuy Medio valley region]." *Journal of the Town Planning Institute* 54 (November): 437–439.

ROSEN, B. C. and M. T. BERLINCK (1968) "Modernization and Family structure in the region of São Paulo, Brazil." *América Latina* 11, No. 3 (July-September): 75–94.

ROSENBLÜTH, G. (1968) "Problemas socio-económicos de la marginalidad y la integración urbana." *Revista Paraguaya de Sociología* 5, No. 11 (April): 11–74.

ROTONDO, H. (1961) "Psychological and mental health problems of urbanization based on case studies in Peru." Pp. 249–257 in P. M. Hauser (ed.) *Urbanization in Latin America.* New York: UNESCO.

SAFA, H. I. (1968) "The social isolation of the urban poor: life in a Puerto Rican shantytown." Pp. 335–353 in I. Deutscher and E. J. Thompson (eds.) *Among the People.* New York: Basic Books.

SALAZAR LARRAÍN, A. (1968) *Lima, teoría y práctica de la ciudad.* Lima.

SALMEN, L. F. (1969) "A perspective on the resettlement of squatters in Brazil." *América Latina* 12, No. 1 (January-March): 73–93.

SANTOS, M. (1968a) "Croissance nationale et nouvelle armature urbaine au Brésil." *Annales de Geographie* 77: 37–63.

——— (1968b) *Cidade dos países subdesenvolvidos.* Rio de Janeiro.

SCHAEFFER, W. G. (1968) "Desenvolvimento urbano: um problema de alocação de recursos." *Revista de Administração Municipal* 15 (September-October): 497–507.

SCHILLER, R. (1968) "Guayana: Venezuela's new El Dorado." *Latin American Report* (New Orleans) 6, No. 12 (July-August): 35–38.

SCHNORE, L. F. (1965) "On the spatial structure of cities in the two Americas." Pp. 347–398 in P. Hauser and L. F. Schnore (eds.) *The Study of Urbanization.* New York: John Wiley.

SECKINGER, R. L. (1968) "Cultural aspects of local government in Brazil." In *Latinamericanist* (Gainesville: University of Florida) December 15.

SEGRE, R. (1968) "Presencia urbana del tiempo libre en Cuba." *Casa de las Américas* (Havana) 9 (July-August): 28–39.

SHULMAN, S. (1966) "Latin American shantytown." *New York Times Magazine* (January 16).

SIMMONS, R. E. *et al.* (1968) "Media and development news in slums of Ecuador and India." *Journalism Quarterly* 45, No. 4: 698–705.

SMITH, C. T. (1968) "Problems of regional development in Peru." *Geography* (Great Britain) 53, Part 3 (July): 260–281.

SMITH, P. H. (1969) "Social mobilization, political participation, and the rise of Juan Perón." *Political Science Quarterly* 84, No. 1 (March): 30–49.

SMITH, T. L. (1968a) "The changing functions of Latin American cities." *The Americas* 25, No. 1 (July): 70–83.

——— (1968b) "El proceso de urbanización y los cambios sociales en América Latina." *Ciencias Sociales* (Venezuela) 4, No. 1 (June): 3–21.

——— (1968c) "Urbanización y la planificación urbana en América Latina: Aspectos demográficos." *Revista de la Sociedad Interamericana de Planificación* 2, No. 5/6 (March-June): 46–51.

SOARES, M. T. DE S. (1969) "Delimitação de áreas metropolitanas." *Revista de Administração Municipal* 94 (May-June): 253–271.

SOBERMAN, R. M. (1968) *Transport Technology for Developing Regions: A Study of Road Transportation in Venezuela.* Cambridge: M.I.T. Press.

SOLBERG, C. (1969) "Immigration and urban social problems in Argentina and Chile, 1890–1914." *Hispanic American Historical Review* 49, No. 2 (May): 215–232.

STODDARD, E. R. (1968) "Comparative structures and attitudes along the United States-Mexican border." Paper presented at the Conference on Urbanization of the United States-Mexican Border, June 15, El Paso, Texas.

STOKES, C. J. (1968) "Tejerias-Valencia Autopista in Venezuela." Pp. 11–74 in *Transportation and Economic Development in Latin America*. New York: Frederick A. Praeger.

STREET, J. H. and G. G. WEIGEND (1967) *Urban Planning and Development Centers in Latin America*. New Brunswick: Rutgers University Press.

TAPER, B. (1968) "Habitação para um mundo que se urbaniza." *Aproximações* (Rio de Janeiro) 1, No. 2: 77–88.

TAPIA, F. X. (1969) "Algunas notas sobre el cabildo abierto en Hispano-américa." *Journal of Inter-American Studies* 11, No. 1 (January): 58–65.

TAPIA MOORE, A. (1968) "Rol social, económico y político de las aglomer-aciones urbanas en Chile." *Revista de Planificación* (Santiago de Chile) 5 (March): 16–20.

TERNER, I. D. and R. C. HERTZ (1968) "Squatter-inspired: Venezuela and Detroit." *Architectural Design* (August): 367–370.

TRAVIESO, F. (1968a) "Sistema de ciudades en Venezuela." *Revista de la Sociedad Interamericana de Planificación* 2, No. 5/6: 18–23.

——— (1968b) "El caso de Venezuela [urbanización]." *Revista de la Sociedad Interamericana de Planificación* 2, No. 5/6: 18–23.

TURNER, J. C. (1968a) "The squatter settlement: architecture that works." *Architectural Design* (August): 355–360.

——— (1968b) "Housing priorities, settlement patterns, and urban develop-ment in modernizing countries." *Journal of the American Institute of Planners* 34, No. 6 (November): 354–363.

——— (1966) "A selected bibliography: uncontrolled urban settlement—prob-lems and policies." Paper prepared for U.N. Centre for Housing, Building and Planning and presented at the Interregional Seminar on Development Policies and Planning in Relation to Urbanization, Pittsburgh.

UNIKEL, L. (1968a) "El caso de México [urbanización]." *Revista de la Sociedad Interamericana de Planificación* 2, No. 5/6: 5–10.

——— (1968b) "Ensayo sobre una nuevo clasificación de población rural y urbana en México." *Demografía y Economía* 2, No. 1: 1–18.

——— (1966) "La urbanización de la Ciudad de México." *Comercio Ex-terior* 16, No. 11 (November): 839–849.

U.N. Economic Commission for Latin America (1968) *Economic Bulletin for Latin America*. "The urbanization of society in Latin America." Vol. 13 (November): 76–93.

U.N. Statistical Office (1967) *Principles and Recommendations for the 1970 Census*. Series M, No. 44. New York: U.N. Statistical Office.

Universidad Central de Venezuela (1969) *Estudio de Caracas: Población, Servicios Urbanos*. Vol. 3. Caracas: Ediciones de la Biblioteca de la Uni-versidad Central de Venezuela.

Universidad de la República (Uruguay), Departamento de Extensión Univer-sitaria (1968) *Los rancheríos y su gente: Viviendas y familias*. Vol. 2. Colec-ción Nuestra Realidad, Montivideo.

URBINA, R. and A. GUROVICH (1968) "Un caso de discusión: El plan regulador de Rancagua." *Revista de Planificación* (Santiago de Chile) 5 (March): 38–68.

URIBE, P. (1967) *Tendencias y perspectivas de la política de vivienda en América Latina*. Santiago: CEPAL (mimeo.).

——— (1966) "Los factores estructurales del desarrollo y el problema de la vivienda en América Latina." *Boletín Económico de América Latina* 11, No. 2 (October).

URQUIDI, V. L. (1969) "El desarrollo económico y el crecimiento de la población." *Demografía y Economia* 3, No. 1: 94–103.

VALENTE, A. (1968) "Problemas de planejamento social." *Revista de Administração Municipal* 15 (November-December): 605–621.

VALLADARES, L. (1968) "Una favela por dentro." *Mundo Nuevo* 29 (November): 19–27.

VAN ES, J. C., E. A. WILKENING and J. B. GUEDES PINTO (1968) *Rural Migrants in Central Brazil—A Study of Itumbiara, Goiás.* Madison: University of Wisconsin Land Tenure Center, June, Research Report No. 29.

VAPNARSKY, C. A. (1968) *La población urbana argentina: Revisión crítica del método y los resultados censales de 1960.* Buenos Aires: Editorial del Instituto Torcuato di Tella.

VAUGHAN, D. R. (1969) *Urbanization in Twentieth Century Latin America: A Working Bibliography.* Austin: Institute of Latin American Studies, University of Texas (mimeo.).

Veritas (Buenos Aires) (1968a) "Esto también es Buenos Aires." Vol. 38 (September 15): 8–12. Interview with Gen. Manuel Iricíbar, Intendente of Buenos Aires.

——— (1968b) "El problema de la vivienda en la Capital Federal." Vol. 38 (August 15): 6–12.

——— (1968c) "¿Qué hace nuestra municipalidad por nuestra cultura?" Vol. 38 (May 15): 4–5.

WAGLEY, C. and M. HARRIS (1965) "A typology of Latin American subcultures." Pp. 42–69 in D. B. Heath and N. Adams (eds.) *Contemporary Cultures and Societies of Latin America.* New York: Random House.

WATTERS, R. F. (1967) "Economic backwardness in the Venezuelan Andes: a study of the traditional sector of the dual economy." *Pacific Viewpoint* (Wellington, N. Z.) 8, No. 1 (May): 17–67.

WILKENING, E. A., J. B. GUEDES PINTO and J. PASTORE (1968) "The role of the extended family in migration and adaptation in Brazil." *Journal of Marriage and the Family* 30, No. 4: 689–695.

WILLEMS, E. (1968) "Urban classes and acculturation in Latin America." Pp. 75–82 in E. M. Eddy (ed.) *Urban Anthropology.* Athens, Georgia: University of Georgia Press.

WILLIAMSON, R. C. (1968) "Social class and orientations to change: some relevant variables in a Bogotá sample." *Social Forces* 46, No. 2 (March): 317–327.

WILSON, A. G. (1968) "Models in urban planning: a synoptic review of recent literature." *Urban Studies* (Glasgow) 5, No. 3 (November): 249–276.

WINGO, L. (1969) *Latin American Urbanization: Plan or Process?* Reprint No. 75. Washington, D.C.: Resources for the Future, Inc., January. Reprinted from B. J. Frieden and W. Nash (eds.) *Shaping an Urban Future.* Cambridge: M.I.T. Press.

——— (1967) "Recent patterns of urbanization among Latin American countries." *Urban Affairs Quarterly* 2, No. 3 (March): 81–110.

WOLFE, M. (1968) "Recent changes in urban and rural settlement patterns in Latin America." *International Social Development Review* (U.N.) 1: 55–62.

YUJNOVSKY, O. *et al.* (1969) *Diagnóstico preliminar del área sudeste de la provincia de Buenos Aires.* 2nd ed. Buenos Aires: Editorial del Instituto Torcuato di Tella.

PART I

URBAN

MIGRATION

AND

MARGINALITY

Chapter 3

THE SOCIAL AND ECONOMIC CONTEXT
OF MIGRATION TO MONTERREY, MEXICO

HARLEY L. BROWNING AND WALTRAUT FEINDT

This study is a report of 904 men aged 21–60 and their last migration to Monterrey, Mexico. It provides a descriptive account of this migration, including conditions (primarily economic) leading to departure from community of origin, the composition of the migratory group, and the conditions attending arrival in Monterrey. It also addresses itself to a problem of more general concern; namely, the appropriateness of some current conceptions of the rural-urban migratory process as it occurs in developing countries today.[1]

THE CHRONOLOGY OF MIGRATION TO MONTERREY

Adequate accounts of what actually takes place in the course of migration from one place to another are uncommon, whether in developed or developing countries. Census-based reports, while useful in plotting migration streams and in comparing socioeconomic characteristics of migrants and natives, provide little if any information on the social and economic context of migration. This means that sample surveys are the one source of information that we can turn to. Although a number of recent survey studies provide some information on the migratory process,[2] it is rare that we can construct in adequate detail the chronology of the move, from its beginnings in the community of departure, during

AUTHORS' NOTE: This research is based on a project jointly sponsored by the Centro de Investigaciones Económicas of the Facultad de Economía, Universidad de Nuevo León and the Population Research Center of the Department of Sociology at The University of Texas at Austin. The research at both institutions was facilitated in part by grants from the Ford Foundation. The directors of the project are Jorge Balán and Elizabeth Jelín (formerly of the Universidad de Nuevo León) and Harley L. Browning.

the move itself, to the initial accommodation in the community of destination.

Since the Monterrey mobility study represents a deliberate effort to obtain such a chronology of migration to a large city, it is well at this point to consider both the choice of Monterrey for such a study and the relevant technical details in the execution of the survey. Monterrey is a large, rapidly-growing metropolitan center in Mexico, a country that has experienced sustained economic development over the last generation. Since 1940, the city grew from 186,000 to an estimated 950,000 at the time of the survey in 1965. Given such rapid growth, it comes as no surprise that more than two-thirds of the adult population was born outside of Monterrey. Another important characteristic of Monterrey is its prominence as the second leading industrial center of Mexico. As the iron and steel center of the nation, to a degree not encountered in the other large cities of Mexico, it is a city with large, modern factories. Monterrey is still very much a blue-collar city, there being less than a quarter of the male labor force in white-collar employment. At the same time, however, an important sector of the labor force is still employed in such marginal occupations as street vendors, construction workers, and so on. Thus the "duality" often encountered in cities of developing countries is also present in Monterrey, although to a lesser degree. What is important is that Monterrey has had impressive economic growth in the last twenty-five years or so and, because of this fact, has exercised a strong attraction for migrants.

Turning to the survey design itself, the sample is of 1,640 men aged 21-60 and resident in the metropolitan area of Monterrey during the summer of 1965. It is a two-stage stratified cluster design, in which older men (41-60) and those living in areas with higher incomes are over-represented. Although it is possible to convert the weighted sample into a representative one, the actual sample is used in this essay because our concern is not primarily with migration rates, but with the migratory process itself. In any event the distributions of the representative and actual samples generally do not differ greatly.[3]

In this essay we deal with migrants only. The distinction between natives and migrants is based not upon where the respondent was born, but on a sociologically more relevant unit, his "community of origin." This is defined as that place where the respondent spent the most time between the ages five through fifteen. Of our 1,640 men, 56 percent (904) were born outside of Monterrey and their community of origin was not Monterrey. Fourteen percent (228) were born outside of Monterrey but migrated there in childhood and spent their formative years in Monterrey.

To determine the social and economic environment in which migration took place, we asked our migrant respondents a series of temporally sequential questions that served to recreate for us the circumstances of their final move to Monterrey. Although 18 percent of the migrants (165 out of 904) had one or more previous migrations to Monterrey with a duration of at least six months, we asked the battery of questions only for last migration to Monterrey because it would have been impractical to do so for all migrations, not to mention the greater unreliability of response for the earlier moves.

In ordering this essay we follow closely the temporal sequence of last migration to Monterrey. The various specific questions were subsumed under the following three headings:

(1) *Factors Influencing the Decision to Come to Monterrey.* Kind of last employment before coming to Monterrey and satisfaction with it; relative importance of work, family, education and community; consideration of alternate destinations; acquaintance with Monterrey by means of prior visits or residence; concreteness of work plans before coming to Monterrey and planned duration of stay; and degree of satisfaction with decision to migrate at the time of the interview.

(2) *Composition of the Migratory Group.* Marital status at time of migration; whether journey was made alone or with relatives or friends; in case of "split" migration (when members of family came at different times) who came with whom, in what order, and at what time.

(3) *Kinds of Contacts and Forms of Assistance in Settling in Upon Arrival to Monterrey.* Who migrants knew in Monterrey prior to arrival; forms of assistance received, if any; presence of relatives and friends in same neighborhood; contact with persons in communities lived in prior to Monterrey.

CONCEPTIONS OF THE MIGRATORY PROCESS

Beyond the descriptive and chronological account of migration lie questions concerning appropriate models of the migratory process as it occurs in developing countries. We are now in a stage when certain older conceptions, mainly deductive in character and derived from European and U.S. theorists, are being challenged by other conceptions that have emerged largely from empirical field investigations of the migratory process. The older conceptions had erected the myth of "migrant man" that shared many of the limitations of "economic man" as created by the economists and "political man" or more narrowly "voter" of the political scientists. All three were based upon two faulty premises: (1) that the individual acted in social isolation; (2) that the decision-making process was a rational one.

Economic man weighed the pecuniary advantages and disadvantages of a given course of action, while political man carefully reviewed all available information provided by competing candidates before casting his ballot. In like manner, migrant man carefully balanced the advantages and disadvantages of remaining in a place and when the scales tipped toward the unfavorable he migrated to that place offering the best prospects for one of his background. The obvious fact that men are attached to social groups, which affect them in ways not maximal for individual self interest, was excluded from consideration. Much of the recent history of economics and political science has reflected the "discovery" of man as a social animal.

The same thing seems to be happening with respect to migration. Probably the most glaring deficiency of older conceptions of migrant man was their neglect of the importance of family and kinship relationships at all stages of the migratory process. Ironically enough, family and kinship were assigned great prominence in the depiction of the social fabric in the community of origin, particularly in rural and village environments. Here we encounter what may be called "the great dichotomy," a powerful theme that has recurred continually in the history of sociology. Its lineage is impressive: from Maine's "status" and "contract," Tönnies's "Gemeinschaft" and "Gesellschaft," Spencer's "military" and "industrial," Durkheim's "mechanical" and "organic," Redfield's "folk" and "urban" down to contemporary variations on "traditional" and "modern."

However useful the great dichotomy may have been in other contexts, its application to migration has had deleterious effects. The reification of the dichotomy, unfettered by any empirical support, led to a conception of the community of origin, the village, that was idealized in terms of the extent, warmth and solidarity of familial and communal interpersonal relations. By definition, therefore, the community of destination, the city, must display opposite characteristics. The migrant is seen as wrenched from his community of origin of which he was an organic part, embarking alone on a lonely journey to the great city. There, unshielded by any sort of social protection, he is exposed to the full force of an impersonal, even hostile, environment. Is it any wonder that migration, from this perspective, can be anything but a traumatic experience where individuals are torn from the deep sociological roots of their community of origin and then exposed, in vulnerable isolation, to all the forms of disorganization and anomie endemic in the urban environment?

Inexplicably, it rarely seems to have occurred to the authors of the above conception of migrant man that family and kin ties need *not* be severed either during the migration itself or when the migrant had arrived in the city. One of the main objectives of this study is to explicitly show how family relationships and kinship networks function at all stages of the migratory process. The former is considered by reference to stage in the family life cycle. We classify our migrants into three groups:

> *Young Bachelors (A)*. Men aged 16-25 who were unmarried at last arrival to Monterrey (274 respondents).
>
> *Young Family Men (B)*. Men aged 26-35 who were married and with children upon last arrival (183 respondents; included are 42 men aged 21-25).

Older Family Men (C). Married men with children who were age 36 or older upon last arrival to Monterrey (205 respondents).

The broader kinship networks are taken up wherever appropriate.

Two other characteristics of the migrants besides their family and kin relationships will warrant attention. We have already alluded to the particular importance of rural-urban migration in the earlier conceptions. One mode of presentation of the results will be to separate migrants engaged in farm unemployment from migrants in nonfarm employment immediately prior to last migration to Monterrey. Since 141 men did not work immediately before coming to Monterrey, there are 303 men with farm and 460 with nonfarm backgrounds.

Finally, we want to introduce a temporal dimension into the discussion, for we cannot assume that in a fast-changing society such as Mexico the patterns we find for one particular time will be present in another. Consequently, we shall introduce time-of-arrival cohorts (always to be understood as last arrival) made up of those who arrived prior to 1941 (159); those between 1941-50 (211); those between 1951-60 (354); and the last arrivals between 1961–65 (180).

THE DECISION TO MOVE

Why do men migrate? More concretely, why did our respondents decide to go to Monterrey? Many factors impinge upon the decision to migrate, ranging from those more remote in a person's past (i.e., level of educational attainment) to those intermediate (i.e., drought conditions over the past several years) down to the immediate precipitant of the move (i.e., loss of job, word from a relative of a good job opening in the city). Most people are scarcely aware themselves of all the considerations that enter into their decision to migrate.

One point has been reasonably well established in a number of studies, however. When men are asked to explain why they migrated, economic factors related to their work invariably are selected as most important.[4] This generalization holds for the Monterrey migrants as well. We first asked our respondents the open question, "What influenced your decision to move?" and then we asked them to select the most important reason. As shown in Table 1, 70 percent of the migrants to Monterrey mentioned work as the most important factor influencing their decision to move. This figure is very close to the 65 percent of male migrants who reported reasons related to work as primary in a national survey conducted by the U.S. Bureau of the Census for the year March, 1962, to March, 1963 (1966) and also similar to the 62.0 percent reported for males migrating to Santiago, Chile by Elizaga (1966).

Next in importance are family reasons. The 17 percent for Monterrey compares with 13.6 for the U.S. sample and 7.6 percent for Santiago.

Family reasons are difficult to interpret because of the diversity of situations subsumed under the family label. It is obviously related to stages in the family life cycle. In Table 1 Young Bachelors have the highest percentage, reflecting the fact that some come to Monterrey not on their own initiative but rather that of their parents'. In contrast, the Young Family Men have their own families and are primarily work oriented. Some family moves are occasioned by a sense of family responsibility, as when a young man comes to assist aging or ailing parents, a move that may be to his own economic detriment.

Table 1. Major Reason for Migrating by Family Life Cycle (in percent)

Major Reason	All Migrants	Young Bachelors	Young Family Men	Older Family Men
Work	70	70	78	68
Family	17	18	11	14
Education	7	6	3	14
Community	3	4	4	1
Other	3	3	4	3
Total	100	101	100	100
N =	(810)[a]	(250)	(183)	(204)

a. This total is not the addition of the Life Cycle Groups A + B + C, but contains all migrants to Monterrey, less the 94 who did not work immediately before coming to Monterrey or who did not work the first year there.

Interestingly enough, education is far more important for Older Family Men than for the other groups; one of every seven of these men migrated primarily for that reason. Clearly the education is not for themselves but for their children. In Mexico, educational facilities in rural areas and small urban places are likely to be lacking or deficient, even on the primary level. If a student is to go on to secondary school and then to university, he must do so in the larger urban centers. Monterrey overall has the best facilities for higher education (a public and a private university) outside of Mexico City. Thus the older migrant, while not regarding migration as a means of directly bettering his own lot, sees it as an opportunity for materially improving the chances of his children.

It is worth mentioning that only three percent of the migrant men select "community" as a principal reason for migrating. They must respond in some degree favorably or unfavorably to Monterrey itself, but it is quite clear that this factor alone only rarely is considered to be decisive in bringing about migration.

THE RELATIONSHIP OF WORK EXPERIENCE
TO MIGRATION

We have established that work-related factors are by far the most important ones influencing the decision to move to Monterrey. Let us therefore first consider the work situation of migrants prior to migration. Table 2 presents the major industry categories in which the men were

Table 2. Last Work Before Migration by Time of Last Arrival (in percent)

TIME OF LAST ARRIVAL

Major Industry	1961-65	1951-60	1941-50	Before 1941	Total
Agriculture	37	46	39	29	40
Mining	4	4	9	8	6
Manufacturing	25	19	16	20	20
Construction	3	9	6	10	7
Commerce	10	9	12	17	11
Transportation, Communications	9	4	6	7	6
Services	12	9	13	9	11
Total	100	100	101	100	101
N =	(172)	(304)	(172)	(115)	(763)[a]

a. This table excludes 141 migrants who either did not work before migrating to Monterrey, or who were already commuting to work in Monterrey, or where industry was insufficiently specified.

employed just before coming to Monterrey by time of arrival. Agricultural employment is most important for each time period but what is unusual and perhaps unexpected is that changes in its importance over time do not correspond to the national trends in agricultural employment, during which there has been a steady proportional decline throughout most of the last 35 years.[5] For our sample, the proportion of the total employed in agriculture is at its lowest point in the years before 1941 and then it gradually builds to a high of 52 percent in the 1951-55 period, only to decline to 37 percent in the 1961-65 period. How are we to account for this U-shaped curve? As urged elsewhere (Browning and Feindt, 1969), migrants to Monterrey before 1941 were positively selective of the populations from which they originated. They were more likely to have higher educational attainment and to be in nonagricultural employment. More recent migrants to Monterrey, however, are much less selective as a

group. This selectivity interpretation also accounts for the elevated proportion we find in manufacturing before 1941, for it will be remembered
that this was before the major thrust of industrialization occurred in
Mexico. Only for the 1961-65 period did the proportion in manufacturing
rise to match that of the earlier period. The other industrial categories
generally show little variation over time. Mining declined, but this is consistent with the decline in mining activity in general over the last several
decades.

Since work is the most important factor influencing the decision to
migrate to Monterrey, it may be assumed that it was the men's dissatisfaction with the conditions of their work that set off the whole migratory process. We asked our respondents, "Were you satisfied with your
last job before coming to Monterrey?" Rather surprisingly, well over
one-half (56 percent) reported themselves satisfied, 14 percent were partly
satisfied, and only 30 percent unequivocably expressed dissatisfaction with
their job.

If most of the men were satisfied with their job, why did they quit?
We asked our men to select the single most important reason for leaving
their last work and this is given by major industry in Table 3. We distinguish between those who reported specific reasons related to work (34
percent for all migrants) and those who only reported a vague desire for
better work (10 percent). There appears, within the context of this table,
to be an approximate balance between those who left their work because
of forces of attraction as compared to forces of repulsion. Twenty-seven
percent reported they wanted more pay or the possibility for advancement while 28 percent left because their work terminated or went badly,
"se iba mal." There are considerable differences within industries. Nearly
four of ten men in agriculture left because they were "forced" off the
land. Only mining approached this figure, doubtless reflecting the decline
of mining in northeastern Mexico. Specific work-related reasons other
than pay and advancement (more stability, better working conditions
and more independence) were of minimal importance save for mining,
where a fifth said they left because they wanted better working conditions. The fact that "more independence" receives almost no mention
is not because the men are ignorant of its significance; when asked elsewhere in the interview to compare their jobs with those of their fathers,
the 26 percent of those in the representative sample who reported themselves worse off than their fathers gave less independence as the main
reason.

Once the migrant has made a decision to terminate his employment
or had this decision made for him by others or by natural factors, the
question arises as to how long an interval exists between leaving work
and the move to Monterrey. One might think that the respondents would
stay in the community for considerable periods of time after their last

Table 3. Principal Reason for Leaving Last Work by Major Industry (in percent)

			MAJOR INDUSTRY				
Principal Reason	*Agriculture*	*Mining*	*Manufacturing*	*Transp. and Constr.*	*Commerce*	*Services*	*Total*
More salary, advancement, etc.	22	17	31	31	36	31	27
More stability	4	5	1	3	1	6	3
Better working conditions	2	21	2	1	3	8	4
More independence	0	0	1	0	0	2	0
Total specific work reasons	(28)	(43)	(35)	(35)	(40)	(47)	(34)
Wanted better work	12	2	10	13	4	10	10
Work discontinued	39	33	20	16	19	13	28
Family reasons	10	10	15	16	21	11	13
Other reasons	11	10	19	21	16	21	15
Total	100	98	99	101	100	102	100
N =	(284)	(42)	(124)	(77)	(75)	(52)	(654)[a]

a. Excluded from this table are 250 migrants who either did not work before migrating to Monterrey or who were transferred, or who did not state reasons.

employment, hoping to find something else before finally moving on to Monterrey. To get at this point we asked the question, "How long after terminating your last employment was it until you moved to Monterrey?" Sixty percent reported coming immediately to Monterrey and 87 percent made the journey within one month. While the results indicate that the men do not generally "hang around" after their last job, it is likely in many cases that the decision to move began to form in the minds of respondents long before actual termination of work and that preparations were made in advance of leaving the job.

Another point of interest in tracing the migratory progress is the number of alternatives regarding place of destination. Of course, we know that our respondents came to Monterrey, but did they consider other destinations before making their choice? Eighty-nine percent said they did not. For the eleven percent who did entertain an alternate destination it was preponderantly a large urban place. Rural or small urban centers had very little attraction for the migrants. About equal proportions considered other urban centers in northeastern Mexico, Mexico City, urban places in other parts of Mexico, and the U.S.A. What tipped the scales in favor of Monterrey? Family and work reasons each are mentioned by about a third, with the other third involving idiosyncratic factors.

The decision to move to Monterrey no doubt was influenced to some extent by direct acquaintance with the city. Nearly two-thirds (63 percent) of the migrants had been to Monterrey prior to the final migration. Even for migrants who arrived before 1941, more than one-half (52 percent) had been to Monterrey. The figure rises to 75 percent for the latest arrivals (1961–65). Clearly, for most migrants, and especially those of recent arrival, the move to Monterrey was no perilous voyage into unknown and uncharted seas. In addition, not all migrations to Monterrey were considered at the time to be permanent changes of residence. We asked our respondents whether their plans had been to remain in Monterrey or eventually to return to their place of origin. Two-thirds (65 percent) reported that they had come to Monterrey with definite expectations of staying; that is, they had sold everything before coming. Twenty percent were more tentative and had come to see what would happen. If they liked Monterrey, they had planned to remain. The rest (16 percent) came with the idea of staying only for a time and then returning to their place of origin.

This figure is a good deal higher for those arriving after 1960 (25 percent) than for the earlier arrivals. The percentage declines to a low of nine percent for those arriving before 1941. Doubtless some part of the 1961-65 arrival cohort will leave Monterrey in the near future. That this group contains a substantial number of transient men (military, business and government) assigned to Monterrey is attested to by the fact that there is a high proportion (11 percent) who arrived with a signed work contract. A substantial part of this group will be gone by the end of a five-year interval, hence their effect is concentrated mainly in the 1961-65 arrival cohort.

Most of the migrants (58 percent) came to Monterrey with nothing more than the hope of finding a satisfactory job. Only 23 percent arrived either with a signed contract or with a definite job promised to them. Another eight percent had a fairly concrete plan for obtaining work. Ten percent did not come to Monterrey to seek work and they are concentrated in the youngest (11-15) and oldest (45-60) age categories. If the major industries in which the migrants were employed before they came to Monterrey are considered, we find that only ten percent of those in agriculture had either a contract or a specific job lined up. By contrast, 27 percent in manufacturing and 41 percent in services had made such an arrangement. This clearly is linked to the marketable skills the migrants can bring to a metropolitan environment.

OVERALL EVALUATION OF THE MOVE
TO MONTERREY

At the end of the series of questions dealing with reasons for leaving their job and for coming to Monterrey we asked the question, "Finally, are you satisfied with having come to Monterrey?" The overwhelmingly positive response (92 percent reported themselves satisfied) to this question was unexpected. (Only three percent gave an unqualified no, while five percent said they were satisfied in part.) That nine of every ten men said they were satisfied with the move no doubt overstates the positive response, for it is well known that people have a tendency to report themselves satisfied with their present situation, no matter what it is. And, of course, although data are lacking, it is undeniable that many of the most dissatisfied migrants had left Monterrey by the time of the survey.

But even if we acknowledge that 92 percent is too high, it still is indisputable that the great majority of migrants were satisfied with their decision to migrate to Monterrey. When asked why they were satisfied, the answers are illuminating. Nine percent expressed general satisfaction. Eighteen percent said in effect that they were content because in Monterrey they were able to satisfy at least the minimal conditions for livelihood ("I have work," "I'm not hungry"). Of those employed in agriculture, mining, and construction before migrating, about a third responded in this manner. This background generally involves risky and undependable work. Moreover, these migrants do not bring skills that have a high value in the urban environment, so it may be that they simply do not have high aspirations.

Although most of our men said they migrated because of work-related reasons, only 19 percent specifically mentioned their work as the reason for their satisfaction in moving. One-fourth (25 percent) said they enjoyed a higher level of living in Monterrey ("earn more," "live better"). Fifteen percent report family reasons and ten percent satisfaction with the community, the latter reason being over-represented among the higher-status migrants.

Since there are only a few cases of expressed dissatisfaction with the decision to migrate to Monterrey, they cannot be analyzed in detail. These men are mainly disappointed with income and level of living (32 percent) and with the community (25 percent). Only 16 percent report dissatisfaction with work itself.

MARITAL STATUS AND COMPOSITION OF
THE MIGRANT GROUP

In this section we will first consider the marital status of the men upon arrival to Monterrey. Then we will deal with the actual migratory act itself in relation to the family group involved. While marital status restricts the possible combinations of the migratory act, it does not permit us to predict who will migrate with whom. For instance, a Young Bachelor obviously cannot migrate with his family of procreation, but he may come alone, with his family of origin, or with other relatives or friends. A married man with children may make it a three-generational group by bringing his parents along. The timing of such a move may even be in three parts: first the father comes alone, then he sends for his wife and children, and finally the parents are called. The patterns of movement can become complex.

Marital status is linked closely to age. Not unexpectedly, men who migrate to Monterrey between ages 16 and 20 are nearly all single, while those 31 and over are nearly all married. There is an even balance between single and married in the 21–30 age group.

Considering marital status by time-of-arrival cohorts, we find a pronounced trend toward a married state from the oldest to the most recent arrivals:

TIME OF LAST ARRIVAL

	1961-65	1951-60	1941-50	Before 1941	Total
Single	23	42	59	79	49
Married	72	55	38	20	48
Widowed, divorced or separated	4	3	3	1	3
Total	99	100	100	100	100
N =	(180)	(354)	(211)	(159)	(904)

This trend is affected by the fact that as a group the men who migrated earlier to Monterrey were younger. There are insufficient cases to present all arrival cohorts by age, but for the men who were aged 21-30 at time of arrival we find that 59 percent of those arriving before 1941 were single. This declines to 43 percent for the 1961–65 period.

Not only are the recent migrants more likely to arrive married, they are also more likely to arrive with children. Table 4 presents those who were at least 21 years upon last arrival to Monterrey and who were married. The proportion arriving with three or more children rises from 19 percent in the earliest period to a peak of 41 in the 1951–60 interval. This pattern is consistent with the declining selectivity hypothesis advanced earlier.

We can now relate marital status, in the form of the Family Life Cycle Groups, to the actual migration itself. Table 5 shows the composition of the migratory group. Note that only one-fifth of the migrants come alone. Does this fit the image of the lone and lonely migrant? Even among the

Table 4. Married Men by Number of Dependent Children by Time of Last Arrival to Monterrey (in percent)

TIME OF LAST ARRIVAL

Dependent Children	1961-65	1951-60	1941-50	Before 1941	Total
None	22	23	21	42	24
One	19	14	19	32	18
Two	27	22	21	6	22
Three	12	16	19	13	15
Four	11	17	10	7	13
Five or more	9	8	10	0	8
Total	100	100	100	100	100
N =	(130)	(196)	(80)	(31)	(437)[a]

a. Married men include only those 21 years or older upon arrival to Monterrey. Dependent children are all those ten years or under.

Table 5. Composition of Migratory Group by Family Life Cycle (in percent)

Migratory Group	All Migrants	Young Bachelors	Young Family Men	Older Family Men
Respondent alone	19	31	8	9
With family of procreation	39	—	72	83
With family of origin	34	66	2	1
With family of origin & procreation	6	—	15	5
Other combinations	2	3	3	1
Total	100	100	100	99
N =	(891)[a]	(274)	(184)	(208)

a. Thirteen cases with no information are excluded.

Young Bachelors only a third come alone. Young Family Men are more likely to arrive in three-generational groups, but such an arrangement is not common in any of the groups.

It is worthy of note that when respondents are examined by time of arrival, 44 percent of the Young Bachelors (and 56 percent of all single men) who arrived in the 1961–65 period came alone. No doubt this reflects the transient status of some of these men in military, industry,

Table 6. Type of Migration by Family Life Cycle and Farm-Nonfarm Background (in percent)

Type of Migration	All Migrants	YOUNG BACHELORS (A)			YOUNG FAMILY MEN (B)			OLDER FAMILY MEN (C)		
		Farm	Non-farm	Total Group A	Farm	Non-farm	Total Group B	Farm	Non-farm	Total Group C
Solitary	20	24	34	31	15	4	8	10	9	9
Simultaneous	38	15	20	18	44	73	62	50	53	52
Split	42	61	46	51	41	23	30	40	38	39
Total	100	100	100	100	100	100	100	100	100	100
N =	(884)[a]	(88)[b]	(146)[b]	(274)	(71)[b]	(112)[b]	(183)	(91)[b]	(110)[b]	(205)

a. Excluded are 20 cases with no information.
b. Based only on migrants who worked before coming to Monterrey.

and government employment. Otherwise, there are no significant changes in this migratory pattern over time.

The dimension of migration we have not yet tapped is the sequence and timing of movement when persons other than the respondent are involved. Logically we may identify: (1) *solitary migration,* when the man comes alone and no one precedes or follows him; (2) *simultaneous migration,* when everyone in the migratory group, however it is made up, comes together; or (3) *split migration,* when the migratory group comes at different intervals. The respondent may be in the avant-garde or rear guard of the group. For example, as a son he may go first to find a job and then prepare for the arrival of his parents and siblings. The possible combinations are many.

Table 6 gives the three types of migration by Family Life Cycle Groups and Farm-Nonfarm background of the migrants. Predictably, it is the Young Bachelors who are most likely to come alone, but nine percent of the Older Family Men come alone. This would include some of the transient 1961–65 migrants or men abandoning their families. Young Family Men understandably travel to Monterrey as part of a group. Migrants who worked in agriculture before coming to Monterrey are less likely to come as a group and more likely to be part of the "bridging" process that is characteristic of split migrations. Among the Young Family Men the difference between those with farm and nonfarm background is particularly strong (44 and 73 percent respectively for simultaneous migration and 41 and 23 percent for split migrations). About the same number of respondents in the split migration category came in the avant-garde as in the rear guard (41 and 42 percent respectively).

Finally, there is the time interval within split migration between the first and last arrival. What is striking is the considerable length of time that is sometimes needed to complete the split migration pattern. Over forty percent of all Young Bachelors with split migration are involved in a sequence that takes more than three years to work itself out. Among Young Family Men this time period is reduced: forty-six percent reunite with their families within six months. Even here, however, almost an equal proportion (44 percent) require more than a year to bring the family together.

This brief survey of split migration patterns touches upon an aspect of migration that is sometimes overlooked. Migration, in this perspective of family units and kinship networks is properly seen as a continuous process, not a movement restricted only to the number of days a person, with or without companions, needs to journey to Monterrey. As we have seen, a sizeable part of the migration extends over a period of years. It is a relatively stable pattern for it does not vary greatly when examined by time-of-arrival cohorts. This suggests that for any specific date we can confidently predict for Monterrey a fair volume of subsequent migration simply as a result of the split migration pattern. This is but another way of saying that migration to Monterrey generates its own momentum and, to a certain extent, becomes independent of economic opportunity.

MIGRATION TO MONTERREY AND FORMS
OF ASSISTANCE

It has been established that most migrants were acquainted with the city prior to last arrival. But did they know anyone there and, if so, did this mean they had an easier time of it? Is assistance made available to the migrants and, if so, in what form? How does this assistance ease the adjustment to life in Monterrey?

The first question is whether the migrants had relatives or friends living in Monterrey at the time of the last migration. A very large proportion (84 percent) had. Because of the heavy flow of migrants into Monterrey during the last decades, the probability of having relatives or friends in Monterrey should be greatest for the more recent arrivals. This is true to the extent that the figure rises from 77 percent for those arriving before 1941 to 86 percent in the 1961–65 cohort. What is striking is how narrow the range is. Evidently, the familial and kinship networks in Monterrey were established well before the migratory surge reached its highest intensity after 1940.

Of course, the mere presence of relatives or friends does not insure that help will be forthcoming. How many of the migrants with these relationships actually received assistance? Two-thirds of those who had friends or relatives living in Monterrey obtained help in some form. Unfortunately, since there were no questions on this point, we do not know what part of the 32 percent who were not aided asked for assistance but were denied it.

The most common form of assistance (70 percent of all aid) is the provision of food and shelter—a highly personal and family-related form of assistance. Our Monterrey data suggest that the kinship network is rather effective in taking care of the basic needs of the migrants immediately after arrival to the metropolis. This pattern is quite stable by time of arrival. All other kinds of aid are much less common. Help in finding a job is of a certain importance (14 percent), especially for the more recent bachelor arrivals. Assistance in finding housing for those families who did not stay with relatives accounted for ten percent of all aid. Direct financial assistance, either by paying for the trip or lending money is rare (seven percent). Migrants cannot expect much help from those "back home." Only thirteen percent of the migrants received any kind of assistance. Most of it takes the form of a one-way bus ticket, predominantly to young, single migrants under 20 years of age. Unquestionably this is related to the forces that bring about migration in the first place—poor economic conditions that generate only little cash income.

At this point, let us consider again the phenomenon of split migration introduced in the last section. Help can flow in two directions: from the arrival(s) in Monterrey to the remaining member(s) of the group in the community of departure and vice versa. For example, a family may send a son to school in Monterrey and pay his expenses. After he has finished schooling and obtained a job he may help the rest of his family to come to Monterrey, or perhaps to assist in the education of his younger brothers and sisters in the city.

In those cases of split migration in which there was at least a six-month interval between the first and last arrivals we inquired as to whether those who remained behind sent money to the avant-garde in Monterrey. Only 19 percent did. A much greater flow of money went from Monterrey to the prior community of residence. Forty-seven percent of the first arrivals reported sending money back to those remaining, a figure showing relatively little variation through time. Given the importance of rural-urban migration and the fact that Monterrey generally provides better economic opportunities (especially in generating cash income) than the previous communities of residence (mainly rural), it is not surprising that such a pattern exists. But there also are forms of aid other than money. Those of the avant-garde who could or did not send money (53 percent) helped the latecomers in various other ways. Finding housing for the latecomers was by far the most common way (78 percent of all non-monetary aid). It may be puzzling that only ten percent of all non-monetary aid is help in finding work until we remember that the latecomers are often wives and children who normally would not be part of the labor force. This relationship shows up too in the category "went to get them" (nine percent of all non-monetary aid). We had not anticipated such a response but the men consider it a type of help and doubtless it is, especially for those unaccustomed to travel, such as women with children or older people.

LIVING ARRANGEMENTS UPON ARRIVAL

Looking at the circumstances surrounding arrival to Monterrey and how it might affect the migrants—particularly those coming directly to Monterrey from small villages—we singled out housing arrangements for closer analysis. Migrants who first live with relatives or friends are more likely to be introduced to the city gradually and by guides they know and trust, while those living independently presumably have to fend for themselves in the new environment. Table 7 shows that more than half of the migrants first lived with relatives or friends already established in Monterrey. This holds not only for the Young Bachelors, but for men with families which, considering the restricted housing space in Monterrey for the great mass of population, certainly entails considerable crowding.

Migrants from farm backgrounds are more likely to receive protection and shelter from relatives than those originating from nonfarm backgrounds. Those most in need of primary group contacts are most likely

Table 7. Living Arrangement upon Arrival to Monterrey by Family Life Cycle and Farm-Nonfarm Background (in percent)

Living Arrangement	All Migrants	YOUNG BACHELORS (A)			YOUNG FAMILY MEN (B)			OLDER FAMILY MEN (C)		
		Farm	Non-farm	Total Group A	Farm	Non-farm	Total Group B	Farm	Non-farm	Total Group C
Lived with relatives or friends already in Monterrey	58	76	57	62	74	42	55	67	51	58
Lived independently	42	24	43	38	26	58	45	33	49	42
Total N =	100 (881)[a]	100 (87)[b]	100 (143)[b]	100 (270)	100 (70)[b]	100 (111)[b]	100 (181)	100 (91)[b]	100 (111)[b]	100 (206)

a. Excluded are 23 cases with no information.
b. Based only on migrants who worked before coming to Monterrey.

to experience the city first through a familial context. An interesting side-light reflecting the male dominance pattern of the Mexican family structure is the fact that of the married migrants who lived with relatives 71 percent resided with relatives of the husband, while only 21 percent lived with relatives of the wife. (Eight percent lived with friends.) It is unlikely that these percentages reflect the lesser availability of wife's relatives in Monterrey. It is more reasonable to assume that the husband will generally avoid a form of dependence upon his wife's relatives for fear that it will weaken his authority within his own nuclear family.

What about those migrants who live independently of established relatives or friends upon their arrival to the metropolis? Did they live independently because they did not know anybody? Table 8 shows that this is true for 41 percent of the migrants who lived independently (18 percent of all migrants). There are significant differences between the family life cycle groups: 53 percent of the Young Bachelors lived independently as compared with 25 percent of the Young Family Men. Most Young Family Men living independently evidently did so by their own choosing; 43 percent of them were aided in finding housing by relatives or friends or by the company employing them.

Table 8. Forms of Assistance to Those Living Independently upon Last Arrival to Monterrey by Family Life Cycle

Forms of Assistance	All Migrants Living Inde- pendently	Young Bachelors	Young Family Men	Older Family Men
Did not know anyone in Monterrey	41	53	25	35
Knew someone but received no help	32	28	31	40
Relatives or friends prepared housing	7	7	11	6
Relatives or friends helped find housing	10	6	14	11
Company helped find housing	11	6	18	8
Total	101	100	99	100
N =	(384)	(107)	(83)	(95)

Looking at Table 8 it appears that the Young Bachelors are the group conforming most closely to the stereotyped image of the migrant alone in the big city. Thirty-eight percent of the Young Bachelors living independently (15 percent of all migrants) were to be found in *pensiones* or similar arrangements. But a Mexican *pensión* is a far cry from an impersonal hotel; it is usually run by a *señora* who provides meals and a certain amount of motherly supervision and the young lodgers more often than not share rooms. Whatever the lot of these Young Bachelors, there is a larger proportion of Young Bachelors (42 percent) who do not lack for family living; they migrated with their family of origin and live with their parents independent of other relatives or friends in the city. Another 20 percent live with their employers, i.e., heads of private households, masters for apprentices, small shopkeepers, the military. Most of the family men (over 90 percent) who do not move in with relatives or friends already in Monterrey live with their own migratory group, that is, their family of procreation.

This discussion of the extent of kinship contacts of migrants upon arrival to Monterrey can be summarized in the following table whereby the migrants are grouped in five categories according to the amount of kin interaction:

		Percent	N
Category 1	Lived with relatives, had additional relatives in neighborhood	20	(171)
Category 2	Lived with relatives, but no additional relatives in neighborhood	38	(337)
Category 3	Lived independently, had relatives in neighborhood	11	(100)
Category 4	Lived independently, no relatives in neighborhood but elsewhere in the city	17	(145)
Category 5	Lived independently, no relatives in neighborhood or in the rest of the city	14	(124)
Total		100	(877)[a]

a. Excluded are 27 cases with no information on one or more of the three questions used to make up the index.

Migrants in Category 1 are most deeply involved in a network of family relations in Monterrey. Not only do they live with relatives, but they are in close contact with other relatives who live in the same neighborhood. When asked how often they visited these relatives during the first year in Monterrey, 60 percent answered "more than once a week," 26 percent "once a week or every 15 days," ten percent "once a month or less," and only four percent "never visited." Migrants in Category 3 visit to a similar extent. We can say, therefore, that migrants in the first three categories (69 percent of all migrants), are members of close-knit family networks. We cannot say that those in Category 4 do not interact with kin, since we do not have information on contacts with relatives in Monterrey who live outside the neighborhood. The migrants in Category 5 (representing one of every seven men) are the ones who had to make their start in the city without the presumed benefit of family relations.

We say "presumed" benefit, for we should not jump to the conclusion that those migrants without extensive kinship contacts in a metropolis necessarily are worse off than those who have them. The benefit derived from kinship networks depends upon the background of the migrants. If they originate from rural or small urban places the kinship network is the only buffer between the migrant and his new environment. It has been shown (Browning and Feindt, n.d.) that of those migrants to Monterrey whose community of origin was rural—and they make up more than one-half of all migrants—59 percent came directly to Monterrey. For these men there is no possibility of prior socialization to the ways of metropolitan Monterrey by virtue of residence in some other urban place. Those coming to Monterrey from metropolitan or large urban places will be less in need of kinship networks to ease the transition.

Table 9. Membership in Kinship Networks by Size Class of Community of Origin, Farm-Nonfarm Background, and Education (in percent)

	NEIGHBORHOOD KINSHIP NETWORK			
Size Class of Community of Origin	*Yes*[a]	*No*[a]	*Total*	N
Rural (−5,000)	73	27	100	(479)
Small urban (5,000–19,999)	70	30	100	(182)
Medium urban (20,000–99,999)	62	38	100	(161)
Large urban (100,000+)	56	44	100	(43)
Last employment before arrival to Monterrey				
Farm	82	18	100	(292)
Nonfarm	62	38	100	(447)
Education				
Primary Education or less	73	27	100	(686)
Beyond primary	55	45	100	(190)

a. Social Contact Categories 1, 2 and 3 are YES; 4 and 5 are NO.

In Table 9 one finds the larger the community of origin (where respondents grew up) the more likely it is that in-migrants will not be part of neighborhood kinship networks. In every case, however, well over one-half are part of such primary groups. Much the same pattern is observed for farm-nonfarm employment immediately prior to last arrival in Monterrey and education. Since we are not concerned in this essay with the long-term adjustment of migrants to the occupational milieu of Monterrey, we will only suggest that, of itself, participation in kinship networks is not requisite for socioeconomic success. It may be, however, that *within* major socioeconomic categories (less than primary school, farm background, etc.) those with kinship networks will do better than those without.

THE MIGRANT'S MAINTENANCE OF CONTACTS WITH PERSONS IN COMMUNITIES OF PREVIOUS RESIDENCE

Most of the migrants to Monterrey had friends or relatives living there before they arrived. But once in Monterrey how close are the ties they maintain to people in communities they have lived in before? Some 88 percent still have relatives and friends there and the more recent the arrival to Monterrey the more likely they are to have relatives or friends in these places (see Table 10). The figure rises from 77 percent in the

Table 10. Kind of Contact with Relatives or Friends in Place Lived in Longest by Time of Arrival to Monterrey (in percent)

TIME OF LAST ARRIVAL

Presence of Relatives	*1961-65*	*1951-60*	*1941-50*	*Before 1941*	*Total*
Respondent has relatives in other place	93	90	85	77	88
Respondent no relatives in other place	7	10	15	23	12
Total	100	100	100	100	100
N =	(179)	(350)	(206)	(155)	(890)[a]
If Relatives, Kind of Contact					
Send money, write and visit	9	5	7	5	6
Write and visit	37	35	35	27	34
Visit only	17	27	32	36	27
Write only	19	13	10	4	12
Other	4	2	1	3	2
No contact	15	18	15	26	18
Total	101	100	100	101	99
N =	(167)	(316)	(176)	(120)	(779)

a. Excluded are 14 cases with no information.

earliest arrival cohort to 93 percent in the latest (1961–65). That is, about three of every four migrants identified friends and relatives in places of previous residence even after the passage of 25 or more years since migrating. Of all respondents who reported affirmatively, 69 percent had relatives or friends only in their community of origin, 18 percent in both community of origin and one or more other places, and 13 percent had relatives and friends only in communities other than their community of origin.

The question remains whether or not our respondents actually maintained contact, and in what form, with their relatives and friends. As Table 10 reveals, of those with relatives or friends still living in communities the respondent had resided in, four out of every five migrants maintain relations of some kind. The most frequent way of maintaining contact is a combination of writing and occasional visits (34 percent), followed by those who visit only (28 percent). The forms which the contacts with relatives or friends in previously lived in communities assume vary by time of arrival. When we consider all forms of contact, those which involve writing occur to a much higher degree among later arrivals. On the other hand, visiting is mentioned significantly more often by the earlier arrivals than by the later ones.

CONCLUSION

The reader who has followed us through the many descriptive details of the chronology of last migration to Monterrey should not require much convincing on the importance of social, particularly familial, factors in the process of migration. The concept of "process" needs to be emphasized. Over many years of sustained heavy in-migration to Monterrey, a relation with other communities, via the kinship and friendship network, has developed so that migration rightfully is to be seen as a continuous process, nearly always involving simultaneously many people in at least two localities.

Within this perspective the migratory pattern is quite stable; it is the individuals who change positions in the process. At any given point in time a person may be labelled differently from the way he would be at another point.[6] Migrants depend upon earlier arrivals for help in establishing themselves and they in turn assist in the accommodation of later arrivals. Migration begets migration in a way not directly related to the economic allure of Monterrey and tends to be self-perpetuating.

Our findings, taken in their totality, lend very little support to some common impressions of migration in Latin America. People are not uprooted from their communities of origin to be driven into a great, grey, hostile, metropolitan environment where they, in vulnerable isolation, are exposed to all forms of disorganization. The great majority of men reported themselves glad they made the change. The experience is not nearly as disruptive or traumatic as it sometimes is portrayed. Only a few of the migrants come alone, and most of them have relatives or friends awaiting them in Monterrey to help ease the period of adjustment.

These conclusions are not novel. For Mexico at least, Oscar Lewis (1952) had suggested some time ago a pattern similar to the one presented here. And we may anticipate that as empirical studies of migration increase in number and as more countries are represented, the older speculative conceptions of migration will be superseded. Cornelius (Chapter 6) has performed a valuable service in his comprehensive comparison of "developmental theorists and Latin Americanists" with "empirically-based studies." His interest is not with the migratory process as such but the consequences of urban environment upon migrants. He is able to demonstrate quite effectively that the "theorists" had posited many negative consequences for migrants (felt deprivation, frustration of socioeconomic expectations, personal and/or social disorganization, alienation, etc.) that were only rarely substantiated in the empirical studies. His finding is also supported by the Monterrey data. In the United States, to cite but one example, Brown, *et al.* (1963) found that migration from a Kentucky locale occurs within a kinship context no doubt similar to that of many migrants to Monterrey. And, of course, African studies of migration, Little (1966) for example, have always placed great emphasis upon the social context of migration.

We should not like to leave the impression that migration to cities in Latin America involves no strain, or that it is always successful. Given the great differences in environments between rural and metropolitan areas, there have to be adjustments, not all of them pleasant. And it must be remembered that our findings are for Monterrey, a city with better than average economic growth. Other urban centers, particularly the stagnant ones, may display somewhat different patterns. We are, however, of the belief that the Monterrey pattern is not atypical in Latin America and that the adaptation of migrants is fairly successful. Man is a far more adaptable animal than he is sometimes given credit for!

NOTES

1. Certain restrictions on the scope of this essay should be seen within the context of the larger project, the Monterrey Mobility Study, from which the data are taken. We do not concern ourselves with the geographic origins of the migrants, the number of moves, conformity to the stage migration hypothesis and the phenomenon of return migration. These features are taken up in another article, "Patterns of Migration to Monterrey, Mexico" (Browning and Feindt, n.d.). The important question of the extent to which migrants differ from comparable populations in their community of origin for such characteristics as education and occupation is considered in "Selectivity of Migrants to a Metropolis in a Developing Country: A Mexican Case Study." (Browning and Feindt, 1969). The problem of how well the migrants fare in the occupational structure of Monterrey when compared with the natives is analyzed elsewhere (Browning and Feindt, 1968). Jorge Balán, "Are Farmers' Sons Handicapped in the City?" (1968) uses Monterrey data to relate social origin to occupational achievement in the city. Finally, the matter of value orientations and attitudes of migrants toward work, family, and so forth, is the subject of a study in progress by Richard Rockwell.

2. Within Latin America, an incomplete listing would include studies sponsored by the Centro Latinoamericano de Demografía (CELADE) for Santiago, Chile

(Elizaga, 1966), and Lima, Peru, that have yet to be reported in detail. There is also the work of Germani (1961) for Buenos Aires, Hutchinson (1963) in Brazil, the MacDonalds (1968) in Venezuela, and Butterworth (1962) for Mexico City, among others.

3. For further details on the Monterrey study see Balán, *et al.* (1967) or an unpublished translation, "Technical Procedures in the Execution of the Monterrey Mobility Survey," available upon request from the Population Research Center, University of Texas at Austin.

4. Henry Shryock (1969) reviews surveys in the United States, Canada, Chile, Turkey, India, Japan, and Korea relevant to this point. He points out that comparability is still limited due to differences in survey design, especially in classification schemes of reasons for moving.

5. Mexican census data on the labor force present problems of comparability from one census date to another, but in 1930, 72 percent of the economically active male population of Mexico was reported in agriculture and other primary activities. This declined to 59 percent for the 1960 census and, no doubt, it had dropped two or three more percentage points by 1965.

6. For example, a Young Bachelor may have come to Monterrey alone at the time of the survey with no intention of bringing any other members of his family. He is classified in the "solitary" category. Five years later he changes his mind and calls for his parents to come. At that time he would be reclassified as a "split" migrant.

REFERENCES

BALÁN, JORGE, E. J. BALÁN and H. L. BROWNING (1967) *Movilidad Social, Migración, y Fecundidad en Monterrey Metropolitano.* Monterrey, Mexico: Centro de Investigaciones Económicas, Universidad de Nuevo León.

BALAN, JORGE (1968) "Are farmers' sons handicapped in the city?" *Rural Sociology* 33 (June): 160–174.

BROWN, JAMES S., H. K. SCHWARZWELLER and J. J. MANGALAM (1933) "Kentucky mountain migration and the stem-family: an American variation on a theme by LePlay." *Rural Sociology* 28 (March): 48–69.

BROWNING, HARLEY and W. FEINDT (1968) "Diferencias entre la población nativa y la migrante en Monterrey." *Demografía y Economía* (México) 2, No. 2, 183–204.

——— (1969) "Selectivity of migrants to a metropolis in a developing country: a Mexican case study." *Demography*.

——— (n.d.) "Patterns of Migration to Monterrey, Mexico." Austin: Population Research Center (mimeo.).

BUTTERWORTH, DOUGLAS S. (1962) "A study of the urbanization process among Mixtec migrants from Tilaltongo in Mexico City." *América Indígena* 22 (July): 257–74.

CORNELIUS, WAYNE JR. (1970) "The political sociology of cityward migration in Latin America: toward empirical theory." Chapter 6 of this volume.

ELIZAGA, JUAN C. (1966) "A study of migration to greater Santiago [Chile]." *Demography* 3, No. 2: 352–377.

GERMANI, GINO (1961) "Inquiry into the social effects of urbanization in a working-class sector of Buenos Aires." Pp. 206–233 in P. M. Hauser (ed.) *Urbanization in Latin America.* New York: International Documents Service.

HUTCHISON, BERTRAM (1963) "The migrant populaton of urban Brazil." *América Latina* 6 (April-June): 41–71.

LANSING, JOHN B. and E. MUELLER (1967) *The Geographic Mobility of Labor.* Ann Arbor, Mich.: Institute for Socal Research.

LEWIS, OSCAR (1952) "Urbanization without breakdown: a case study." *Scientific Monthly,* 75 (July): 31–41.

LITTLE, KENNETH (1966) *West African Urbanization: A Study of Voluntary Associations in Social Change.* London: Cambridge University Press.

MACDONALD, LEATRICE D. and J. S. MACDONALD (1968) "Motives and objectives of migration: selective migration and preferences toward rural and urban life." *Social and Economic Studies* 17 (December): 417–434.

SHRYOCK, HENRY (1969) "Survey statistics on reasons for moving." Paper presented at the meetings of the International Union for the Scientific Study of Population, London (September 3–11).

U.S. Bureau of the Census (1960) "Reasons for Moving: March 1962 to March 1963." *Current Population Reports, Population Characteristics,* P-20, No. 154 (August 22).

Chapter 4

URBANIZATION AND URBAN MIGRATION IN LATIN AMERICA: AN ECONOMIST'S VIEW

BRUCE HERRICK

Latin American urbanization reflects a pervasive and profound phenomenon, characterized most simply by unprecedented rates of growth of the largest cities. Vast tides of human migration are a dynamic element within this process. They result in rates of urban population growth forty to seventy per cent larger than would occur in the presence of natural increase alone (Arriaga, 1968). Higher rates of natural increase in rural areas than in urban ones merely serve to accentuate the impulses in favor of internal population redistribution.

An economist viewing urbanization either impressionistically or statistically wants to devise explanations at once simple and general. At first, these theories might be judged on their ability to explain the motives of migrants, the rates of resultant migration or at least changes in these rates, and the directions of internal migration in terms of origin and destination. In short, migrants' individual decisions might be examined.

But as usual, the macroeconomic impact of urbanization on the society as a whole poses an even more difficult question. The urban migrant leaves one area and arrives in another. Does his movement affect human welfare in either area, and if so, how?[1]

As little as five years ago, satisfactory responses to these questions were difficult to render. Our task has been made easier now, both by theoretical advances and by a considerable amount of empirical work on the subject. Internal migration and resultant urbanization in all countries have been sufficiently dramatic to attract systematic examination from a variety

AUTHOR'S NOTE: M. J. Frankman, W. P. McGreevey, and C. T. Nisbet made particularly helpful comments upon reading an earlier draft of this paper.

of intellectul disciplines. But, it is interesting, if a bit discouraging, to note the amount of misinformation still accepted as conventional wisdom about Latin American urbanization. Even so distinguished a research organization as the United Nations' Economic Commission for Latin America can be found announcing that "the population shift from the country to the town mainly involves surplus agricultural workers and their families, who come from the poorest and least skilled sectors of the rural population." Their migration is "responsible for the concentration in the cities . . . of unskilled workers with little chance of finding productive employment." (Slawinski, 1965: 164). No knowledgeable person takes a Panglossian view that all's for the best in Latin American cities. But at the same time if we explore possibilities for the application of economic analysis to the phenomenon of Latin American urbanization no detailed empirical study confirms the assertions quoted above. And, economic theory is more consistent with the empirical observations than with the impressionistic vision cited.

URBAN MIGRANTS AND THE RATE OF RETURN

Migration can be pictured as a process involving investment in human capital (Sjaastad, 1962; Becker, 1964). The migrant incurs costs in order to reap future benefits. His migration decision is hypothesized to depend on the rate of return from so doing.

The act of migration then becomes a function of three variables: differential returns (the difference between returns accruing to the migrant before migration and after[2]), differential costs, and length of time over which the returns are received. We would thus hypothesize the higher rates of migration among those individuals or groups whose rates of return from migration were highest, that is, among potential migrants with high differential returns, low differential costs, and long periods during which the returns would flow.

Differential returns are related to an older formulation of migration theory that postulates movement on the basis of pulls and pushes (Fischlowitz, 1965, 1966; Sahota, 1968). Urban pulls include higher wages or more job opportunities in the cities. Rural push factors involve trends toward more *minifundos*, insecure land tenure, or increasing concentration of farm ownership. The concept of differential returns clearly encompasses both push and pull, and implies that trying to separate them is an intellectually empty exercise.

Similarly dated are gravity models (e.g., Stouffer, 1940; Lee, 1966). Their concept of intervening opportunites (pulls) is more simply and generally represented by differential returns. Furthermore, migration in gravity models is discouraged by distance. In the rate-of-return model, increasing distance implies increasing costs of transport and information. Insofar as there also exist costs of migration which are functionally unrelated to distance, the rate-of-return hypothesis once again appears a more general formulation.[3]

Several objections to using this framework have been offered. The most common is concerned with its exclusive emphasis on measurable economic factors. To reduce migration or any other human action to its economic elements is, of course, to rob analysis of potential richness that would follow from a less unidimensional point of view. At the same time the nature of models in the social sciences as elsewhere is to strip away details and to concentrate on a simplified view of human action.

Evidence supporting migrants' economic orientation appears in their responses to surveys. Whatever may be the shortcomings of these responses, they always indicate a large proportion of migration, as explained by the migrants themselves, as economically motivated (Instituto de Economía, 1959; Elizaga, 1966; Peru, Dirección Nacional de Estadística y Censos, 1966). Included as "economically motivated" are moves by wives and children to join breadwinners already resident at the destination. Without dealing directly with the well-known problems of accuracy of survey response, it seems significant that so many migrants are aware of the plausibility of an economic answer, even if it lacks completeness or oversimplifies complex decision-making processes that may precede migration.

Finally, some scientists would judge a theory on its capability for prediction. Migrants may not (indeed, do not) make calculations of discounted present values and corresponding rates of return. But the theory, following this view, is vindicated if they behave *as if* they do. Accordingly, this section tries merely to show the consistency between observed behavior and the rate-of-return theory without claiming that rate-of-return is the only possible perspective from which to view the process.

The most generally observed aspect of differential migration, namely, the relative youth of the migrants (Arias, 1963; Bogue, 1963; Chen, 1968; Ducoff, 1963; Elizaga, 1965, 1966; Latin American Demographic Center, 1963; Peru, Dirección Nacional de Estadística y Censos, 1966; Rivarola, 1967; Wingo, 1967; to cite only a few studies dealing with Latin-American cities) is explained under the rate-of-return hypothesis by the expected length of working life. Younger people tend more to migrate owing to the longer periods over which they can reap the benefits from having done so. It is therefore unnecessary to resort to introspective impressions about the greater flexibility of youth or the more settled habits of older people in order to explain the age selectivity of movement.

Similarly the predominance of females among Latin American urban migrants (Arias, 1963; Burnight, 1963; Ducoff, 1963; Elizaga, 1965; Latin American Demographic Center, 1963) is consistent with a rate-of-return hypothesis. Employment opportunities for women on farms or even in villages are rare; cities, by contrast, are characterized by a multitude of low-skill, low-productivity jobs in domestic service and petty commerce. Of course, the low levels of skill and productivity asserted here refer to absolute rather than relative standards. Relative to pre-migration employment or self-employment alternatives, these jobs may be highly productive. Although their absolute returns may be thought low by outsiders, only differential returns affect movement based on rate of return. By contrast to opportunities for females, the possibilities for high *differentials* in earnings for men are lower, although absolute earnings in the city are considerably higher, and accordingly fewer males engage in urban migration in Latin America.

The economic desirability of avoiding unemployment has suggested a job opportunity hypothesis that predicts net migratory flows toward places with low unemployment rates. This hypothesis regards low measured rates of unemployment in the countryside as specious because they ignore disguised unemployment and underemployment in agricultural activities. However, high unemployment rates in cities would discourage migration only to the extent that they reduced the statistically expected value of differential returns and in turn lowered the rate of return from investment in migration to a value below that of alternative investments.[4] The lack of alternatives to migration frequently posited for *campesinos* implies migration's insensitivity to high measured rates of urban unemployment. This insensitivity, in turn, is reflected in some empirical studies (Herrick, 1965; Slighton, 1968; Tekse, 1967). But measurement of unemployment is sufficiently difficult to make uncritical acceptance of such conclusions risky.

Educational attainment and occupational compositon of the urban migrants lends additional support to the rate-of-return hypothesis. Investment in secondary and higher education generally requires initial migration to urban centers with educational facilities. The cost of movement and of the education itself is seen as recompensed by higher future earnings. The importance of curriculum for potential migrants' decisions to move is frequently, although not universally, ignored in the literature. If formal education revolves around a classic curriculum—languages, philosophy, history, law, even engineering—the graduate or drop-out will try to maximize his returns from such knowledge. Demand for labor with these skills and aptitudes is centered in government, commerce, and to a lesser extent, industry. These activities are largely concentrated in major urban centers. The initial migration to school thus results in further economic incentive, quite beyond whatever urban amenities may exist, for continued residence in a city (Tekse, 1967).

Regardless of the relation between educational attainments of urban migrants and urban natives—in some countries migrants are better educated (Herrick, 1965; Latin American Demographic Center, 1963; McGreevey, 1968), in others, not quite so well (Ducoff, 1963; Elizaga, 1966; Peru, Dirección Nacional de Estadística y Censos, 1966)—there seems no doubt about migrants' educational superiority to the population groups from which they come (Herrick, 1965; McGreevey, 1968).[5] These findings shed additional light on the degree of rationality present in the migration process. Economic folklore sometimes attributes a large degree of irrationality to the process of urban migration, owing to alleged higher unemployment in the biggest cities, the more taxing pace of urban life, etc. It is hard to reconcile however, the relatively high levels of education of migrants with allegations of their irrational decisions to migrate, the more so since migration has continued and perhaps even increased in strength during the entire post-World War II period.

Occupational composition of migrants is in turn heavily influenced by their education. Since their educational attainment approaches or surpasses that of urban natives, most studies have *not* verified the common skill than natives (Bradfield, 1965; Elizaga, 1966). As always in studies impression that male migrants are employed in occupations requiring less involving large subgroups from the population, spurious results may be generated by a failure to standardize by age.

A stronger contrast exists between occupational distributions of female migrants and natives. Most women, especially those newly arrived, work in domestic service (Peru, Dirección Nacianal de Estadística y Censos, 1966). More settled female migrants are distributed by occupation in a manner more resembling natives: when active in the labor force, higher proportions are found in self-employment, especially in commerce, and in wage employment as factory operatives. Retail trade, clerical work, and factory assembly jobs seem economically the most attractive opportunities for urban women. Domestic service probably claims a disproportionately large number of recent migrants owing to their relative lack of information on arrival about alternative employment possibilities. "Lack of information," of course, can be viewed more revealingly as a high cost of obtaining information about these alternatives. With continued urban residence, these costs to the individual fall, and occupational composition shifts accordingly.

A further characteristic of migration to the largest cities in Latin America is internationally observed. Inter-urban migration, in which the persons moving to the largest cities are not unlettered and unskilled country bumpkins, but rather come from other, smaller cities seems the most prevalent pattern (Elizaga, 1966; Herrick, 1965; McGreevey, 1968). Insofar as the migrant either has been reared in or has already adjusted to the exigencies of urban life, problems of further adjustment in the big city are lessened. In economic terms, where productivity and wages are affected by morale, the inter-urban migrant is less handicapped than would be the more commonly pictured rural-urban migrant.[6]

Urban migrants' high educational attainments, substantial skills, and previous familiarity with urban life are reinforced by the amounts of information they possess about their expected economic circumstances at their destination. This information flows through many channels: previous

visits to the destination, presence there of friends and relatives, and the
increased circulation of mass media of all kinds (Herrick, 1965; Margulis,
1967; Rivarola, 1967). Greater amounts of information decrease the un-
certainty associated with moving, and may increase the expected value of
a move. If migrants are risk averters, lessened risks associated with more
complete information will therefore spur movement.

The presence in town of friends and relatives, besides increasing the
amounts of information readily (i.e., inexpensively) available to migrants,
stimulates further movement—sometimes called "chain migration" (Caldwell, 1968)—in another way. Migration is hypothesized to be greater the
lower are its costs. If a migrant can lodge cheaply with anyone already
located in the city, the expenses directly incurred by him and associated
with migration will be lower than if he were forced to stay in more ex-
pensive public accommodations. Impressionistic observations within the
biggest cities of colonies composed of migrants from a given provincial
origin is consistent with and economically explained by the increased
expected differential returns and lower differential costs associated with
the previous arrival there of people from that area.

It should be clear that the rate-of-return framework operates as easily
in international as in domestic applications. Thus, the international emigration from the West Indies (Tekse, 1967) or Paraguay (Rivarola, 1967)
can be cast in the mold of migrants incurring the costs of migration to
seek higher earnings at their destinations: London and other industrial
English cities, and Buenos Aires, respectively.

Even political exile, probably accounting only for a small fraction of
international movement, can be explained if we view earnings possibilities in the home country as impaired by threats of imprisonment or restricted movement (house arrest) and compare these with present earnings
possibilities in the exiles' new home. Extending the analysis further, we
should recognize that political exiles are free to plan changes of governmnt
while residing abroad, changes that might accrue to their economic benefit.
Thus, not only are present earnings possibilities increased by political
exile, but future income streams may also rise as a result of unhampered
planning in their new homes.

ECONOMIC IMPACT OF URBANIZATION

If the world were characterized by equality of individual[7] and social
products, fewer analytical problems with respect to the economic effects
of urbanization would arise. The urban migrants would earn their marginal product in the cities, their presence neither benefiting nor injuring
those already there. Because the migrants increase their welfare by moving (or expect to), and others remain at an already achieved level of
utility, a Pareto-optimal state of welfare has been more closely approached.

Unfortunately, it is at once clear that such an analytical viewpoint is simplistic at best and incorrect at worst. The migrant's presence in the city yields both external economies and external diseconomies whose benefits he is incapable of capturing and whose costs he need not pay. The largest single source of external economies probably comes from the larger labor market to which the migrant belongs. His presence in a large urban labor market, together with that of other migrants, allows the development of occupational specialties. Insofar as his skills can be used in more than one firm, costs of training are borne by the worker himself (Becker, 1964). Thus, the prospective employer is confronted by a greater number af individuals in the labor market, some of whose training he need not subsidize.

By contrast, the migrant also imposes costs on others which he need not pay. The well-known urban characteristics associated with population density such as physical crowding, transportation congestion, and air pollution all might be partly attributed to unchecked inflows of urban workers and their families, responding to private incentives.

Two strands of thought about these processes should be distinguished. The first suggests that the population in a developing country tends to concentrate itself in a single so-called primate city, whose functions are largely parasitic rather than generative and whose effects on the country as a whole are therefore negative. Primacy, measured simply by deviations from some assumed normal rank-size rule, is more frequently observed in small countries than in larger ones.[8] And even where primate cities are observed, systematic investigation has failed to demonstrate their parasitic or degenerative effects on the economic system as a whole (Mehta, 1964).

Another impression, now almost completely dispelled by empirical studies about the mechanisms of urbanization, suggested that its greatest social ill lies in the concentration af the migrant population in noisy shantytowns constructed at the margins of the cities. We have already noted that urban migrants are not individuals distinguished by lack of preparation or inherent incapability to deal with urban situations. This in itself might lead to skepticism about claims that migration was responsible for the establishment of socially undesirable neighborhoods. Careful and systematic study of shantytowns in most of the capitals of Latin America has effectively reinforced this skepticism (Flinn, 1968; Mangin, 1967; Peru, Dirección Nacional de Estadística y Censos, 1966). Once again, a difference arises between absolute and relative standards. Life, economic and otherwise, in the new shantytowns may be thought disordered or unpleasant by those who apply absolute standards. However, when compared either with living conditions in the countryside or in the central city slums from which many shantytown dwellers emigrate, conditions in the shantytowns are relatively orderly and considerably above those in the place of origin.

The macro-economic view of urbanization suggests not necessarily the concentration of population in a single primate city, but rather the concentration of population in urban regions as a whole. This phenomenon, labeled hyperurbanization by at least one pair of investigators (Friedmann and Lackington, 1967) has been hypothesized to have the following effects: encouraging high consumption, discouraging agricultural production, diverting investment into less productive uses, aggravating inflationary pressures, and distributing income more regressively. None of these effects seems conducive to the commonly held goal of industrialization and economic growth, and insofar as hyperurbanization can be convincingly identified with these phenomena, its resulting from "natural" (individually motivated) population movements calls into question the desirability of those movements from the standpoint of the society as a whole.

CONCLUSIONS

In reviewing Latin American urbanization from a perspective stressing economic considerations, I hope that several related facets of this phenomenon have been made clearer:

(1) Migrants are rational. A stronger statement, consistent with empirical observations, is that migrants display economic rationality.

(2) An hypothesis that pictures urban-oriented population redistribution as a type of investment in human capital allows us to explain observations that formerly lacked a rigorous theoretical framework. The socio-economic data describing migrants and migration are seen to be consistent with the rate-of-return hypothesis,

(3) The rate-of-return hypothesis assumes equality of individual and social costs and benefits, an assumption which has been questioned within the context of developing countries. Further hypotheses and observations of hyperurbanization may, in fact, serve to reinforce skepticism about the overall beneficence of Latin American urbanization.

NOTES

1. Contrasts among models that emphasize individuals' decisions, those that concentrate on success of the assimilation or acculturation process, and those that center on economic adjustment are made by Graves (1966).

2. More strictly, differential returns are the difference between the migrant's earnings at the destination and what he would have earned had he remained at the origin.

3. Interestingly enough, Schultz (1969) finds distance *positively* associated with rates of emigration in Colombia, suggesting that remoteness in itself may be conducive to that decision. His tests appropriately treat remoteness independently from a measure of *la violencia*, a phenomenon which might superficially be thought to explain the positive relationship.

4. The expected value of earnings at the destination is simply the probability of employment times the wage rate. The same calculation, of course, is relevant for the place of origin.

5. Compare these empirical findings with the following statement by the United Nations' Economic Commission for Latin America (1963: 52): 'A very rapid increase in the number of persons seeking urban employment, particularly if their levels of education and skills are too low to permit ready integration with the urban employment structure, implies that many of them will have to fall back either on little-capitalized traditional ways of livelihood or on intermittent and insecure activities affording incomes so low as to place them in an economically and socially marginal category. It is well known that this is occurring on a large scale in the Latin American cities." The logic of these statements, however persuasive, is simply at variance with more detailed observations about initial levels of education and about comparative occupational structures and resulting incomes.

6. Once again, an impressionistic assertion by the United Nations' Economic Commission for Latin America provides a strikingly contrasting view (1963: 60): " . . . urbanization taking place largely through migration concentrated upon the largest cities implies a maximum break in cultural and occupational continuity for the migrant, with a likelihood of multiple maladjustments."

7. Economists should read "private" for "individual" here.

8. The dangers implicit in making any generalization are aptly demonstrated by this one. Berry (1961) points out that Brazil and El Salvador have log-normal (rank size) distribution, while Peru, Mexico, the Dominican Republic, and Guatemala tend toward a primate distribution. Clearly, generalized comparisons about city size distributions in "big" countries and "small" ones admit of important Latin American exceptions.

REFERENCES

ARIAS, B. J. (1963) "Internal migration in Guatemala." Pp. 395–404 in *Proceedings of the International Population Conference, New York, 1961*. London: UNESCO.

ARRIAGA, EDUARDO E. (1968) "Components of city growth in selected Latin American countries." *Milbank Memoral Fund Quarterly* 46, No. 2, part 1 (April): 237–252.

BECKER, GARY (1964) *Human Capital*. New York: National Bureau of Economic Resarch.

BERRY, BRIAN J. L. (1961) "City size distributions and economic development." *Economic Development and Cultural Change* 2, No. 4 (July): 573–588.

BOGUE, DONALD J. (1963) "Techniques and hypotheses for the study of differential migration: Pp. 405–411 in *Proceedings of the International Population Conference, New York, 1961*. London: UNESCO.

BRADFIELD, STILLMAN (1965) "Some occupational aspects of migration." *Economic Development and Cultural Change*, 14, No. 1 (October): 61–70.

BURNIGHT, R. G. (1963) "Estimates of net migration, Mexico, 1930–1950." Pp. 412–419 in *Proceedings of the International Population Conference, New York, 1961*. London: UNESCO.

CALDWELL, J. C. (1968) "Determinants of rural-urban migration in Ghana." *Population Studies* 22, No. 3 (November): 361–378.

CHEN, CHI-YI (1968) *Movimientos migratorios en Venezuela*. Caracas: Instituto de Investigaciones Económicas de la Universidad Católica Andrés Bello.

DUCOFF, L. J. (1963) 'The migrant population of a metropolitan area in a developing country: a preliminary report on a case study of San Salvador."

Pp. 428–436 in *Proceedings of the International Population Conference, New York, 1961.* London: UNESCO.

ELIZAGA, JUAN C. (1965) "Internal migration in Latin America." In Clyde Kiser (ed.) *Components of Population Change in Latin America,* Milbank Memorial Fund Quarterly 43, No. 4, part 2 (October).

—— (1966) "A study of migration to greater Santiago." *Demography,* 3, No. 2: 352–377.

FISCHLOWITZ, ESTANISLAO (1965) "Driving forces in internal migration in Brazil." *Migration News* 14, No. 6 (November-December).

—— (1966) "Driving forces in internal migration in Brazil." *Migration News* 15, No. 1 (January-February).

FLINN, WILLIAM (1968) "The process of migration to a shantytown in Bogotá." *Inter-American Economic Affairs* 22, No. 2 (Autumn): 77–88.

FRIEDMANN, JOHN and TOMÁS LACKINGTON (1967) "Hyperurbanization and national development in Chile: some hypotheses." *Urban Affairs Quarterly* 2, No. 4 (June): 3–29.

GRAVES, T. D. (1966) "Alternative models for the study of urban migration." *Human Organization* 25 (Winter): 295–299.

HERRICK, BRUCE (1965) *Urban Migration and Economic Development in Chile.* Cambridge: M.I.T. Press.

Instituto de Economía de la Universidad de Chile (1959) *La Población del Gran Santiago.* Santiago: Instituto de Economía.

Latin American Demographic Center (1963) "Differential migration in some regions and cities of Latin America in the period 1940–1950: methodological aspects and results." Pp. 468–482 in *Proceedings of the International Population Conference, New York, 1961.* London: UNESCO.

LEE, EVERETT S. (1966) "A theory of migration." *Demography* 3, No. 1: 47–57.

MANGIN, WILLIAM (1967) "Latin American squatter settlements: a problem and a solution." *Latin American Research Review* 2, No. 3 (Summer): 65–98.

MARGULIS, MARIO (1967) "Análisis de un proceso migratorio rural urbano en Argentina." *Aportes* 3 (January).

McGREEVEY, WILLIAM (1968) "Causas de la migración interna en Colombia." Pp. 211–221 in *Empleo y desempleo en Colombia.* Centro de Estudios Sobre Desarrollo Económico (CEDE). Bogotá: Ediciones Universidad de los Andes.

MEHTA, SURINDER K. (1964) "Some demographic and economic correlates of primate cities: a case for revaluation." *Demography* 1, No. 1: 136–137.

Peru, Dirección Nacional de Estadística y Censos (1966) *Encuesta de inmigración de Lima metropolitana.* Lima: Dirección Nacional de Estadística y Censos.

RIVAROLA, DOMINGO M. (1967) "Aspectos de la migración Paraguaya." *Aportes* 3 (January): 24–71.

SAHOTA, GIAN S. (1968) "An economic analysis of internal migration in Brazil." *Journal of Political Economy* 76, No. 2 (March-April): 218–245.

SCHULTZ, T. PAUL (1969) "Population growth and internal migration in Colombia." Rand Corporation Memorandum RM-5765. Santa Monica: Rand Corporation.

SJAASTAD, LARRY (1962) "The costs and returns of human migration." *Journal of Political Economy* 70, No. 5 part 2 (October): 80–93.

SLAWINSKI, ZYGMUNDT (1965) "Structural changes in development within the context of Latin America's economic development." *Economic Bulletin for Latin America* 10, No. 2 (October): 163–187.

SLIGHTON, ROBERT L. (1968) "Urban unemployment in Colombia: measurement, characteristics, and policy problems." Rand Corporation Memorandum RM-5393-AID. Santa Monica: Rand Corporation.

STOUFFER, SAMUEL A. (1940) "Intervening opportunities: a theory relating mobility and distance." *American Sociological Review* 5 (December): 845–867.

TEKSE, KALMAN (1967) *Internal Migration in Jamaica.* Kingston, Jamaica: Department of Statistics.

U.N. Economic Commission for Latin America (1963) "Geographic Distribution of the population of Latin America and regional development priorities." *Economic Bulletin for Latin America* 8, No. 1 (March).

WINGO, LOWDON (1967) "Recent patterns of urbanization among Latin American countries." *Urban Affairs Quarterly* 2, No. 3 (March): 81–109.

Chapter 5

RURAL AND INTRA-URBAN MIGRATION IN COLOMBIA: TWO CASE STUDIES IN BOGOTÁ

WILLIAM L. FLINN

The study reported in this essay traces two random samples of residents of barrios El Carmen and El Gavilán in Bogotá from their birthplace to their present locations. More specifically, it seeks answers to the following questions: How much of this rural-to-urban migration involves a multi-stage or step process, i.e., farm to village, village to town, town to city? What interval of time is involved in the migration process to the city? How much of the intra-city migration? What factors are related to the intra-city movement? What are the experiences of rural migrants in terms of their satisfaction with their urban conditions?

MIGRATION TO BOGOTÁ

A prevalent theory is that migration to Bogotá occurs by a series of stages or steps. The step-migration theory, which characterizes the process as one in which people move from small population centers to successively larger ones can be traced to Ravenstein's (1885) nineteenth-century study of England. He observed a universal shifting or displacement of the population which produced migration streams in the direction of the large cities. The gaps were filled by migrants from more remote districts.

In both cases reported here, the majority of migrants moved directly

AUTHOR'S NOTE: These studies were supported by the Agricultural Development Council, Inc., The Midwest Universities Consortium for International Activities, The Land Tenure Center, and the Agency for International Development. The work was done with the cooperation of the Faculty of Sociology at National University of Bogotá, Colombia. The author wishes to thank Professor Marion Brown for his comments on an early draft of this paper.

Table 1. Number of Intermediate Steps in Migration by Rural-to-Urban Migrant Residents of Barrios El Carmen and El Gavilán (in percent)

	BARRIOS	
Steps	*El Carmen*	*El Gavilán*
Direct to Bogotá	66	70
One step	12	15
Two steps	8	8
Three steps	6	5
Four steps	6	1
Five steps	1	1
Six steps	1	0
Total	100	100
N =	106	87

to Bogotá without intermediate stops (see Table I). On the other hand, at least 30 percent of both samples made intermediate stops of widely varying lengths. (See Table 2.) Even for these migrants, however, the pattern is not fully consistent with step theory, since several of them apparently did not move to larger population centers before migrating to Bogotá. Table 3 indicates that some *campesinos* who were born in the *vereda* (more or less equivalent to a rural U.S. school district) did move to the *cabecera* (a small village, town, or city). This does not, however, present a clear picture of the step-migration process since the population of a *cabecera* is not always greater than that of a *vereda*. In the present studies slightly

Table 2. Time Interval Between Departure from Area of Origin and Arrival in Bogotá of Residents of Barrios El Carmen and El Gavilán (in percent)

	BARRIOS	
Years	*El Carmen*	*El Gavilán*
Less than one year	66	70
1 to 5 years	13	15
6 to 10 years	6	5
11 to 15 years	6	5
16 to 20 years	4	1
21 to 25 years	3	2
More than 25 years	2	2
Total	100	100
N =	106	87

more than half the in-migrants who made intermediate stops moved to successively larger population centers before migrating to Bogotá. The others moved to population centers of the same size or smaller.

Table 3. Place of Birth and Last Place of Residence Before Bogotá of In-Migrant Household Heads of Barrios El Carmen and El Gavilán (in percent)

	BARRIOS			
	El Carmen		El Gavilán	
Place	*Birth Place*	*Last Residence*	*Birth Place*	*Last Residence*
Cabecera	60	74	56	67
Vereda	40	26	44	33
Total	100	100	100	100
N =	106	106	87	87

These data seem to show that step-migration does not always occur. Several other Colombian studies, however, indicate that the migration steps take place, but that the steps are not necessarily made by the same generation and probably are not (Facultad de Sociología, 1963; Urrutia, 1963; Reyes, Durán, and Hanneson, 1965). Small towns around Bogotá have experienced large in-migration. For example, in 1963, 60 percent of the population of Chía was composed of in-migrants, while the population of Facatativá, Zipaquirá, and Chiquinquirá contained 48, 42, and 30 percent in-migrants respectively (Urrutia, 1963). The data from these towns indicated that the majority of the in-migrants came from surrounding areas. The growth rates for these municipalities were approximately the same as the national average, indicating that out-migration is also taking place. Reyes, Durán, and Hanneson (1965) stated that 68 percent of the emigrants from the Suárez River Valley, a *municipio* 36 miles from Bogatá, moved directly to Bogotá. The researchers also noted that the largest amount of in-migrants to the area were from the surrounding areas. A study of the Subachoque River Valley, near Bogotá, indicated that 10 percent of the heads of households were not natives of Subachoque, but were from areas near Subachoque (Facultad de Sociología, 1963: 14). The major focal point for the emigrants was Bogotá.

Perhaps rural-to-urban migration processes are best summed up by McGreevey (1965: 23–25) who notes that there are two predominant patterns. One he calls "fill-in" migration where people who move out of rural areas generally go to nearby small towns, and natives of small towns move up to larger cities. The other major pattern is direct migration from farms to the large cities.

INTRA-CITY MIGRATION

Even though the majority of shantytown residents migrate from farms or small towns, research shows they come to the shantytowns largely by way of the tenement houses and back alley slums within the central city (Mangin, 1967: 68). This is contrary to the commonly espoused notion that "thousands of discontented farmers are moving to the cities and building shantytowns called *barrios* on the edge of town. . . ." (Leonard, 1969: 5). It is also counter to some descriptions of Latin American cities as made up of a plaza-centered commercial core, an adjacent upper-class residential zone, and a periphery af slums (Morse, 1962: 485). This conception of the spatial structure does not include an intra-city slum or transition zone as noted in the theory devised for the North American city by Burgess (1925).

Evidence suggests that the former notion is a myth while the latter ecological pattern is indicative of Latin American cities which are experiencing little growth (Hayner, 1944; Hayner, 1945; Leonard, 1948; Caplow, 1949; Dotson and Dotson, 1954). It has been suggested that cities in different technological epochs will display dissimilar spatial structures (Schnore, 1965: 372). With growth, the ecological processes of invasion and succession of land uses is set into motion (Burgess, 1925). As the city's business district expands along with accompanying improvements in tranportation, the spatial structure begins to reverse itself. The upper classes shift from central to peripheral residence and the lower classes increasingly take up occupancy in the central areas abandoned by the élite. The old mansions are converted into tenement houses and cheap hotels. This transition area or zone is inhabited by rural-urban immigrants and otherwise dispossessed residents. Most live there, not by preference, but because the cost of transportation to work in the center of the city is low. This reversal in spatial structure produces a pattern of concentric circles: central business district, transition zone, zone of working men's homes, residential zone, and the commuter zone. (For other theories see Hoyt, 1939; Harris and Ullman, 1945.) Breese (1966: 106) notes that this concentric pattern of growth is subsequently replaced by a sector pattern of growth. This view holds that different income groups tend to locate themselves in distinct sectors of the city centered around the central business district and along particular axes of transportation.

In Bogotá, which was founded in 1538, the prominent families lived in the *barrios* surrounding the main plaza until the late nineteenth century (Amato, 1968: 97) Then the reversal started with the upper classes moving north of the plaza until the beginning of the 1940s when they abandoned the central city for residence in the northern suburbs. Neissa (1965) demonstrates that Bogotá has passed through the reversal stage and has developed a transition zone (zona negra) in the areas evacuated by the élites. The patio-centered houses in this area have been converted into *vecindades* (a family per room with the kitchen and other services shared) and *inquilinatos* (rental apartments and housing). These rental slum dwellings and *hoteluchos* contain migrants from nearly every region of Colombia.

Both Amato (1968: 97–98) and Neissa (1965: 50) demonstrate that beyond the transition zone, the sector theory prabably best describes Bogotá's spatial structure. The industrial zone extends westward from the central business district to the edge of the city. The élite residential areas are concentrated in the north, middle group in the west, the lower classes in the south. The lower-class residential area is divided into at least three types: (1) *barrios piratas* or *clandestinos,* illegal "pirate" or "clandestine" subdivisions in which small parcels of unimproved land are sold without official permits; (2) *invasiones* or *tugurios* (rustic shacks), squatter settlements on public and private lands (Instituto de Crédito Territorial, 1966: 7; Ludgerio Camues F., 1966); (3) public-housing projects and *urbanizaciones,* legal subdivisions designed according to city specifications and provided with some public services.

If intra-city migration is a two-step process, we would expect to find that in-migrants move first to the central city, especially in *inquilinatos* or *vecindades,* in the transition and then later to *barrios clandestinos* or *tugurios* in Bogotá. This is what Cardona (1968: 69) found in a study of two *barrios de invasiones* or *tugurios* in Bogotá. Over 65 percent of the in-migrants in both invasion *barrios* had lived in *inquilinatos* or *vecindades* in the central city while still others had lived with relatives in the central city before moving to the squatter settlements. Somewhat similar patterns were noted among residents of *barrios clandestinos* (Departamento Administrativo de Planificación, 1963a and 1963b). Both *barrios* in the present study are clandestine. Thirty-eight percent of the in-migrant residents of El Carmen and 45 percent of the residents of El Gavilán lived in the central city (transition zone or workingmen's houses) prior to moving to their respective *barrios.*

One study established that some in-migrants to *barrios clandestinos* had experienced social mobility prior to moving to the "shantytown suburbs" (Flinn, 1968). Another study suggests that *barrios de invasiones* or *tugurios* provide a means for securing land for those in-migrants who do not possess the capital to purchase a lot in a *barrio clandestino* (Flinn and Converse, forthcoming). This desire for home ownership seems to be one of the major motivating forces in the migrants moving to the "shantytown suburbs." In the studies conducted by the City Planning Office (Departamento Administrativo de Planificación Distrital, 1963a and 1963b) on clandestine *barrios,* research indicates that approximately 40 percent of the respondents were motivated to reside in the various *barrios* by the desire to own a homesite. Approximately another fifth of the respondents moved to the areas because of cheaper rent, even though for most of the respondents this meant higher transition costs and an hour or an hour and a half commuting time to their jobs in *el centro*.

In the present study, a majority of the respondents in both *barrios* listed home ownership or desire for property as the major reason for moving to the area. A follow-up study on Barrio El Gavilán indicated that those who own property in the *barrio* are the least likely to move, while nearly 90 percent of the renters had moved away during a three-year period.

Table 4 shows that the majority of the in-migrants did not move directly to El Carmen or El Gavilán. In fact, the majority lived in the

Table 4. Number of Intra-City Moves by the In-Migrant Residents of Barrios El Carmen and El Gavilán (in percent)

	BARRIOS	
Number of Moves	*El Carmen*	*El Gavilán*
Present *barrio* only	31	13
One move	28	41
Two moves	23	25
Three moves	12	10
Four moves	4	5
Five moves	1	2
Six moves	1	2
Seven moves	0	0
Eight moves	0	1
Total	100	100
N =	106	87

Table 5. Time Interval Between Arrival in Bogotá and Moving to Barrio El Carmen or El Gavilán (in percent)

	BARRIOS	
Years	*El Carmen*	*El Gavilán*
Less than one year	44	24
1 to 5 years	28	33
6 to 10 years	16	28
11 to 15 years	6	8
16 to 20 years	3	5
21 to 25 years	1	0
More than 25 years	1	2
Total	100	100
N =	106	87

transition zone, zone of workingmen's homes, or in other shantytowns between one and ten years before they moved to either El Carmen or El Gavilán (see Table 5).

How do in-migrants like city life? Eighty-nine percent of the residents of El Carmen and 75 percent of the residents of El Gavilán stated that

Table 6. Satisfaction of In-Migrant Residents of Barrio El Carmen with Barrio and Social Conditions in Comparison With Their Previous Residence (in percent)

| | | PRIOR RESIDENCE | | |
| | Outside Bogotá | Central City | Other Shanty-town | Total |
Social Conditions				
1. Household head's satisfaction with *barrio*				
—more satisfied	46	72	67	62
—equally satisfied	24	18	12	18
—less satisfied	30	10	18	19
—no data	0	0	3	1
Total	100	100	100	100
2. Wife's satisfaction with *barrio*				
—more satisfied	39	63	55	53
—equally satisfied	28	15	15	19
—less satisfied	24	18	18	20
—no data	3	2	3	3
—no wife	6	2	9	5
Total	100	100	100	100
3. Household head's satisfaction with house				
—better housing	52	73	63	63
—equal housing	12	5	28	14
—worse housing	33	20	6	20
—no data	3	2	3	3
Total	100	100	100	100
4. Household head's satisfaction with income				
—better income	42	55	46	48
—equal income	21	33	33	29
—worse income	37	12	18	22
—no data	0	0	3	1
Total	100	100	100	100
N =	33	40	33	106

they prefer city life to the country. Only 26 percent of the in-migrant residents of El Gavilán reported being less satisfied with their present residence than they were with their last residence prior to moving to Bogotá.

Tables 6 and 7 show the residents' satisfaction with the *barrio* and services in relation to their previous residence. It is interesting to note that in both *barrios*, migrants whose prior residence was the central city are

Table 7. Satisfaction of In-Migrant Residents of Barrio El Gavilán with Social Conditions of Barrio in Comparison With Their Previous Residence (in percent)

Social Conditions	Outside Bogotá	Central City	Other Shanty-town	Total
1. Household head's satis- faction with house				
—better housing	45	64	52	56
—equal housing	36	5	5	9
—worse housing	18	31	43	35
Total	100	100	100	100
2. Household head's satis- faction with income				
—better income	36	31	19	26
—equal income	36	33	38	26
—worse income	28	36	38	36
—no data	0	0	5	2
Total	100	100	100	100
3. Household head's satis- faction with public services				
—better	36	26	11	21
—same	36	20	11	18
—worse	28	54	76	60
—no data	0	0	2	1
Total	100	100	100	100
4. Household head's satis- faction with educa- tional opportunities for children				
—better	64	38	22	34
—same	27	26	30	28
—worse	0	31	40	31
—no data	9	5	8	7
Total	100	100	100	100
N =	11	39	37	87

more satisfied than migrants whose previous residence was another shanty-town. Most of the migrants from the central city lived in *inquilinatos* or *vecindades* and view this move to the "shantytown suburb" as a big move upward.

CONCLUSION: POLICY IMPLICATIONS

In Bogotá, the various governmental agencies offer at least four solutions to the problems of *tugurios* and *barrios clandestinos*: (1) eradication of squatter settlements; (2) urban renewal for intra-city slums; (3) low-cost public housing; (4) improvement and renovation of peripheral shanty-towns (Instituto de Crédito Territorial, 1966; 23–27).

As Mangin (1967) notes, the most commonly espoused solution to the problem is eradication. The Department of Planning of the Special District of Bogotá, however, has embarked upon a number of urban renewal projects (Departamento Administrative de Planificación Distrital Bogotá 1964: 216). Unfortunately, these projects primarily benefit the élites and the upper-middle classes by producing luxury housing, cleaning up central city blight, and improving land values in the central business district (Amato, 1968: 239). For example, the National Civic Center project envisions a revitalization and improvement of the old colonial area of the city by destroying or renovating many deteriorated residences around the headquarters of the Colombian Government near the central plaza. This plan would displace many low-income groups from the *zona negra* or transition zone.

On the other hand, the building and location of public low-cost housing projects such as Ciudad Kennedy has not solved the squatter problem. It has only led to further segregation of the population by social class. Amato (1968: 257) indicates that the Colombian Government, acting through its various housing agencies, has developed several huge low-income self-contained projects which are completely isolated from the other social classes within the city. Many residents complain they are too far from their place of work and transportation costs are high.

Another solution sometimes offered is the renovation of *tugurios* through loans and self-help house building projects. The Instituto de Crédito Territorial has lowered construction costs and loans to about U.S. $3,000 per dwelling, and has a policy of lending money only to families whose personal holdings are valued at less than U.S. $8,000 (Fletcher, 1968: 30). They admit, however, that even with these measures, credit is not within the reach of the average *tugurio* resident whose income is only 40 or 50 percent of the legal minimum daily wage of 14 *pesos* (less than U.S. $1 at mid-1969 rates) (Instituto de Crédito Territorial: 20).

In the course of the present study it was observed that many people who moved within the city, moved to a shantytown because of a desire to own a homesite. This implies that financial resources play a major role in determining place of residence. As in-migrants accumulate capital, they move from the crowded tenements of the central city to what they see as a relatively better situation in a *barrio clandestino* on the edge of the city. The purchasing of property becomes a stabilizing agent in the migrant's life. It provides him with security and a hedge against inflation. Once they have some form of title security, residents of *tugurios* and *piratas* make considerable improvements on their property such as adding additional rooms or stories. A study in Barranquilla shows similar results. One-quarter of the residents of three *barrios de invasiones* had spent from 1,000 to 6,000 pesos (approximately U.S. $75 to $450 at 1965 rates) in improvements on their properties (Usandizaga and Havens, 1966). Perhaps the municipal and federal governments would receive greater return from investments designed to speed up the distribution of secure titles in existing settlements than from unrealistic efforts to eradicate shantytowns.

REFERENCES

AMATO, PETER W. (1968) *An Analysis of the Changing Patterns of Elite Residential Areas in Bogotá, Colombia.* Ithaca: Cornell University, Latin American Studies Program, Dissertation Series (mimeo.).

BREESE, GERALD (1966) *Urbanization in Newly Developing Countries.* Englewood Cliffs: Prentice-Hall.

BURGESS, ERNEST W. (1925) "The growth of the city: an introduction to a research project." In R. E. Park, E. W. Burgess, and D. McKenzie, *The City.* Chicago: University of Chicago Press.

CAMUES F., LUDGERIO (1966) *El Tugurio: Problemática Social de las "Invasiones."* Bogotá: Editorial Kelly, folletos de divulgacíon, No. 4.

CAPLOW, THEODORE (1949) "The Social Ecology of Guatemala City." *Social Forces* 28 (December): 113–133.

CARDONA G., RAMIRO (1968) "Migración, Urbanización y Marginalidad." In *Asociación Colombiana de Facultades de Medicina, Urbanización y Marginalidad.* Bogotá: Tercer Mundo.

Departamento Administrativo de Planificación Distrital Bogotá (1963a) "Encuesta Socio-Económica, Barrio San Vicente." Bogotá: unpublished paper.

———— (1963b) "Encuesta Socio-Económica, Barrios Córdoba and Santa Inés." Bogotá: unpublished paper.

———— (1964) *La Planificación en Bogotá.* Bogotá: Imprenta Distrital de Bogotá.

DOTSON, FLOYD and LILLIAN OTA DOTSON (1954) "Ecological Trends in the City of Guadalajara, Mexico." *Social Forces* 32 (May): 367–374.

Facultad de Sociología (1963) *Factores Sociales que Inciden en el Desarrollo Económico de la Hoya del Rio Subachoque.* Bogotá: Universidad Nacional de Colombia.

FLETCHER, DAVID F. (1968) "Squatter settlements in Colombia." Los Angeles: University of California Latin American Center, unpublished paper.

FLINN, WILLIAM L. (1968) "The process of migration to a shantytown in Bogotá, Colombia." *Inter-American Economic Affairs,* 22 (Autumn) 77–88.

FLINN, WILLIAM and JAMES CONVERSE (forthcoming) "The Rural-to-Urban Migration Process of Residents of Three Types of Barrios." Land Tenure Center Research Paper. Madison: University of Wisconsin.

HARRIS, CHARENCY D., and EDWARD L. ULLMAN (1945) "The nature of cities." *Annals of the American Academy of Political and Social Science* 242, (November): 7–17.

HAYNER, NORMAN S. (1944) "Oaxaca: city of old Mexico." *Sociology and Social Research* 29 (December): 87–95.

——— (1945) "Mexico City: its growth and configuration." *American Journal of Sociology* 50: 295–304.

HOYT, HOMER (1939) *The Structure and Growth of Residential Neighborhoods in American Cities.* Washington, D.C.: Federal Housing Administration.

Instituto de Crédito Territorial (1966) *Seminario sobre Tugurios.* Bogotá: Instituto de Crédito Territorial (mimeo.).

LEONARD, OLIN E. (1948) "La Paz, Bolivia: its population and growth." *American Sociological Review* 13 (August): 448–454.

LEONARD, RICHARD H. (1969) "U.S. AID vital for Colombia's growth." *The Milwaukee Journal. Accent* (Milwaukee) May 18, pp. 1, 5.

McGREEVEY, WILLIAM P. (1965) *Change in Rural Colombia: Population Movement and Strategies for Change.* Berkeley: University of California Latin American Center (mimeo.).

MANASTER, KENNETH A. (1968) "The problem of urban squatters in developing countries: Peru." *Wisconsin Law Review* 1: 23–61.

MANGIN, WILLIAM (1967) "Latin American squatter settlements: a problem and a solution." *Latin American Research Review* 2 (Summer): 65–98.

MORSE, RICHARD M. (1962) "Latin American cities: aspects of function and structure." *Comparative Studies in Society of History* 47 (July): 473–493.

NEISSA R., CARLOS (1965) "Ecología General y Ecología Urbana." *Universidad Libre Revista de Cultura Moderna* 19 (June and July): 37–65.

RAVENSTEIN, E. G. (1885) "Laws of Migration." *Journal of the Royal Statistical Society* 48 (June): 167–227.

REYES, MARCO C., RAFAEL DURÁN PRIETO, and WILLIAM HANNESON (1965) *Agro-Económico de la Hoya del Río Suarez.* Bogotá: Universidad de los Andes.

SCHNORE, LEO F. (1965) "On the spatial structure of cities in the two Americas." In Phillip M. Hauser and Leo F. Schnore (eds.) *The Study of Urbanization.* New York: John Wiley.

URRUTIA M., MIGUEL (1963) *Estudio Económico Social de los Centros de la CAR.* Bogotá: Corporación Autónoma Regional.

USANDIZAGA, ELSA and A. EUGENE HAVENS (1966) *Tres Barrios de Invasión.* Bogotá: Tercer Mundo.

and propositions derived from Anglo-European experience have come to be accepted as the working truth, forming a part of the conceptual framework of numerous government officials, politicians, and academicians— both North American and Latin-American—dealing with Latin American affairs. Constant repetition in innumerable books and articles (particularly textbooks) has given these concepts and propositions continuing currency, despite early warnings by some investigators urging caution in the utilization of conventional theory not grounded in the empirics of Latin American experience.[1] Latter-day field researchers working in this area of Latin American urban studies have been fond of isolating and attacking the various elements of "urban mythology" which have held sway over the past several decades (see Mangin, 1967; Leeds and Leeds, 1969). They themselves—and many of their Latin American colleagues writing in this area—seem to have largely rejected the models developed in conventional urban theory. But a glance at the stream of scholarly and popular writings on Latin American social and political development indicates beyond doubt that the confidence of many other Latin Americanists in these formulations remains unshaken.

The tendency toward uncritical acceptance of theory and research findings not deriving from the Latin American context cannot, however, be attributed solely to the lack of essential data from Latin America available to U.S.-based area specialists. Apparently it has been reinforced by the overall research perspective shared by many political scientists working in the Latin American field, especially those who have been trained in modern research techniques and who are sensitive to the type of work which has been done in more "advanced" areas of the discipline. Such persons, correctly perceiving Latin American politics as a largely tradition-bound, underdeveloped subfield of the discipline, have felt the need to "return to the mainstream of political science" through the borrowing and testing of conceptual formulations emanating from other areas of the discipline and related behavioral sciences which appear to be isomorphic to their particular set of concerns. The temptation to engage in this kind of "greener pastures" ploy would appear to be strongest with respect to uncharted areas of inquiry in which there is still relatively little systematic, data-based literature, such as Latin American voting behavior, community power structure and decision-making, or socio-political correlates of city-ward migration (see Fennell, 1967; Rabinovitz, 1968; Martz, 1966: 80). Yet in exploring these and other areas, it might be beneficial to confront at the present stage the methodological implications of research strategies now in favor. To what extent is it actually feasible, and desirable, to draw upon conceptual frameworks and techniques developed in more "advanced" areas of social science in the study of migrant political behavior and attitude formation in Latin America? If widespread transfer of conceptual apparatus derived from non-Latin American experience *has* occurred, what are the evident consequences for research and theory in the recipient field of study? And if the negative consequences of "borrowing-and-testing" do appear to outweigh the positive benefits, what alternative approaches to research and theory construction should be pursued in attempting to deal with problems of migrant assimilation in the Latin American socio-political context? These are the questions of general theoretical and methodological import to be taken up in this paper. With specific reference to the political sociology of migrant assimilation as a substantive research area, we shall attempt to (1) identify the origins of existing propositions and generalizations in this area; (2) assess the validity and explanatory power of such propositions in dealing with Latin American phenomena; and (3) suggest some possible reasons for the inadequacy of our "borrowed" propositions. Finally we will propose some alternative emphases or foci of empirical research and theory-building which might be adopted in developing this area of Latin American urban studies.

SOURCES OF EXISTING THEORY

There is no integrated, formal theory of migrant assimilation and political behavior which informs textbook discussions and other non-data-based treatments of the subject by Latin Americanists. What has been widely diffused through the literature is, rather, an amalgam of generalizations and propositions derived from the work of European social theorists, North American urban specialists and political sociologists, and political scientists in the American politics and political development fields. The borrowed propositions appear to cluster around three basic themes: (1) Material deprivation and frustration of mobility expectations; (2) personal and social disorganization; and (3) political radicalization and disruptive behavior. Migrants entering urban centers are assumed to experience instigating conditions (1) and (2), become alienated toward the existing socio-political order, and undergo political radicalization leading to various forms of disruptive activity. Reduced to barest essentials, this is what has served as the most commonly accepted, "working theory" regarding political correlates of migrant assimilation in contemporary Latin America. Intervening variables are sometimes introduced, but these are generally regarded as mediating conditions which may influence the degree of radicalization or intensity of disruptive behavior, which are still regarded as the most probable outcomes of migrant assimilation into Latin American urban environments under existing circumstances. These circumstances, which are said to hold now and in the foreseeable future, include (1) the high rate and volume of in-migration; (2) the limited absorptive capacity of urban centers, capacity being defined primarily in terms of provision of housing, sanitation, educational facilities, public transportation, and other basic urban services; and (3) the large discrepancy between urbanization and industrialization rates, frequently referred to by economists as the condition of "overurbanization" or "hyperurbanization" (Friedmann and Lackington, 1967; Kamerschen, 1969), which ostensibly creates a severe shortage of employment opportunities.

Before attempting to assess the validity and explanatory power of the "conventional wisdom" in this area, it is helpful to retrace its origins in diverse bodies of theory developed largely without reference to Latin American phenomena. The major theoretical input has come from the so-called "Chicago School" of urban sociology and its European background.[2] Within modern urban sociology in the United States, Louis Wirth's conception of "urbanism as a way of life" has been perhaps the most widely cited and influential theoretical orientation.[3] The propagation of Wirth's ideas in largely unmodified form in major urban sociology texts down to the present day testifies to their enormous impact and acceptance as virtual unshakeable truths.[4] In formulating his vision of the city and its life style, Wirth drew heavily upon the work of such European theorists as Durkheim and Simmel, as well as his predecessors at Chicago, notably Park (Park, 1928, 1967; Park *et al.*, 1967; Simmel, 1950). The resulting description emphasized the anomic, disintegrative, disorienting, depersonalizing features of urban life and entry into the urban environment, manifested in psychological maladjustment, poorly defined social roles, breakdown of traditional value systems and controls on deviant behavior, the weakening of family and kinship ties, and the decline of religious life. The total picture is one of disorganization, normlessness, anonymity, social isolation, and insecurity. Such conditions are assumed necessarily to accompany exposure to the urban environment, and then incidences of various forms of personal and social pathology in areas heavily settled with in-migrants (crime, delinquency, prostitution, alcoholism, divorce, suicide, mental illness, drug addiction, etc.) are listed as indicators.[5] Implicitly or explicitly, elaborators and reformulators of the Park-Wirth conception of urbanism and urban migration have contrasted the urban center with the traditional rural community or "folk society." Robert Redfield was most explicit in this regard, viewing the large city and the rural, closed community as representing the extremes of a folk-urban continuum of social organization (Redfield, 1941, 1947, 1961). Redfield and his following in anthropology perceived personal and social disorganization as an inevitable concomitant of urbanization because it was believed that the strong ties that integrated the individual into the folk or peasant community and traditional social controls on deviant behavior were invariably loosened or destroyed by the growth of urban society. Thus the negative consequences of urban development could be viewed both in terms of changes in community life style as the "folk" society metamorphosed into urban society, and in terms of changes in the life style of individuals who, through rural-urban migration, bridged in their own lifetime the distance between the polar extremes of the folk-urban continuum. In the late 1950s the models of urban society created by Redfield and Wirth were incorporated and elaborated by political sociologists concerned with the loss of identity, alienation, or anomie in urban-based, "mass societies" (Kornhauser, 1959; Selznick, 1960; Stein, 1960; Gusfield, 1962; Bensman and Rosenberg, 1963). These writers, who, like Wirth and Redfield, conceived of the urban way of life in terms of secularization, atomization of social relations, and the like, implied that the modern city is the quintessence of mass society, with its high potential for political radicalism and totalitarian movements. Kornhauser places special emphasis on the rate at which urbanization proceeds (the higher the rate, the more likely that the process will generate "available masses"), and upon the disintegration of intermediate social and political structures between cities and masses, making the latter susceptible to manipulation and recruitment into totalitarian movements of the far left or right.

Another type of theoretical input derives from the work of European social theorists and latter-day psychological frustration/aggression theorists, with respect to the attitudinal and behavioral consequences of material deprivation. Both Marx and Durkheim assumed that mass alienation and orientation toward protest would increase as a result of felt or relative deprivation (though not of mere *objective* deprivation, not perceived by the individual actor relative to some external standard of well-being). More recent theorists of revolution and civil violence have also drawn a fundamental distinction between objective and relative deprivation, the latter being defined primarily as the individual's perception of a discrepancy or "frustration gap" between the goods and living conditions to which he believes he is justifiably entitled and the amounts of goods and quality of conditions that he thinks he is able to obtain and retain.[6] Some Latin Americanists who have been influenced by this body of theory nevertheless appear to posit a direct linear relationship between mass economic deprivation—in absolute terms—and urban unrest or potential for unrest, with little or no attention to mediating perceptual or structural variables (see K. Johnson, 1963, 1964; Burnett and Johnson, 1968: 518–19). Others appear to have made an implicit assumption of perceived deprivation, reinforced by a "revolution of rising expectations" or "demonstration effect," as a necessary precondition for political radicalism in urban areas, even while lacking explicit data to support such an assumption (see Soares, 1965).

Still another type of theoretical input has been provided by the literature on urbanization and political participation as developed by political scientists working in the American politics and political development fields. The American politics specialists were first to posit a positive association between degree of urbanization and degree of electoral participation and party competition. While the research findings presented to date are far from conclusive, and even contradictory, a number of studies based primarily on aggregate electoral and census data have demonstrated that in some American states urbanization does appear to have facilitated the development of attitudes conducive to higher electoral participation rates

Table 1. Informal Content Analysis of Recent Discussions of Socio-Political Consequences of Urban Migration by Developmental Theorists and Latin Americanists

Theme	Developmental Theorists																				Latin Americanists																				
	Black (1966: 31-34, 81-84)	Breese (1968)	Coleman (1960: 536-537)	Eisenstadt (1966: 20-32)	DeGregory–Pi-Sunyer (1969: 95-100)	Hagen (1962: 252-255, 404-405)	Hauser (1963: 209-212)	Howton (1969)	Huntington (1968: 53-54, 278-283)	Kerr et al. (1964: 170-172)	McCord (1965: 33-43)	Moore (1963: 101-105)	Mountjoy (1968)	Olson (1963: 534-535)	Pye (1969)	Russett (1965: 130-131)	Rustow (1967: 245)	Tangri (1966)	Ward (1964)	Weiner (1967)	Andreski (1969: 6-19)	Angell (1966: 313-316)	Bagu-Palermo (1966)	Blanksten (1960: 475-478)	Burnett-Johnson (1968: 50-55, 518-519)	Edelmann (1969: 51-53, 77-78)	Fernández (1969: 16-17, 32-33)	Fitzgibbon (1967: 40-41)	Haar (1963)	Hopper (1964: 264-265)	Horowitz (1969)	K. Johnson (1967: 18)	Needler (1968)	Nehemkis (1966: 183-188)	Rogers (1967: 65-71)	Schmitt-Burks (1963: 84)	Scott (1964: 51-52, 76-77)	Soares-Hamblin (1967)	Szulc (1965: 49-54)	Wagner (1962)	Welfort (1966)
Felt deprivation, frustration of socioeconomic expectations	x		x		x	x	x	x			x			x	x	x	x	x	x		x	x	x		x	x		x	x	x		x		x	x	x	x	x	x	x	x

Social and personal dis-
organization, maladjust-
ment, anomie, insecurity,
primary-group breakdown

Alienation, non-supportive
legitimacy orientations

Increased politicization,
demand-creation

Mass availability, atom-
ization of social rela-
tions, "reintegration" need

Political radicalization,
disruptive behavior (1st
or 2nd generation
in-migrants)

and competitive party voting patterns.[7] The notion that urbanization produces an increase in political awareness, electoral participation, and demand-creation by bringing larger numbers of people into close contact
with highly salient partisan political activity, a wider range of educational
and industrial employment opportunities, and the mass media of communication also proved attractive to comparative politics specialists, who
subsequently incorporated it into their multivariate models of social mobilization and political development.[8] In many of these studies hypotheses
were constructed outlining relations among independent variables such as
urbanization, literacy, access to mass communications, income distribution,
and other social and economic attributes of national populations, on one
hand; and the dependent variable of stable, participant democracy on the
other (see Cnudde and Neubauer, 1969: 516–517). In other studies there is
emphasis on urbanization as a politicizing agent which exacerbates inter-
group tensions within a developing society and creates conditions for
mass involvement in radical political activity (see Pye, 1969; Dyckman,
1966; Leggett, 1963). It is this latter emphasis which has become most
widely diffused through the social science literature on contemporary
Latin America.

The extent to which this eclectic body of theory has been drawn upon
by Latin American specialists as well as general developmental theorists
whose analyses purport to be applicable to Latin America, can be gauged
roughly from Table 1 below. This table summarizes the results of an
informal content analysis of discussions of urban migration and its consequences for attitudes and behavior, appearing during the past decade
in texts, journals, conference papers, and "popular," non-academic studies
of contemporary Latin American affairs. The presence or absence of six
themes prominent in conventional urban theory is coded for each selection.
Themes are coded as present (x) if the author appears to posit one or more
of the specified attitudinal and behavioral patterns as outcomes (or potential outcomes) of the migrant assimilation process in cities of Latin
America and/or the developing areas in general. It must be emphasized
that this is an informal thematic analysis. The number of themes embodied
in conventional theory which are also incorporated in these discussions of
urban migration is no doubt more a function of the length and detail
of treatment which the topic receives than of a conscious desire on the
part of an author to downgrade the importance of one or another aspect
of the migrant assimilation experience. In those cases where urban migration is the main substantive concern of the source consulted, the
writers tend to pick up the full range of themes listed here in the course
of their discussion.

THE ADEQUACY OF "BORROWED" THEORY

The adequacy of conventional theory in this area can be determined
in two ways: (1) by bringing to bear empirical evidence from field studies

upon the specific propositions embodied in it, with a view toward verification or falsification; and (2) by examining the overall explanatory power of the theory in accounting for broad patterns or macro-phenomena of urban political behavior, as revealed in over-time data for nations and sub-national units. In Table 2 we summarize the findings of empirically based country studies bearing directly or indirectly upon standard conceptualizations of cityward migration and its consequences for political behavior and attitude formation. Thirty-seven of these studies take the form primarily) of analyses of sample survey data on individual attitudes and behavioral predispositions; eleven are anthropological studies of urban populations; seven are basically analyses of aggregate electoral and/or demographic data; and one study presents clinical phychological case data. The number of Latin American countries represented here is only 12 out of 21, but all of the major nations which have experienced the highest rates of internal migration since World War II are included in our sample. Finally it should be noted that the studies summarized here focus primarily upon lower-class populations. Although these sectors continue to comprise the bulk of migratory streams to Latin American cities, there has also been significant upper and middle-class migration. Two field studies now in progress (Kahl, 1968b; Reis, forthcoming) will provide data on middle and upper-class migrants in Brazil and Chile, but there are no published studies with such a focus available as of this writing.

Collectively the studies cited in Table 2 provide evidence suggesting that urban migration in Latin America does not necessarily result in severe frustration of expectations for socioeconomic improvement or widespread personal and social disorganization; and that even where these conditions are present, they do not necessarily lead to political alienation. Nor does alienation necessarily lead to political radicalization or disruptive behavior. Indeed, the apparent disjuncture between attitudes and behavioral predispositions among urban dwellers of migrant background is one of the most significant findings of those studies focused primarily upon political behavior (see Bonilla, 1961; 7–9; Goldrich, 1964: 332–333; Goldrich *et al.*, 1967–68: 14–15; Cornelius, 1969; Mangin, forthcoming). With few exceptions these studies find that urban migrants fail in most respects to conform to the usual conception of a highly politicized, disposable mass. On the contrary, the persistent non-politicization or even de-politicization of these sectors over time appears to be one of their most prominent characteristics as political actors (see Goldrich *et al.*, 1967–68: 14–16; Inkeles, 1969; Roberts, 1968b, 201). There is as yet no firm evidence to support frequent expectations of markedly increased political cognition or development of participant orientations among migrants as a consequence of exposure to the urban environment. A detailed analysis of the various factors operating to retard the politicization of in-migrant populations in Latin America is beyond the scope of this paper. Certainly one of the most powerful of these negative factors is lower socioeconomic status *per se,* with the severe restrictions on time and energy for political in-

Table 2. Summary of Empirically Based Studies Bearing Upon Conventional Theory on Socio-Political Consequences of Urban Migration*

Migrant attitude or behavior pattern†

Columns by country and study:

ARGENTINA: Critto (1969)[a]; Friedman (1968)[a]; Germani (1961)[a]; Inkeles (1969, 1970)[a f]; Margulis (1968)[a]; Yalour de Tobar (1967)[a]

BRAZIL: Bonilla (1961)[a]; Ferrari (1962)[a]; Hutchinson (1963a, 1963b)[a]; Kahl (1968a)[a]; Leeds and Leeds (1969)[c]; Lopes (1965)[a]; Nilo Tavares (1962)[a]; Pearse (1958, 1961)[a]; Rios (1960)[c]; Rosen-Berlinck (1968)[a]; Soares (1967)[a]; Soares and Noronha (1960)[b]

CHILE: Briones-Waisanen (1967)[a]; Goldrich et al. (1967-68),[a] Goldrich (n.d.)[a]; Gurrieri (1965)[a]; Halperin (1965)[b]; Herrick (1965)[a]; Inkeles (1969, 1970)[a f]; Jones (1967)[b]; Portes (1969b)[a]; Soares-Hamblin (1967)[b]

COLOMBIA: Flinn (n.d.),[a] Flinn-Camacho (1969)[a]; Williamson (1968)[a]

COSTA RICA: Goldrich (1964)[a]

GUATEMALA: Gonzáles (1965)[c]; Roberts (1968a,b,c)[c]

Pattern	Argentina	Brazil	Chile	Colombia	Costa Rica	Guatemala
(1)	o o i o	i o o o o	i i o o i i	o	o	o o
(2)	x x o o x	i o o o o	o o	o x	o	o o
(3)	x x	x	o o		o	x
(4)	o o o o	o o i o o o x	i o	o		x
(5)	o	o o o				o
(6)	o i	o o o x o o x	o i i o i	o	o	o

Symbols for Research Findings:
   x–Positive finding.
   o–Negative finding.
   i–Evidence inconclusive, ambivalent, or no direct relationship established between urban experience and dependent variable indicated.

* *Data-base key:*
   a. Sample survey data.
   b. Aggregate electoral and/or demographic data.
   c. Qualitative anthropological data.
   d. Psychological test data and/or clinical case data.
   e. Results of secondary analysis of survey data reported in Cornelius (1969), in addition to survey findings in original source (Kahl, 1968a).
   f. Results of secondary analysis of survey data reported in Nelson (1969) in addition to survey findings reported in Inkeles (1969).
   g. Partial report of CENDES survey data gathered in Caracas *rancho* districts.

† *Migrant attitude or behavior pattern predicted:*
   (1) Felt deprivation, frustration of socioeconomic expectations.

formation-seeking and involvement which it imposes (see Goldrich, 1965: 364–366; Inkeles, 1969; Toness, 1967: 39–40; Whiteford, 1964; 120). Other frequently mentioned constraints include segmented patterns of social organization and interaction in urban settlement zones inhabited

Table 2. (Continued)

	MEXICO										NICARAGUA [?]	PANAMA			PERU													EL SALVADOR	VENEZUELA					
Alschuler (1967)[b]	Balán-Browning (1967a)[a]	Butterworth (1962)[c]	Cornelius (1969)[a]	Kahl (1968a)[a e]	Kaufman (1968)[a]	Lewis (1952, 1959)[c]	Nutini-Murphy (1968)[c]	Olivé Negrete (1962)[a]	Ríos Hernández (1961)[c]	Valencia (1965)[a]	Toness (1967)[a c]	Goldrich (1964)[a]	Lutz (1968b)[a]	Bourricaud (1964)[b]	Briones (1963)[a]	Fried (1959)[d]	Goldrich et al. (1967-68),[a] Goldrich (n.d.)[a]	Mangin (1965b, 1967, 1968, forthcoming)[a c]	Mangin-Cohen (1965)[c d]	Matos Mar (1961)[a]	Powell (1969)[b]	Rotondo (1961)[a]	Seguín (1962)[d]	Turner (1965, 1967, 1968)[c]	Williamson (1963)[a]	Brisseau (1963)[b]	CENDES (1967)[b]	Jones (1967)[b]	Pan American Union (1955)[a]	Peattie (1968a, 1969)[g]	Ray (1969)[a c]	Silva Michelena (1965)[a]
o	o	o	o	i	o		o				o	x	i		o	x	i	o		x				x	x		o			o		o	o
o	o	o			o	o		x	o		o	o			x	o	o	o	x		x	x	i	x	x		o	o			o	x
	o	i	o	o	x			x	x	x				x	x												o					
o		o		i	o			x		o				o	i								o				o			x	x	x
	o	o						o	o		o		o					i					o				i			o	o	

(2) Personal and/or social disorganization, maladjustment, anomie, insecurity, primary-group breakdown.

(3) Alienation, non-supportive legitimacy orientations.

(4) Increased politicization and/or demand-creation.

(5) Mass "availability," atomization of social relations, felt reintegration need.

(6) Political radicalization, support for or participation in disruptive political activity (as a modal pattern of behavior).

N.B.: In the only two studies reporting positive evidence of political radicalization, the survey studies by Nilo Tavares (1962) and Soares (1967) conducted in Belo Horizonte and Rio de Janeiro, Brazil, respectively, the index of "radicalism" was expressed preference for the Partido Brasileiro Trabalhista (PTB). There is considerable reason to question the appropriateness of this indicator as a measure of predisposition toward political violence or radical solutions to social and economic problems. Many Brazilian specialists would argue that PTB support may well indicate no more than a desire for reformist change, unaccompanied by radical restructuring of the social order. In other cases it may reflect no issue preferences at all, but rather the personalistic identification of the respondent with authoritarian-populist candidates who have run on the PTB ticket (see Weffort, 1965).

primarily by in-migrants (see Huntington, 1968: 280–281; Roberts, 1968c: 15–19); a low sense of subjective competence as political actors, attributable in part to the persistence in the urban setting of rural value systems and orientations toward authority structures (Ray, 1969: 152); Sherwood, 1964: 15); and previous experience with negative sanctions and other forms of governmental response to squatter settlements formation and improvement efforts (Goldrich *et al.,* 1967–68; Kaufman, 1966; Lindenberg, 1969; Toness, 1967: 57).

Even in those few reported cases in which urban experience has been accompanied by ample awareness of political and governmental activity and perception of a range of possibilities for extracting benefits from local political systems (see Leeds and Leeds, 199; E. Leeds, 1969), it has apparently failed to induce a stronger orientation toward protest among the in-migrant population. Prominent among this sector are not large numbers of political extremists threatening to respond to persisting deprivation with "increasingly antisocial activities" (Pye, 1969: 402), but rather numerous politically moderate-to-conservative individuals seeking small-scale improvements in living and working conditions without recourse to violence or radical restructuring of the social order. Beyond these limited, short-term, highly localized objectives, the mass of migrants to Latin American cities apparently see little or nothing to be gained by direct political action aimed at influencing government decision-makers. Indeed, they have demonstrated relatively little inclination toward collective, broadly-based political activity on any front, let alone for "revolutionary" agitation against incumbent elites (see Bamberger, 1968: 712; Machado da Silva, 1967: 37–38; Mangin, 1968: 418–420; Powell, 1969: 15–16; Ray, 1969: 81–83, 151; Roberts, 1968b, 1968c). Under certain conditions they may become recruitable for such activity; but on the whole they exhibit no well-developed sense of class antagonism toward the upper strata of society, do not see politics (especially partisan politics) as instrumental to the attainment of personal aims, and frequently acquiesce in regimes that sustain the status quo. After six years of field work among migrant residents of Lima's burgeoning squatter settlements, one investigator (Mangin, 1967: 83; cf. Ray, 1969: 157) concluded that

> "a paternalistic ideology, combined with a 'don't let them take it away' slogan, would be more appealing [to *barriada* dwellers] than a revolutionary 'let's rise and kill the oligarchy' approach. Probably not many inhabitants of the squatter settlements would have regrets if someone else took the latter action, but they themselves are too busy."

Such attitudes undoubtedly reflect in-migrant perceptions of improvement in living conditions and life chances (however small by objective standards) usually experienced as a result of cityward migration, as well as their belief in the potential for future socioeconomic betterment within the ongoing system and their low level of tolerance for the risks and uncertainties of anti-system political action, in the face of their considerable investment of energy and resources in the acquisition and improvement of homesites on the urban periphery.

Of course, in attempting to treat the political behavior of populations such as these—a topic which is still *terra incognita* in terms of hard data, particularly of the type which might be gathered in cross-national field studies employing a structured survey instrument—there is need to exercise caution in interpreting the evidence now available. But the thrust of the findings to date, fragmentary and tentative though they may be, is clearly that the generalizations and relationships embodied in prevailing theoretical orientations do not hold for most of the Latin American populations which have been examined. Whether the explanatory and predictive power of conventional formulations may be greater with regard to second or third generation in-migrants than to the first generation, as argued by proponents of the so-called "second-generation theory," is an open question, certainly not answerable on the basis of existing evidence. What data *are* available, however, fail to reveal any marked radicalization of the second generation expressed in terms of extremist party preference (Goldrich, 1964: 332–333), negative evaluations of political system performance (Friedman, 1969: 88), or lack of confidence in existing socio-political institutions as potential vehicles of upward mobility (Gurrieri, 1965: 16–18, 24–27). Nelson (1969: 49–51) in her analysis of survey data from the Harvard Project on Sociocultural Aspects of Economic Development, finds lower levels of job and status satisfaction among urban-born as opposed to first-generation migrant respondents, but these data do not permit an actual test of the "second-generation" thesis, since city-born sons of migrants are not separable from other social types included in the "urban-born" category. It is certainly conceivable that higher levels of education, life-long exposure to urban political activity, and a lack of personal awareness of how much less satisfactory the living conditions in rural areas can be, may predispose the second generation of urban dwellers to be less satisfied with their socioeconomic and political status than the first generation (see Friedman, 1969; Ray, 1969: 175–176). But even so, it is far too early to conclude deterministically, as some developmental theorists seem all too eager to do, that in Latin America, as in North America and Asia, "urban violence, political and criminal, is due to rise as the proportion of natives [i. e., second-generation in-migrants] to immigrants [first-generation internal migrants] in the city rises" (Huntington, 1968: 283). Such notions overlook the fact that even now, most large cities in Latin America contain high proportions of second and even third generation in-migrants, who have had the benefit of improved education and opportunities for political experience and whose environmental satisfaction clearly does not depend on retrospective comparison of rural/urban socioeconomic differentials. Yet in most countries of the region the incidence of mass participation in urban political violence has been dropping rapidly, while elite-initiated violence involving primarily university students and the military has predominated (see Anderson, 1967: 98; Bwy, 1968: 202; Hobsbawm, 1967: 60; Horowitz, 1969: 166;

J. Johnson, 1967: 333). Indeed, the only major documented cases of large-scale involvement of the newly-urbanized masses in civil violence in recent Latin American experience (i.e., since the 1948 riots in Bogotá, Colombia) are the Dominican revolt of 1965 and the Venezuelan revolt of 1958. In the Dominican case, disruptive political behavior among the marginal settlement residents of Santo Domingo occurred under conditions of high unemployment and in the wake of armed clashes between opposing factions of the armed forces (Corten, 1965; Moreno, forthcoming: chap. 5). In the Venezuelan case, the *rancho* dwellers were mobilized after nearly a year of careful organizational effort by a united front of anti-Pérez Jiménez party, student, and military leaders, against an incumbent regime which had pursued a consistently hostile line toward the half million peasants who had migrated to the cities during its tenure (Ray, 1969: 31–32, 142–145, 159, 162–163). Thus in both cases it is likely that structural and situational variables not specified in conventional theory were more important as determinants of migrant political behavior than the socio-psychological factors which it stresses.

Electoral data from a number of countries reveal that conservative *políticos* (including former military dictators such as Manuel Odría of Peru) have been supported more heavily in working-class districts of some of the large cities than in the hinterland, and that in most cases low-income urban settlement zones containing large proportions of migrants have not voted disproportionately for radical opposition candidates (nor abstained from voting in response to extremist directives), relative to other working-class districts or to all electoral subunits of the cities of which they are a part (see Bourricaud, 1964; Halperin, 1965; Jones, 1967; Powell, 1969; Ray, 1969: 124, 130–131; Ferrari, 1962). Moreover, these patterns have been observed in such rapidly urbanizing countries as Chile and Mexico, where real per capita income among the urban poor as a whole has actually declined in the post-World War II period (cf. Alexander, 1962: 6; Navarrete, 1967: 170). The explanation for such phenomena clearly does not lie in prevailing conceptualizations of the attitudinal and behavioral concomitants of rapid in-migration.

SOME DEFICIENCIES OF CONVENTIONAL THEORY

A number of reasons for the inadequacy of conventional theory in this area could be suggested. Part of its inadequacy no doubt arises from the fact that many of the generalizations and hypotheses of which it is constructed were insufficiently grounded in empirical evidence to begin with. In many cases, it would seem, they were never adequately tested even within the Anglo-European context.[9] The work of the Chicago School of urban theorists is particularly vulnerable to criticism on these grounds. A number of less provincially-minded urban sociologists have pointed out the extremely narrow empirical base of the Park-Wirth *et al.* conceptualizations of city life and cityward migration, derived as they were from a limited number of case studies and impressionistic accounts of urban conditions, mainly in the United States.[10] These were supplemented by "spot mapping" of aggregate data on various indices of deviant behavior in large cities and in urban areas as contrasted with rural areas, with little or no attention to variations in reporting and public record-keeping which invariably exaggerate rural-urban and even intra-city differentials on such indices. The generalizations resulting from this research tend to be extremely time-bound as well as culture-bound; they appear to be no more empirically relevant to the emerging cities of Latin America and the developing world than to the North American metropoli of the 1970s.

Apart from the fact that the data base for Chicago School conceptualizations of "urbanism as a way of life" left much to be desired, and the fact that the data used to generate them represent a highly selective sampling of cities, countries, and cultural areas, their validity and usefulness is further compromised by strong normative bias. For example, it is easy to recognize that the Park-Wirth *et al.* writings reflect the ethos of the 1920s and 1930s in the United States, a period when many American intellectuals—Chicago School sociologists among them—were attempting to account for and and cope with the stresses and strains of urban life arising from such forces as World War I, the absorption of millions of immigrants coming from diverse foreign cultures (as well as being mainly of rural origin), and the Great Depression (see Faris, 1967: 57–58; M. Fried, 1969; Thomas and Znaniecki, 1958). Redfield's writings were strongly colored by his retrospectively idealized conception of the people of "folk societies" as socially cohesive, personally contented, nonconflictual, and well-adjusted. Folk societies were inherently good; urban industrial development was undesirable, since it destroyed the peasant community and with it, the idyllic folk culture.[11] Kornhauser and other "mass society" theorists seem obsessed by the fear that the "atomized" individuals in urban society will form undifferentiated, highly "available" masses that can be easily manipulated by demagogues of extremist persuasion (cf. Bramson, 1961; Neal and Seeman, 1964: 216; Gusfield, 1962). Such essentially anti-urban bias has led to the development of a body of theory largely incapable of accommodating both positive and negative aspects of urban development and its impact on political life.

Still another type of deficiency afflicting conventional theory in this area stems from inadequate specification of concepts, and imprecision in their use. For example a single concept, "social disorganization," has been used for ordering much of the research and writing on migrant assimilation and urban problems in general (Burgess and Bogue, eds., 1964: 488; Matras, 1965; Thomas, 1966: chap. 1; Tilly, 1965: 16–17). However, as Joseph Kahl has noted, the comparative base of "organization" is never clearly specified in the literature. "Does the concept refer to a lack of close relationship between various segments of a culture, as Redfield defines it? Then what is the standard of proper integration?—a complex urban culture will, *when well organized,* show more variation, more alternatives, than a simple rural culture. Does the concept refer to social control over individual behavior [as Kornhauser implies]? Then what is a proper standard of homogeneity within a given type of society and its various segments? American urban life is called disorganized by some observers, over-conformist by others" (Kahl, 1959: 70). What then, is actually being conceptualized through use of the term "disorganization"?[12] While separate from questions of theoretical validity or explanatory power, such conceptual confusion markedly impairs the utility of conventional theory for research on urban phenomena in Latin America and other developing areas.

But perhaps the most serious deficiency of the conventional wisdom in this area lies in its broad conceptualization of the population flow into urban areas as an undifferentiated mass responding in uniform fashion to a given set of conditions or stimuli, to which all migrants to large cities are presumably exposed. This has led to research which attempts to gauge the potential for political protest, anti-system voting, or anomic agitation in urban centers by examining gross changes in urban population composition attributable to in-migration, often through the technique of ecological correlation.[13] In the non-empirical literature the same type of perspective is reflected in references to the "vast and inchoate migrant masses" as "social dynamite of megaton proportions . . . flooding the cities and seething with discontent" (Edelmann, 1969: 53), or as "teeming urban populations . . . so highly politicized that they have become in a sense loaded revolvers pointed at the responsible governments, and on the verge of being triggered off at the slightest provocation" (Pye, 1969: 404). It becomes increasingly apparent, however, that this macro-level, aggregate-data perspective is no more satisfactory today in research on urban migration in Latin America than it was in the 1930s when Chicago School sociologists pored over census data and crime statistics in order to arrive at generalizations about "urbanism as a way of life."[14] Such generalizations are simply too gross. They leap from macro-societal processes of demographic change to conjecture about individual attitudes and behavior. Such inferential leaps might be justified *if* the results of macro-analysis could be tested against sample survey data, as they are, for example, in recent studies of population movement and voting behavior in the United States (see Campbell, *et al.,* 1964: 231–249; Wolfinger and Greenstein, 1969: 77–78). In the absence of such data, however, there remain substantial doubts as to the long-term promise of research seeking to make statements about personal political predispositions or psychological traits of urban migrants on the basis of aggregate data for macro units such as cities, states, or provinces.

Why should this be so? What theoretically relevant variables are ignored in such studies, and to what extent is this a consequence of the analytical perspectives dictated by conventional theory in this area? First let us return to the notion of the in-migrant population as an undifferentiated, disposable mass reacting uniformly to the urban environment. It turns out that in the Latin American context, relatively few individuals sharing the common experience of "cityward migration" actually go through the same type of migration experience. Some are direct rural-to-urban, or inter-urban, migrants, engaging in a single migratory movement from communities of origin to the city of destination with no extended intermediate steps.[15] Others experience what should properly be described as step-migration, involving sequential movements from village to small town to medium-sized city to metropolis.[16] It is probable that several types of population movement are occurring in varying degree in most Latin American countries. Certainly there is no single, generic pattern of cityward migration for the Latin American region, as some analysts have contended (see Quijano, 1966). In actuality the migrant population of a large city contains a large and disparate array of social types, who vary not only in terms of migration and socialization experiences but on a number of indices of pre-migration status and preparation as well. Moreover, there is evidence that in some countries socioeconomic differentiation has proceeded to such an extent in the post-migration situation that distinct sub-classes or sub-cultures of in-migrants with different life styles, value orientations, and levels of subjective political competence are now discernible (see Peattie, 1968b; Ray, 1969; 51–73, 172). Given such heterogeneity, how could we assume uniformity of response to urban environmental stimuli on the part of in-migrant populations? Yet this assumption clearly underlies both conventional theory on socio-political correlates of urban migration and much recent writing on Latin American urban conditions which has been influenced by it.

The foregoing discussion of differential migration experience implies that what the migrant transfers to the city in the way of cognitions, attitudes, and behavior patterns is a key determinant of behavior and attitude-formation in the post-migration situation. This may seem obvious, but it is nevertheless one of the most frequently underrecognized and least understood aspects of the urban migration process in modern Latin America. Certainly there is little in conventional urban theory that would suggest the persisting importance of rural community orientations within the big city ambience. On the contrary, the commonly accepted dichotomization of rural-urban life styles would lead us to assume that the "flight" to the city of individuals of rural or semi-rural origin results in virtually instantaneous "deculturation," giving way to anomie and disorganization. Nevertheless, field studies have shown clearly that what might be termed "residual ruralism" mediates importantly between pre- and post-migration situations in Latin American countries. Germani (1967: 179) has defined this as the "transference from the rural areas of institutions, values, and behavior patterns and their persistence or adaptation to the specific requirements of the urban setting." Thus we may find replicated among in-migrants traditional rural patterns of kinship and *compadrazgo* (godparenthood) relations, of religious observance, health practices, etc. (see Lewis, 1952, 1965; Butterworth, 1962). There may even be direct carry-over of attitudinal patterns such as leadership role expectations (Cooper, 1958, 1960) and concepts of authority (Ray, 1969: 50–51, 58–59). Such persistence may result from the effects of residential clustering of migrants from a given locality or region in urban settlement zones, or from the continued importance of small-scale urban production and service enterprises that keep in-migrants in a life style close to that of their rural counterparts. The urban work situation is often comparable to that of the communities of origin, and the social organizational arrangements surrounding it are reinforced by many of the same factors that operated in the rural setting. The same types of mutual aid networks and other arrangements which provided insurance for family survival in the place of origin continue to function (Adams, 1967: 53–55; Browning, in this volume). Lewis (1965: 495) has found that the *vecindad* or central-city settlement zone within the Mexico City metropolitan area tends to "act as a shock absorber for the rural migrants to the city because of the similarity between its culture and that of rural communities. Indeed, we find no sharp differences in family structure, diet, dress, and belief systems of the *vecindad* tenants, according to their rural-urban origins." Such findings have important implications for any attempt at theorizing about the political consequences of urban migration in Latin America. To assume, for example, that the in-migrant has a completely free choice in matters of political participation, aside from that more or less dictated by the existing situation or political organization of the community in which he finds himself, is probably erroneous and misleading. His total background and experience—including socialization into certain attitudinal and behavioral patterns in the rural environment—may have been such that he finds it easy to accept a very limited area of political involvement and competition. This would seem to be especially true in the case of migrants who have lived under the traditional peon-patron system in rural areas, and who now find themselves in an urban-industrial environment with an employer, labor union leader, government agency, or the machine of an authoritarian-populist politician assuming the role of patron.[18] It seems likely that residual ruralism of this form would have a direct bearing on orientations toward protest among urban migrants and their relative "availability" for recruitment into anti-system political movements.

The phenomenon of rural carry-over illustrates the need for a theoretical orientation which places more emphasis on the ecological settings from which migrants have emerged and into which they have moved.[19] Available evidence indicates that such factors as proportion of work force employment in large-scale industrial enterprises and other social, economic, and political attributes of the community of origin, the city of destination, and the particular socio-residential environments in which the migrant finds himself at various stages of the assimilation process, are likely to be of greater importance as determinants of behavior and life chances in the urban setting than the personal characteristics of migrants or internal characterological changes stimulated by the experience of migration.[20] In fact there would appear to be a wide range of environmental and situational variables external to the individual migrant which may strongly influence both attitude formation and the translation of attitudes into behavior.[21] The theoretically relevant variables of this type which may be identified on the basis of existing studies can be grouped into three general categories: (1) those relating to non-political structural and contextual properties of the metropolitan sub-communities or settlement zones in which migrants reside; (2) historical antecedents and political-cultural factors peculiar to the host city and its sub-units; and (3) factors relating to governmental response to large-scale in-migration, as determined by the structural attributes and performance capabilities of the political system at local and national levels. A brief discussion of several potential determinants of in-migrant behavior drawn from these variable clusters will have to suffice here for illustrative purposes.

The squatter settlements which have developed in such profusion in and around major metropolitan areas throughout Latin America represent major points of concentration for in-migrant populations, although they may also contain large proportions of native-born urban dwellers (see Leeds and Leeds, 1969; Portes, 1969b). Field studies conducted in recent years have shown that these settlement zones represent a wide range of environmental properties which have important consequences for attitudes and behavior patterns among their inhabitants.[22] The settlements have been found to vary along a number of dimensions, some of which are purely demographic in nature (e.g., size and density of population, stability of residence, and per capita land ownership), others of a physical, structural, or organizational nature (e.g., the type of terrain on which dwellings are built, relative security of land tenure, type of housing construction, presence or absence of formal voluntary associations, and extent of dependence relationships with external political and governmental agencies). Settlement zones may also be expected to vary importantly according to age, the process by which the settlement is formed (e.g., by organized squatter invasion, gradual, spontaneous accretion, or government initiation as part of an urban renewal program), proximity to employment sources in the central city, and access to basic urban services. Thus we may find a pattern of significant ecological variation among settlement zones within a single city. A squatter settlement may contain several hundred families, constituting practically a small community in itself, with a distinctive sub-culture of its own. John Turner (1965, 1967, 1968: 116–120, and forthcoming) has described sharply divergent sets of characteristics and functions particular to the "bridgehead" and "consolidation" settlements of metropolitan Lima. A similar pattern of ecological differentiation was revealed by a recent comparative study of marginal settlement districts in three cities in Colombia, Peru, and Puerto Rico (Rogler, 1967). The investigator found that even geographically contiguous *barrios* or settlement zones may differ sharply in the degree to which they and their inhabitants are integrated socially and economically into urban life. Some settlements are afflicted with recurrent waves of tension, antagonism, and conflict; others show no evidence of such stress. In each type of settlement the entering migrant is subject to a distinctive mix of socioeconomic pressures, social controls, and political influences (see Germani, 1967: 188; Patch, 1968: 178, 219; Stokes, 1962). The important point to be made here is that the set of environmental conditions or stimuli to which the in-migrant population of a city responds is by no means fixed and uniform, as conventional formulations would lead us to assume. There is clearly no such thing as a generic Latin American squatter settlement, or even a generic Brazilian *favela* or Peruvian *barriada*. Once again, given the diversity of conditions which has been found to exist, both among peripheral squatter settlement types and among the centrally located, high-density, "conventional slums" often inhabited by migrants in the early stages of urban assimilation, expectations of uniformity of response in terms of attitudinal and behavioral patterns seem rather fanciful.[23] Yet the social science literature on contemporary Latin America and other developing areas persists in indiscriminately lumping together all squatter settlements as "tension-ridden zones of transition" (Howton, 1969: 444), "seed-beds of political unrest" (Thein, 1965: 469), or "lost cities of parasitic misery where promiscuity, vagrance, prostitution, vices, and the worst crimes flourish" (Vargas Martínez, 1961: 151–152); places where "it takes only a clever and willful demagogue to whip into a frenzy the barely latent discontent" of the residents (Schnore and Lampard, 1968: 46); Given the importance of the internal differentiation of the Latin American city into distinctive subcommunities, such broad-brush descriptions of squatter settlements and the types of political appeals to which their inhabitants will respond remain mere statements of faith.

Insufficient attention to the squatters settlement as an agent of socialization and integration for migrants in Latin American urban centers, coupled with the traditional emphasis on social disorganization as an inevitable concomitant of "urbanism as a way of life" has caused Latin Americanists to overlook yet another theoretically relevant phenomenon: informal associational activity among in-migrant populations. Apparently many informal networks of social relations do exist that were overlooked or never searched for; networks which may serve to facilitate adjustment to the urban environment as effectively as formal organizational structures. For this reason it seems that, by relying upon participation in formal voluntary associations as a key indicator of "successful assimilation" into urban life (also a carry-over from U.S. urban sociology), the investigator actually engages in "stacking the cards" against the migrant (see A. Leeds in Field, ed., 1967: 78; Segal and Meyer, 1969: 218–219; Shannon and Shannon, 1968: 61–62). Surveys in both Latin America and the United States have shown consistently that migrant participation in formal voluntary associations in urban areas is scant, and may even decline with longer residence in the city.[24] By contrast, high levels of migrant involvement in informal networks or non-associational groupings within marginal settlement zones have been noted by anthropologists. This pattern appears to have developed most strongly in the Brazilian *favelas,* where numerous forms of *both* associational and non-associational group activity have been observed, including mutual aid networks, credit cooperatives, *ad hoc* systems for distribution of water and electricity, cooperative marketing arrangements, group activity to raise money to buy illegally occupied land, and a variety of recreational groupings (see Hoenack, 1966; Leeds, 1966; Leeds, Leeds, and Morocco, 1966; Leeds and Leeds, 1967: 27–30, 37–39; Machado da Silva, 1967: 41; Morocco, 1966; Wygand, 1966). Similarly intricate sets of informal organizational arrangements have been observed in the squatter settlements of Venezuela and Guatemala (Field, ed., 1967: 78; Peattie, 1968: 55–57; Roberts, 1968a, 1968b, 1968c). The existence of such informal networks, however short-lived and ineffectual they may be in terms of actual performance, is pertinent to our main theoretical concerns, for it indicates that disorganization and atomization of social relations as a basis for political radicalism may not be as severe a problem as standard conceptualizations of urban life and migrant assimilation would lead us to believe.

Yet another major class of theoretically relevant variables external to the individual migrant—those relating to governmental response—can only be touched upon here. We lack sufficient data on which to base an adequate discussion of these factors. Political scientists are confronted with this dilemma at least in part because, in their haste to plunder the sociological and psychological literature in search of concepts and theories to apply in their research, they have neglected a host of matters involving the operation of the political system itself which bear importantly upon the behavior of in-migrant populations. The study of comparative politics begins with the knowledge that different political regimes make different responses to widely experienced but similar problems. Rapid urbanization in contemporary Latin America is such a problem; yet with very few exceptions (e.g., Daland, 1969; Friedmann, 1968, 1969; Leeds, 1968) the extant literature contains little or no recognition of the possibility that differential responses to the problem are in fact being made by political systems throughout the region, and by specific administrations within single nations over time, and that such differences might be important in accounting for variations in migrant political attitudes and behavior. To what extent is political alienation or commitment to the system keyed to the absolute level of basic urban services and physical improvements provided to in-migrants? Or to governmental performance in coping with their needs for housing, education, and medical care? Or to the extent of deliberate efforts by incumbent elites and opposition groups to mobilize and integrate the newly urbanized into the political system in supportive or non-supportive roles? How are rates and directionality of migrant politicization affected by hostile or permissive administrative responses to the illegal land seizures through which most marginal settlements have been formed, or by subsequent government actions in granting or withholding tenure rights?[25] How are internal organizational patterns and propensities for direct political action within the settlements affected by government programs and by attempts of local political party organizations to coöpt *barrio* association leaders and other key activists in such zones?[26] Are such efforts at coöptation and control related to the widely-noted tendency of migrant organizational activity directed toward political goals to decline over time as a settlement consolidates (Goldrich *et al.*, 1967–68: 20; Lutz, 1968a: 27–29; Mangin, 1968: 416; Ray, 1969: 45; Roberts, 1968c: 20; Turner, 1968: 120)? How are the structural attributes of the national political system (e.g., party structure, extent of bureaucratic role specialization, distribution of political resources within the system, elite accessibility to vertical communication within the system) related to success in coping with the socio-political consequences of rapid in-migration?[27]

Unfortunately we can do little more than pose these problems as a string of rhetorical questions, and hope that in future political research on cityward migration and its consequences they will receive adequate attention. It is doubtful that the explanatory power of theory in this area can be raised significantly unless such matters are satisfactorily accommodated in future studies. This will entail a drastic overhaul of conventional theoretical formulations—or a decision to abandon them entirely and concentrate on the generation of new theory from the data of political research. The field studies summarized above strongly suggest that the conventional models of urbanism and urban migration do not stand up to cross-cultural, or even cross-national, comparisons. Indeed, they appear to be of such low relevance to the empirical situation in most Latin American nations today that progress could be made most rapidly through a reorientation of research away from refuting or establishing limits on existing propositions and toward discovering new relationships and formulating new hypotheses.[28]

CONCLUSION

A United Nations conference on urbanization in Latin America concluded in 1957 with a resolution recognizing that "further empirical research, and especially comparative survey research of a cross-national character, was necessary to provide a framework more adequate to Latin America for understanding the impact of urbanization" (Medina Echavarria and Hauser, 1961: 55). This statement remains essentially as valid today as it was over a decade ago. Although more extensive experimentation with aggregate data analysis is possible, the major research task for those concerned with the political sociology of urban migration in the years ahead is clearly the design of comparative survey studies which will help to determine in a systematic way how the "universal" concomitants (if any) of city migration combine with local and national political cultures, social stratification patterns, and other types of contextual and situational variables to create distinctive attitudinal and behavioral patterns among in-migrant populations. An example of this type of research is the "Comparative Class Cultures" project of "El Grupo Interamericano de Sociología Comparativa," directed by Joseph Kahl. This study will provide systematic data on the social and cultural patterns of the different social classes which absorb migrants to the St. Louis (U.S.), Santiago (Chile), and Rio de Janeiro metropolitan areas, as well as qualitative case studies of migrant assimilation experiences in these three urban centers (see Kahl, 1968b).

The intensive, comparative study of urban settlement zones within single metropolitan areas, on a cross-national or single-country basis, would seem to be another highly promising area of investigation and source of new theoretical insights. Such a research focus, providing data on both individual attitudes and the distribution of attitudes within settlement zones, should illuminate more fully than previous studies the impact of immediate urban environments on the social and political integration of migrants. This attention to the socio-political context of individual responses stems from the general expectation that the likelihood that an individual will internalize a given preference, and act on the basis of such a preference, is related to the proportion of those around him who share that preference (cf. Berelson and Steiner, 1964: 567). Stated in alternative terms, we may expect that living in a settlement zone with a high concentration of people sharing the same value orientation will accentuate the effect of that orientation as a source of individual political behavior.[29]

Yet there is also need for recognition of the inherent limitations of even the best survey research which might be conducted in Latin American urban areas. Most surveys attempt to describe the situation as it exists at a given point in time. Thus we might collect data on what proportion of migrants seem to be minimally politicized, or psychologically adjusted, or economicaly assimilated, at that moment. But only indirectly can these studies focus on the dynamic change processes which characterize the migrant assimilation experience and which are of central concern to construction of empirical theory regarding the social and political outcomes of the assimilation process. For this latter purpose, the crucial

data do not concern the proportion of migrants who appear to be alienated or successfully integrated into supportive roles within the political
system at a given moment, but rather the processes which integrate or
alienate them and the attitudinal and behavioral changes which they
undergo as a consequence of integration or alienation. For an adequate
understanding of such change processes, we need in each urban settlement zone or city being surveyed a number of detailed life histories derived
through open-ended depth interviewing and over-time observation of
behavior.[30] In survey studies steps can be taken in questionnaire construction (Balán *et al.,* 1967b), sample design (Cornelius, forthcoming),
and data analysis (Balán *et al.,* 1969) to probe such topics as the decision
to migrate, intra-city residential and occupational histories, socialization
experience, and perceived changes in life style and environmental satisfaction in the post-migration period. Nevertheless, we cannot depend alone
on survey techniques to provide us the needed information; retrospective,
cross-sectional survey data is always a poor substitute for longitudinal
data when change through time under certain defined circumstances is the
main focus of interest.

In surveying the extant literature on urban migration in Latin America,
one is struck by the fact that studies by social anthropologists are perhaps the closest thing we have to a rounded portrait of migration and its
impact on Latin American social and political life.[31] This would seem to
recommend some combination of the quantitative sample survey approach
now being employed in most systematic studies of urban political behavior
in Latin America with more intensive anthropological field methods.
Ideally, application of such techniques would begin in the pre-migration
situation with administration of questionnaires and intensive participant-
observation of the group situations in which decisions to migrate are discussed and made, thus enabling us to compare the attributes, motivations,
and behavioral predispositions of migrants before and after departure from
the place of origin, and perhaps even at various stages of migratory movement en route to the metropolis (see Germani, 1965: 172–176; Margulis,
1968: chaps. 5–7).[32] It would thus be possible to determine more precisely,
for example, the relative potency of anticipatory urban socialization as
an explanatory variable in migrant assimilation and attitude formation
(cf. Stycos and Dobyns, 1963: 41). The point to be emphasized is that,
although a good deal may become known about the characteristics of
in-migrants at specific stages of urban assimilation, and how they compare with non-migrant groups in urban areas, this would still leave us
with little or no systematic data on the assimilation process itself, conceived in terms of a "developmental sequence" (Richardson, 1967), "role
path" (Hanson and Simmons, 1968), or "experiential chain" (Simmons,
1967). Although we may recognize implicitly the dynamic, processual
nature of "deculturation," "enculturation," "resocialization," "urban accommodation," or "politicization," the approaches and concepts that have been

employed most frequently in research and writing on urban migration in Latin America and elsewhere have been static.[33] Of greatest importance from the standpoint of general theory-building, however, are not the static aspects of the problem but the types and sequences of events and experiences through which the migrant becomes exposed to and then internalizes the value systems and behavior patterns of the larger urban society and polity. Thus it seems likely that truly useful generalizations concerning the dynamics of the urbanizing process and its impact on Latin American political life and political culture may be arrived at more speedily through adequate attention to the "role paths" and "event sequences" which have long preoccupied anthropological investigators in their labors in both metropoli and provinces.

NOTES

1. One such early, and unheeded, warning is contained in Lewis (1952). This article was based on Lewis's initial anthropological study of migrants to the Mexico City metropolitan area. Corroborative findings based on a much larger number of cases were reported in Lewis (1959). This research on in-migrant populations should not be confused with Lewis's subsequent work on the "culture of poverty" in Mexico and elsewhere (see especially his *The Children of Sánchez*, 1961). These later studies focused on both migrant and non-migrant families in central-city slum zones, and were not concerned explicitly with the migrant assimilation process. Yet the literature abounds with instances in which analysts have generalized from the few cases treated intensively in Lewis's work since 1960 to in-migrant populations at large. Examples of this tendency to impute to all or most migrants the attitudinal and behavioral syndrome described by Lewis as the "culture of poverty" may be found in De Gregori and Pi-Sunyer (1969: 98–100) and Duff and McCamant (1968: 1128). The "culture of poverty" concept itself has been widely criticized; see especially Irelan *et al.* (1969), A. Leeds (1970), Portes (1969a), Valentine (1968: chaps. 3,5), and Valentine *et al.* (1969).

2. Overviews of the Chicago School's work are provided in Burgess and Bogue, eds. (1964: 1–14); and Faris (1967).

3. The classic statement of Wirth's position is his article, "Urbanism as a Way of Life" (1938). See also other essays collected in Reiss, ed. (1964).

4. See, for example, Anderson (1959), Clinard (1966), and Gist and Fava (1964). On the persisting influence of Wirth and other early Chicago School theorists in the sociological literature, see Bell (1968: 134–137), Strauss (1968: 80), and Tilly and Brown (1967: 139–140).

5. See Berelson and Steiner (1964: 606–610); Cartwright (1969: 164–166). The fact that Wirth regarded these attributes of urban life as inevitable concomitants occurring together in the development of cities is of major importance for the cross-cultural transmission of his theory. Wirth saw the deleterious effects of urbanization as distinctive and independent of those stemming from industrialization; these latter are "held constant." According to this reasoning, all cities, regardless of national or regional culture or degree of industrialization, supposedly share this set of characteristics. It has thus been possible to transfer the theory to Latin American contexts, where national and regional culture diverge markedly from those of Anglo-European nations, and where urbanization has proceeded in advance of, or largely out of phase with, industrial development.

6. See especially Bienen (1968: 88–89), Davies (1962 and forthcoming), Gurr

(1968a, 1968b, and forthcoming), Lupsha (1969: 284–285), Masotti and Bowen, eds. (1968: part 3), Moore (1966: 453–59), Morrison and Steeves (1967), Nieburg (1969: 39–45), Runciman (1966: 9–35), Southwood (1967: 41–46), Tanter and Midlarsky (1967).

7. The positive and negative findings reported thus far are found in Casstevens and Press (1963), Cutright (1963), Dawson and Robinson (1963), Eulau (1957), Dye (1966), Fenton (1966: 44 ff.), Gatlin (1968), Gold and Schmidhauser (1960), Golembiewski (1958), Gordon and Coulter (1969), Hofferbert (1966), Key (1956: 218–227), Masters and Wright (1958), Reeves (1964), Young and Moreno (1965). Attempts at explaining the various contradictions and discrepancies in this body of research are provided in Coulter and Gordon (1968) and Fenton and Chamberlayne (1969).

8. The extent to which this notion is embedded in the developmental literature can be gauged by consulting Adelman and Morris (1967: 25–26, 167), Alker (1966), Almond and Coleman, eds. (1960: 475–478, 536–544), Apter (1965: 454–458), Cutright (1966), Cutright and Wiley (1969–70), Deutsch (1961), Feierabend and Feierabend (1966: 258), Huntington (1968: 47), von Lazar and Kennedy (1968: 97–98), Lerner (1958: 60), Lipset (1963: 37–38), McCrone and Cnudde (1967), Neubauer (1967), Olsen (1968), Ranis (1968–69: 23), A. Smith (1969), Simmons *et al.* (1968), Solari (1965), and Tanter (1967). More recent analysis of cross-national survey data has shown that the correlation between urbanization and mass political participation posited in the developmental literature and apparently "demonstrated" in aggregate data studies using many nations at varying levels of development as the units of analysis is essentially spurious, as indicated by the absence of a relationship between urban residence and participation *within* each nation for which survey data was examined, and derivative of the greater levels of urbanization and political participation in the more highly developed nations (see Nie, Powell, and Prewitt, 1969: 365–368). Comparative survey analyses by Inkeles (1969) and Main (1966) have also shown that urbanization is associated with higher political participation rates primarily in those advanced countries possessing "participant" political cultures, and may even depress participation levels in nations having traditional ("parochial") or "subject" political cultures.

9. As two North American urban specialists recently observed with reference to the Chicago School conceptualization of urbanism and the migrant assimilation process, "The curious thing about the theory is not that many people have found it plausible, but that it has passed into sociological writing as an explanatory principle with very little elaboration and precious little testing. If there is a general correlation between the mobility of an area's population and some measure of social disorganization, it hardly seems worth determining whether the most mobile inhabitants contribute most vigorously to that disorganization. If cities in rapidly urbanizing countries are often politically turbulent, it seems natural to attribute some of the turbulence to the disruptive effects of large-scale migration. If new arrivals to American cities pose problems of public welfare, it goes almost without saying that they are personally maladjusted. Yet these connections among mobility, personal maladjustment, and social disorganization are in fact neither firmly established nor well understood" (Tilly and Brown, 1967: 139–140).

10. See Gans (1952), Gibbs, ed. (1961: 5), Greer (1962: 23), Kolb (1954), Sjoberg (1959, 1960: 13–24; 1965), and Reissman (1964: 130–134). Of course, the Chicago School formulations have not gone unchallenged among sociologists concerned primarily with urban life in the United States. See, for example, Freedman (1964), Greer (1962), Greer *et al.* (1968), Mizruchi (1969), Murphy (1965), Bell and Boat (1957), Sussman and Burchinal (1962), and Tilly (1968a). An extended critique of Wirth's ideas in particular, from the standpoint of general urban theory,

is provided in Morse (1968: 15–38, 160–172). A recent data-based defense of the Wirth conception of urban life is Guterman (1969).

11. For detailed criticism of Redfield's folk-urban theory see Benet (1963), Hauser (1965), Lewis (1951, 1965), Lopreato (1967: 123–130), McGee (1964), Mintz (1953). It should be noted that Redfield's emphasis on the non-conflictual, socially cooperative nature of peasant life in the "folk community" is not supported by much subsequent anthropological research. See especially the work of Foster (1962: 51 ff.) and Lewis (1951, 1965).

12. A number of sociologists have attempted to bring a semblance of order out of this confusion, but without notable success: see especially Beshers (1962: 7–8 ff.) and Hillery (1968: 112–113). Such terminological problems do not exist in isolation; they are more often than not symptomatic of basic unresolved theoretical dilemmas. For further discussion of this point see Bendix (1963: 533–535).

13. See, for example, K. Johnson (1967: 16–18), Soares and Hamblin (1967: 1062 ff.), Stepan (1966: 231), and Weiner (1967). A recent cross-national analysis of Latin American voting behavior (McDonald, 1969) also attempts to explain the high incidence of opposition voting in urban "core" areas by reference to large-scale in-migration and other social change processes, but concludes that in the Mexican case the capital's pattern of anti-system voting is essentially unrelated to such demographic and social factors. For detailed discussions identifying some of the numerous analytical and methodological pitfalls of such ecological analyses see Cartwright (1969), Dogan and Rokkan, eds. (1969: chaps. 2–5), Shively (1969), and Sterne (1967).

14. Some North American demographers, it would appear, have also adopted this perspective in speculating about the implications of their data for socio-political change and areal behavior pattterns. For example, one demographer has advanced the thesis that the proliferation of bizarre religious sects and radical political organizations in Southern California might be attributed to the fact that the area is also the greatest recipient of internal migrants in the United States (Tomlinson, 1965: 233). There is, however, an abundance of survey data which fails to support either the proposition that the mass of new migrants who continue to flood into the region constitute the seedbed of Southern California ultra-conservatism (see Wolfinger and Greenstein, 1969: 77–78), or the popular notion that collective violence in Los Angeles and other major cities across the nation in recent years is the product of "culture shock" or failure to acculturate to the urban environment on the part of recent migrants (see Lupsha, 1969: 280–281; National Advisory Commission on Civil Disorders, 1968: 130–131; Sears and McConahay, 1967: 5–10).

15. This pattern seems to have been dominant in such nations as Argentina, Chile, Colombia, Ecuador, Mexico, and possibly Peru, although confirmation must await more extensive analysis of sample survey data. See Alers and Appelbaum (1968: 8), Butterworth (1962: 261), Balán et al. (1967a: 73–75), Deneke (1966: 92), Elizaga (1966: 359–361), Flinn (1968: 81), Forni and Mármora (1967: 53–55), Foster (1967: 273–274), Margulis (1968: 147–148), Martínez (1968: 155), McGreevy (1968: 216), Molina S. (1965: 49), and Schultz (1968: 29). Note, however, that many of those involved in "direct" (i.e., one-step) migration in these countries are actually *inter-urban* migrants born and raised in towns and provincial cities, and who subsequently have moved to the capital or some other major metropolitan area. This appears to be the case in Chile, for example (see Herrick, 1965: 53–103; cf. Sahota, 1969: 85).

16. This pattern seems to predominate in Venezuela and Brazil. See Briones (1963: 65), Hutchinson (1963a: 43–46), Hill et al. (1959: 19), Leeds and Leeds (1967: 5–6), and Ray (1969: 69).

17. It should be noted, however, that the operation of "residual ruralism" in

Latin American urban environments is only imperfectly understood at present, as evidenced by the continuing debate over "ruralization of the city" among Latin American specialists. Some have stressed the existence of true urban "folk enclaves" on the rural, closed-community model, and imply that through preservation of rural values and ways of life such groupings impede the assimilation of migrants (see Bonilla, 1961, 1962; Critto, 1969: 352 ff.; Gumucio, 1967; Matos Mar, 1961: 174–176; Willems, 1968). Mangin (1967: 80–82) has taken issue with extreme statements of this "country-in-the-city" view, particularly those asserting a direct carry-over of rural social structural features into the urban squatter settlements. He adds that although migrants continue to preserve many elements of provincial culture in the city, internal organizational patterns of the squatter settlements are often new and follow no rural pattern. Anthony Leeds has also stressed the "essentially urban character" of the experience and values of *favela* and *barriada* residents, and argues that those peasant values or ways of doing things which *are* transferred to the city are in fact highly adaptive in the urban setting (Leeds in Field, ed., 1967: 68–80; Leeds and Leeds, 1967; cf. Micklin, 1968). Still others have observed that rigidly unchanging, non-adaptive replication of rural living patterns within the city is more characteristic of non-Spanish-speaking, Indian migrants than of non-Indian peasants who migrate (Bataillon, 1964: 83–85). Clearly there is need for more empirical research aimed at specifying to what extent migrants carry over their previous values, institutions, expectations, and needs; and at what rates, under what conditions, and with what consequences they undergo "deculturation" within the urban environment.

18. On the migrant's tendency to seek out such paternalistic clientage relationships, see especially Adams (1967: 186–187), Bamberger (1968: 710–711), Hobsbawm (1967: 61), Lopes (1966), Pearse (1961: 199–205), Pécaut (1968: 678), Ray (1969: 60–63), Rios (1960: 34–35), and Weffort (1965). For indications that under certain types of external constraint systems such relationships in an urban setting may often be highly political and manipulative in character, from the standpoint of both urban squatters and *políticos,* see Cotler (1967–68: 242), Leeds and Leeds (1967: 7, 26, 47), and A. Leeds (1969). Lutz (1968b: 30–33) has presented evidence suggesting that in Panama City orientations toward paternalism and dependency upon political-governmental agencies among migrant populations may be strongly influenced by the presence or absence of voluntary associations (*barriada* improvement societies) dealing with common problems within settlement zones.

19. Such an emphasis is also advocated by A. Leeds in Field, ed. (1967: 131), Safa (1966), and Shannon (1965).

20. For supporting evidence and arguments see Balán (1967, 1968), Bock and Iutaka (1969), Bryce-Laporte (1968), Forni and Mármora (1967), González (1965: 277–278), Inkeles (1969, 1970), Margulis (1968: chaps. 5, 7), Ray (1969: 24, 63–71), Roberts (1968b: 193, 201; 1968c: 9), Safa (1964, 1967), Sherwood (1967: 27–29), Touraine (1961: 34), Willems (1968: 76–77), and Williamson (1964). For evidence drawn from non-Latin American contexts see Fried (1967), Lane (1959: 267–269), Nelson (1969), and Tilly (1969c: 35–36).

21. See the excellent general discussion of internal versus external determinants of migrant assimilation outcomes in Shannon and Shannon (1968: 56–58), and the empirical work of Heiss (1967, 1969), which tests a number of general hypotheses concerning the relative potency of individual pre-migration traits and various aspects of the early post-migration situation in predicting assimilation outcomes, with data on Italian immigrants.

22. The only detailed descriptions of life in the central-city slum zones are found in Lewis (1961, 1968) and Patch (1961, 1968: 219). See also Harris (1969: 194–197). Central-city slums are currently being examined in survey studies conducted in Mexico City and Lima (Cornelius, forthcoming; Eckstein, forthcoming; Collier, forthcoming).

23. The only detailed descriptions of life in the central-city slum zones are found in Lewis (1961, 1968) and Patch (1961, 1968: 219). See also Harris (1969: 194–197). Central-city slums are currently being examined in comparative survey studies conducted in Mexico City and Guadalajara (Cornelius, forthcoming; Eckstein, forthcoming).

24. See, for example, Beyer, ed. (1967: 203), Dotson (1953), Frank (1966: 78–79), Goldrich *et al.* (1967–68: 7–9), Margulis (1968: 171), Portes (1969b: 26–29), and DESAL (1969: 304–308). For U.S. data see Windham (1963) and Zimmer (1955: 218–222). The major exceptions have been observed in Peru, where neighborhood or citywide "sons of the region" clubs provide recent Indian migrants with ties among each other and between them and their regions of origin (see Doughty, 1969; Mangin, 1965a, and forthcoming; Matos Mar, 1966). A. Leeds has observed that in squatter settlements in Rio de Janeiro and Lima overall levels of participation in settlement associations do not decline appreciably over time but fluctuate in response to changes in the internal political organization of settlements and changes in the external constraint structure (personal communication, November, 1969).

It appears that formal associational structures play a more significant role in migrant assimilation in African cities than in Latin America (see Bogdan, 1969; Hanna, 1967: 16–17; Little, 1964, 1966; Meillassoux, 1968; Middleton, 1969; Parkin, 1966), although even for Africa the evidence is still far from conclusive (see Jenkins, 1967: 73–76). Africanists have attributed the salience of voluntary associations in the migrant assimilation process in that region to the fact that they largely substitute for the traditional institutions of family, kinship, and local community left behind in the act of migration or modified significantly in the urban setting in response to changed economic circumstances (Gutkind, 1965, 1967). The fact that such institutions appear to have persisted in largely unmodified form among inmigrants in Latin American cities may help to explain their lesser dependence upon association-based groupings as adaptive, integrative mechanisms.

25. Goldrich *et al.* (1967–68), Lutz (1969), Pratt (1968), and Ray (1969: 31–33, 36) are among the very few studies by political scientists which even begin to shed light on this and the following question in the Latin American context. For related findings from anthropological and sociological investigations, see R. M. Morse (1965: 55), Smith (1966), and Toness (1967). Fried (1967) has provided a valuable analysis of the political impact of Italian urbanization focusing in part on these questions.

26. For some highly suggestive anthropological analyses bearing on patterns and consequences for interaction between squatter settlements and various supralocal political structures, see A. Leeds (forthcoming), E. Leeds (1966), Olien (1968), Machado da Silva (1967: 38 ff.), Toness (1967), and Vaughan (1968).

27. The potentialities of longitudinal analysis employing extant historical data for illuminating this type of problem seem considerable. See especially the work of Charles Tilly and his associates on the evolution of collective violence in western Europe under the impact of urbanization and industrialization in the 19th and 20th centuries (C. Tilly, 1968b, 1968c, 1969a, 1969b; R. Tilly, 1969); Lane's analysis of the relationship between urbanization and criminal violence in the state of Massachusetts in the nineteenth century (Lane, 1969); and the studies conducted as part of the Project on Historical Crises and Political Development at Stanford University (see Almond, 1969). This type of approach might be applied fruitfully to the case of Argentina under Perón, which is frequently cited in connection with prevailing theory regarding socio-political consequences of urban migration (see Andújar, 1966; Barager, ed., 1968: 24; Daland, 1969: 24–25; Ray, 1969: 177–179; P. Smith, 1969b). While it is apparent that newly arrived urban migrants formed a large part of Perón's constituency during the 1940's, and that even today a high

proportion of the in-migrant population of Argentine cities could be classified as *Peronistas,* at least in terms of partisan preferences (Imaz, 1961; Margulis, 1968: 174), it is far less clear that migrant support for the Perón regime derived primarily from those psychologically disorienting, politically mobilizing effects of cityward migration predicted in conventional urban theory. Historical accounts of the period suggest that the effects of rapid in-migration were mediated by a variety of structural and performance variables unrelated to the migration process, such as systemic constraints on lower-class political participation and access to decisional elites, the differential effectiveness of *Peronista* and non-*Peronista* leadership in securing material benefits for the urban poor, and so forth (see Germani, 1962: 220–231; Germani, 1969: 138–139; Butler, 1969: 427–433; P. Smith, 1969a: chap. 9; P. Smith, 1969b: 47–49). Intensive analysis of available time-series data and other quantitative and qualitative evidence relating to Argentine social and political change over the 1940–1955 period, along the lines of the Tilly and Stanford Project studies cited above, might be of considerable assistance in evaluating the relative importance of socio-psychological variables and structural/performance factors of a political nature in Perón's rise to power. The beginnings of such an analysis are provided in Cantón (1966) and Kirkpatrick (1968). This type of detailed, diachronic examination of the urbanizing experiences of single nations constitutes a needed corrective to correlational and causal-modelling studies employing cross-sectional designs. These studies, which pursue an analysis across scores of countries at many different stages of development, have served as the basis for many of the most commonly accepted generalizations about urbanization and its social, economic, and political concomitants. Careful longitudinal analyses have already cast some of these popular notions into serious question (see especially Anderson and Anderson, 1959; Ferejohn, 1969; Sovani, 1964; and the studies by C. and R. Tilly cited above).

28. Essentially the same conclusion is reached in a recent review essay with respect to research on urbanization and its impact on patterns of social and political participation in the United States. See Marshall (1968: 215).

29. For empirical confirmation of this expectation with respect to metropolitan subunits in the United States, see Bell (1965: 257), Foladare (1968: 529), Greer and Orleans (1968: 204), Putnam (1966), and Segal and Meyer (1969). The case for such contextually grounded survey research and analysis in comparative politics and political sociology is well made in Barton (1968) and Verba (1969). Survey studies which employ contextual designs in the sampling of Latin American urban populations for political research include Cornelius (forthcoming), Goldrich *et al.* (1967–68), and Ornelas (forthcoming). Demographic and sociological studies employing such survey designs include Calderón Alvarado (1963), Caplow *et al.* (1964), Cuevas (1965), Eckstein (in progress), Rogler (1967), Usandizaga and Havens (1966).

30. For illustrative case histories of migrant assimilation experiences in Lima, Peru, see Patch (1968) and Dietz (1969). See also the case histories of Puerto Rican migrant families presented in Lewis (1968: 87–106).

31. The previously cited work of William Mangin and Bryan Roberts is particularly valuable in this regard. See also Southall and Bruner, eds. (forthcoming) and Eddy, ed. (1968).

32. For additional arguments supportive of this type of research design, see Beshers (1967: chap. 5) and Germani (1965: 172–176). The only full-scale attempt at such a study to be undertaken thus far is that of Margulis (1968), which analyzes migratory movements from a group of isolated rural villages in the La Rioja (Chilecito) region of Argentina to the Buenos Aires metropolitan area, using sociological survey as well as anthropological community study techniques, "focussed" key-informant interviews, and psychological tests in both the communities of origin and the host city. A sample consisting of in-migrant relatives of the families studied

in the La Rioja communities was interviewed in Buenos Aires. A smaller survey study conducted in Venezuela by MacDonald and MacDonald (1968) sampled migrant and non-migrant populations in Ciudad Guayana and its hinterland, comparing the in-migrant respondents with non-related respondents residing in the same two counties from which the migrants originated. A similar research design was employed by Critto (1969) in a study of rural-urban migration in the Córdoba region of Argentina.

33. Essentially the same complaint has been made by Shannon and Shannon (1968: 56 ff.). A significant exception is the work being done on assimilation paths of Spanish-American migrants to Denver, Colorado, by members of the project on "Urbanization of the Migrant: Processes and Outcomes," at the Institute of Behavioral Science, University of Colorado, Boulder. This research involves computer simulation of assimilation experiences based on complex life history data gathered from migrant informants. See Hanson and Simmons (forthcoming), Hanson *et al.* (1968), Rendon (1968), and Simmons *et al.* (forthcoming).

REFERENCES

ABRAMS, CHARLES (1965) *Squatter Settlements: The Problem and the Opportunity.* Special Report to the U.S. Agency for International Development. New York: Dept. of Housing and Urban Development.

ADAMS, RICHARD N. (1967) *The Second Sowing: Power and Secondary Development in Latin America.* San Francisco: Chandler.

ADELMAN, IRMA and CYNTHIA T. MORRIS (1967) *Society, Politics, and Economic Development: A Quantitative Approach.* Baltimore: Johns Hopkins Press.

ALERS, J. OSCAR and RICHARD P. APPELBAUM (1968) "La migración en el Perú: un inventario de proposiciones." *Estudios de Población y Desarrollo* (Peru) 1, No. 4: 1–43.

ALEXANDER, ROBERT J. (1962) *Labor Relations in Argentina, Brazil, and Chile.* New York: McGraw-Hill.

ALKER, HAYWARD (1966) "Causal inference and political analysis." Pp. 7–43 in J. L. Bernd (ed.) *Mathematical Applications in Political Science,* II. Dallas: Arnold Foundation–Southern Methodist University.

ALMOND, GABRIEL A. (1969) "Determinacy-choice, stability-change: some thoughts on a contemporary polemic in political theory." Unpublished paper, Center for Advanced Study in the Behavioral Sciences, Stanford, California, August.

ALMOND, GABRIEL A. and J. S. COLEMAN, eds. (1960) *The Politics of the Developing Areas.* Princeton: Princeton University Press.

ALSCHULER, LAWRENCE R. (1967) Political Participation and Urbanization in Mexican Cities. Ph.D. dissertation, Northwestern University.

ANDERSON, CHARLES W. (1967) *Politics and Economic Change in Latin America.* Princeton: D. Van Nostrand.

ANDERSON, NELS (1959) *The Urban Community.* New York: Henry Holt.

ANDERSON, ROBERT and GALLATIN ANDERSON (1959) "Voluntary associations and urbanization: a diachronic analysis." *American Journal of Sociology* 65: 265–273.

ANDRESKI, STANISLAV (1969) *Parasitism and Subversion: The Case of Latin America,* 2nd ed. New York: Schocken Books.

ANDÚJAR, GERARDO (1966) "Migración urgano-rural y autoritarismo político." *Revista Paraguaya de Sociología* 6: 43–56.

ANGELL, ALAN (1966) "Party systems in Latin America." *Political Quarterly* 37: 309–323.

BAGÚ, SERGIO and EPIFANIO PALERMO (1966) "Las condiciones de vida y salud entre los trabajadores migrantes y sus familias en América Latina." *Cuadernos Americanos* (Mexico) 145, No. 2: 15–34.

BALÁN, JORGE (1968) "Are farmers' sons handicapped in the city?" *Rural Sociology* 33, No. 2: 160–174.

—— (1969) "Migrant-native socioeconomic differences in Latin American cities: a structural analysis." *Latin American Research Review* 4, No. 1: 3–29.

BALÁN, JORGE, HARLEY BROWNING and ELIZABETH JELÍN DE BALÁN (1967a) *Movilidad social, migración, y fecundidad en Monterrey metropolitano*. Monterrey, Mexico: Centro de Investigaciones Económicas, Universidad de Nuevo León, and Austin: Population Research Center, Dept. of Sociology, University of Texas.

—— (1967b) "Technical procedures in the execution of the Monterrey Mobility Study." Unpublished paper. Population Research Center, Dept. of Sociology, University of Texas, Austin.

BALÁN, JORGE, HARLEY BROWNING, ELIZABETH JELÍN, and LEE LITZLER (1969) "A computerized approach to the processing and analysis of life histories obtained in sample surveys." *Behavioral Science* 14, No. 2: 105–120.

BAMBERGER, MICHAEL (1968) "A problem of political integration in Latin America: the *barrios* of Venezuela." *International Affairs* 44, No. 4: 709–719.

BARAGER, JOSEPH R., ed. (1968) *Why Perón Came to Power*. New York: Alfred A. Knopf.

BARTON, ALLEN H. (1968) "Bringing society back in: survey research and macro-methodology." *American Behavioral Scientist* 12, No. 2: 1–9.

BATAILLON, CLAUDE (1964) "La geografía urbana de la ciudad de México." *América Latina* (Rio de Janeiro) 7, No. 4: 77-86.

BELL, WENDELL (1965) "Urban neighborhoods and individual behavior." Pp. 253–264 in Muzafer Sherif and Carolyn W. Sherif (eds.) *Problems of Youth*. Chicago: Aldine.

—— (1968) "The city, the suburb, and a theory of social choice." Pp. 132–168 in Scott Greer et al. (eds.) *The New Urbanization*. New York: St. Martin's Press.

BELL, WENDELL and MARION D. BOAT (1957) "Urban neighborhoods and informal social relations." *American Journal of Sociology* 62: 391–398.

BENDIX, REINHARD (1963) "Concepts and generalizations in comparative sociological studies." *American Sociological Review* 28: 532-539.

BENET, FRANCISCO (1963) 'Sociology uncertain: the ideology of the rural-urban continuum." *Comparative Studies in Society and History* 6: 1–23.

BENSMAN, JOSEPH and BERNARD ROSENBERG (1963) *Mass, Class, and Bureaucracy*. Englewood Cliffs: Prentice-Hall.

BERELSON, BERNARD and GARY A. STEINER (1964) *Human Behavior: An Inventory of Scientific Findings*. New York: Harcourt, Brace, & World.

BESHERS, JAMES M. (1962) *Urban Social Structure*. New York: Free Press.

—— (1967) *Population Processes in Social Systems*. New York: Free Press.

BEYER, GLENN H., ed. (1967) *The Urban Explosion in Latin America: A*

Continent in Process of Modernization. Ithaca, N.Y.: Cornell University Press.

BIENEN, HENRY (1968) *Violence and Social Change*. Chicago: University of Chicago Press.

BLACK, CYRIL E. (1966) *The Dynamics of Modernization*. New York: Harper & Row.

BLANKSTEN, GEORGE I. (1960) "The politics of Latin America." Pp. 455–531 in G. A. Almond and J. S. Coleman (eds.) *The Politics of the Developing Areas*. Princeton: Princeton University Press.

BOCK, E. WILBUR and SUGIYAMA IUTAKA (1969) "Rural-urban migration and social mobility: the controversy on Latin America." *Rural Sociology* 34, No. 3: 343–355.

BOGDAN, ROBERT (1969) "Youth clubs in a West African city." Pp. 223–241 in P. Meadows and E. H. Mizruchi (eds.) *Urbanism, Urbanization, and Change: Comparative Perspectives*. Reading, Mass.: Addison-Wesley.

BONILLA, FRANK (1961) "Rio's *favelas*: the rural slum within the city." *American Universities Field Staff Reports, East Coast South America Series*, 8, No. 3: August.

———— (1962) "The *favelas* of Rio: the rundown rural *barrio* in the city." *Dissent* 9: 383–386.

BOURRICAUD, FRANÇOIS (1964) "Lima en la vida política peruana." *América Latina* (Rio de Janeiro) 7, No. 4: 85–95.

BRAMSON, LEON (1961) *The Political Context of Sociology*. Princeton: Princeton University Press.

BREESE, GERALD (1968) "Some dilemmas in poverty, power, and public policy in cities of underdeveloped areas." Pp. 443–464 in Warner Bloomberg, Jr., and H. J. Schmandt (eds.) *Power, Poverty, and Urban Policy: Urban Affairs Annual Reviews*. Vol. 2. Beverly Hills, Calif.: Sage Publications.

————, ed. (1969) *The City in Newly Developing Countries: Readings on Urbanism and Urbanization*. Englewood Cliffs: Prentice-Hall.

BRIONES, GUILLERMO (1963) "Movilidad ocupacional y mercado de trabajo en el Perú." *América Latina* (Rio de Janeiro) 6, No. 3: 63–76.

BRIONES, GUILLERMO and F. B. WAISANEN (1967) "Aspiraciones educacionales, modernización, e integración urbana." *América Latina* (Rio de Janeiro) 10, No. 4: 3–21. An earlier, English-language version is reprinted in P. Meadows and E. H. Mizruchi (eds.) *Urbanism, Urbanization, and Change*. Reading, Mass.: Addison-Wesley, 1969, pp. 252–264.

BRISSEAU, JANINE (1963) "Les 'barrios' de Petare: faubourgs populaires d'une banlieue de Caracas." *Les Cahiers d'Outre Mer* (Bordeaux, France) 16, No. 61: 5–42.

BROWNING, HARLEY and WALTRAUT FEINDT (1968) "Diferencias entre la población nativa y la migrante en Monterrey." *Demografía y Economía* (Mexico) 2, No. 2: 183–204.

BRYCE-LAPORTE, ROY S. (1968) "Family adaptation of relocated slum dwellers in Puerto Rico: implications for urban research and development." *Journal of the Developing Areas* 2, No. 4: 533–540.

BURGESS, E. W. and DONALD J. BOGUE, eds. (1964) *Contributions to Urban Sociology*. Chicago: University of Chicago Press.

BURNETT, BEN G. and KENNETH F. JOHNSON (1968) *Political Forces in Latin*

America: Dimensions of the Quest for Stability. Belmont, Calif.: Wadsworth.
BUTLER, DAVID J. (1969) "Charisma, migration, and elite coalescence: an interpretation of Peronism." *Comparative Politics* 1, No. 3: 423–439.
BUTTERWORTH, DOUGLAS S. (1962) "A study of the urbanization process among Mixtec migrants from Tilaltongo in Mexico City." *América Indígena* (Mexico) 22, No. 3: 257–274.
BWY, D. P. (1968) "Dimensions of social conflict in Latin America." Pp. 201–236 in L. H. Masotti and D. R. Bowen (eds.) *Riots and Rebellion: Civil Violence in the Urban Community*. Beverly Hills, Calif.: Sage Publications.
CALDERÓN ALVARADO, LUIS (1963) *Poder retentivo del 'área local urbana' en las relaciones sociales*. Fribourg. Switzerland: Centro Internacional de Investigaciones Sociales de Fédération Européenne de Recherche Economique et Social.
CAMPBELL, ANGUS et al. (1964) *The American Voter: An Abridgement*. New York: John Wiley.
CANTÓN, DARÍO (1966) *Universal Suffrage as an Agent of Mobilization* [in Argentina]. Documento de Trabajo No. 19. Buenos Aires: Editorial del Instituto Torcuato Di Tella.
CAPLOW, THEODORE et al. (1964) *The Urban Ambience: A Study of San Juan, Puerto Rico*. Totowa, N.J.: Bedminster Press.
CARTWRIGHT, DESMOND S. (1969) "Ecological variables." Pp. 155–218 in E. F. Borgatta and G. W. Bohrnstedt (eds.) *Sociological Methodology, 1969*. San Francisco: Jossey-Bass.
CASSTEVENS, THOMAS W. and CHARLES PRESS (1963) "The context of democratic competition in American state politics." *American Journal of Sociology* 68: 536–543.
Centro de Estudios del Desarrollo, Universidad Central de Venezuela (CENDES) (1967) *Estudio de conflictos y consenso*. Caracas, Venezuela: Imprenta Universitaria.
CLINARD, MARSHALL B. (1966) *Slums and Community Development*. New York: Free Press.
COLEMAN, J. S. (1960) "Conclusion." Pp. 532–576 in G. A. Almond and J. S. Coleman (eds.) *The Politics of the Developing Areas*. Princeton: Princeton University Press.
COLLIER, DAVID (forthcoming) Aspects of *barriada* politics in Lima, Peru [title approx.]. Ph.D. dissertation, Dept. of Political Science, University of Chicago.
COOPER, KENNETH J. (1958) "A comparative study of leadership in Mexican peasant and industrial environments." Paper presented at the Annual Meeting of the American Anthropological Association, Washington, D.C.
———— (1960) "The modified Q technique in rural-urban field research." Pp. 338–351 in R. N. Adams and J. J. Preiss (eds.) *Human Organizational Research*. Homewood, Ill.: Dorsey Press.
CORNELIUS, WAYNE A., JR. (1969) "Urbanization as an agent in Latin American political instability: the case of Mexico." *American Political Science Review* 63, No. 3.
———— (forthcoming) Political Correlates of Migrant Assimilation in Mexican Urban Environments. Ph.D. dissertation, Dept. of Political Science, Stanford University.

CORTEN, ANDRÉ (1965) "Como vive la otra mitad de Santo Domingo: estudio de dualismo estructural." *Caribbean Studies* 4, No. 4: 3–19.

COTLER, JULIO (1967–68) "The mechanics of internal domination and social change in Peru." *Studies in Comparative International Development* 3, No. 12: 229–246.

COULTER, PHILIP and GLEN GORDON (1968) "Urbanization and party competition: critique and redirection of theoretical research." *Western Political Quarterly* 21, No. 2: 274–288.

CRITTO, ADOLFO (1969) "Análisis del campo y la ciudad después de la migración: campo-ciudad en Córdoba [Argentina]." Pp. 339–359 in J. E. Hardoy and R. P. Schaedel (eds.) *El Proceso de urbanización en América desde los orígenes hasta nuestros días.* Buenos Aires: Editorial del Instituto Torcuato Di Tella.

CUEVAS, MARCO ANTONIO (1965) "Análisis de tres áreas marginales de la ciudad de Guatemala y su incidencia en una política urbana nacional." Pp. 47–77 in *Seminario de Integración Social Guatemalteca, Problems de la urbanización en Guatemala.* Guatemala City: Departamento Editorial "José de Pineda Ibarra," Ministerio de Educación.

CUTRIGHT, PHILLIPS (1963) "Urbanization and competitive party politics." *Journal of Politics* 25: 552–564.

―――― (1966) "National political development: social and economic correlates." Pp. 569–581 in Nelson W. Polsby *et al.* (eds.) *Politics and Social Life.* Boston: Houghton Mifflin.

CUTRIGHT, PHILLIPS and JAMES A. WILEY (1969–70) "Modernization and political representation: 1927–1966." *Studies in Comparative International Development* 5, No. 2.

DALAND, ROBERT T. (1969) "Urbanization policy and political development in Latin America." *American Behavioral Scientist* 12, No. 5: 22–33.

DAVIES, JAMES C. (1962) "Toward a theory of revolution." *American Sociological Review* 27, No. 1: 5–19.

―――― , ed. (forthcoming) *When Men Revolt—and Why.* New York: Free Press.

DAWSON, RICHARD E. and J. A. ROBINSON (1963) "Inter-party competition, economic variables, and welfare policies in the American states." *Journal of Politics* 25, No. 2: 265–289.

DE GREGORI, THOMAS R. and ORIOL PI-SUNYER (1969) *Economic Development: The Cultural Context.* New York: John Wiley.

DELGADO, CARLOS (1969) "Three proposals regarding accelerated urbanization problems in metropolitan areas: the Lima case." *American Behavioral Scientist* 12, No. 5: 34–45.

DENEKE, JORGE A. H. (1966) *The Colonias Proletarias of Mexico City: Low-Income Settlements of the Urban Fringe.* M.A. thesis, Dept. of City Planning, M.I.T.

DESAL (Center for the Economic and Social Development of Latin America) (1969) *Marginalidad en América Latina: Un ensayo de diagnóstico.* Santiago de Chile and Barcelona, Spain: DESAL–Editorial Herder.

DEWEY, RICHARD (1960) "The rural-urban continuum: real but relatively unimportant." *American Journal of Sociology* 66: 60–66.

DIETZ, HENRY (1969) "Urban squatter settlements in Peru: a case history and analysis." *Journal of Inter-American Studies* 11, No. 3: 353–370.

DOGAN, MATTEI and STEIN ROKKAN, eds. (1969) *Quantitative Ecological Analysis in the Social Sciences.* Cambridge: M.I.T. Press.

DOTSON, FLOYD (1953) "A note on participation in voluntary associations in a Mexican city." *American Sociological Review* 18, No. 4: 380–386.

DOUGHTY, PAUL L. (1969) "La cultura del regionalismo en la vida urbana de Lima, Perú." *América Indígena* (Mexico) 29, No. 4: 949–981.

DUFF, ERNEST A. and JOHN F. MCCAMANT (1968) "Measuring social and political requirements for system stability in Latin America." *American Political Science Review* 62, No. 4: 1125–1143.

DYCKMAN, JOHN W. (1966) "Some conditions of civic order in an urbanized world." *Daedalus* 95, No. 3: 797–812.

DYE, THOMAS R. (1966) *Politics, Economics, and the Public: Policy Outcomes in the American States.* Chicago: Rand McNally.

ECKSTEIN, SUSAN (forthcoming) Social, Economic, Political, and Cultural Integration of the Urban Poor in Mexico City [title approx.]. Ph.D. dissertation, Columbia University.

EDDY, ELIZABETH M., [ed.] (1968) *Urban Anthropology: Research Perspectives and Strategies.* Southern Anthropological Society Proceedings, No. 2. Athens, Georgia: University of Georgia Press for the Southern Anthropological Society.

EDELMANN, ALEXANDER T. (1969) *Latin American Government and Politics: The Dynamics of a Revolutionary Society.* Rev. ed. Homewood, Ill.: Dorsey Press.

EISENSTADT, S. N. (1966) *Modernization: Protest and Change.* Englewood Cliffs: Prentice-Hall.

ELIZAGA, JUAN C. (1966) "A study of migration to Greater Santiago [Chile]." *Demography* 3, No. 2: 352–377. Reprinted in Breese (ed.), 1969: 332–359.

EULAU, HEINZ (1957) "The ecological basis of party systems: the case of Ohio." *Midwest Journal of Political Science* 1: 125–135.

FARIS, ROBERT E. L. (1967) *Chicago Sociology, 1920–1932.* San Francisco: Chandler.

FEIERABEND, IVO K. and ROSALIND L. FEIERABEND (1966) "Aggressive behaviors within polities, 1948–1962: a cross-national study." *Journal of Conflict Resolution* 10: 249–271.

FENNELL, LEE C. (1967) "Critical elections and voter salience: the Argentine case." *The Latinamericanist* (Center for Latin American Studies, University of Florida) 3, No. 4: 1–3.

FENTON, JOHN H. and DONALD W. CHAMBERLAYNE (1969) "The literature dealing with the relationships between political processes, socioeconomic conditions, and public policies in the American states: a bibliographical essay." *Polity* 1, No. 3: 388–404.

FEREJOHN, JOHN (1969) "Causal models and dynamic analysis." Paper presented at the Annual Meeting of the American Political Science Association, New York City, September.

FERNÁNDEZ, JULIO A. (1969) *Political Administration in Mexico.* Boulder: Bureau of Governmental Research and Service, University of Colorado, Boulder.

FERRARI, ALFONSO TRUJILLO (1962) "Atitude e comportamento político do inmigrante nordestino em São Paulo." *Sociologia* (Brazil) 24, No. 3: 159–180.

FIELD, ARTHUR J., ed. (1967) *Urbanization and Work in Modernizing Societies.* Detroit: Glengary Press.

FITZGIBBON, RUSSELL H. (1967) "Political implications of population growth in Latin America." *The Sociological Review* 11: 23–46.

FLINN, WILLIAM A. (n.d.) "Rural-to-urban migration: a Colombian case." Research publication No. 19, Land Tenure Center, University of Wisconsin, Madison (mimeo.).

———— (1968) "The process of migration to a shantytown in Bogotá." *Inter-American Economic Affairs* 22, No. 2: 77–88.

FLINN, WILLIAM A. and ALVARO CAMACHO (1969) "The correlates of voter participation in a shantytown *barrio* in Bogotá, Colombia." *Inter-American Economic Affairs* 22, No. 4: 47–58.

FOLADARE, IRVING S. (1968) "The effect of neighborhood on voting behavior." *Political Science Quarterly* 83, No. 4: 516–529.

FORNI, FLOREAL and LELIO MÁRMORA (1967) "Migración diferencial en comunidades rurales." *Cuadernos del Centro de Estudios Urbanos y Regionales* (Buenos Aires) 10: 1–95.

FOSTER, GEORGE M. (1962) *Traditional Cultures and the Impact of Technological Change.* New York: Harper.

FRANK, ANDREW GUNDER (1966) "Urban poverty in Latin America." *Studies in Comparative International Development* 2, No. 5: 75–84.

FREEDMAN, RONALD (1964) "Cityward migration, urban ecology, and social theory." In E. W. Burgess and D. W. Bogue (eds.) *Contributions to Urban Sociology.* Chicago: University of Chicago Press.

FRIED, JACOB (1959) "Acculturation and mental health among Indian migrants in Peru." in Marvin K. Opler (ed.) *Culture and Mental Health.* New York: Macmillan.

FRIED, MARC (1969) "Deprivation and migration: dilemmas of causal interpretation." Pp. 111–159 in Daniel P. Moynihan (ed.) *On Understanding Poverty: Perspectives from the Social Sciences.* New York: Basic Books.

FRIED, ROBERT C. (1967) "Urbanization and Italian politics." *Journal of Politics* 29, No. 3: 505–534.

FRIEDMAN, HERBERT D. (1968) Squatter Assimilation in Buenos Aires, Argentina. Ph.D. dissertation, M.I.T.

———— (1969) "Los adolescentes de las villas de emergencia de Buenos Aires." *Revista Latinoamericana de Sociología* 5, No. 1: 80–93.

FRIEDMANN, JOHN (1968) "A strategy of deliberate urbanization." *Journal of the American Institute of Planners* 34, No. 6: 364–373.

———— (1969) "The role of cities in national development." *American Behavioral Scientist* 12, No. 5: 13–21.

FRIEDMANN, JOHN and TOMAS LACKINGTON (1967) "Hyperurbanization and national development in Chile." *Urban Affairs Quarterly* 2, No. 4: 3–29.

GANS, HERBERT (1952) "Urbanism and suburbanism as ways of life." Pp. 625–648 in Arnold Rose (ed.) *Human Behavior and Social Processes.* Boston: Houghton Mifflin.

GATLIN, DOUGLAS S. (1968) "Toward a functionalist theory of political parties:

inter-party competition in North Carolina." In William J. Crotty (ed.) *Approaches to the Study of Party Organization*. Boston: Allyn & Bacon.

GERMANI, GINO (1961) "Inquiry into the social effects of urbanization in a working-class sector of Buenos Aires." Pp. 206–233 in P. M. Hauser (ed.) *Urbanization in Latin America*. New York: International Documents Service.

——— (1962) *Política y sociedad en una época de transición*. Buenos Aires: Editorial Paidós.

——— (1965) "Migration and acculturation." Pp. 159–178 in P. M. Hauser (ed.) *Handbook for Social Research in Urban Areas*. Paris: UNESCO.

——— (1967) "The city as an integrating mechanism: the concept of social integration." Pp. 175–189 in Glenn H. Beyer (ed.) *The Urban Explosion in Latin America*. Ithaca: Cornell University Press.

——— (1969) "The transition to a mass democracy in Argentina." Pp. 121–141 in Arpad von Lazar and R. R. Kaufman (eds.) *Reform and Revolution: Readings in Latin American Politics*. Boston: Allyn & Bacon.

GIBBS, JACK P., ed. (1961) *Urban Research Methods*. Princeton: D. Van Nostrand.

GIST, NOEL P. and SYLVIA F. FAVA (1964) *Urban Sociology*. 5th ed. New York: Thomas Y. Crowell.

GOLD, DAVID and J. R. SCHMIDHAUSER (1960) "Urbanization and party competition: the case of Iowa." *Midwest Journal of Political Science* 4: 62–75.

GOLDRICH, DANIEL M. (n.d.) Politics and the pobladore: political behavior in four lower class settlements. Unpublished paper. Dept. of Political Science, University of Oregon, Eugene.

——— (1964) "Peasants' sons in city schools: an inquiry into the politics of urbanization in Panama and Costa Rica." *Human Organization* 23, No. 4: 328–333.

——— (1965) "Toward the comparative study of politicization in Latin America." Pp. 361–378 in Dwight Heath and R. N. Adams (eds.) *Contemporary Cultures and Societies of Latin America*. New York: Random House.

——— et al. (1967–68) "The political integration of lower-class urban settlements in Chile and Peru." *Studies in Comparative International Development* 3, No. 1: 1–22.

GOLEMBIEWSKI, ROBERT T. (1958) "A taxonomic approach to state political party strength." *Western Political Quarterly* 11: 494–513.

GONZÁLEZ, NANCIE L. SOLIEN DE (1965) "Black Carib adaptation to a Latin urban milieu." *Social and Economic Studies* (Jamaica) 14: 272–278.

GORDON, GLEN and PHILIP COULTER (1969) "The sociological bases of party competition: the case of Massachusetts." *The Sociological Quarterly* 10, No. 1: 84–105.

GREER, SCOTT (1962) *The Emerging City: Myth and Reality*. New York: Free Press.

——— et al., eds. (1968) *The New Urbanization*. New York: St. Martin's Press.

GREER, SCOTT and PETER ORLEANS (1968) "The mass society and the parapolitical structure." Pp. 201–221 in S. Greer et al. (eds.) *The New Urbanization*. New York: St. Martin's Press.

GUMUCIO, MARIANO BAPTISTA (1967) "La ruralización de las ciudades latinoamericanas." *Política* (Venezuela) 6, No. 58: 13–24.

GURR, TED (1968a) "Psychological factors in civil violence." *World Politics* 20, No. 2: 245–278.

———— (1968b) "A causal model of civil strife: a comparative analysis using new indices." *American Political Science Review* 62, No. 4: 1104–1124.

———— (forthcoming) *Why Men Revolt.* Princeton: Princeton University Press.

GURRIERI, ADOLFO (1965) *Situación y perspectivas de la juventud en una po-blación urbana popular.* Doc. No. E/LACCY/BP/L.2. Santiago de Chile: U. N. Economic Commission for Latin America.

GUSFIELD, JOSEPH R. (1962) "Mass society and extremist politics." *American Sociological Review* 27: 19–30.

GUTERMAN, STANLEY S. (1969) "In defense of Wirth's 'Urbanism as a Way of Life.'" *American Journal of Sociology* 74, No. 5: 492–499.

GUTKIND, PETER C. W. (1965) "African urbanism, mobility, and the social network." Pp. 48–60 in Ralph Piddington (ed.) *Kinship and Geographic Mobility.* Leiden, Netherlands: E. J. Brill. Reprinted in Breese, ed., 1969: 389–400.

———— (1967) "The energy of despair: social organization of the unemployed in two African cities: Lagos and Nairobi." *Civilisations* (Belgium) 17: 186–214 (Part I), 380–405 (Part II).

HAAR, CHARLES M. (1963) "Latin America's troubled cities." *Foreign Affairs* 41, No. 3: 536–549.

HAGEN, EVERETT E. (1962) *On the Theory of Social Change: How Economic Growth Begins.* Homewood, Ill.: Dorsey Press.

HALPERIN, ERNST (1965) "The decline of Communism in Latin America." *The Atlantic Monthly* 215 (May): 65–70.

HANNA, WILLIAM J. (1967) "The integrative role of urban Africa's middle-places and middlemen." *Civilisations* (Belgium) 17, No. 1/2: 12–29.

HANSON, ROBERT C. and OZZIE G. SIMMONS (1968) "The role path: a con-cept and procedure for studying migration to urban communities." *Human Organization* 27, No. 2: 152–158.

———— (1970) "Differential experience paths of rural migrants to the city." Pp. 145–166 in Eugene B. Brody (ed.) *Behavior in New Environments.* Beverly Hills, Calif.: Sage Publications.

HANSON, ROBERT C. *et al.* (1968) "Quantitative analyses of the urban experi-ences of Spanish-American migrants." Pp. 65–83 in *Proceedings of the 1968 Annual Spring Meeting of the American Ethnological Society.*

HARRIS, WALTER D. (1969) "Urban quality in the context of the developing society." Pp. 187–210 in H. J. Schmandt and W. Bloomberg, Jr. (eds.) *The Quality of Urban Life: Urban Affairs Annual Reviews.* Vol. 3. Beverly Hills, Calif.: Sage Publications.

HAUSER, PHILIP M. (1963) "The social, economic, and technological problems of rapid urbanization." Pp. 199–217 in B. F. Hoselitz and W. E. Moore (eds.) *Industrialization and Society.* The Hague: UNESCO-Mouton.

HEISS, JEROLD (1967) "Factors related to immigrant assimilation: the early post-migration situation." *Human Organization* 26, (Winter): 265–272.

———— (1969) "Factors related to immigrant assimilation: pre-migration traits." *Social Forces* 47, No. 4: 422–428.

HERRICK, BRUCE H. (1965) *Urban Migration and Economic Development in Chile.* Cambridge: M.I.T. Press.

HILL, GEORGE W., JOSÉ A. SILVA MICHELENA, and RUTH OLIVER DE HILL (1959) "La vida rural en Venezuela." *Revista de Sanidad y Asistencia Social* (Venezuela) 24, January-April.

HILLERY, GEORGE A., JR. (1968) *Communal Organizations: A Study of Local Societies.* Chicago: University of Chicago Press.

HOBSBAWM, E. J. (1967) "Peasants and rural migrants in politics." Pp. 43–65 in Claudio Véliz (ed.) *The Politics of Conformity in Latin America.* London and New York: Oxford University Press.

HOENACK, JUDITH (1966) "Marketing, supply, and their social ties in Rio *favelas.*" Paper presented at the 37th International Congress of Americanists, Mar del Plata, Argentina, September. Forthcoming in Leeds, ed.

HOFFERBERT, RICHARD I. (1966) "The relation between public policy and some structural and environmental variables in the American states." *American Political Science Review* 60: 73–82.

HOPPER, REX D. (1964) "Research on Latin America in sociology." Pp. 243–289 in Charles Wagley (ed.) *Social Science Research on Latin America.* New York: Columbia University Press.

HOROWITZ, IRVING L. (1969) "Electoral politics, urbanization, and social development in Latin America." Pp. 140–176 in I. L. Horowitz *et al.* (eds.) *Latin American Radicalism.* New York: Random House.

HOWTON, F. WILLIAM (1969) "Cities, slums, and accultrative process in developing countries." Pp. 431–447 in P. Meadows and E. H. Mizruchi (eds.) *Urbanism, Urbanization, and Change: Comparative Perspectives.* Reading, Mass.: Addison-Wesley.

HUNTINGTON, SAMUEL P. (1968) *Political Order in Changing Societies.* New Haven: Yale University Press.

HUTCHINSON, BERTRAM (1963a) "The migrant population of urban Brazil." *América Latina* (Rio de Janeiro) 6, No. 2: 41–71.

——— (1963b) "Urban social mobility rates in Brazil related to migration and changing occupational structure." *América Latina* (Rio de Janeiro) 6, No. 3: 47–71.

INKELES, ALEX (1969) "Participant citizenship in six developing countries." *American Political Science Review* 63, No. 4.

———, and DAVID H. SMITH (1970) "The fate of personal adjustment in the process of modernization." *International Journal of Comparative Sociology* 11: forthcoming.

IRELAN, LOLA M. *et al.* (1969) "Ethnicity, poverty, and selected attitudes: a test of the 'culture of poverty' hypothesis." *Social Forces* 47, No. 4: 405–413.

JENKINS, GEORGE (1967) "Africa as it urbanizes: an overview of current research." *Urban Affairs Quarterly* 2, No. 3: 66–80.

DE JESUS, CAROLINA MARIA (1962) *Child of the Dark.* Trans. David St. Clair. New York: Dutton.

JOHNSON, JOHN J. (1967) "The United States and the Latin American left wings." *Yale Review* 56, No. 3: 321–336.

JOHNSON, KENNETH F. (1963) Urbanization and political change in Latin America. Ph.D. dissertation, University of California, Los Angeles.

——— (1964) "Causal factors in Latin American political instability." *Western Political Quarterly* 17, September: 432–446.

———— (1967) *The Guatemalan Presidential Election of March 6, 1966: An Analysis.* Washington, D.C.: Institute for the Comparative Study of Political Systems.

JONES, GEORGE F. (1967) Urbanization and Voting Behavior in Venezuela, 1958–1964. M.A. thesis, Latin American Studies, Stanford University.

KAHL, JOSEPH A. (1959) "Some social concomitants of industrialization and urbanization." *Human Organization* 18, No. 2: 53–74. Reprinted in W. J. Hanna (ed.) *Independent Black Africa.* Chicago: Rand McNally, 1964: 86–136.

———— (1968a) *The Measurement of Modernism: A Study of Values in Brazil and Mexico.* Austin: University of Texas Press.

———— (1968b) "Comparative class cultures: a research project of 'El Grupo Interamericano de Sociología Comparativa'." Unpublished paper. Washington University, St. Louis.

KAMERSCHEN, DAVID R. (1969) "Further analysis of overurbanization." *Economic Development and Cultural Change* 17, No. 2: 235–253.

KAUFMAN, CLIFFORD (1966) Urbanization, Personal Welfare, and Politicization: The Lower Class in Santiago, Chile. Ph.D. dissertation, University of Oregon.

———— (1968) "Urbanization and political involvement: limited reflections on the case of Mexico City." Paper presented at the Annual Meeting of the American Political Science Asociation, Washington, D.C., September.

KERR, CLARK et al. (1964) *Industrialism and Industrial Man.* 2nd ed. New York: Oxford University Press.

KEY, V. O., JR. (1956) *American State Politics.* New York: Alfred A. Knopf.

KIRKPATRICK, JEANE J. (1968) The mass base of the Peronist movement: composition, expectations, and demands. Unpublished Ph.D. dissertation, Columbia University.

KOLB, WILLIAM L. (1954) "The social structure and function of cities." *Economic Development and Cultural Change* 3, October: 30–46.

KORNHAUSER, WILLIAM (1959) *The Politics of Mass Society.* New York: Free Press.

LANE, ROBERT E. (1959) *Political Life: Why and How People Get Involved in Politics.* New York: Free Press.

LANE, ROGER (1969) "Urbanization and criminal violence in the 19th century: Massachusetts as a test case." Pp. 445–459 in H. D. Graham and T. R. Gurr (eds.) *Violence in America: Historical and Comparative Perspectives.* New York: New American Library.

LEEDS, ANTHONY (1966) "Future orientation: the investment climate in Rio *favelas.*" Paper presented at the 37th International Congress of Americanists, Mar del Plata, Argentina, September. Forthcoming in Leeds, ed.

———— (1968) "The anthropology of cities: some methodological issues." Pp. 31–47 in Elizabeth M. Eddy (ed.) *Urban Anthropology: Research Perspectives and Strategies.* Athens, Georgia: University of Georgia Press for the Southern Anthropological Society.

———— (1969) "The significant variables determining the character of squatter settlements." *América Latina* (Rio de Janeiro) 12, No. 3: forthcoming.

———— (1970) "The culture of poverty concept: conceptual, logical, and empirical problems, with perspective from Brazil and Peru." In E. Leacock (ed.) *The Culture of Poverty: Review and Critique.* New York: Simon and Schuster.

───── (forthcoming) "Locality power in relation to supra-local power institutions." In E. Bruner and A. Southall (eds.) *Urban Anthropology.* Chicago: Aldine.

─────, ed. (forthcoming) Rio's *Favelas.* Austin: University of Texas Press.

LEEDS, ANTHONY and ELIZABETH LEEDS (1969) "Brazil and the myth of urban rurality: urban experience, work, and values in 'squatments' of Rio de Janeiro and Lima." In A. J. Feld (ed.) *City and Country in the Third World.* Cambridge, Mass.: Schenkman.

LEEDS, ANTHONY and ELIZABETH LEEDS, and D. A. MOROCCO (1966) "Electricity and social power in Rio's favelas." Paper presented at the 37th International Congress of Americanists, Mar del Plata, Argentina, September. Forthcoming in Leeds, ed.

LEEDS, ELIZABETH R. (1966) "Political complementarity of *favelas* with the larger society of Rio de Janeiro." Paper presented at the 37th International Congress of Americanists, Mar del Plata, Argentina, September. Forthcoming in Leeds, ed.

───── (1969) "The myth of politicization: a comparison of urban proletarian political articulation in Rio de Janeiro and Lima." Unpublished manuscript, University of Texas, Austin.

LEGGETT, JOHN C. (1963) "Uprootedness and working-class consciousness." *American Journal of Sociology* 68: 682–692.

LERNER, DANIEL (1958) *The Passing of Traditional Society.* New York: Free Press.

LEWIS, OSCAR (1951) *Life in a Mexican Vilage: Tepoztlán Restudied.* Urbana, Ill.: University of Illinois Press.

───── (1952) "Urbanization without breakdown: a case study." *Scientific Monthly* 75, July: 31–41. Reprinted in D. Heath and R. N. Adams (eds.) *Contemporary Cultures and Societies of Latin America.* New York: Random House, 1965.

───── (1959) "The culture of the *vecindad* in Mexico City: two case studies." Pp. 387–402 in *Actas del III Congreso Internacional de Americanistas, San José, Costa Rica.* Vol. I.

───── (1961) *The Children of Sánchez: Autobiography of a Mexican Family.* New York: Random House.

───── (1965) "Further observations on the folk-urban continuum and urbanization with special reference to Mexico City." Pp. 491–503 in P. M. Hauser and L. F. Schnore (eds.) *The Study of Urbanization.* New York: John Wiley.

───── (1968) *A Study of Slum Culture: Backgrounds for* La Vida. New York: Random House.

LINDENBERG, KAREN (1969) The Effect of Negative Sanctions on Politicization Among Lower Class Sectors in Santiago, Chile, and Lima, Peru. Ph.D. dissertation, University of Oregon.

LITTLE, KENNETH (1964) "The functions of regional associations in urbanization: West Africa and Peru." Paper presented at the Wenner-Gren Symposium on Cross-Cultural Similarities in the Urbanization Process, Burg Wartenstein, Austria. Forthcoming in Southall and Bruner, eds.

———— (1966) *West African Urbanization: A Study of Voluntary Associations in Social Change*. London: Cambridge University Press.

LOPES, JUAREZ RUBENS BRANDÃO (1965) "Adaptación de migrantes rurales a São Paulo." Pp. 188–202 in J. A. Kahl (ed.) *La industrialización en América Latina*. Mexico, D. F.: Fondo de Cultura Económica.

———— (1966) "Some basic developments in Brazilian politics and society." Pp. 59–77 in E. N. Baklanoff (ed.) *New Perspectives of Brazil*. Nashville, Tenn.: Vanderbilt University Press.

LOPREATO, JOSEPH (1967) *Peasants No More: Social Class and Social Change in an Underdeveloped* Society. San Francisco: Chandler.

LUPSHA, PETER A. (1969) "On theories of urban violence." *Urban Affairs Quarterly* 4, No. 3: 273–295.

LUTZ, THOMAS (1968a) "Some aspects of community organization and activity in the squatter settlements of Panama City." Unpublished manuscript, Dept. of Government, Georgetown University.

———— (1968b) "The developing political orientations among urban squatters in Panama City: a comparison of organized and unorganized squatter settlements." Unpublished manuscript, Georgetown University.

———— (1969) "Political socialization and the developing political subcultures among urban squatters in Panama City, Guayaquil, and Lima: comparisons of attitudes in organized and unorganized squatter settlements." Ph.D. dissertation, Georgetown University.

MACHADO DA SILVA, L. A. (1967) "A política na favela." *Cadernos Brasileiros* (Brazil) 9, No. 3: 35–47.

MCCORD, WILLIAM (1965) *The Springtime of Freedom: Evolution of Developing Societies*. New York: Oxford University Press.

MCCRONE, DONALD J. and CHARLES F. CNUDDE (1967) "Toward a communications theory of democratic political development." *American Political Science Review* 61: 72–79.

MACDONALD, LEATRICE D. and JOHN S. MACDONALD (1968) "Motives and objectives of migration: selective migration and preferences toward rural and urban life." *Social and Economic Studies* (Jamaica) 7, No. 4: 417–434.

MCDONALD, RONALD H. (1969) "National urban voting behavior: the politics of dissent in Latin America." *Inter-American Economic Affairs* 23, No. 1: 3–20.

MCGEE, T. G. (1964) "The rural-urban continuum debate, the preindustrial city, and rural-urban migration." *Pacific Viewpoint* 5, No. 2: 159–181.

MCGREEVEY, WILLIAM P. (1968) "Causas de la migración interna en Colombia." Pp. 211–221 in Centro de Estudios Sobre Desarrollo Económico (CEDE), *Empleo y desempleo en Colombia*. Bogotá, Colombia: Ediciones Universidad de los Andes. Reprinted in Latin American Reprint Series (No. 301), Center for Latin American Studies, University of California, Berkeley, 1968.

MAIN, ELEANOR (1966) The Impact of Urbanization: A Comparative Study of Urban and Non-Urban Political Attitudes and Behavior. Ph.D. dissertation, University of North Carolina, Chapel Hill.

MANGIN, WILLIAM P. (1965a) 'The role of regional associations in the adaptation of rural migrants to cities in Peru." Pp. 311–323 in D. B. Heath and

R. N. Adams (eds.) *Contemporary Cultures and Societies of Latin America.* New York: Random House.

———— (1965b) "Mental health and migration to cities: a Peruvian case." Pp. 546–555 in D. B. Heath and R. N. Adams (eds.) *Contemporary Cultures and Societies of Latin America.* New York: Random House.

———— (1967) "Latin American squatter settlements: a problem and a solution." *Latin American Research Review* 2, No. 3: 65–98.

———— (1968) "Poverty and politics in cities of Latin America." Pp. 397–432 in Warner Bloomberg, Jr., and H. J. Schmandt (eds.) *Power, Poverty, and Urban Policy: Urban Affairs Annual Reviews.* Vol. 2. Beverly Hills, Calif.: Sage Publications.

———— (forthcoming) "Sociological, cultural, and political characteristics of some urban migrants in Peru." In E. M. Bruner and A. W. Southall (eds.) *Urban Anthropology.* Chicago: Aldine.

MANGIN, WILLIAM P. and JEROME COHEN (1965) "Cultural and psychological characteristics of mountain migrants to Lima." *Sociologus* 14, No. 1: 81–88.

MARGULIS, MARIO (1968) *Migración y marginalidad en la sociedad Argentina.* Buenos Aires: Editorial Paidós.

MARSHALL, DALE R. (1968) "Who participates in what?—a bibliographical essay on individual participation in urban areas." *Urban Affairs Quarterly* 4, No. 2: 201–224.

MARTÍNEZ, HÉCTOR (1968) "Las migraciones internas en el Perú." *Aportes* (Paris) 10: 136–60.

MARTZ, JOHN D. (1966) "The place of Latin America in the study of comparative politics." *Journal of Politics* 28: 57–80.

MASOTTI, L. H. and D. R. BOWEN, eds. (1968) *Riots and Rebellion: Civil Violence in the Urban Community.* Beverly Hills, Calif.: Sage Publications.

MASTERS, N. A. and D. S. WRIGHT (1958) "Trends and variations in the two-party vote: the case of Michigan." *American Political Review* 52: 1079–1088.

MATOS MAR, JOSÉ (1961) "The *barriadas* of Lima: an example of integration into urban life." Pp. 170–190 in P. M. Hauser (ed.) *Urbanization in Latin America.* New York: International Documents Service.

———— (1966) *Estudio de las barriadas limeñas.* Lima, Peru: Departamento de Antropología, Universidad Nacional Mayor de San Marcos.

MATRAS, JUDAH (1965) "Social and personal disorganization." Pp. 179–191 in P. M. Hauser (ed.) *Handbook for Social Research in Urban Areas.* Paris: UNESCO.

MEDINA ECHAVARRIA, J. and P. M. HAUSER (1961) "Rapporteurs' report." Pp. 19–74 in P. M. Hauser (ed.) *Urbanization in Latin America.* New York: International Documents Service.

MEILLASSOUX, CLAUDE (1968) *Urbanization of an African Community: Voluntary Associations in Bamako.* Seattle, Wash.: University of Washington Press.

MICKLIN, MICHAEL (1968) "Methodological problems in the anthropological study of cities in Latin America." Paper presented at the annual meeting of the Southern Anthropological Society.

MIDDLETON, JOHN (1969) "Labour migration and associations in Africa: two case studies." *Civilisations* (Belgium) 29, No. 1: 42–50.

MINTZ, SIDNEY (1953) "The folk-urban continuum and the rural proletarian community." *American Journal of Sociology* 59, No. 2: 136–143.

MIZRUCHI, EPHRAIM H. (1969) "Romanticism, urbanism, and small town in mass society: an exploratory analysis." Pp. 243–251 in P. Meadows and E. H. Mizruchi (eds.) *Urbanism, Urbanization, and Change: Comparative Perspectives.* Reading, Mass.: Addison-Wesley.

MOLINA, S., JUAN (1965) *Las migraciones internas en el Ecuador.* Quito, Ecuador: Editorial Universitaria.

MOORE, WILBERT E. (1963) *Social Change.* Englewood Cliffs: Prentice-Hall.

MORENO, J. A. (1970) *Barrios in Arms: Revolution in Santo Domingo.* Pittsburgh: University of Pittsburgh Press.

MOROCCO, DAVID (1966) "*Carnaval* groups: maintainers and intensifiers of the *favela* phenomenon in Rio." Paper presented at the 37th International Congress of Americanists, Mar del Plata, Argentina, September. Forthcoming in Leeds, ed.

MORRISON, DENTON E. and ALLAN STEEVES (1967) "Deprivation, discontent, and social movement participation." *Rural Sociology,* December: 414–435.

MORSE, RICHARD M. (1965) "Recent research on Latin American urbanization: a selective survey with commentary." *Latin American Research Review* 1, No. 1: 35–74.

———— (1967) "Urban society in contemporary Latin America." *Ventures* 7, No. 2: 39–48.

MORSE, R. N. (1968) *Urban Sociology.* New York: Frederick A. Praeger.

MOUNTJOY, ALAN B. (1968) "Million cities: urbanization and the developing countries." *Geography* (London) 53, Part 4, No. 241: 365–374.

MURPHY, H. B. M. (1965) "Migration and the major mental disorders: a reappraisal." In Mildred Kantor (ed.) *Mobility and Mental Health.* Springfield, Ill.: Charles C. Thomas.

National Advisory Commission on Civil Disorders (1968) *Report of the Commission.* New York: New York Times Company.

NAVARRETE, IFIGENIA M. DE (1967) "Income distribution in Mexico." Pp. 133–172 in Enrique Pérez López *et al. Mexico's Recent Economic Growth.* Austin: University of Texas Press.

NEAL, ARTHUR C. and MELVIN SEEMAN (1964) "Organizations and powerlessness: a test of the mediation hypothesis." *American Sociological Review* 29: 216–226.

NEEDLER, MARTIN C. (1968) "The political implications of urbanization in Mexico." Paper presented at the Conference on Urbanization in the United States-Mexican Border Area, University of Texas, El Paso, June.

NEHEMKIS, PETER R. (1966) *Latin America: Myth and Reality.* 2nd ed. New York: Mentor Books-New American Library.

NELSON, JOAN M. (1969) *Migrants, Urban Poverty, and Instability in Developing Nations.* Cambridge: Center for International Affairs, Harvard University.

NEUBAUER, DEANE E. (1967) "Some conditions of democracy." *American Political Science Review* 61: 1002–1009.

NIE, N. H., G. BINGHAM POWELL, JR., and K. PREWITT (1969) "Social structure and political participation: developmental relationships, I." *American Political Science Review* 63: 361–378.

NIEBURG, H. L. (1969) *Political Violence: The Behavioral Process.* New York: St. Martin's Press.

NILO TAVARES, JOSÉ (1962) "Marginalismo social, marginalismo político?" *Revista Brasileira de Estudos Políticos* (Brazil) 13: 71–81.

NUTINI, HUGO G. and TIMOTHY D. MURPHY (1968) "Labor migration and family structure in the Tlaxcala-Puebla area, Mexico." Unpublished Manuscript, Dept. of Anthropology, University of Pittsburgh.

OLIEN, MICHAEL D. (1968) "Levels of urban relationships in a complex society: a Costa Rican case." Pp. 83–92 in Elizabeth M. Eddy (ed.) *Urban Anthropology: Research Perspectives and Strategies*. Athens, Georgia: University of Georgia Press for the Southern Anthropological Society.

OLIVÉ NEGRETE, JULIO CÉSAR and BEATRIZ BARBA DE PIÑA CHÁN (1962) "Estudio de las clases sociales en la ciudad de México: experiencias con un grupo obrero." *Anales del Instituto Nacional de Antropología e Historia* (Mexico) 14, No. 43: 219–281.

OLSEN, MARVIN E. (1968) "Multivariate analysis of national political development." *American Sociological Review* 33: 699–711.

OLSON, MANCUR, JR. (1963) "Rapid growth as a destabilizing force." *Journal of Economic History* 23: 529–552.

ORNELAS, CHARLES (forthcoming) *Land Tenure, Sanctions, and Politicization in Mexico City*. Ph.D. dissertation, Dept. of Political Science, University of California, Riverside.

PAN AMERICAN UNION (1955) *Causas y efectos del éxodo rural en Venezuela*. Washington, D.C.: Inter-American Economic and Social Council, Pan American Union.

PARK, ROBERT E. (1928) "Human migration and the marginal man." *American Journal of Sociology* 33: 881–893.

——— (1967) *On Social Control and Collective Behavior*. Chicago: University of Chicago Press. Selected papers edited by R. H. Turner.

——— et al. (1967) *The City*. 2nd ed. Chicago: University of Chicago Press.

PARKIN, D. J. (1966) "Urban voluntary associations as institutions of adaptation." *Man* 1, No. 1: 90–95.

PATCH, RICHARD (1961) "Life in a *callejón*: a study of urban disorganization." *American Universities Field Staff, West Coast South America Series* 8, No. 6: June.

——— (1968) "La Parada, Lima's market—part III: *serrano* to *crillo*, a study of assimilation." Pp. 207–223 in American Universities Field Staff Associates, *City and Nation in the Developing World: AUFS Readings*. Vol. II New York: American Universities Field Staff.

PEARSE, ANDREW (1958) "Notas sobre a organização social de uma favela do Rio de Janeiro." *Educação e Ciencias Sociais* (Brazil) 3, No. 7: 9–32.

——— (1961) "Some characteristics of urbanization in the city of Rio de Janeiro." Pp. 191–205 in P. M. Hauser (ed.) *Urbanization in Latin America*. New York: International Documents Service.

PEATTIE, LISA R. (1968a) *The View from the Barrio*. Ann Arbor, Mich.: University of Michigan Press.

——— (1968b) 'Social mobility and economic development." In Lloyd Rodwin (ed.) *Regional Planning for Development: The Experience of the Guayana Program of Venezuela*. Cambridge: M.I.T. Press.

——— (1969) "Social issues in housing." Pp. 15–34 in Bernard J. Frieden and W. W. Nash, Jr. (eds.) *Shaping an Urban Future.* Cambridge: M.I.T. Press.

PÉCAUT, DANIEL (1968) "The urban working class." Pp. 674–680 in Claudio Véliz (ed.) *Latin America and the Caribbean: A Handbook.* New York: Frederick A. Praeger.

PORTES, ALEJANDRO (1969a) "Los grupos urbanos marginados: un nuevo intento de explicación." Unpublished manuscript, Dept. of Sociology, University of Wisconsin, Madison.

———— (1969b) *Cuatro poblaciones: informe preliminar sobre situación y aspiraciones de grupos marginados en el Gran Santiago.* Santiago, Chile: Programa Sociología del Desarrollo de la Universidad de Wisconsin.

POWELL, SANDRA (1969) "Political participation in the *barriadas*: a case study." *Comparative Political Studies* 2, No. 2: 195–215.

PRATT, RAYMOND B. (1968) Organizational Participation, Politization, and Development: A Study of Political Consequences of Participation in Community Associations in Four Lower Class Urban Settlements in Chile and Peru. Ph.D. dissertation, University of Oregon.

PUTNAM, ROBERT D. (1966) "Political attitudes and the local community." *American Political Science Review* 60: 640-654.

PYE, LUCIAN W. (1969) "Political implications of urbanization and the development process." Pp. 401–406 in Gerald Breese (ed.) *The City in Newly Developing Countries: Readings on Urbanism and Urbanization.* Englewood Cliffs: Prentice-Hall.

QUIJANO, ANÍBAL (1966) *El proceso de urbanización en América Latina.* Santiago de Chile: CEPAL.

RABINOVITZ, FRANCINE F. (1968) "Sound and fury signifying nothing?: a review of community power research in Latin America." *Urban Affairs Quarterly* 3: 111–122.

RANIS, PETER (1968-69) "Modernity and political development in five Latin American countries." *Studies in Comparative International Development* 4, No. 2: 19–41.

RAY, TALTON F. (1969) *The Politics of the Barrios of Venezuela.* Berkeley and Los Angeles: University of California Press.

REDFIELD, ROBERT (1941) *The Folk Culture of Yucatán.* Chicago: University of Chicago Press.

———— (1947) "The folk society." *American Journal of Sociology* 52: 293–308.

———— (1961) *Peasant Society and Culture.* Chicago: University of Chicago Press.

REEVES, EARL (1964) "Ecological change and political competition in Kansas." Pp. 224–250 in R. L. Stauber (ed.) *Approaches to the Study of Urbanization.* Topeka, Kan.: Governmental Research Center, University of Kansas.

REIS, FABIO WANDERLEY (forthcoming) Ph.D. dissertation, Department of Government, Harvard University.

REISS, A. J., ed. (1964) *Louis Wirth on Cities and Social Life.* Chicago: University of Chicago Press.

RENDON, GABINO, JR. (1968) Prediction of Adjustment Outcomes of Rural Migrants to the City. Ph.D. dissertation, University of Colorado, Boulder.

Rios, José Artur (1960) 'El pueblo y el político." *Política* (Venezuela) 6: 11–36.

———— et al. (1960) "Aspectos humanos da favela carioca." *O Estado de São Paulo* (São Paulo, Brazil), Special Supplements, April 13, April 15.

Rios Hernández, Onésimo (1961) "Algunos procesos de aculturación negativa indígena en la ciudad de México." *Revista de Economía* (Mexico) 24, No. 8: 282–286.

Roberts, Bryan R. (1968a) "Protestant groups and coping with urban life in Guatemala City." *American Journal of Sociology* 73: 753–767.

———— (1968b) "Politics in an urban neighborhood of Guatemala City." *Sociology* (London) 2, No. 2: 185–204.

———— (1968c) "Poverty and politics in Guatemala City." Paper presented at the Annual Meeting of the American Anthropological Association, Washington, D.C., November.

Rogers, William D. (1967) *"The Twilight Struggle: The Alliance for Progress and the Politics of Development in Latin America.* New York: Random House.

Rogler, Lloyd H. (1967) "Slum neighborhoods in Latin America." *Journal of Inter-American Studies* 9, No. 4: 507-528.

Rosen, Bernard C. and Manoel T. Berlinck (1968) "Modernization and family structure in the region of São Paulo, Brazil." *América Latina* (Rio de Janeiro) 11, No. 3: 75–96.

Rosenblüth López, Guillermo (1968) "Problemas socio-económicos de la marginalidad y de la integración urbana." *Revista Paraguaya de Sociología* (Paraguay) 11.

Rotondo, H. (1961) "Psychological and mental health problems of urbanization based on case studies in Peru." Pp. 249–257 in P. M. Hauser (ed.) *Urbanization in Latin America.* New York: International Documents Service.

Runciman, W. G. (1966) *Relative Deprivation and Social Justice: A Study of Social Inequality in 20th Century England.* Berkeley and Los Angeles: University of California Press.

Russett, Bruce M. (1965) *Trends in World Politics.* New York: Macmillan.

Rustow, Dankwart A. (1967) *A World of Nations: Problems of Political Modernization.* Washington, D.C. Brookings Institution.

Safa, Helen I. (1966) "Comparative study of the assimilation of urban poor." Paper presented at the 133rd Annual Meeting of the American Anthropological Association, December.

———— (1964) "From shantytown to public housing: a comparison of family structure in two urban neighborhoods in Puerto Rico." *Caribbean Studies* 4, No. 1: 3–12.

———— (1967) *An Analysis of Upward Mobility in Low Income Families: A Comparison of Family and Community Life Among Negro and Puerto Rican Poor.* Syracuse, N.Y.: Youth Development Program, Syracuse University.

Sahota, Gian S. (1969) "An economic analysis of internal migration in Brazil." Pp. 73–90 in Charles T. Nisbet (ed.) *Latin America: Problems in Economic Development.* New York: Free Press.

Schmitt, Karl M. and David Burks (1963) *Evolution or Chaos: Dynamics* of Latin American Government and Politics. New York: Frederick A. Praeger.

SCHNORE, L. F. and ERIC E. LAMPARD (1968) "Social science and the city: a survey of research needs." Pp. 21–47 in L. F. Schnore (ed.) *Social Science and the City: A Survey of Urban Research.* New York: Frederick A. Praeger.

SCHULTZ, T. PAUL (1968) *Internal Migration in Colombia: A Quantitative Analysis.* Santa Monica: Rand Corporation.

SCOTT, ROBERT E. (1964) *Mexican Government in Transition.* 2nd ed. Urbana, Ill.: University of Illinois Press.

SEARS, DAVID O. and JOHN B. McCONAHAY (1967) *The Los Angeles Riot Study: The Politics of Discontent.* Los Angeles: Institute of Government and Public Affairs, University of California, Los Angeles.

SEGAL, DAVID R. and MARSHALL W. MEYER (1969) "The social context of political partisanship." Pp. 217–232 in M. Dogan and S. Rokkan (eds.) *Quantitative Ecological Analysis in the Social Sciences.* Cambridge: M.I.T. Press.

SEGUÍN, CARLOS ALBERTO, ed. (1962) *Psiquiatría y sociedad: estudio sobre la realidad peruana.* Lima, Peru: Universidad Nacional Mayor de San Marcos.

SELZNICK, PHILIP (1960) *The Organizational Weapon.* Glencoe, Ill.: Free Press.

SHANNON, LYLE W. (1965) "Urban adjustment and its relationship to the social antecedents of immigrant workers." *International Review of Community Development* 13–14: 177–188.

SHANNON, LYLE W. and MAGDALINE SHANNON (1968) "The assimilation of migrants to cities: anthropological and sociological contributions." Pp. 49–76 in L. F. Schnore (ed.) *Social Science and the City: A Survey of Urban Research.* New York: Frederick A. Praeger.

SHERWOOO, FRANK P. (1964) "Industrialization and urbanization in Brazil: local government implications." Paper presented at the Annual Meeting of the American Political Science Association, Chicago, Ill., September.

—————— (1967) *Institutionalizing the Grass Roots in Brazil: A Study of Comparative Local Government.* San Francisco: Chandler.

SHIVELY, W. PHILLIPS (1969) "Ecological inference: the use of aggregate data to study individuals." *American Political Science Review* 63, No. 4.

SILVA MICHELENA, JOSÉ A. (1965) "Estructura social y el diseño de políticas." Pp. 141-159 in *Memoria del VIII Congreso Latinoamericano de Sociología.* Vol. I. Bogotá, Colombia: Asociación Colombiana de Sociología.

SIMMEL, GEORG (1950) "The metropolis and mental life." Pp. 409–422 in Kurt H. Wolff (ed. and trans.) *The Sociology of Georg Simmel.* New York: Free Press.

SIMMONS, OZZIE G. et al. (forthcoming) "The rural migrant in the urban world of work." In *Proceedings of the XI Interamerican Congress of Psychology,* Mexico City, December, 1967.

SIMMONS, ROBERT E. et al. (1968) "Media and developmental news in slums of Ecuador and India." *Journalism Quarterly* 45: 698–705.

SJOBERG, GIDEON (1960) *The Preindustrial City: Past and Present.* Glencoe, Ill.: Free Press.

SMITH, ARTHUR K., JR. (1969) 'Socioeconomic development and political democracy: a causal analysis." *Midwest Journal of Political Science* 13: 95–125.

SMITH, NANCY (1966) "Eviction in a Rio favela: leadership, land tenure, and legal aspects." Paper presented at the 37th International Congress of Americanists, Mar del Plata, Argentina, September. Forthcoming in Leeds, ed.

SMITH, PETER H. (1969a) *Politics and Beef in Argentina: Patterns of Conflict and Change.* New York: Columbia University Press.

——— (1969b) "Social mobilization, political participation, and the rise of Juan Perón." *Political Science Quarterly,* 84: 30–49.

SOARES, GLÁUCIO A. D. (1965) "Desarrollo económico y radicalismo político." Pp. 516–559 in J. A. Kahl (ed.) *La industrialización en América Latina.* Mexico City and Buenos Aires: Fondo de Cultura Económica.

——— (1967) "The politics of uneven development: the case of Brazil." Pp. 467–496 in S. M. Lipset and S. Rokkan (eds.) *Party Systems and Voter Alignments: Cross-National Perspectives.* New York: Free Press.

SOARES, GLÁUCIO A. D. and R. L. HAMBLIN (1967) "Socio-economic variables and voting for the radical left: Chile, 1952." *American Political Science Review* 61: 1053–1065.

SOARES, GLÁUCIO A. D. and A. M. NORONHA (1960) "Urbanização e dispersão eleitoral." *Revista de Direito Público e Ciência Política* (Brazil) July-Dec.: 258–270.

SOLARI, ALDO (1965) "Impacto político de las diferencias internas de los países en los grados e índices de modernización y desarrollo económico." *América Latina* (Rio de Janeiro) 8, No. 1: 5–22.

SOUTHALL, AIDAN W. and EDWRD M. BRUNER, eds. (forthcoming) *Urban Anthropology.* Chicago: Aldine.

SOUTHWOOD, KENNETH (1967) "Riot and revolt: sociological theories of political violence." *Peace Research Reviews* 1, No. 3: 1–75.

SOVANI, N. V. (1964) "The analysis of 'over-urbanization.'" *Economic Development and Cultural Change* 12, No. 2: 113–122. Reprinted in Breese, ed., 1969: 322–330.

STEIN, M. R. (1960) *The Eclipse of Community.* Princeton: Princeton University Press.

STEPAN, ALFRED (1966) "Political development theory: the Latin American experience." *Journal of International Affairs* 20: 223–234.

STERNE, RICHARD S. (1967) "Components and stereotypes in ecological analyses of social problems." *Urban Affairs Quarterly* 3, No. 1: 3–21.

STOKES, CHARLES J. (1962) "A theory of slums." *Land Economics* 38, No. 3: 187–197.

STRAUSS, ANSELM L. (1968) "Strategies for discovering urban theory." Pp. 79–98 in L. F. Schnore (ed.) *Social Science and the City: A Survey of Urban Research.* New York: Frederick A. Praeger.

STYCOS, JOSEPH and CARA RICHARDS DE DOBYNS (1963) "Fuentes de la migración en la Gran Lima." In Henry F. Dobyns and Mario C. Vásquez (eds.) *Migración e integración en el Perú.* Monografía Andina No. 2. Lima, Peru: Editorial e studios Andinos.

SUSSMAN, MARVIN B. and LEE BURCHINAL (1962) "Kin family network: unheralded structure in current conceptualizations of family functioning." *Marriage and Family Living* 24: 231–240.

Szulc, Tad (1965) *Winds of Revolution: Latin America Today and Tomorrow.* 2nd ed. New York: Frederick A. Praeger.

Tanter, Raymond (1967) "Toward a theory of political development." *Midwest Journal of Political Science* 11: 145–172.

Tanter, Raymond and Manus Midlarsky (1967) "A theory of revolution." *Journal of Conflict Resolution* 11: 264–280.

Thein, U Aung (1965) "Some aspects of urban explosions in developing countries." In U.N., Dept. of Economic and Social Affairs, *Proceedings of the World Population Conference, 1965.* Doc. No. E/CONF.41/5, Vol. 4. New York, 1967.

Thomas, W. I. (1966) *On Social Organization and Social Personality.* Chicago: University of Chicago Press. Selected papers edited by Morris Janowitz.

Thomas, W. J. and Florian Znaniecki (1958) *The Polish Peasant in Europe and America.* 3rd ed. 2 vols. New York: Dover Publications.

Thomlinson, Ralph (1965) *Population Dynamics: Causes and Consequences of World Demographic Change.* New York: Random House.

Tilly, Charles (1968a) "Race and migration to the American city." Pp. 135–158 in James Q. Wilson (ed.) *The Metropolitan Enigma: Inquiries into the Nature and Dimensions of America's Urban Crisis.* Cambridge: Harvard University Press.

——— (1968b) "Urbanization and protest in Western Europe." Paper presented at the Annual Meeting of the American Political Science Association, Washington, D.C., September.

——— (1968c) "Collective violence in European perspective." Paper prepared for the National Commission on the Causes and Prevention of Violence, November.

——— (1969a) "A travers le chaos des vivantes cités." Pp. 379–394 in P. Meadows and Mizruchi (eds.) *Urbanism, Urbanization, and Change.* Reading, Mass.: Addison-Wesley.

——— (1969b) "How protest modernized in France, 1845–1855." Paper presented at the Conference on Applications of Quantitative Methods to Political, Social, and Economic History, University of Chicago, Chicago, Ill., June.

——— (1969c) "Community: City: Urbanization." Unpublished paper, Center for Advanced Study in the Behavioral Sciences, Stanford, California, January.

Tilly, Charles and C. Harold Brown (1967) "On uprooting, kinship, and the auspices of migration." *International Journal of Comparative Socialogy* 8: 139–164.

Tilly, Charles and James Rule (1965) *Measuring Political Upheaval.* Research Monograph No. 19. Princeton: Center of International Studies, Princeton University.

Tilly, Richard (1969) "Popular disorders in nineteenth-century Germany: a preliminary survey." Unpublished manuscript, Münster, Germany.

Toness, Odin Alf, Jr. (1967) Power Relations of a Central American Slum. M.A. thesis, University of Texas, Austin.

Touraine, Alain (1961) "Industrialización y conciencia obrera en São Paulo." *Sociologie du Travail* (Paris) 4, Oct.-Dec.: 7–38.

Turner, John F. C. (1965) "Lima's *barriadas* and *corralones*: suburbs vs. slums." *Ekistics* (Greece) 19, No. 112: 152–156.

———— (1967) "Four autonomous settlements in Lima, Peru." Paper presented at the Latin American Colloquium, Dept. of Sociology, Brandeis University, May.

———— (1968) "Uncontrolled urban settlement: problems and policies." *International Social Development Review* (United Nations) 1: 107–130. Reprinted in Breese, ed., 1969: 507–534.

———— (forthcoming) *The Squatter Revolution: Autonomous Urban Settlement and Social Change in Transitional Economies.* Cambridge: M.I.T. Press.

USANDIZAGA, ELSE and A. EUGENE HAVENS (1966) *Tres barrios de invasión: estudio de nivel de vida y actitudes en Barranquilla* [Colombia]. Bogotá, Colombia: Ediciones Tercer Mundo.

VALENCIA, ENRIQUE (1965) *La Merced: estudio ecológico y social de una zona de la ciudad de México.* Serie Investigaciones No. 11. Mexico, D.F.: Instituto Nacional de Antropología e Historia.

VALENTINE, CHARLES A. (1968) *Culture and Poverty: Critique and Counter-Proposals.* Chicago: University of Chicago Press.

———— *et al.* (1969) "Culture and poverty: critique and counter-proposals" *Current Anthropology* 10, No. 2–3: 181–201. Author's summary, book reviews, and commentaries.

VAUGHAN, DENTON R. (1968) "Links between peripheral lower income residential areas and political parties in a Latin American city." Unpublished paper, Dept. of Anthropology, University of Texas, Austin, January.

VARGAS MARTÍNEZ, UBALDO (1961) *La ciudad de México, 1935–1960.* Mexico, D.F.: Departamento del Distrito Federal.

VERBA, SIDNEY (1969) "The uses of survey research in the study of comparative politics: issues and strategies." Pp. 56–106 in Stein Rokkan *et al. Comparative Survey Analysis.* The Hague: Mouton.

VON LAZAR, ARPAD and VIRGINIA KENNEDY (1968) "Movilización social, gobierno, y crecimiento: un análisis trans-nacional." *Revista de Ciencias Sociales* (Puerto Rico) 12, No. 1: 93–112.

WAGNER, PHILIP L. (1962) "Political implications of rapid urbanization in Caribbean countries." Paper presented at the 57th Annual Meeting of the Association of American Geographers, Miami Beach, Florida.

WARD, BARBARA (1964) "The uses of prosperity." *Saturday Review,* Aug. 29: 191–192.

WEFFORT, FRANCISCO C. (1965) "Raizes sociais do populismo em São Paulo." *Revista Civilização Brasileira* (Brazil), 1, No. 2: 39–60.

———— (1966) "State and mass in Brazil." *Studies in Comparative International Development,* 2, No. 12: 187–196.

WEINER, MYRON (1967) "Urbanization and political protest." *Civilisations* (Belgium) 17, No. 1/2: 44–52.

WHITEFORD, ANDREW (1964) *Two Cities of Latin America: A Comparative Description of Social Classes.* Garden City, N.Y.: Doubleday-Anchor Books.

WILLIAMSON, ROBERT C. (1963) "Some factors in urbanism in a quasi-rural setting: San Salvador and San José." *Sociology and Social Research* 47: 187–200.

———— (1964) "Psychological correlates of housing in Central America." *Journal of Inter-American Studies* 6: 489–499.

———— (1968) "Social class and orientation to change: some relevant variables in a Bogotá sample." *Social Forces* 46: 317–327.

WILLEMS, EMILIO (1968) "Urban classes and acculturation in Latin America." Pp. 75–82 in Elizabeth M. Eddy (ed.) *Urban Anthropology: Research Perspectives and Strategies.* Athens, Georgia: University of Georgia Press for the Southern Anthropological Society.

WINDHAM, GERALD O. (1963) "Formal participation of migrant housewives in an urban community." *Sociology and Social Research* 47: 201–209.

WIRTH, LOUIS (1938) "Urbanism as a way of life." *American Journal of Sociology* 44: 1–24.

WOLFE, MARSHALL (1968) "Recent changes in urban and rural settlement patterns in Latin America." *International Social Development Review* (United Nations) 1: 55–62.

WOLFINGER, RAYMOND E. and FRED I. GREENSTEIN (1969) "Comparing political regions: the case of California." *American Political Science Review* 63: 74–85.

WYGAND, JAMES (1966) "Water networks: their technology and sociology in Rio favelas." Paper presented at the 37th International Congress of Americanists, Mar del Plata, Argentina, September. Forthcoming in Leeds, ed.

YALOUR DE TOBAR, MARGOT R. *et al.* (1967) "Clase obrera: anomia y cambio social; el proceso de socialización urbana; marginalidad y alienación en la clase obrera." *Cuadernos del Centro de Estudios Urbanos y Regionales* (Buenos Aires) 9: 1–171.

YOUNG, RUTH C. and JOSÉ A. MORENO (1965) "Economic development and social rigidity: a comparative study of the forty-eight states." *Economic Development and Cultural Change* 13: 439–452.

ZIMMER, BASIL G. (1955) "Participation of migrants in urban structures." *American Sociological Review* 20: 218–224.

PART II

URBAN

CULTURE

—VALUES

AND

NORMS

Chapter 7

SÃO PAULO: CASE STUDY OF A LATIN AMERICAN METROPOLIS

RICHARD M. MORSE

During the past fifteen years, São Paulo has been one of the Latin American cities most extensively studied by social scientists, and its bellwether role as an industrial, "anti-traditional" metropolis invites an assessment of their findings. With no claim to exhaustiveness this paper attempts the task. At the risk of my playing Oscar Lewis to my own Robert Redfield, it also provides a coda to my own book on the city (1954; 1958).

At the time of my basic research in 1947–1948, my few notions of urban societies were gleaned largely from Lewis Mumford and Redfield. At that time, moreover, large Latin American cities were scarcely a field for social-science inquiry. In São Paulo some preliminary data on social classes, ethnic groups, and living standards had been gathered by Samuel Lowrie, Horace B. Davis, Donald Pierson, and Oscar Egydio de Araujo (much of it published in the *Revista do Arquivo Municipal*). Some conceptual orientation could be found in Florestan Fernandes' early papers on folklore and immigrants, Lucila Herrmann's studies of occupational distribution and functional urban areas, and the ecological studies of Caio Prado Júnior. (See the bibliography in Morse, 1958.) Otherwise there were few benchmarks.

Today's researcher works in a context of mushrooming research on urban societies throughout Latin America and the world and must conjure with existing formulations for São Paulo in such areas as regional ecology, entrepreneurship, social mobility, recruitment and politicization of the proletariat, revitalization movements, and ethnic attitudes. Schemes for historical periodization (discussed below) have also been devised, but history along with cultural anthropology—once the two mainstays of social-science research on Latin America—are lagging partners on the São Paulo scene. Sociologists of race relations and labor movements have, in fact, generated their own historical studies. One implicit purpose of the present paper is to suggest themes of contemporary interest which merit historical investigation.

THE CITY IN TIME AND SPACE

Periodization. In discussing how to periodize Latin American urban histories Carrera Damas (1967) issues several caveats: the histories of a large city and its nation may obey different sets of imperatives and therefore require different temporal divisions; factors of extra-national origin, such as immigration or foreign investment, may affect the phasing of urban development; contemporary perspective may efface colonial watersheds and exaggerate recent ones. For the history of Caracas, Carrera Damas balances extra-national, national, and regional factors to produce five periods.[1] Caracas and São Paulo offer interesting parallels: an inland, elevated urban site; modest, semi-isolated, agrarian-oriented colonial development; nineteenth-century prolongation of the colonial mold; a stylish European face-lifting in the 1870s and '80s; tumultuous growth effacing visible remnants of the past, triggered by export revenues; industrialization. There are also discrepancies. Colonial São Paulo was more impoverished than Caracas; its *bandeiras* were unique; its eighteenth-century bureaucratic and cultural development was less pronounced; São Paulo was less plagued by military upheaval during and after independence; its coffee boom antedated Caracas' oil prosperity by some sixty years, producing earlier crystallization of the industry-immigration-metropolis complex.

Carrera Damas calls his periodization a pioneer attempt, given the *costumbrista* character of most histories of Caracas. The historian of São Paulo, on the other hand, has several formulae to choose from, four of which are considered here (see Table A). The criterion of Silva Bruno (1954) can be called *impressionistic.* He is less concerned with interlinking the components of historical change than with seizing upon an era's distinctive trait ("student town," "coffee metropolis"). G. L. de Barros (1967) more nearly meets the specifications of Carrera Damas with his *pluralistic* criterion that identifies successive configurations of loosely interrelated factors: economic activities, customs and social structure, bureaucratization, rationalization, physical change, regional ecology. My book (1954; 1958, in English) deals with such themes but, with its shorter time span, raises the question of *generational* change. It tries to re-create the ethos of successive ten- to twenty-year periods on the assumption that certain agents for urban change must find leverage in attitude and mind-set. Some catalysts operate inconspicuously until the generation nurtured by them comes into its own.

Unlike the others, the vantage point of architect-planner Luiz Saia (1963; 1966) is external to the city, a spatial, *ecological* perspective focused on the nature of urban-rural relations. From the city's founding to the present, he looks for periods of urban-rural polarity or "binary" (i.e., when the city functioned as a self-contained outpost, sanctum, geometric enclave or bastion of privilege) and periods of urban-rural interpenetration and accommodation. Saia's approach is appealing because he organizes the whole of São Paulo's history around a few key questions; he suggests cyclical as well as developmental trends; his concept of "city" has no artificial spatial limits; he is boldly normative in keeping the *health* of city and hinterland (social, institutional, economic, technological) constantly in focus.

The schematic comparison in Table A helps to identify the authors' criteria more clearly than they themselves may have done. An obvious discrepancy is in the characterization of the late eighteenth century; Silva Bruno and Saia call it a period of lethargy and impoverishment while Leite de Barros, who is alert to signs of bureaucratization, routinization and primary capital accrual, finds it a pivotal if unspectacular time of change.[2] A second discrepancy is in the use of the term "metropolis." Silva Bruno and Leite de Barros apply it to the city of the 1870s; I apply it to the post-1890 period; Saia speaks of "metropolitanization" after 1929. Thus the term is used variously to signify rapid growth and prosperity, cosmopolitan life style, power over a tributary region or, for Saia, the evaporation of "city limits" when urban technology and industrial forms erupt across the hinterland.

Causes for Metropolitan Growth. The challenge to explain São Paulo's explosive growth from a town of 31,000 in 1872 to a metropolis of some 7,000,000 holds continuing fascination. Standard explanations advance three interrelated sets of factors: (1) temperate climate, favorable site, transportation linkages; (2) the coffee boom, whch created capital for industry and attracted foreign immigration; (3) industrialization, facilitated by immigrant workers and entrepreneurs, availability of raw materials and hydroelectric power, and a regional market for manufactures. Some add to the mixture a regional *bandeirante* mystique (discussed below).

Two recent analyses sacrifice inclusiveness for sharper focus. Cardoso (1960b; 1961) warns against attributing *paulista* industrialization simply to capital accumulated from coffee production, for this might have been invested elsewhere in the country. Of equal importance, he feels, are: the shift of coffee planting from the Paraíba valley to the western lands, which made Santos the nation's leading coffee port; the growth of towns and a petty bourgeoisie in the *paulista* interior which provided a market for home industry; the impetus which coffee planting gave to the profit motive and to rationalization of entrepreneurship. The last point requires qualifications supplied by Cardoso's subsequent research on *paulista* entrepreneurs (discussed below).

In providing a geographic context for such hypotheses Momsen (1964: 143–171) speculates why São Paulo and not Santos experienced runaway growth.[3] His three central points are: first, the single route-zone between

Table A. Four Periodizations of the History of São Paulo

ERNANI SILVA BRUNO (1954) *Time Span: 1554–1954*	GILBERTO LEITE DE BARROS (1967) *Time Span: 1554–1889*	RICHARD M. MORSE (1954; 1958) *Time Span: 1820–1950*	LUIZ SAIA (1963) *Time Span: 1554–1963*
1554–1828: "campsite for pathfinders" Religio-military determination of site. 17th-century town an expeditionary base for *bandeiras*. 18th-century lethargy and poverty, though with modest commercial development and urban improvements. [For a subsequent study of the whole *paulista* region Bruno (1966) refined his colonial periodization as follows: pioneer period (1500–1580), Indian slave-hunting (1580–1640), search for gold (1640–1730), cattle trade (1730–1775), sugar industry (1775–1822).] 1828–1872: "student town" Urban society still provincial, patriarchal, traditional. Effect of economic catalysts of 1850s (such as coffee planting) not felt till 1870s. Law students dominant as agents of social and intellectual change.	1554–1600: Founding and consolidation. Base for Jesuit catechizing; imperial politico-military functions. 1600–1765: Agrarian economy of scarcity. Isolation; bridgehead to *sertão*; geographic mobility; miscegenation. Call of the backlands stronger than appeal of sedentary municipal life. Military heroic life, becoming tranquil by 18th-century. 1765–1822: Stabilization of life; routinized trade and farming; city becomes trade and transport hub. Mule trade creates capital for sugar and coffee cycles. Firmer urban control over surrounding nuclei and hinterland. More complex socio-economic-political organization; patriarchal system strengthened. Public services; physical "urbanization." 1822–1850: Bureaucratization of city as provin-	1820–1830: Modest agro-commercial economy; persistence of patriarchal customs and social structure; isolation, xenophobia; sense of face-to-face community. Modernizing catalysts: national political involvement; city becomes provincial capital; law faculty; printing press. 1830–1845: Period of suspension and malaise; catalysts of 1820s not yet effective; unruliness of law students; continued poverty and parochialism. 1842 revolution and emperor's visit in 1846 erode city's isolation. 1845–1855: Vitality of law academy; students adopt romantic style; modernizing of customs and behavior; clerical reform. Economic development; urban improvements; start of coffee boom. 1855–1870: Influx of foreign merchants, engineers, teachers, ministers.	1554–1600: Town settled as a garrison of sea-borne empire and a utopian Jesuit sanctum; urban-rural polarity or "binary." 1600–1727: first phase Colonist-Jesuit conflict over secularization of the urban nucleus; Jesuits' Renaissance idealism yields to halfbreed warrior society. second phase Negation of urban-rural polarity and of chessboard planning. *Bandeirismo* causes depopulation, impoverishment and collapse of military social structure. 1727–1848: No clear expression of the individuality of city and region; city's destiny passively determined by circumstance and bureaucratic fiat. 1848–1929: central theses Colonial coffee monoculture; fan-shaped rail system centering on São Paulo.

1872–1918:
"coffee metropolis"
Coffee boom: commercial development; city a rail center; European immigration.
City's customs and appearance cosmopolitanized.
Rapid, unplanned physical growth.

1918–1954:
"contemporary São Paulo"
Continued high rate of population and spatial growth.
High-rise construction; traffic arteries laid out.
Industrial growth after World War I.
Green belt of truck farms created.
Universities, libraries, sports facilities; modernism in the arts.

cial capital; rationalization of public life.
Class distinctions sharpened.
Exodus of entrepreneurs to coffee lands.

1850–1875:
Coffee boom leads to urbanization, trade, capital accrual, commercial credit.
Coffee plantations lose autarky, become dependent on city.
Urban professions multiply; family system loosened; liberalizing influence of law students; Europeanization of urban life.

1875–1889:
Beginnings of a "metropolitan" economy; growth of domestic capital; industrialization; city becomes a rail center.
European immigration; population and spatial growth.
Sweeping physical change.

Overextension of credit.
Railway link to Santos.
Paraguayan War breeds nationalism; students oriented to politics and science.

1870–1890:
Era of positivism; decline of law academy; faith in material progress; city a base for abolitionism.
Economic expansion; start of industrialization; massive European immigration; physical growth of city; prosperity; cosmopolitanization.

1890–1950:
"Metropolitan temper"; labor movements; bureaucratization; secularization; social mobility; industrialism and its problems; city's apathy in the 1924 revolt, its militancy in 1932; obstacles to social action.
Modernist renovation in the arts.
Uncontrolled growth and sprawl; functional specialization of the metropolitan area; urban-rural discontinuities.
[No special attempt was made to subdivide the 1890–1950 period except for the arts, where the Modernist movement simplifies the task. However, the cultural periods (1890–1920, 1920–1945, 1945–present) seem useful for other realms of urban change, particularly as artistic expression often provides cues for the "generational" criterion.]

subtheses
Predatory pioneering of coffee zones; linear spacing of towns along interfluvial ridges; new urban-rural polarity; abstract, reticulated management of urban and rural lands; São Paulo functionally absorbs port of Santos.

1929–1945:
Metropolitanization; larger region acquires energy potential sufficient to overcome underdevelopment; radical shift in regional planning needs unperceived by elites and professionals.

1945–present:
central thesis
Mounting of a regional industrial system erodes urban-rural polarity.

subtheses
Restoration and reinterpretation of original urban site; integration of the geometric, reticulated settlement pattern; reformulation of problems of public services, transport, electric power.

São Paulo and Santos which prevents the regional transportation arteries from interconnecting at the port city; second, the high productivity of the hinterland served by the routes converging on São Paulo. Inasmuch as agricultural exports alone could not trigger the main growth of São Paulo, the final ingredient needed was industrial development based on regional raw materials. This obviated the double crossing of the coastal escarpment that had been necessary as long as raw materials were exchanged for foreign manufactures. Thus the critical moment when São Paulo pulled decisively ahead of its port came when the value and volume of traffic between São Paulo and its hinterland exceeded those of its overseas traffic via Santos. This formula suggests comparisons with other "coupled nuclei" (Curitiba-Paranaguá, Barra Mansa-Angra dos Reis, Caracas-La Guaira) and has possible predictive value for a case such as Governador Valadares-Vitória.

Bases for City Planning. São Paulo's tumultuous growth has posed monumental problems for planners. Many have been met ineffectively if at all. Jorge Wilheim (1965) echoes the despair of Saia (1963) over this fact, yet Wilheim attributes the *paulistas*[4] lack of civic concern (in contrast to the *cariocas'* pride in Rio) to the same historical legacy—erosion of the urban-rural dichotomy—which Saia finds appealing. The long era when the urban patriciate was dispersed and ruralized, Wilheim claims, created a tradition of alienation from municipal affairs, reflected in the weak and intermittent action of the town council. The nineteenth-century afflux of population to the city was composed of floating groups (students, traveling venders, freed slaves, immigrant workers) who carried weak traditions of civic loyalty. After 1870, the release of vacant city lands to real-estate speculation minimized the possibilities for organic, concentric growth. Expansion was a disorderly process of filling in empty spaces and connecting up those peripheral settlements which, in Saia's analysis, had once been a healthy hallmark of rural-urban interpenetration.

Wilheim's recommendations are addressed not to Saia's broad hinterland but to the immediate São Paulo-Santos zone of conurbation which will contain at least 20,000,000 inhabitants by the end of this century. In particular, he stresses the need to revolutionize the city's circulation system, which is still constricted by a unicentric loop-and-spoke plan imposed in the 1920s. Wilheim suggests: (1) A spacious parking ring around the inner city designed as a circular terminus for the radial arteries. Inner-city transportation would then be handled by buses, microtaxis, moving sidewalks and the future subway. (2) Depollution and channelization of the waterways (Tietê, Pinheiros) to allow incorporation of the river basins into the urban system as residential-recreation areas and as transportation arteries. (See Sanson, 1950.) (3) Replanning of the city's arterial system so that it no longer converges on the traditional city center (site of the ancient Jesuit palisade), but takes advantage of the city's "most important topographic accident," a long, curving ridge *(espigão central)* which divides the basins of the Tietê and Pinheiros rivers.[5] Developed as an elevated eight-mile traffic artery, the *espigão* would become a distribution axis for many city *barrios,* supplanting the unicentric radials-perimeter plan with a vertebrate, pluricentric one.

Cultural features are as important to Wilheim's diagnosis as those of urban topography. His emphasis, for example, on a well-knit transport system reflects a conviction that the city cannot be reconstructed on the basis of work-residence neighborhood units. São Paulo's case is quite different from that of Lima, Peru, where 600,000 people, roughly a quarter of the 1968 urban population, live in squatter settlements.[6] With proper industrial site-planning the Lima *barriadas* seem capable of being developed into self-contained neighborhoods for residence, work, commerce, schooling, and recreation. Only a small fraction of the *paulistas,* however, live in *favelas,* the Brazilian equivalent of *barriadas.* Of São Paulo's 700,000 inhabitants who lived under "subhuman conditions" in 1960 (20 percent of the population) only one in ten were *favelados;* the rest were *cortiço* dwellers (Lagenest, 1962).[7] *Cortiços* are less suited than *favelas* for planning territorial neighborhoods.[8] And certainly São Paulo's prominent middle-class zones are no better adaptable as work-residence communities, given that rent control and the high cost of land for home-buyers cause residential mobility to lag far behind job mobility. Neighborhood communities, formerly widespread, are now limited to *favelas,* to occasional old-time *barrios,* and to dwelling clusters beyond easy reach of public transportation. (Goldman, 1965: 535)

These conditions pose obstacles to schemes like that of Delorenzo Neto (1967: 124) and the late Father Lebret (Resumo do estudo, 1958) to reorganize the city's administration into a six-level pyramid based on neighborhood units of 500 meters' radius, combined in larger units of one-, two- and four-kilometer radius, and culminating in "urban units" and a supreme "supra-urban unit." In somewhat Durkheimian language Wilheim suggests that we conceive São Paulo neighborhoods in terms, not of physical, but of social distance: "Social cohesion no longer arises as a product of community sentiments but through free *association of interests.*" Planners, he feels, should give priority not to the territorial neighborhood, but to functional gathering points that already exist: places of work, places of education and recreation, markets and shopping centers, public meeting-places for speeches, rallies, plays and worship, and the embarkation points for public transportation. The final item has special importance. For if one accepts the city as it is and abjures the herculean task of replanning it on a basis of territorial neighborhoods, then an effective transportation system assumes high priority as a factor of urban integration, perhaps even higher than the need for urban housing.[9]

The Regional Impact of Urbanization. In 1962, the Interstate Commission of the Paraná-Uruguay Basin produced a report on demography, migrations, economic development, urbanization, and urban systems in a vast area comprising seven states of southern Brazil: Minas Gerais, São Paulo, Paraná, Santa Catarina, Rio Grande do Sul, Mato Grosso, and Goiás (Costa-Kowarick, 1963). The Basin was found to gravitate around two urban poles. The São Paulo complex in the north and the Pôrto Alegre complex in the south. A secondary complex centers on Belo Horizonte and an incipient one on Curitiba. The *paulista* system, however, is "the dynamic center of the whole region." Containing six of the state's seven cities of over 100,000 inhabitants (as of 1960), it extends along four axes from the state capital, three of them penetrating the neighboring states of Minas, Mato Grosso and Paraná. It produces 90 percent of the manufactures of the state and 67 percent of those of the whole Basin; it employs 85 percent of the state's industrial workers and 57 percent of the Basin's; it contains 68 percent of the state's urban population and 36 percent of the Basin's.

The report finds that settlement density in the area is highly uneven and the infrastructures for urban systems too restricted in number and regional influence. It indicates the desirability of two complementary systems along an axis from Curitiba into the coffee zone of Londrina, with southern extensions into Santa Catarina, and along an axis joining Belo Horizonte to the agricultural zone of Governador Valadares and Teófilo Otoni along the River Doce. The latter would offset the polarization of that zone by Rio de Janeiro.

The isolation and self-containment of the chief urban systems raise questions about their internal structure. Is the morphology of the whole Basin replicated within single urban systems? Even the impressive *paulista* system exhibits weak dispersion of urban functions. Of the state's 16,194,-892 inhabitants in 1967, 5,247,120 lived in São Paulo city and 7,035,420, or 43.4 percent, in the thirty-three municipalities comprising Greater São Paulo.[10] If higher education and certain sectors of public administration have been decentralized, commercial and most administration functions are still heavily concentrated in the state capital. Industry has expanded into the interior, but along continuous, well defined zones radiating from the metropolis.[11]

> "The question here is not the lack of cities sufficiently large to assume the role of regional centers but the powerful dominance exercised by the agglomeration of the capital. . . . Despite the great density of urbanization in the system, Ribeirão Prêto is the only city beyond the direct influence of the capital with a population of over 100,000 and a substantial development of industry and regional services, or the minimum conditions for a real regional center. Other cities like Bauru, President Prudente or Araçatuba will acquire these characteristics in rounded, balanced form only when an appropriate strategy can be defined." [Costa-Kowarick 1963: 395][12]

In Latin America, then, even a "dynamic" industrial metropolis recalls features of the old bureaucratic, patrimonial capital. Impulses for regional development tend to originate centrally and magnetize the periphery into dependency relationships.[13] In his analysis of transportation development and urbanization in São Paulo state from 1940 to 1960, Gauthier (1968) tests whether the two processes are in "balanced" interaction or whether one significantly "leads" the other. He finds an "unbalanced" relationship, with highway accessibility (created by decisions and resources at the center) acting as a "lead" factor for regional industrialization and, to a less extent, urban population growth.

The analysis of inter-city relationships within the urban system should extend to include the consequences of urbanization for the tributary rural population. (See Pinho, 1964.) Two contrasting approaches may be cited. Haller (1967) uses quantitative methods to test the Marxist hypothesis that the economic growth of cities has deleterious effects upon surrounding rural populations—namely, proletarianization of the labor force, decrease in real incomes, and polarization of social strata.[14] He establishes indices for each dependent variable, then collects data for the base years 1953 and 1962 from sample households in four ecologically diverse farm communities located 35 to 75 miles from the metropolis. He finds that (1) rapid proletarianization occurred during the decade, not primarily because independent farm operators lost status but because many workers rose "from a subproletariat stratum of sharecroppers" to the stratum of wage earners; (2) monetary income and land ownership showed little change, whether up or down, while non-monetary income (radio listening, education) showed substantial increase; (3) there was little evidence to prove either polarization or equalization of the social strata.

Without questioning the accuracy of Haller's data, one can challenge the meliorist implications of his finding that the "relative impoverishment" hypothesis is untenable for rural populations of the Rio hinterland. For his analysis is silent on the cultural and psychological stress which looms so important in the qualitative field study of Antônio Cândido (1964). Cândido's chapter, "The *caipira*[15] confronting urban civilization," suggests how deceptive Haller's indicators are, because even if they hold true for Cândido's *paulista* zone they fail to illuminate the central fact of rural social change: "The *caipira* no longer lives in a precarious balance determined by the resources of the immediate environment and the sociability of isolated groups. He lives in clear economic disequilibrium vis-à-vis the resources provided by modern technology." A social revolution is suddenly occurring. Rural and urban types, subsistence farmers and *fazendeiros,* farm and factory wage earners find themselves "brusquely colliding in geographic and social space, sharing a universe which lays economic and cultural discrepancies painfully bare." In this new cacophonous dialogue the weakest and most neglected voice "is beyond doubt the *caipira's.*"

What Haller perceives as a situation partly of equilibrium, partly of "relative enrichment," Antônio Cândido designates a "crisis situation" in which traditional culture traits vanish more swiftly than they can be replaced because the *caipira* has no means to acquire new ones. The encroachment of urban culture forces persons and families into dramatic decisions which undermine the solidarity of social groups that have traditionally yielded consolation and support. Obliged to abandon "material and social techniques elaborated for a bygone way of life," the *caipira* may even exhibit "regressive adaptation" and fall back upon archaic social patterns "incompatible with fully developed cultural life."

PRESSURES AND PROCESS IN URBAN SOCIETY

Entrepreneurship. In the city reputed to be South America's largest industrial park, the question of entrepreneurship has a priority claim on our attention. Ever since the late nineteenth-century travelers who admired the drive and modernity of *paulista* businessmen, observers have referred to a regional *paulista* or *bandeirante* mystique in explaining the emergence of this Brazilian Chicago or Milan. There are two recent formulations of the theme.

Warren Dean (1964; 1966) adopts a historical perspective to ask whether this regional culture is indeed more congenial to the capitalist spirit than others in Latin America. His conclusion is negative; he finds it more plausible to assume that entrepreneurial talent was distributed more or less evenly throughout Brazil. The success of *paulista* planters who turned to urban enterprise he attributes not to cultural or psychological factors but to historical and economic ones, such as the nature of coffee cultivation (which favored "capitalistic" planters who reinvested profits), prior capital accumulation, a profitable market economy, and a free labor market. Despite the importance he ascribes to the market economy, Dean (1966: 152) paradoxically adds to his explanatory list those "factors discouraging competition from other groups, or encouraging their assimilation."

Dean's argument tends to be circular. He accounts for successful entrepreneurship by commercial and institutional preconditions that seem as much result as cause of a "rational" economic outlook. At the same time, he appears to consider entrepreneurial spirit as a ubiquitous reservoir of energy, releasable by happy conjunctions of transcultural factors. Only indirectly does he hint at the cultural conditioning of this energy, as when he speaks of the *paulista* planters' "thoroughly politicized view of economic development," their preference for government clientage arrangements, or their co-opting and neutralization of potential immigrant élites.

In his studies of industrial entrepreneurship in Brazil, which rely heavily on the *paulista* case, Cardoso (1961; 1963; 1964; 1965) formulates the problem differently. He is not concerned with the causal role of either psychocultural or circumstantial factors in São Paulo's industrial revolution. Nor does he conceive of entrepreneurial spirit as a standard unit of psychic energy. His premise is that entrepreneurship in Brazil can be studied only as a function of the institutional context which sustains it. "I was less concerned with the innovative capacity of a talented entrepreneur than with the social conditions that permit the deployment of entrepreneurial skills under the form of industrial capitalism" (1964: 8). São Paulo, therefore, ceases to be an idiosyncratic case of industrial "progressivism" and antitraditionalism, and becomes an exemplary case of the complex forms of industrialism in the Ibero-American cultural world.

From this perspective, Cardoso (1964: 80–92, 159–166) interprets the "frames of reference" of *paulista* industrialists as having been "relatively restricted" until as late as the 1950s.[16] The choice of manufactures was traditional; business practices were routine; and the political pressures generated by industrialists were weak. Cardoso therefore challenges the familiar thesis that "private initiative—or, the entrepreneurial bourgeoisie —constitutes the original motive force for development and modernization in Brazil." Rather than calling entrepreneurship an engine of modernization, he suggests that only recently has the institutional, political, and cultural climate become supportive of industrial innovation. Frequently, in fact, this public climate encounters resistances to change precisely from family-controlled entrepreneurial groups with "pioneering" traditions. The industrial élite is so heterogeneous that it fails to exert coherent political pressure upon national leadership; its members perceive themselves primarily in the light of private status criteria and only secondarily as an entrepreneurial group; their view of the social order inhibits them from construing their personal or class situation in terms of economic interests; and their response to market requirements is the "minimum necessary for enterprises to survive as economic organizations with a profit-making objective." In short, Cardoso finds *paulista* entrepreneurship to be less innovative than accommodative with respect to economic attitudes and social change.

Social Mobility. Just as Cardoso's study alerts us against exaggerating the "dynamism" of *paulista* industry during the first half of the twentieth century, so the studies of the Hutchinson group (1960: 9–16, 192–229) warn us not to overestimate the structural social change caused in this period by industrialization, immigration, and education. As of 1960, their conclusion was that in comparison to England, the education system in São Paulo (particularly the traditional primary and secondary systems) tended to maintain the *status quo* and discourage social mobility. "That is, available resources for education do not correspond to the requirements for economic development." The seeming antitraditionalism of São Paulo society must therefore be explained by a distinction between "structural mobility," which results from the creation of new middle- and upper-level positions by an expanding economy, and "exchange mobility" (or in Gino Germani's term, "replacement mobility"), which results from promotion and demotion of talent up and down the occupational ladder on a merit basis. São Paulo obviously offers considerable mobility of the first or structural type but is said to exhibit relatively little of the second.

The Hutchinson studies of Italian immigrants to São Paulo indicate that their cultural or motivational make-up advantaged them for upward mobility in comparison to native Brazilians.[17] Their new environment, however, encouraged them to abandon the very ethic of work which had assured their survival and early advancement and to adopt its prevalent status orientations. The cultural reality worked against the economic to stigmatize physical labor and petty commerce. The new middle class, composed largely of immigrants, "tends at the start to contribute to an artificial overpopulation of the traditional professions, which continue to retain social prestige if not economic predominance." It was further found that many immigrants achieved success with little education and that the education received by their children has a largely symbolic value. This means that there is little correlation between a person's intelligence and his chances for improving his social status; that "personality" rather than capacity is the critical motive force for upward mobility; and that schools and family conventions tend to produce "an average individual who sets a higher value on the preservation of status than on the risks inherent in mobility."

These conclusions are reinforced by Leeds' description of how informal primary groups function to establish and sustain careers in Brazilian urban society.[18] Such a group, or *panelinha* (saucepan), characteristically contains a customs official, an insurance man, a lawyer, a businessman, an accountant, a local or federal deputy and a banker. It serves "both status and contractual ends" to provide linkage, horizontal and vertical, among the otherwise weakly interrelated institutions and formal organizations of Brazilian society. The *panelinha* places a premium on the talent for ingratiation, for perception of cues relating to career possibilities, for energetic cultivation of "connections," and for mobilizing *igrejinhas* (little churches) of loyal supporters. By excluding the poor from access to "cue-transmitted information" the system perpetuates institutionalized poverty and the dichotomy between "masses" and "classes." "Furthermore, the great degree of control exercised over the masses tends to force them to look to the classes for support, thus reinforcing the system structurally and ideologically through institutions generally described as 'paternalistic.' "

Proletarianization. Like entrepreneurial and middle-class groups, the urban proletariat and subproletariat—referred to by Leeds as the "masses" —have received increasing attention. Many who study urban workers in Latin America or the *tiers monde* emphasize that in these areas urbanization has outrun or been unlinked to industrialization. This leads to the inference that the new urbanization merely transfers poverty from rural to urban areas, inflating the urban work force (particularly the tertiary or "services" sector) with unskilled and irregularly employed laborers, street vendors and disguised mendicants.[19] Whatever the merits of this thesis, it seems of limited relevance to the case of São Paulo, where employment in the secondary sector (industry, construction, public utilities) is relatively high in relation to the tertiary. J. F. de Camargo (1968: 68–71) notes that in 1950, São Paulo had only 53.7 percent of its population in tertiary employment while Rio had 71.2 percent. The former's occupational structure was "more solid," with a larger secondary sector, more favorable distribution of the tertiary, and fewer people in unremunerated activities.[20] (In contrast even with Rio, however, Salvador and Recife are called "pathological.")

One need not accept all the normative implications of Camargo's comparisons; nor can one deny the existence of marginally employed persons in São Paulo and an unemployment rate which at times reaches 15 percent or more. The point is that opportunities for secondary-sector employment here, unlike many parts of Latin America, seem more or less to have increased at a pace with population growth. Balán (1969) suggests that the capacity of Latin American cities to absorb migrants can be classified by two variables: (a) "credentialism," that is, the formal entry requirements of the urban occupational structure (not identical with *skill* requirements), and (b) the rate of increase of urban jobs in high-productivity sectors. São Paulo he ranks high on both counts; in other words, Brazilian migrants with few credentials are initially disadvantaged with respect to native urbanites, but the expanding job structure eventually absorbs them or their children.[21]

Touraine's study of São Paulo workers (1961; also Cardoso 1962a; Touraine-Pécaut 1967–68) stresses psychological adaptation rather than economic opportunity. He starts from the contrast between contemporary Brazil and pre-World War I Europe with respect to the formation of a proletarian consciousness.[22] In Europe, he points out, the urban worker felt himself partly *outside* the national society. The era of mass consumption had not yet arrived, and the worker could not aspire to a comfortable middle-class style of life. This motivated him to organize as a proletarian class and sensitized him to the appeals and ideologies of international communism, socialism, and anarcho-syndicalism. As late as the eve of World War I, European socialists wavered between patriotic allegiance to nation and class allegiance to an international proletariat. The European worker won his social democracy only gradually. The achievement of a mass-consumption society is only the recent end-product of a long history of industrialization and political reform. Workers' movements never separated problems of economic policy from the goals of social change, and never faltered in the objective of placing the forces of production under control.

The Brazilian migrant to the large city, on the other hand, soon feels himself part of the national society in transition and eligible to consume its products.[23] The appeal of nationalism strikes more deeply than that of class solidarity. What in fact attracted him to the city was not so much the prospect of occupational training and lifelong identification with a single professional career and social class as vague promises of the urban environment, exemplified in the middle- or upper-class style of life. In this situation Touraine finds that São Paulo's industrial workers adopt three different forms of socialization: (1) The individual search for opportunities, which diminishes worker solidarity in the factory. (2) Solidarity with small primary groups, uninformed by ideology or class consciousness. This camaraderie is kindled in time of crisis and in the face of concrete issues, but dissipates when provocation fades away. (3) Acceptance of a vague, generalized image of the society at large. This outlook recognizes the opposition between the weak, disinherited majority and the powerful minority, but without calling into question the appropriateness of existing economic institutions or the social role of capital. It is concerned more with assessing the moral behavior of the élite than with discovering a point of leverage for social revolution. The state-supported labor syndicate to which workers appeal for defense functions more as a sovereign granting relief from oppression than as an agent for sociopolitical change created by its members.

These three orientations are not mutually exclusive and may be found in combination, but none is compatible with the grand tradition of proletarian class solidarity. They seem to reflect the fact that the worker who comes to São Paulo from a rural or small-town background is guided in his behavior by personal criteria rather than by requirements of a system, whether a factory routine or a class ideology. The most notorious aspect of this complex of personalism is a quest for a dependency or clientage relationship, the search for a *bom patrão*. The natural complement to dependency, however, is personal independence. As Touraine (1961) has said, Brazilian workers tend more than their French counterparts to resist "the social organization of firms; they do not want masters and they wish to preserve a freedom which is at once reminiscent of bygone working conditions and a sign of nonintegration into the industrial scene." This conclusion is confirmed by Brandão Lopes (1964: 22–95; see also Ferrari, 1962), who found that the usual goal of migrants to São Paulo is to work independently as a taxi driver, shopkeeper or artisan. His explanation is that migrants have already internalized rural norms linked to independent economic activities, including a sense of "obligation." Their lack of experience with urban forms of impersonal, "rational" association together with their knowledge that workers exercise little control in such organizations causes them to redefine their interests on a highly individual basis. The lack of group consciousness which Cardoso notes among industrialists is therefore replicated among workers.

Populism. The political corollary to the situation just described is the politics of populism. Among the first to identify its Brazilian version was Morazé (1954: 135), who interpreted what was later called "populism" as an urban mutation of the traditional politics of the old rural bosses—the colonels, or *coronéis*. He claimed that a hybrid, new-style politics could first be glimpsed in São Paulo's 1932 revolt against the Vargas régime, when *coronelismo* became allied to urban reformism:

"By 1945 one witnesses throughout Brazil a curious amalgam of rejuvenated republican *coronelismo* and new urban political structures which, adapted to the patterns of traditional Brazilian functions, deserves the name 'urban *coronelismo.*'

A whole mass of voters is detached from the old colonels; they become partisans of the reforms of the New State and, even before elections take place, they display steadfast confidence in Getúlio Vargas.

There are undoubtedly analogies between *coronelismo* and populism insofar as the latter is institutionalized in local clientage systems whose key figures *(patrão, pistolão, cabo eleitoral, pelego)* have rural counterparts.[24] However, it is an oversimplification—and in the case of industrial São Paulo an inaccuracy—to say that the larger Brazilian cities are becoming "ruralized" by the influx of rural and small-town migrants.[25] As a broadly Latin-American phenomenon, populism has been said to draw its strength from upper- and middle-level élites who harbor anti-*status quo* motivations (also called "counterélites"); a mass which has become available or mobilized because of a revolution of expectations; and an ideology or widespread emotional state which fosters communication between leaders and followers, creating collective enthusiasm. Di Tella (1965), Weffort (1965a and 1965b), and Lopes (1966) contrast Brazilian *coronelismo* and populism as follows:

coronelismo	*populism*
1. Social and economic contacts of the populace are restricted to single rural localities.	Adherence of the urban mass to a leader presupposes freedom from local constraints.
2. Political relation between leader and voter is merely one dimension of a broader social dependency.	Political relation between leader and voter is frequently their only relation.
3. Reflects a compromise between public and private power.	Exalts the power of the State, placing it in direct relation with the people.

Weffort and Ferrari (1962: 178–179) have analyzed two divergent styles of populist leadership emanating from São Paulo: the "politics of love" of Ademar de Barros with its benign, conservative, patriarchal appeal to marginal and threatened sectors of the petty bourgeoisie who felt themselves impotent to seize and direct the historical process; and the "politics of hate" of Jânio Quadros with its ascetic, moralistic appeal to proletarian groups who had made their peace with the industrial order but resented the injustices of a society ridden with privilege and favoritism.[26]

Revitalized Primary Groups. So long as populist politics rests on the charismatic appeal of state- and national-level leaders to the masses without mediating programs tailored to specific groups and localities; and so long as patronage structures are opportunistic, imposed from above and inadequate in their rewards, one may expect innovative political responses to provide alternatives to—and eventually an infrastructure for—the politics of populism. These responses may be characterized as "clientage" and "secessionist" associations. An example of the former are organized neighborhood committees (the *juntas de vecinos* of Spanish-American cities) which aspire to legitimation and assistance from private and official sources, and cannot be indefinitely appeased by the token hand-outs of old-style political clientage. Goldman (1965: 536) observed these in the São Paulo *favelas*.

An alternative response is the secessionist association. City dwellers who despair of finding accommodation within "the system" may turn to groups which allow them to secede, at least psychologically, from it. A prime example in Brazil are non-Catholic religious movements such as Pentecostalism, Spiritism, and Umbanda. They have special appeal for the lower classes and occur characteristically in rural frontier areas and large cities, where changes strongly affecting the traditional structure of society are taking place (Willems, 1966, 1967; C. P. F. de Camargo, 1961a, 1961b; Warren, 1968). In varying styles these sects symbolically subvert the existing power structure, reject upper-class paternalism, and offer the initiate a chance to rebuild his personal community. The convert feels needed and relied on as a "brother." If he possesses "powers" he is accorded the recognition of personal capacity which the outer world denies. The cults provide therapy for anxieties and personality disorder. They aim toward radical reorganization of society and of the personal habits of converts. Some of them sponsor programs of social assistance through hospitals, asylums, shelters and schools. Because their vitality comes from primary groups, the non-Catholic sects are not effectively organized into regional or city-wide associations. Nonetheless they are now recognized as representing an important sector of the electorate. More important, their accomplishments in reorienting personalities and energizing small groups may be contributing to the more effective political mobilization of the urban lower classes. Willems (1967: 259) feels that "the organizational schism [of the Pentecostal sects] seems to be a more adequate means of expressing rebellion against the traditional social order than the doctrinal schism." Religious cult groups, like squatters' movements and guerrilla bands, are rehabilitating the single anonymous man and his family to assert their force in the metropolitan mass societies of Latin America.

Race and Class. The most sustained and penetrating sociological study of São Paulo ever written is probably Florestan Fernandes' analysis (1964) of the incorporation of the Negro into urban society. Fernandes conclusively demonstrates the presence of color prejudice in São Paulo, bringing to light its origins, functions, effects and resultant dilemmas. (See also Bastide-Fernandes, 1955.) He does less to disprove earlier scholars who linked color prejudice to social prejudice than to show that they failed to take account of developments since 1930 in Brazil's leading industrial metropolis. Here, appreciable numbers of Negroes have achieved socioeconomic mobility without corresponding relief from pressures of color prejudice. In other words, the parallelism between racial and social attitudes has been broken. Fernandes explodes the myth of "racial democracy," showing how the reality of prejudice is camouflaged by the "external cordiality" and "mask of civility" which, in his clinical view, reflect a cultural paucity of "social techniques for manipulating tensions."

Two special strengths of Fernandes' presentation are: (1) his generous temporal perspective, which allows one to perceive discriminatory patterns as a form of inertial traditionalism rather than an innovative defense mechanism, and thus to gauge their historical logic and momentum; (2) his unmasking of the color-related psychological stress experienced by both whites and Negroes, a feature which escapes many other analyses. If there is oversimplification in his otherwise elaborate treatment of color prejudice, it may lie in his failure to contrast the position of "Negroes" with that of "mulattoes." There are only occasional hints as to whether he accepts the distinction made by Nogueira (1955) between "prejudice of origin" and "prejudice of mark" or, in the terms applied to Caribbean societies by M. G. Smith (1955), "genealogical" and "phenotypical color." (Bastide and van den Berghe [1957] detect both forms of discrimination in São Paulo.)

As the book's title indicates, however, the author is concerned, not simply with clarifying the forms and prevalence of color prejudice, but also with identifying obstacles to the incorporation of Negroes into urban society at various periods since the emancipation of Brazil's slaves in 1888. It is a study in sociology as well as social psychology. The key proposition is that a "bourgeois revolution" has transformed São Paulo society into one that is competitive and class-based for increasing numbers of white citizens, yet keeps the Negro and mulatto population subject to archaic forms of domination inherited from the "society of estates and castes" of the nineteenth century.[27]

In light of other research discussed above, the most challenging part of this proposition is the assertion that whites themselves participate in an open, competitive class society. This assumption needs to be reconciled with the fact that several writers deny that the proletariat has a class identity (Ianni, 1963; Cardoso, 1960a, 1962; Touraine, 1961; Lopes, 1964); Weffort (1966) denies that the middle groups have one; and Cardoso (1964) finds entrepreneurs perceiving their situation in the light of status rather than class criteria.[28] Fernandes' description of how Negroes commonly achieve social mobility by using techniques of ingratiation with white protectors corresponds to the Hutchinson finding that white immigrants' children often get ahead on the basis of "personality" and not capacity.[29] Fernandes' analysis of the "acephalization" of the Negro community, which occurs as successful members infiltrate the "world of the whites" and lose their identification with "the great mass of the colored," corresponds to Touraine's description of how successful workers who obtain steady jobs and syndical protection abrogate their allegiance to the subproletariat. Indeed, the three forms of Negro personality adjustment to white dominance which Fernandes (1964: 508–518) identifies correspond with remarkable fidelity to the three ways in which Touraine (1961: 84) finds workers adapting psychologically to the society at large:

Forms of Negro personality adjustment (Fernandes)	*Forms of worker personality adjustment (Touraine)*
1. passivity and conformism	apathetic adaptation a. *conscience segmentée* b. *conscience éclatée*
2. complex of fear which causes the Negro to make ineffective use of opportunities for upward mobility	utopian nonconformism; submissiveness combined with hopes for own or children's advancement
3. reactive mechanism permitting a dynamic response to concrete possibilities	reinterpretation of present situation leading to integration of attitudes

If Leeds' estimate that the larger urban societies of Brazil are composed of 40 percent of privileged "classes" and 60 percent of underprivileged "masses" is anywhere near correct,[30] it means that a large sector of the white population, as well as the majority of Negroes, is denied access to positions of opportunity. In his analysis, the *panelinha* and the *cabide* ("coat hanger" for multiple job holding) are the main structural entities that create a virtually impermeable boundary between "classes" and "masses."[31] Within the "classes," Leeds observes, the ascension of persons from lower strata is selectively controlled from above. Aspirants must therefore try to secure favor and protection from higher strata, reinforced by the small-group support and connections afforded by the *panelinha*. Again, the similarity to Fernandes' description of mobility patterns for successful Negroes is evident. One is therefore led to question the assertion that "the 'white' stocks of the São Paulo population soon acquired the psychosocial and sociocultural traits which characterize class formation" (Fernandes 1964: 253). For social success in São Paulo society seems to depend less on the strength and militancy of class identifications[32] than on the capacity of socioeconomic strata or ethnic minorities to develop primary-group organizations as *trampolins* ("springboards" for careers), given the *relatively* limited importance of personal merit as a criterion for advancement. Fernandes in effect recognizes this point (1964: 495) when he attributes "the failure of the 'Negro' vis-à-vis the Italian, the 'Turk' and especially the Japanese" to the superior capacity of the latter groups to generate mutual aid and cooperativism (i.e., precisely the forms of solidarity which, in Marxist literature, are *antecedent* to the formation of class consciousness). The point is also implicit when he observes that many Negroes now appreciate the importance of establishing the "integrated Negro family" as a firm, small-group basis for socializing the child and providing "support for the ambitions of the young" (1964: 524). Another form of small-group organization available to Negroes, which may well be of greater significance than their potential for "class" militancy, is the spiritist and Pentecostal sects discussed above; it is revealing that he pays them no attention.

In short, Fernandes claims that the historical and cultural imperatives of the "society of estates" of the nineteenth century no longer govern relations among urban whites but continue to govern those between whites and urban Negroes. Evidence from other sociologists and from Fernandes' own research, however, lays the first part of this proposition under question. It seems more accurate to say that the whole of urban society is permeated with vigorous survivals from the agro-commercial régime of the past (status ascription, hierarchical patterns of deference, masks of etiquette, clientage systems, forms of primary-group organization) which have been reworked in answer to structural and psychological requirements of industrialism and urbanization. The Negro is severely disadvantaged in his quest for opportunities because: (1) he has not inherited a position of prestige and authority, such as that long monopolized by the "traditional whites"; (2) he has been handicapped vis-à-vis immigrant groups because of their focused motivations and their cultural resources for family and mutual-assistance organization; (3) he is victimized by color prejudice. Negroes are a negatively privileged but not an outcast group. Their hopes for the future would seem to depend less on their ability to develop "class consciousness" or a "racial self-image" than on their success at discovering and revitalizing forms of action more consistent with the traditions of the culture which they share.

Cultural Tradition and Social Change. None of the sociological studies that have been cited endorses the simplistic notion that the *paulista* industrial region is merely recapitulating the historic stages of socioeconomic development of the northern industrial countries. They emphasize configurations of tradition and innovation, linkages between political and economic change, attitudes toward work, authority and social action that are largely without precedent in nineteenth-century industrial societies. Analysts of social change in contemporary Brazil recognize what Brandão Lopes (1964) calls the "juxtaposition of epochs."

By virtue of their primary focus on change or process, however, most of these descriptions of urban society make it appear that present configurations are "transitional" toward a more standard or universal ethos of industrialism. The idiosyncrasy or "asymmetries" of prevailing patterns are attributed to alterations of the phasing and sequences associated with nineteenth-century industrialization. Little attention is paid to the enduring belief system which not only influences "transitional" patterns but may significantly determine the features of the more completely industrialized society of the future. Thus, for example, Cardoso (1964: 159–187) is concerned with how the "industrial bourgeoisie" is to attain ideological consistency in a society en route from "irrational" to "rational" patterns of economic action, from "traditional" forms of behavior to "collective modernizing aspirations."[33] Hutchinson (1958: 19) observes that a unilinear process of "disintegration of the immigrant primary group, and of the consanguine family pattern, follows closely in São Paulo the lines suggested by Talcott Parsons' analysis of the rise of western society." Leeds (1965: 379–382) describes his research as a case study for a broader inquiry into "regularities of developmental sequences" from "static-agrarian" to "expansive-industrial" societies. Goldman (1965: 539) predicts that the *paulista* worker may acquire class consciousness "following patterns like those of Europe," while Fernandes (1964) defines the problem of the Negro as one of integrating to a society which has *already* moved from a basis of castes or estates to one of classes.[34]

No one would deny the appropriateness of this concern with change to a study of São Paulo society. Moreover, the versions of development theory just cited all fit respectively within Durkheim's classic paradigm for the transformation of societies from régimes of mechanical to those of organic solidarity in response to the requirements of division of labor. What must be remembered, however, is that Durkheim's model is transcultural. It attempts to identify the generic, universal requirements for complex industrial societies. As he made clear in his preface to the second edition of the *Division of Labor,* he himself was uncertain as to the specific institutional arrangements that industrial division of labor might dictate in any particular society. He was also aware that unpropitious conditions might cause the model to assume "abnormal forms." Contemporary analysts of São Paulo society tend to identify such conditions as temporary rigidities caused by the "juxtaposition of epochs." Few give serious attention to the long-term cultural imperatives which will help to shape the institutions of that eventual society variously described as rational (Cardoso), individualistic (Hutchinson), expansive-industrial (Leeds) and open-competitive (Fernandes).

Some researchers, who mistake correlation for comparison, syndromes for matrices, and "values" for belief, have cast off completely from cultural and institutional moorings. The result is anarchy. In his study of family patterns, for example, Rosen (1962) finds that U. S. boys of all social classes attain higher achievement motivation scores than Brazilian boys of all classes. Thus: "Nationality seems to be more important than class in determining achievement motivation." Kahl's study (1968) of modernizing values "proves" the opposite. Industrialism is found to homogenize national value schemes into a universal syndrome of modernism. Upper-class city-dwellers in Brazil, Mexico, and the United States show "striking" similarities of value orientation. Whereas Rosen's upper-class Brazilians have lower achievement motivation than the *Lumpen,* Kahl finds that "the higher the status, the more modern the response." Thus for Kahl: "It seems that position in the social structure determines the degree of modernism, and nationality differences are not important."[35] Such research, compared with the best done by Brazilians, suggests inverse correlation between economic development and sociological imagination.

Rosen's intimation that the Brazilian family pattern is an unfortunate psychological aberration and Kahl's cavalier dismissal of national culture differences[36] illustrate the confusion that occurs when researchers shy away from examining belief systems and confine themselves to ephemeral expressions of belief in the form of style, ideology and "values." In the case of Brazil, social attitudes and social action continue to be informed by the pervasive Catholic ethic, however lax or heterodox Brazilian churchgoers may be. The language and ideologies of belief may change from one decade to the next; but the premises of belief—the often unspoken assumptions about how people are to enter a state of grace, singly or collectively—are far more durable. A primary task in analyzing the industrialization and urbanization of Brazil is, therefore, to chart present and foreseeable patterns of accommodation between the psychology of a Catholic society and Durkheim's requirements for organic solidarity produced by division of labor.

What partly accounts for neglect of this point is the fact that Max Weber so persuasively identified the Protestant ethic with "rational" economic organization and capital accumulation. To emphasize the tenacity of the Catholic ethic in Brazil might seem—to any but a staunch Catholic ideologue—to condemn its society to penury, atrophy, and tumult.[37] Societies, however, do not abrogate spiritual commitments easily. The secret of an effective educational reform or a successful "revolution" is that it returns to and reinterprets such commitments. Even the evangelical Protestant movements of contemporary Brazil represent an age-old form of protest and renovation within the Catholic order. It is misleading to construe them as tropical outposts of Protestant, industrial civilization. Sociologically, they are more akin to the radical sects or congregations of pre-Protestant, medieval Europe.[38] Whatever resistances the Catholic ethic may offer to the Weberian requirements for "rational" economic and organizational behavior, one must recognize its historic traditions of protest and "revolution" as well as its therapeutic promise for pathological conditions of depersonalization, cut-throat competitiveness and anomie.

The role of the religious ethic in Brazil's social and economic development becomes clearer when we call to mind the Japanese case, a comparison which receives only perfunctory notice from Kahl (1968: 7). In his study of Japanese city life, Dore (1965) shows how private ambition, or "getting on," was legitimized during the early Meiji period in the framework of a morality oriented toward the collectivity.[39] The leaders of the Meiji Restoration were mostly samurai of lower grades who rose to positions of power by virtue of ability. They had no vested interest in the existing feudal hierarchy and were concerned "to dismantle the class structure from the top" and to design egalitarian reforms. "A unified non-discriminatory school system was established and has persisted to the present day with, at the primary and secondary level, only a very limited

development of private-school alternatives." Upward channels of mobility
were opened—bureaucratic, military, entrepreneurial; and although patronage continued to lubricate the advancement of talent, bureaucratic
status became ascribed to persons rather than families, and individual
enterprise was encouraged as necessary to the state.

In São Paulo, according to the Hutchinson studies, the situation was
almost the reverse. Social ascension certainly took place, but as a by-
product of economic change, not as the fruit of systematic promotion of
ability. Successful climbers tended to adopt an élitist outlook, and the
educational process functioned more to validate privilege than to recruit
talent. The merits of individual enterprise were publicized, but its exercise
was enjoyed principally by élitist groups and foreign concessionaires; its
contributions to national welfare or to strengthening the state were for-
tuitous.

Urban Japan and urban Brazil of the late nineteenth and early twentieth centuries both exhibit preindustrial survivals: familialism, paternalism, patron-client relations, hierarchical attitudes of deference, weak class
identifications. But in Japan these features were accommodated to a
state-supported system which required identification and release of talent
from lower social strata. "The masses, in short, had minds, not simply
souls, to be saved" (Dore, 1964: 235). In Brazil, the wellborn and most
foreigners were immensely advantaged for careers, and the state was not
erected into an engine for social reorganization and economic development.

The contrast between these two industrializing societies can be related
to a difference in social ethic. In Japan the reformulation of Shinto and
Confucian ideals promoted the mystique of a strong, integrated, imperial
nation while encouraging social attitudes that served the needs of personal self-development, among them consideration for others, loyalty to
principles, frank expression of opinion, equality before the law, equality
of the sexes, the duty of personal accomplishment and the right to self-
fulfillment. Except for its failure to include liberation of private conscience, this list corresponds to conventionally cited moral requirements
for an industrial society, or to features of Durkheim's organic solidarity.

Catholicism, unlike Shinto, is a universal faith and therefore a less
reliable source of mystique for nation-building. Furthermore, although the
resources of Catholicism for personal consolation are impressive, it is not
a faith which conspicuously motivates and rewards personal accomplishment. The Catholic community, as Weber (1964: 186–190) analyzes it, is
one in which grace is institutionally dispensed. In such a society the
personal qualifications of those seeking "salvation" are a matter of in-
difference to the institution distributing grace. Salvation is universal and
therefore accessible to other than "virtuosi"; in fact, the virtuoso falls
under suspicion if he seeks to attain grace by his unaided power. The
expectation of personal accomplishment is modestly defined, for the conduct of life is largely patterned by distribution of grace by institutions

and charismatic persons. The vouchsafing of grace facilitates the individual's capacity to bear guilt and "largely spares him the necessity of developing an individual planned pattern of life based on ethical foundations. . . . Hence, value is attached to concrete individual acts rather than to the total personality pattern which has been produced by asceticism, contemplation, or eternally vigilant self-control." This typology is consistent with many of the recent sociological findings in São Paulo, and it helps to place them in historical and cultural perspective.

Juxtaposing Durkheim's transcultural moral requirements for industrialization with Weber's paradigm for the ethos of Catholicism has important advantages for the study of urbanization in Brazil, assuming that idiosyncratic historical circumstances are not lost sight of. This approach draws attention to psychological commitments and to the morphology and logic of institutions rather than to artificial historical stages and dynamisms. It leads us to construe urban change in Brazil as the transactions between an enduring social ethic and the flexible preconditions, both moral and organizational, for any industrial society—and not as an extraneous ethic impinging upon an "archaic" social system, or as the collision of two closed and alien systems. For all its apparent resistance to the "rationalism" of an industrial, market society, the ethic in question has historically demonstrated considerable resilience and innovative potential. It may in the long run help to preserve certain affective modes of fellowship and moral bases for action which in other technified Western societies seem lost beyond retrieve.

The Mirror of Literature. Turning from social science to literature refreshes one's sense of the immediacies of a city. São Paulo is often a setting for prose fiction (Antônio, 1966), but in this case one finds the city's personality projected less forcefully in the genre of the urban novel than in periodic bursts of creativity in the several literary and art forms. Antônio Cândido (1965: 167–199) identifies five historical "moments" since 1750 when groups of writers and artists have, in community, imaginatively rendered "the social and spiritual life of São Paulo city." The two most vigorous groups were the Romantics of 1845 and the Modernists who rallied at Modern Art Week in 1922. The Romantics were law students—marginated by their society, given to amorous idealism, melancholia, sarcasm, satanism, and necrophilia—who contributed a *"paulista* tonality" to the whole of Brazilian romantic literature. The style of the Modernists has an equally strong regional accent. Their mission, however, was not to secede from urban society, which was by now complex and dynamic enough to accommodate them, but to defy academicism and cultural snobbery and to break the artistic monopoly of the élite.

Both Silva Brito (1964) in his exhaustive study of the origins of Modern Art Week and Wilson Martins (1965) in his conspectus of the Modernist movement agree upon the urban, *paulista* inspiration of Modernism. Silva Brito quotes an article of 1920 in which the *paulista* poet

Menotti del Picchia spoke of "the agitation of the great city, the great fair" and of how "the agricultural, commercial, industrial struggle with machinery and banks instead of blunderbusses chilled the nerves of our artists." The historian concludes: "Modernism at that stage is a city movement, gushing from the urban age, and, more than Brazilian, it is *paulista.*" Martins similarly emphasizes "the identification of Modernism with the city, that is, with a fact of civilization, but also with São Paulo city."

The Modernist movement, lasting until about 1945, went through several phases and split into many currents. Its primary phase reflected the impudence, iconoclasm, and experimentalism of a generation born in the 1890s, the first to be formed in the ethos of bustling commercialism and dynamic change. If, however, our preceding sociological analysis holds true—if the dynamism of the present has reworked without effacing the patriarchal heritage from the past—we would expect the post-Modernist writer to come to grips with this theme. Such is indeed the case with São Paulo's foremost contemporary playwright, Jorge Andrade, whose theater documents a personal quest for the vitalities and meanings of the old patriarchal order and their implications for the fragmented, anonymous world of today.[40]

Jorge Andrade's plays illuminate this theme precisely because he is not an "urban" playwright but takes a whole society as his subject. He perceives city energies as fermenting and eroding the old agrarian order, yet also as being dampened, deflected or turned upon themselves in a setting vaguely hostile to them. An "urban" play such a *A Escada* (The Staircase) must therefore be considered in a context with: *Pedreira das Almas* (Quarry of Souls), which turns back in history to render the archetypal ancestral family with epic, sculptural strength; *A Moratória* (The Moratorium), which catches the plantocracy at its moment of collapse, weaving an ironic temporal counterpoint between the threshold and aftermath of disaster; and *O Telescópio* (The Telescope), which shows the ideals and accomplishments of a coffee planter's family being undermined by the hedonism, slovenliness, and city-bred acquisitiveness of the young generation.

A Escada transports the generational conflict to the urban setting. Whereas *O Telescópio* measures children against the norms of their parents in the domain of the *fazenda*, the aging father and mother in *A Escada* dwell in the city, where they appear as living ghosts through the eyes of their married children. The children have made their respective adjustments to city life—save for the perplexity, guilt, and exasperation created by the sentimental burden of the past in the form of their anachronistic parents. Condescendingly, the children allow the parents their "illusions" and freedom, take turns caring for them, explain away their idiosyncrasies to outsiders. Yet the presence of the senile couple becomes cumulatively more oppressive. Their recollections and remarks and actions continually interfere with the domestic routine, personal relations and business affairs of the children's families. Oblivious to the human dramas about them, they live unreachably in a fantasy world of the past. ("The past is a monster!" one son finally cries out.) Filial duty prevents the children from following their separate interests and moving to homes of their choice. Just as the staircase linking their four adjoining apartments symbolizes the forced solidarity of the young generation, so, ironically, does it afford the parents free access to the city, where their business schemes and acts of hauteur create repeated family embarrassments. At length the children prove incapable of handling the burden of the past; they send their parents to an institution and in "great anguish" watch them depart as the curtain falls.

The tension of Jorge Andrade's theater derives not from the universal theme of generational conflict but from this unrelenting quest to locate the "reality" of his own world, and from his honest struggle with the suspicion that it may reside irrecoverably in the more solid, rounded lives of tradition and memory. This is the question, the ambivalence, the fear expressed by the son in *A Escada* who tells why he likes his parents to live with him:

> "It's as though a whole world were caught in my hands! A completely different world that we alone possess! no one else! They stay inside there, locked in . . . you only hear a murmur! And I always have the feeling that if I open this door I'll find the answer to so much that torments me . . . and I don't know just what it is! But I don't want to open it! I don't know what holds me back!"

Who then inhabits the world of fantasy? The old couple lost in reveries of the Empire? Or their children who dare not acknowledge the force and consistency of those dreams? Only the Italian nouveau riche in Jorge Andrade's comedy, *Os Ossos do Barão* (The Bones of the Baron), can relate fearlessly, generously, comprehendingly to those who "carry the caravel of Martim Afonso de Sousa on their backs." But he is an immigrant, born of another "reality." This play provides a palliative but no resolution for the tension of the playwright. His most intimate drama, *Rasto atrás* (Backtracking), suggests in fact that this resolution must be pursued on a very personal plane.

If Jorge Andrade has explored the nostalgia and ambivalences of the *haute bourgeoisie,* then—as we recall Leeds' classes and masses, or Goldman's upper and "popular" classes—it is Plínio Marcos who renders the desperate, elemental world of the *Lumpenproletariat.* His *Navalha na carne* (Razor in the Flesh) has been called a poor man's *Huis-Clos.* The single scene is a shabby hotel room where three characters—a prostitute, her pimp and a male homosexual—are trapped in a primitive drama of self-preservation. Obscenity, braggadocio, selfishness, duplicity, threats, and sadomasochism are the coin of their personal relations. When the prostitute relents for an instant, she forfeits her money and her brief interlude of sexual release with the pimp. What cripples their life is not economic deprivation, but moral infantilism. "Sometimes I even wonder," sighs the prostitute, "*pôxa,* am I really a person? Are you and I and Veludo people? I almost doubt it!"

The plays of Plínio Marcos are neither militant proletarian theater nor a theater of the absurd in a morally anarchic world. He gives us a "pre-morality play." Like the razor that flashes between pimp and whore as a surrogate for the mutuality they can never attain, so the play itself is a blade against the flesh of the larger society. Beyond even this, it bares the stubborn core of yearning, fright and egotism that lies beneth the masks of Everyman.[41]

A literary reconstruction of the city should compose such strokes of the private imagination against a generalized, anonymous image from its popular culture. Mário de Andrade (1942: 26–28) referred to the latter in explaining why the Modernist movement exploded in São Paulo rather than the nation's capital. São Paulo, he wrote, was the "highland *caipira* who has preserved till now a servile, provincial spirit" yet who, because of his commercialism and industrialism, lived "in more spiritual and technical contact with the realities of the world." In São Paulo there was a classic bourgeoisie to be shocked. Rio had the cosmopolitanism and "vibrant malice" of a port city and national capital, fused with folkloric exoticism and "a traditional, arrested character"—a blend less conducive to cultural revolution.

The folklore studies of Florestan Fernandes (1961: 9–35) confirm this characterization of São Paulo. He finds that the style of urban life developed "in a convergence of cultural legacies somewhat alien to the old rural tradition that had dominated the city." There was less continuity here than in Rio, Salvador, or Recife between inherited and imported cultural forms. Disparaged for its rusticity and provincialism, *paulista* folklore could not accompany the evolution of the city to become a true "urban folklore." Research yields only "residues of the old inherited traditions which managed to survive the general liquidation of the disdained rural past." Fernandes predicts not the eventual emergence of a coherent body of urban folklore, but a pluralistic reworking of traditional themes, assisted by technology and mass media (newspapers, recordings, radio, television) and serving diverse functional uses in such areas as recreation, relations with the supernatural, or ethical and esthetic guidance.

The confluence of folk and highbrow currents which produced the São Paulo school of samba in the 1960s sharpens our image of the cultural personality of the city. According to Regis (1966) the internationalism and technical sophistication of bossa nova created problems of self-trained composers and led in 1964 to the appearance of three distinct schools of samba in Salvador, Rio, and São Paulo. Although there is continual exchange among these schools, their local inspiration differs. The Bahian samba reflects systematic research into folkloric traditions. It is a samba "forged close to the roots," liberated from classical forms, bringing freshness and originality to the national musical scene. The Rio samba (*samba de morro, samba de carnaval*) is also of popular inspiration but has explored social and agrarian themes at an ideological level. Folk and highbrow music had not found their synthesis here as of 1966, partly because of the composers' immaturity, partly because of the city's limited facilities for reaching a mass audience. Consumption of good popular music tended still to be an upper-class privilege.

São Paulo has more fully developed mass media than Rio (television, press, promotional organizations) and more ample facilities for bringing performances direct to a democratic public of workers and students. The environment encourages dialogue between an intellectual composer and his mass audience. Chico Buarque de Holanda is the prototype of the contemporary *paulista* musician; the fact that he composes from a narrower base of folkloric research than the Bahian group is compensated "by the depth of his general vision of the diverse cultures of Brazil." Regis (1966) ascribes his success to his ability to blend an educated middle-class outlook with the culture of the university intelligentsia and produce a music which is popular in fact as well as in name, "which can be and is sung by the people in their daily life and has possibilities for pleasing and illuminating that people."[42]

With Kubler (1964), then, we can give the term "metropolis" cultural as well as ecological definition. It is a city having a distinctive ethos which imbues without circumscribing its cultural expression. It originates styles, ideas, and expressive forms because as a window both to a regional or national culture and to the world it performs a task of innovative mediation. São Paulo is assuming such a role, and one may expect its cultural self-definition to affect and be affected by the perception of problems in the political, economic and social orders. This indeed is the burden of the "confession" of Mário de Andrade (1942: 79–80), the high priest of São Paulo's Modernist movement:

> "I feel that the modernists of Modern Art Week should serve as an example to no one. But we can provide a lesson. Man is passing through an integrally political phase of humanity. . . . And despite our contemporaneity, our nationalism, our universalism, there is one thing we didn't take part in: the politico-social betterment of man. And this is the very meaning of our times."

In retrospect the self-criticism seems unduly harsh, for the achievement of the Modernists was to democratize the arts and revitalize their cultural roots. This, surely, is a *sine qua non* for "the politico-social betterment of man."

NOTES

1. 1567–1821: belated founding; base for expansion and consolidation of settlement; precarious existence; hierarchical society; accrual of bureaucratic functions.

1821–1864: survival of colonial "morphology" and "dynamic"; gradual changes in physical appearance and life tempo.

1864–1900: superficial transformation into a "little Paris" under Guzmán Blanco, followed by a new "hibernation."

1900–1945: quickening of city life; strengthening of urban bourgeoisie; impact of oil wealth; city bursts its spatial perimeter; nation's industrial capital after 1929.

1945–   : violent, disarticulated metropolitan growth; heavy in-migration; anarchic real-estate speculation; the hypertrophic capital threatens national stability.

2. Taunay's history of São Paulo (1953), covering the period 1554 to 1920, is too diffuse for schematization; he does, however, call the years 1701 to 1821 a time of "stagnation and decadence." Petrone (1968) supports Leite de Barros with her conclusion that from 1765 to 1851 sugar-growing linked the São Paulo region to the world market and created an infrastructure (transportation and commercial facilities, investment capital) for the coffee economy.

3. A century ago at the start of the coffee boom one observer predicted that "Santos will be the great commercial emporium of São Paulo [province]" (Godoy, 1869: 4–15).

4. Strictly speaking, *paulistas* are inhabitants of São Paulo state, *paulistanos* of the city.

5. For a full description of the *espigão* see Azevedo (1958: I, 183–195).

6. Delgado (1968) estimates that by 1980, squatters will account for 40 percent of the Lima-Callao population.

7. The *cortiço,* generally located in the inner city, takes three typical forms: the humid, unventilated *porão* (basement), the *meia-agua* (U-shaped cluster of ten or fifteen one-room dwellings around a narrow court), and the *andar superior* (rented room in a converted mansion). For earlier descriptions see Teles (1940–41) and Relatorio (1894).

8. Moreover, while a Lima *barriada* is often formed by an invasion of inner-city slum-dwellers acquainted with city ways, the *paulista favela* tends to be a reception camp for rural and semirural migrants. (Goldman, 1965: 526)

9. Lowe (1969) gives a preview of the São Paulo master plan initiated in 1967 by the vigorous mayor, José Vicente de Faria Lima.

10. The three next-largest cities dropped off to populations (as of 1964) of 271,267 (Santos), 249,264 (Campinas) and 159,560 (Ribeirão Prêto).

11. Of São Paulo state's industrial workers 59.1 percent were located in the state capital in 1947 and only 54.8 percent in 1964 (Crespo, 1968: 79).

12. The *paulista* urban system is described in IBGE (1957–64: esp. XI, 136–184), Geiger (1963: 249–273), and Azevedo (1966). Serviço Estadual de Planejamento (1964) assembles statistics for a comprehensive state development plan.

13. This point is expanded elsewhere (Morse, 1968).

14. Although Haller claims no universal validity for his findings, which apply to the rural zone of Rio, his methods would presumably yield similar results for the São Paulo hinterland.

15. Cândido distinguishes the *caipira,* a small landholder living in an isolated, mutual-aid neighborhood community, from the *caboclo,* typically of Indian descent and showing a tendency to social parasitism and anomie.

16. Pereira (1967: 16–32) confirms that the 1950s witnessed a "qualitative change in the industrial park" marked by mechanization, renovation, a jump in

per capita production, heavy capitalization, and a shift from traditional manufactures to electrical, communications and transportation equipment.

Industrial Indices for São Paulo state

year	No. of workers (index)	Value of production adjusted for inflation (index)
1939/40	100.0	100.0
1949/50	179.0	176.9
1958	233.0	329.4

17. Hopkins' study (1968) of late-nineteenth-century Atlanta, Georgia, shows that foreign immigrants were about as mobile as native whites and much more mobile than Negroes. In São Paulo one surmises that immigrants were advantaged over natives of all races, which gives special bite to the phrase "racial democracy" often applied to Brazil.

18. Leeds' research (1965) was conducted in six cities including São Paulo.

19. Lambert (1965) and Mattelart-Garretón (1965) state the case for Latin America. For more perceptive, rounded discussions, see Higgins (1967), Friedmann-Lackington (1967), Cardoso-Reyna (1968).

20. See also Bazzanella (1963) and J. A. Rodrigues (1959).

21. Silva (1967) describes typical occupational paths leading the migrant and his children toward absorption into the urban work force. An atypical path is that of Carolina M. de Jesus, an ex-*favelada* whose now-classic diary (1960) relates how she kept her family alive by collecting old newspapers in the streets; once her book became a best seller she moved into a brick house and wrote the sequel (1961). Sarno (1967) presents some more conventional life histories. Ferrari (1959) describes cultural adaptations of immigrants from northeast Brazil.

22. Germani (1966: 233–252) makes a similar comparative analysis for Buenos Aires. Touraine's argument is generalized for Latin America by Faletto (1964).

23. Crespo (1968) contrasts the behavior of São Paulo's predominantly foreign proletariat of the pre-1930 period with the subsequent behavior of native-born in-migrants. For histories of São Paulo's proletariat see Dias (1962), L. Rodrigues (1966), and Simão (1966).

24. Ferrari (1962: 171) contrasts the rural *cabo eleitoral* of northeast Brazil with the urban version encountered by migrants to São Paulo. See also Pearse (1961).

25. A. and E. Leeds (1967) insist on "the essentially urban character of the experience and values of *favela* and *barriada* residents."

26. Debrun (1964) observes that Weffort sees populist nationalism as being of petty-bourgeois inspiration and aimed at the radical incorporation of the masses into the national polity, while Ianni (1963) sees it serving the needs of the urban industrial bourgeoisie by soothing the political conscience of the proletariat and restraining the process of politicization. Cardoso's recent analysis (1968a), which takes post-1964 developments into account, suggests a transitional, more complex situation, while his Argentine comparison (1968b) helps clarify the Brazilian case.

27. The analysis of a two-stage "bourgeois revolution" (1875–1930, 1930–   ) is expanded in Fernandes (1968: 107–199).

28. Queiroz (1965) generalizes the thesis of weak class-identifications of Brazilian society as a whole.

29. From his study of family patterns in São Paulo, Rosen (1962: 623) concludes: "And submission in the form of ingratiation and obedience is the dominant adjustment to authority in Brazil."

30. By "classes" Leeds (1965: 395) does not mean integrated, self-conscious strata "for which the Marxian term 'class' would be appropriate."

31. By calling the barrier between classes and masses impermeable, Leeds virtually

reverses the opinion of Beals (1953: 334), who found only "mild" breaching of barriers between middle and upper classes in urban Brazil and increasing mobility from lower to middle. Goldman (1965: 530) confirms Leeds when he finds greater social distance between the upper-middle and lower-middle class in São Paulo than between the lower-middle and the "urban popular'" class. In effect, he claims, there are only two "clearly visible" classes, the upper-middle and the "popular," which supports the "polarization" thesis advanced by Morse (1965: 63) and Soares (1967: 41).

32. The immigrant-led socialist organizations and strikes of *paulista* workers in the early twentieth century were apparently no more effective in creating permanent "class" ideology and militancy than the Negro protest movements aimed toward the "Second Abolition" in the period 1927–1945.

33. Cardoso (1961: 163) does however hint that "rationality" requires comparative cultural definition, while Cardoso-Reyna (1968) criticize the "dual" or "polar" mode of sociological analysis.

34. Hoetink (1965) and Soares (1967) have criticized "unilinear" evolutionary frameworks for Latin American development, although Soares emphasizes structural and international factors, while my discussion below emphasizes cultural and psychological ones.

35. Rosen's Brazilian data came from the capital and interior of São Paulo state, Kahl's from Rio de Janeiro and small towns in Minas Gerais and Rio Grande do Sul.

36. For which he sheepishly apologized in advance (Kahl, 1959: 74).

37. Fernandes (1964: 629), for example, finds that Catholic morality is more suited to coating the pill of prejudice with artifices and rationalizations than to effecting a reform of attitudes and social organization.

38. "Further, just as the objectification of the Church was achieved in connection with the feudal society of the Early Middle Ages, the reappearance of the tendency to form sects was connected with the social transformation, and the new developments of city-civilization in the central period of the Middle Ages and in its period of decline—with the growth of individualism and the gathering of masses of people in the towns themselves—and with the reflex effect of this city formation upon the rural population and the aristocracy" (Troeltsch, 1960: I, 343).

39. Dore (1964) has perceptively developed the Japanese-Latin American comparison.

40. In this sense Jorge Andrade's plays recapitulate the dominant motif of Gilberto Freyre's work; but whereas Freyre's sentimental and psychological ambivalences remain largely subliminal, Jorge Andrade persistently objectifies his in dramatic form.

41. Jorge Andrade's one "proletarian" play (*Vereda da salvação,* Path of Salvation) deals with rural workers. Although more deprived and, in the conventional sense, exploited than the threesome in *Navalha* (indeed, they are finally massacred), their tiny community still has reference points in the social order and in the cosmos. Political, moral, and religious options are available and indeed must be exercised.

42. Galvão (1968) criticizes the lack of ideological content of the contemporary samba, especially Chico Buarque's compositions. They offer consolation and fraternity, she observes, only for the duration of the song; the message is one of fatalism and scepticism.

REFERENCES

ANDRADE, JORGE (1960) *Pedreira das Almas; O telescópio.* Rio de Janeiro.
———— (1964) *A escada; Os ossos do Barão.* São Paulo.
———— (1965a) *A moratória.* 2nd ed. Rio de Janeiro.

—— (1965b) *Vereda dá salvação.* São Paulo.

—— (1967) *Rasto atrás.* São Paulo.

ANDRADE, MÁRIO DE (1942) *O movimento modernista.* Rio de Janeiro.

ANTÔNIO, JOÃO (1966) "Inquérito: o romance urbano." *Revista Civilização Brasileira,* 1, No. 7: 190–220.

AZEVEDO, AROLDO DE (1958) *A cidade de São Paulo, estudos de geografia urbana.* 4 vols. São Paulo.

—— (1966) "A rêde urbana paulista," pp. 65–75 in Ernani Silva Bruno (ed.) *São Paulo terra e povo.* Pôrto Alegre.

BALÁN, JORGE (1969) "Migrant-native socioeconomic differences in Latin American cities: a structural analysis," *Latin American Research Review* 4, No. 1: 3–51.

BARROS, GILBERTO LEITE DE (1967) *A cidade e o planalto, processo de dominância da cidade de São Paulo.* 2 vols. São Paulo.

BASTIDE, ROGER and FLORESTAN FERNANDES (1955) *Relações raciais entre negros e brancos em São Paulo.* São Paulo.

BASTIDE, ROGER and PIERRE VAN DEN BERGHE (1957) "Stereotypes, norms and interracial behavior in São Paulo, Brazil." *American Sociological Review* 22, No. 6: 689–694.

BAZZANELLA, WALDEMIRO (1963) "Industrialização e urbanização no Brasil." *América Latina* 6, No. 1: 3–27.

BEALS, RALPH L. (1953) "Social stratification in Latin America." *American Journal of Sociology* 58, No. 4: 327–339.

BRITO, MÁRIO DA SILVA (1964) *História do modernismo brasileiro: I, Antecedentes da Semana de Arte Moderna.* 2nd ed. Rio de Janeiro.

BRUNO, ERNANI SILVA (1954) *História e tradições da cidade de São Paulo.* 2nd ed. 3 vols. Rio de Janeiro.

CAMARGO, CÂNDIDO PROCÓPIO FERREIRA DE (1961a) *Aspectos sociológicos del espiritismo en São Paulo.* Freiburg and Bogotá.

—— (1961b) *Kardecismo e Umbanda, uma interpretação sociológica.* São Paulo.

CAMARGO, JOSÉ FRANCISCO DE (1968) *A cidade e o campo, o êxodo rural no Brasil.* Rio de Janeiro.

CÂNDIDO, ANTÔNIO (1964) *Os parceiros do Rio Bonito, estudo sôbre o caipira paulista e a transformação dos seus meios de vida.* Rio de Janeiro.

—— (1965) *Literatura e sociedade.* São Paulo.

CARDOSO, FERNANDO HENRIQUE (1960a) "Proletariado e mudança social em São Paulo." *Sociologia* 22, No. 1: 3–11.

—— (1960b) "O café e a industrialização da cidade de São Paulo." *Revista de História* 20, No. 42: 471–475. São Paulo.

—— (1961) "Condições e fatôres sociais da industrialização de São Paulo." *Revista Brasileira de Estudos Políticos* 11: 148–163.

—— (1962) "Proletariado no Brasil: situação e comportamento social." *Revista Brasiliense* 41: 98–122.

—— (1963) *El empresario industrial en América Latina, 2, Brasil.* Economic Commission for Latin America, E/CN.12/642/Add. 2, Feb. 10.

—— (1964) *Empresário industrial e desenvolvimento econômico.* São Paulo.

—— (1965) "The structure and evolution of industry in São Paulo: 1930–1960." *Studies in Comparative International Development* 1, No. 5: 43–47.

——— (1968a) "Hegemonia burguesa e independência econômica: raízes estruturais da crise política brasileira." *Revista Civilização Brasileira* 4, No. 17: 67–95.

——— (1968b) *Política e desenvolvimento em sociedades dependentes: ideologias do empresariado industrial argentino e brasileiro.* São Paulo.

CARDOSO, FERNANDO HENRIQUE and JOSÉ LUIS REYNA (1968) "Industrialization, occupational structure, and social stratification in Latin America," pp. 19–55 in Cole Blasier (ed.) *Constructive Change in Latin America.* Pittsburgh.

CARRERA DAMAS, GERMÁN (1967) "Principales momentos del desarrollo histórico de Caracas." *Estudio de Caracas* (Caracas: Universidad Central de Caracas) 2, No. 1: 23–102.

COSTA, LUIZ CARLOS and LÚCIO FREDERICO KOWARICK (1963) "Estudos da Bacia Paraná-Uruguai: aspectos demográficos e desenvolvimento." *Sociologia* 25, No. 4: 345–397.

CRESPO, MAURÍCIO (1968) "Proletariado brasileiro e seu comportamento político." *II Colóquio de Estudos Luso-Brasileiros, Anais:* 68–88. Tokyo.

DEAN, WARREN (1964) São Paulo's industrial elite, 1890–1960. Ph.D. dissertation, University of Florida. (Revised as *The Industrialization of São Paulo 1880–1945.* Austin, Texas, 1969.)

——— (1966) "The planter as entrepreneur: the case of São Paulo." *The Hispanic American Historical Review* 46, No. 2: 138–152.

DEBRUN, MICHEL (1964) "Nationalisme et politiques du développement au Brésil." *Sociologie du Travail* 6, Nos. 3 and 4: 235–257, 351–380.

DELGADO, CARLOS (1968) *Tres planteamientos en torno a problemas de urbanización acelerada en áreas metropolitanas: el caso de Lima.* CIDU, Universidad Católica de Chile. Santiago (mimeo.).

DELORENZO NETO, A. (1967) *O município de capital São Paulo e a região metropolitana.* Osasco, São Paulo.

DIAS, EVERARDO (1962) *História das lutas sociais no Brasil.* São Paulo.

DI TELLA, TORCUATO S. (1965) "Populism and reform in Latin America." In Claudio Véliz, ed. *Obstacles to Change in Latin America.* London.

DORE, R. P. (1964) "Latin America and Japan compared," pp. 227–249 in John J. Johnson (ed.) *Continuity and Change in Latin America.* Stanford.

——— (1965) *City Life in Japan.* Berkeley and Los Angeles.

DURKHEIM, ÉMILE (1933) *Division of Labor in Society.* New York.

FALETTO, ENZO (1964) *Incorporación de los sectores obreros al proceso de desarrollo.* Economic Commission for Latin America document. Santiago.

FERNANDES, FLORESTAN (1961) *Folclore e mudança social na cidade de São Paulo.* São Paulo.

——— (1964) *A integração do negro à sociedade de classes.* São Paulo. (English edition: *The Negro in Brazilian Society.* New York, 1969).

——— (1968) *Sociedade de classes e subdesenvolvimento.* Rio de Janeiro.

FERRARI, ALFONSO TRUJILLO (1959) *Movimientos migratorios internos y problemas de acomodación del inmigrante nacional en São Paulo* [Brasil]. UN document General E/CN.12/URB/12, UNESCO/SS/URB/LA/12.

——— (1962) "Atitude e comportamento político do imigrante nordestino em São Paulo." *Sociologia* 24, No. 3: 159–180.

FRIEDMANN, JOHN and TOMÁS LACKINGTON (1967) "Hyperurbanization and national development in Chile: some hypotheses." *Urban Affairs Quarterly* 2, No. 4: 3–29.

GALVÃO, WALNICE NOGUEIRA (1968) "MMPB: uma análise ideológica." *aParte* 2: 18–31.

GAUTHIER, HOWARD L. (1968) "Transportation and the growth of the São Paulo economy." *Journal of Regional Science* 8, No. 1: 77–94.

GEIGER, PEDRO PINCHAS (1963) *Evolução da rêde urbana brasileira*. Rio de Janeiro.

GERMANI, GINO (1966) *Política y sociedad en una época de transición*. Buenos Aires.

GODOY, JOAQUIM FLORIANO DE (1869) *Ligação do valle do Parahyba á via ferrea de Santos*. Rio de Janeiro.

GOLDMAN, FRANK PERRY (1965) "Big metrópole, América do Sul." *Journal of Inter-American Studies* 7, No. 4: 519–540.

HALLER, ARCHIBALD O. (1967) "Urban economic growth and changes in rural stratification: Rio de Janeiro 1953–1962." *América Latina* 10, No. 4: 48–67.

HIGGINS, BENJAMIN (1967) "Urbanization, industrialization, and economic development," pp. 117–155 in Glenn H. Beyer (ed.) *The Urban Explosion in Latin America*. Ithaca, N.Y.

HOETINK, HARRY (1965) "El nuevo evolucionismo." *América Latina* 8, No. 4: 26–42.

HOPKINS, RICHARD J. (1968) "Occupational and social mobility in Atlanta, 1870–1896." *The Journal of Southern History* 34, No. 2: 200–213.

HUTCHINSON, BERTRAM (1958) *Conditions of immigrant assimilation in urban Brazil*. UN document GENERAL E/CN.12/URB/13. Santiago.

——— (1960) *Mobilidade e trabalho, um estudo na cidade de São Paulo*. Rio de Janeiro.

IANNI, OCTÁVIO (1963) *Industrialização e desenvolvimento social no Brasil*. Rio de Janeiro.

Instituto Brasileiro de Geografia e Estatística (IBGE) (1957–64) *Enciclopédia dos municípios brasileiros*. 32 vols. Rio de Janeiro.

JESUS, CAROLINA MARIA DE (1960) *Quarto de despejo, diário de uma favelada*. 8th ed. São Paulo. English edition: *Child of the Dark, the Diary of Carolina Maria de Jesus*. New York, 1962.

——— (1961) *Casa de alvenaria, diário de uma ex-favelada*. Rio de Janeiro.

KAHL, JOSEPH A. (1959) "Some social concomitants of industrialization and urbanization." *Human Organization* 18, No. 2: 53–74.

——— (1968) *The Measurement of Modernism, a Study of Values in Brazil and Mexico*. Austin, Texas.

KUBLER, GEORGE A. (1964) "Cities and culture in the colonial period in Latin America." *Diogenes* 47: 53–62.

LAGENEST, H.-D. BARRUEL DE (1962) "Os cortiços de São Paulo." *Anhembi* 12, No. 139: 5–17.

LAMBERT, DENIS (1965) "L'urbanisation accélérée de l'Amérique Latine et la formation d'un secteur tetiaire refugé." *Civilisations* 15, No. 2–4: 158–174, 309–325, 477–492.

LEEDS, ANTHONY (1965) "Brazilian careers and social structure, a case history and model." Pp. 379–404 in D. B. Heath and R. N. Adams (eds.) *Contemporary Cultures and Societies of Latin America*. New York.

LEEDS, ANTHONY and ELIZABETH LEEDS (1967) "Brazil and the myth of urban rurality: urban experience, work, and values in 'squatments' of Rio de Janeiro and Lima." Paper for Conference on Urbanization and Work in Modernizing Societies, St. Thomas, V. I.

LOPES, JUAREZ RUBENS BRANDÃO (1964) *Sociedade industrial no Brasil*. São Paulo.

——— (1966) "Some basic developments in Brazilian politics and society." Pp. 59–77 in E. N. Baklanoff (ed.) *New Perspectives of Brazil*. Nashville, Tenn.

LOWE, ARBON JACK (1969) "São Paulo 1990." *Américas* 21, No. 1: 28–31.

MARCOS, PLÍNIO (1968) *A navalha na carne*. São Paulo.

MARTINS, WILSON (1965) *O modernismo*. São Paulo.

MATTELART, ARMAND and MANUEL A. GARRETÓN (1965) *Integración nacional y marginalidad, ensayo de regionalización de Chile*. Santiago.

MOMSEN, RICHARD P., JR. (1964) *Routes over the Serra do Mar*. Rio de Janeiro.

MORAZÉ, CHARLES (1954) *Les trois âges du Brésil, essai de politique*. Paris.

MORSE, RICHARD M. (1954) *De comunidade a metrópole, biografia de São Paulo*. São Paulo. (Revised ed.: *Formação histórica de São Paulo*. São Paulo, 1970.)

——— (1958) *From Community to Metropolis, A Biography of São Paulo. Brazil*. Gainesville, Florida.

———(1965) "Recent research on Latin American urbanization: a selective survey with commentary." *Latin American Research Review* 1, No. 1: 35–74.

——— (1968) "Planning, History, Politics." Paper for the Seminar on Social Science and Urban Development in Latin America. Jahuel, Chile. In R. A. Gakenheimer and J. Miller (eds.) *Latin American Urban Policies and the Social Sciences*. Beverly Hills: Sage Publications, forthcoming.

NOGUEIRA, ORACY (1955) "Preconceito racial de marca e preconceito racial de origem." *Anhembi* 5, No. 53: 279–299.

PEARSE, ANDREW (1961) "Some characteristics of urbanization in the city of Rio de Janeiro." Pp. 191–205 in Philip M. Hauser (ed.) *Urbanization in Latin America*. New York.

PEREIRA, JOSÉ CARLOS (1967) *Estrutura e expansão da indústria em São Paulo*. São Paulo.

PETRONE, MARIA THEREZA SCHORER (1968) *A lavoura canavieira em São Paulo, expansão e declínio (1765–1851)*. São Paulo.

PINHO, DIVA BENAVIDES (1964) *Cooperativismo e desenvolvimento das zonas rurais do Estado de São Paulo*. São Paulo.

QUEIROZ, MARIA ISAURA PEREIRA DE (1965) "Les classes sociales dans le Brésil actuel." *Cahiers Internationaux de Sociologie*, 39: 137–169.

REGIS, FLÁVIO EDUARDO DE MACEDO SOARES (1966) "A nova geração do samba." *Revista Civilização Brasileira* 1, No. 7: 364–374.

Relatorio apresentado á Câmara Municipal de São Paulo pelo Intendente Municipal Cesario Ramalho da Silva, 1893. (1894) São Paulo.

"Resumo do estudo da estrutura urbana de São Paulo." (1958) *Cuadernos Latinoamericanos de Economía Humana* 1, No. 3: 268–295.

RODRIGUES, JOSÉ ALBERTINO (1959) "Condições econômico sociais da mão de obra em São Paulo," *Anhembi* 35, No. 103: 44–63.

RODRIGUES, LEÔNCIO (1966) *Conflito industrial e sindicalismo no Brasil.* São Paulo.

ROSEN, BERNARD C. (1962) "Socialization and achievement motivation in Brazil." *American Sociological Review* 27, No. 5: 612–624.

SAIA, LUIZ (1963) "Notas para a teorização de São Paulo." *Acrópole* 25, Nos. 295/6: 209–221.

――― (1966) "A arquitetura em São Paulo." Pp. 229–251 in Ernani Silva Bruno (ed.) *São Paulo terra e povo.* Pôrto Alegre.

SANSON, LOUIS ROMERO (1950) "Contribuição para oestudo do aproveitamento da zona de lagos de São Paulo." *Anhembi* 1, No. 1: 117–124.

SARNO, GERALDO (1967) "Três emigrantes em São Paulo." *Teoria e Prática* 1: 121–130.

Serviço Estadual de Planejamento, Estado de São Paulo (1964) "Pladi," Plano de Desenvolvimento Integrado, 1964–1966. São Paulo.

SILVA, ARMANDO CORRÊA DA (1967) "Estrutura e mobilidade social do proletariado urbano em São Paulo." *Revista Civilização Brasileira* 3, No. 13: 57–90.

SIMÃO, AZIS (1966) *Sindicato e estado, suas relações na formação do proletariado de São Paulo.* São Paulo.

SMITH, M. G. (1955) *A Framework for Caribbean Studies.* Mona, Jamaica.

SOARES, GLAUCIO ARY DILLON (1967) "A nova industrialização e o sistema político brasileiro." *Dados* 2/3: 32–50.

TAUNAY, AFONSO D'E (1953) *História da cidade de São Paulo.* São Paulo.

TELES, GUIOMAR URBINA (1940–41) "O problema do cortiço." *Serviço social* 2–3, Nos. 23–27.

TOURAINE, ALAIN (1961) "Industrialisation et conscience ouvrière à São-Paulo." *Sociologie du Travail* 3, No. 4: 77–95.

TOURAINE, ALAIN and DANIEL PÉCAUT (1967–68) "Working-class consciousness and economic development in Latin America." *Studies in Comparative International Development* 3, No. 4: 71–84.

TROELTSCH, ERNST (1960) *The Social Teachings of the Christian Churches.* 2 vols. New York.

WARREN, DONALD, JR. (1968) "Spiritism in Brazil." *Journal of Inter-American Studies* 10, No. 3: 393–405.

WEBER, MAX (1964) *The Sociology of Religion.* Boston.

WEFFORT, FRANCISCO (1965a) "Raízes sociais do populismo em São Paulo." *Revista Civilização Brasileira* 1, No. 2: 39–60.

――― (1965b) "Política de massas." Pp. 159–198 in Octávio Ianni *et al. Política e revolução social no Brasil.* Rio de Janeiro.

――― (1966) "State and Mass in Brazil." *Studies in Comparative International Development* 2, No. 12: 187–196.

WILHEIM, JORGE (1965) *São Paulo metrópole 65.* São Paulo.

WILLEMS, EMÍLIO (1966) "Religious movements and social change in Brazil." Pp. 205–232 in E. N. Baklanoff (ed.) *New Perspectives of Brazil.* Nashville, Tenn.

――― (1967) *Followers of the New Faith, Culture Change and the Rise of Protestantism in Brazil and Chile.* Nashville, Tenn.

The following important items were consulted too late for use in preparing this study:

BERLINCK, MANOEL TOSTA (1969) *The Structure of the Brazilian Family in the City of São Paulo*. Cornell University Latin American Studies Program Dissertation Series 12. Ithaca, New York.

MARCÍLIO, MARIA LUIZA (1968) *La ville de São Paulo, peuplement et population 1750–1850*. Rouen, France.

Prefeitura do Município de São Paulo, Grupo Executivo do Planejamento (1970) *Plan Urbanístico básico*. 6 vols. São Paulo.

Secretaria da Economia e Planejamento, GEGRAM (Grupo Executivo da Grande São Paulo) (1969) *Diagnóstico definitivo, análise macroeconômica da região da Grande São Paulo*. 3 vols. São Paulo.

SINGER, PAUL (1968) *Desenvolvimento econômico e evolução urbana (análise da evolução econômica de São Paulo, Blumenau, Pôrto Alegre, Belo Horizonte e Recife)*. São Paulo.

SOUZA, BEATRIZ MUNIZ DE (1969) *A experiência da salvação, Pentecostais em São Paulo*. São Paulo.

SOUZA, HEITOR FERREIRA DE (1968) *Área metropolitana de São Paulo*. São Paulo.

WILHEIM, JORGE (1969) *Urbanismo no subdesenvolvimento*. Rio de Janeiro.

PART III

GOVERNMENT

INSTITUTIONS

AND

DECISION-MAKING

Chapter 8

THE DECISION-MAKING PROCESS IN SAN SALVADOR

ROLAND H. EBEL

THE ROLE OF LOCAL GOVERNMENT IN
LATIN AMERICAN POLITICS

For Juan Gómez it is in the community and not in the nation where things happen. The *plaza*, bordered by church, market, and town hall, competes only with the *cantina*, the soccer field, and the cemetery as the focus of his life. And while the better-educated urbanite enjoys a wider vista, for many city people the *barrio* or the *barranco* (shantytown) pretty largely fills their horizon. Ultimately, whether for a cosmopolite or a parochial, the services which lighten the day and enliven the night are largely local in character. Sewage and water, light and power, transportation, recreation, and justice emanate from City Hall.

Although the Latin American municipality is weak, it is not unimportant. Urban centers are growing at the rate of 6 percent per year and they generate most of their countries' education wealth, skill, art, and crime. And while the attention of North Americans has been upon the succession of unstable governments at the national level, the "revolution of rising expectations," which is the most current and widely-held explanation of this instability is, within the nations themselves, concerned largely with the price of bus fares or the deteriorating state of the municipal vegetable market—matters of predominantly local concern.

Thus, although unrecognized by most observers, community politics is at the heart of national politics. For one thing, Latin American political systems are made up of local and regional systems capped by the political network of the capital city which is a political entity in its own right.

AUTHOR'S NOTE: This research was made possible by a Tulane-Ford Research Grant, summer, 1967.

That is, although most of the members of the metropolitan political élite are concerned with national issues and are working within national governmental and political institutions, the loyalties and rivalries, interests and issues involved are those of the city. In other words, much of what passes as national politics has to do primarily with the concerns of the capital city. This is particularly true in the smaller countries of the area which contain "primate cities"—single urban agglomerations which monopolize the political, economic, cultural, and social resources of the nation and serve as the center of these activities.

This essay will describe the political decision-making process in a primate city of Latin America. The primary focus will be on the city as a political system in its own right.[1] Considerable attention will also be paid to the relationships between national and local political institutions and processes; that is, the role played by national governmental institutions in municipal decision-making and the place of the city's political organizations in the national political structure. The study is based upon an investigation of sixteen issues or problems confronting the municipal government of San Salvador between 1964 and 1967.[2]

FORMAL GOVERNMENTAL ORGANIZATION

The city of San Salvador, as is true of the municipalities of Latin America, has a very ambiguous juridical status. That is, the Constitution of 1962 does not make clear whether the Salvadoran municipality is considered to be solely an administrative unit of the nation or an autonomous corporation with sufficient power to act in response to local needs. The relevant constitutional clauses are contradictory. Article 105, for example, states that "The law shall specify the powers of the municipal councils, *which shall be purely economic and administrative.*"[3] (Italics mine). Section 2, however, states that "The municipal councils are *autonomous* in the exercise of their functions." In similar fashion, the constitution grants to municipal councils the power "to administer their resources for the benefit of the community . . ." (Article 104) but requires that schedules of local taxes "be submitted to the Legislative Assembly for enactment as laws, and that body may make any changes deemed necessary" (Article 105).

One expert on Salvadoran municipal law solves the problem by stating that although the legal philosophy underlying the juridical status of the municipality was based upon the idea of simple administrative decentralization, the specific constitutional dispositions permit the *municipios* both to serve as instruments for the development of their populations through the exploitation of their own resources and to do this through the electoral process (Chávez Mena, 1966). The specific constitutional dispositions upon which this conclusion is based are (1) the right of the citizen to elect town councils (Article 103, Sec. 2); (2) the power of the councils to appoint their own officials (Article 106); and (3) the prohibitions against the absorbing of municipal funds into the general treasury of the nation (Article 104, Sec. 1).

The problem is compounded further by the broad grant of powers and responsibilities to local government by the National Municipal Law (Ley del Ramo Municipal). Under Article 50 of this law, the municipality is responsible, among other things, to collect municipal revenues, to maintain public order, to construct and repair streets, to regulate transactions in the municipal markets, to promote primary education including the construction and maintenance of schools and libraries, to publish books and notebooks and diffuse "useful knowledge," to promote institutions to improve public morality, to promote commerce, to maintain public transportation, to regulate the use of roads, streets and bridges relative to subsurface drains, power lines and automobiles, to maintain nocturnal pharmaceutical services, to establish *Juntas de Sanidad* to protect public health, to maintain a *registro civil* (births, deaths, weddings, and so forth) and a *registro cívico* (voter list), to protect the forests, to notarize contracts between individuals and to enact such ordinances and regulations as are deemed useful or required by the civil code.

Whatever the exact constitutional position of Salvadoran municipalities, the powers and duties delegated by the National Municipal Law, or the theoretical views of the proponents of municipal autonomy, the fact remains that in actual practice, San Salvador's decision-making system is inextricably intertwined with that of the nation. This is to be seen, first of all, in the area of fiscal policy where the Ley del Ramo Municipal requires that the national executive (usually the Ministry of the Interior) approve all loans for public works, all sales or donations of municipal property, all expenditures of over $2250.00 (until 1965, the maximum amount under the control of San Salvador was $450.00) and all contracts in excess of $2250.00.[4] Furthermore, all changes in the city's tax schedule require the approval of the Legislative Assembly.[5]

If strict fiscal controls are one side of the coin of municipal dependency, the role of the central government in many of the city's services is the other. Of the 21 services investigated (see Table 1) only two (street cleaning and street nomenclature) were totally in the hands of the municipality. Five services (sewers and drainage, traffic control, telecommunications, the airport and provision of public school faculty) were the sole responsibility of an agency of the central government, and two (bus transportation and water) were the joint responsibility of the central government and a private company and an international lending agency respectively. The municipality and a national agency shared in providing ten city services while street lighting and the educational plant were undertaken by the municipality, the central government and a private and/or international agency. Finally, fire protection was provided by a volunteer organization. Six services involve three or more agencies in some aspect of

Table 1. Responsibility of Governmental Agencies for Municipal Services in San Salvador

TYPE OF GOVERNMENTAL ACTIVITY

Service	*Planning*	*Financing*	*Const. & Maint.*	*Admin. & Reg.*
1. Water	ANDA	ANDA BID	ANDA	ANDA
2. Police	Int. Mpl.	Int. Mpl.	Int. Mpl.	Int. Mpl.
3. Public transportation	Trans.	Priv.	Priv.	Trans.
4. Streets	DUA Mpl.	DUA Mpl.	DUA Mpl.	DUA Mpl.
5. Street nomenclature	Mpl.	Mpl.	Mpl.	Mpl.
6. Street cleaning	Mpl.	Mpl.	Mpl.	Mpl.
7. Street lighting	Mpl. CAESS CNP	BNR CAESS Mpl.	CAESS	Mpl.
8. Drainage	ANDA SP	ANDA	ANDA	ANDA SP
9. Fire protection	Vol.	Vol.	Vol.	Vol.
10. Telephones	ANTEL	ANTEL	ANTEL	ANTEL
11. School buildings	ME Mpl.	ME Mpl. Alianza	ME Mpl.	ME
12. School equipment	ME Mpl.	ME Mpl.	—	—
13. School faculty	ME	ME	—	—
14. Building code	—	—	—	IVU DUA Mpl.
15. Municipal fair	Mpl. DUA	Mpl.	Mpl. DUA	Mpl.
16. Cemeteries	Mpl. CNP	Mpl.	Mpl.	Mpl.
17. Airport	OP	—	OP	—
18. Slaughtering	OP Mpl.	OP	OP	OP Mpl. MA

19. Markets	Mpl. OP	Mpl.	Mpl.	Mpl.
20. Traffic control	DT	—	—	—
21. Urban zoning	DUA Mpl.	—	—	DUA Mpl.

ABBREVIATIONS:

ANDA–Administración Nacional de Acueductos y Alcantarillados
ANTEL–Administración Nacional de Telecomunicaciones
BID–Inter American Development Bank
BNR–Banco Nacional de Reserva
CAESS–Compañía de Alumbrado Eléctrico
CNP–Consejo Nacional de Planificación y Coordinación
DT–Departamento de Tránsito

DUA–Dirección de Urbanismo e Arquitectura
IUV–Instituto de Vivienda Urbana
MA–Ministerio de Agricultura
ME–Ministerio de Educación
MI–Ministerio de Interior
Mpl.–Municipality of San Salvador
OP–Ministerio de Obras Públicas
Sp–Ministerio de Salud Pública
Priv.–private corporation
Trans.–Departamento de Transportes
Vol.–Volunteer

their administration. As a case in point, San Salvador's new street lights were planned by the municipality, the private Compañía de Alumbrado Eléctrico de San Salvador (CAESS) and the National Planning Council, financed jointly by the National Reserve Bank, the municipality and CAESS, constructed by the CAESS and administered by the municipality. By the same token, to obtain a building permit one must obtain approval of the National Housing Institute, the Department of Urban Affairs (DUA), and the municipality. Luckily, the three agencies have established a joint office to expedite applications.

It is obvious from the above that there are very few decisions which the city can take without becoming involved in a hideously complex network of competing governmental agencies and jealous politicians. Before describing the decision-making process itself, it is necessary to outline the formal organization of city government.

The Council. The primary decision-making body of the City of San Salvador is the *consejo municipal* composed of the *alcalde* (mayor), *síndico* (trustee or chief legal officer) and twelve *regidores* (aldermen). These officials are elected for two-year terms on party slates (*planillas*), with the winning slate capturing all of the posts for the bienium. Candidates for the council are chosen by the political parties in a series of caucuses and conventions. The head of the ticket, the *alcalde,* is determined by the national conventions of those parties which are legally inscribed with the Central Electoral Commission some three months before the election. The rest of the *planilla* is chosen in a caucus of the city party organization after a period of negotiation between the candidate for *alcalde*, the party leaders, and the potential candidates. It should be remembered, however, that, unlike the municipalities in the rest of the nation, the local committee in San Salvador is primarily made up of the national party leadership which lives and works in the city.

Table 2. Composition of Party Slates in Municipal Elections in San Salvador, 1964, 1966, 1968

			Number
I.	Business-managerial		
	1.	Business	5
	2.	Managers	4
	3.	Agriculturalists	3
	4.	Bankers-economists	4
		Total	16
II.	Higher professions		
	1.	Medical-dental	14
	2.	Law	16
	3.	Engineering	19
	4.	Architecture	3
	5.	University teaching	3
	6.	University students	5
		Total	60
III.	Lower professions		
	1.	School teaching	7
	2.	Chemistry	2
	3.	Pharmacy	1
	4.	Accounting	12
	5.	Music and art	2
	6.	Technical	3
		Total	27
IV.	Clerical		
	1.	Secretary	2
	2.	Clerk	5
		Total	7
V.	Small business		
	1.	*Comerciantes*	20
	2.	Salesmen	1
	3.	Market vendors	4
		Total	25

SOURCE: *Prensa Gráfica,* March, 1964, 1966, 1968.

An attempt is made to balance the ticket. As can be seen from Table 2, each party *planilla* contains its quota of professionals, small businessmen, and workers. The bulk of the candidates come from the higher professions, particularly law, medicine, and engineering, followed at some distance by the lower professions and small businessmen. The predominance of professionals follows the time-honored pattern of the Latin American political culture, according to which political leadership has been traditionally recruited from the middle sectors, and also reflects the assumption that the electorate expects that the city should be run by competent professionals. In El Salvador, however, a nation noted for its aggressive entrepreneurial spirit and lack of employment opportunities in the countryside, the small shopkeeper, sidewalk vendor, and market woman are a potent political force in the capital city. This fact is reflected in the popular saying: "He who controls the market runs the nation." In fact, it is well known that Don Napoleón Duarte, the Christian Democratic incumbent mayor and son of a *comerciante del mercado,* hopes to do just that, and considers the support of the market women to be essential to his political ambitions. To secure this support, each of the major parties attempts to establish a committee of market vendors to assist in the campaign.

The council meets in regular session once a month although extraordinary sessions may be convened by the *alcalde* or a majority of the *regidores*. Issues before the council are decided by a simple majority vote, the *alcalde* being permitted a second vote to break a tie.[6]

To facilitate its work, the *consejo municipal* is organized into committees (*comisiones*). Four are established by law: (1) public instruction, police, penal institutions, and public works; (2) roads, streets, plazas, and sanitation; (3) public lighting, street cleaning, and taxation; and (4) markets, slaughterhouses, water service, and weights and measures. An additional six were established by the incumbent council: (1) services; (2) community action; (3) finance; (4) administration and personnel; (5) engineering and (6) planning. The commissions have the power to demand reports and data from the administration in their areas of competence but cannot make decisions or expend funds independently of the entire council. Although it would be expected that the commissions would be a major point of access to the decision-making system, the prevailing cultural patterns of *caudillismo* and patronalism tend to direct demands to the *alcalde*. The commissions, thus, are primarily advisory bodies to him.

The Alcalde. As the major political figure in the municipal administration and, by virtue of his dual role as chief administrative officer and member of the council, the *alcalde* constitutes the central point in the decision-making system. Although his formal powers are not numerous, they provide him with broad areas of discretionary action. He presides over meetings of the council, convenes special sessions and administers its decisions. More important, however, is his power to take action "on all matters of public interest" falling under the jurisdiction of the municipality. These are, however, subject to ratification by the council at its next meeting. He is head of the police force, responsible for patrolling the city and empowered to notify the departmental governor of any episode requiring action by that official. Finally, he can insist upon a good-conduct certificate from anyone seeking a domicile in the city.

These formal powers are reinforced by his political position. Next to the President, he holds the most visible elected office in the nation. This is due to a number of factors. First, in a country the size of El Salvador, practically all political activity centers in the capital city. Second, all of the news media are located there. Furthermore, under contemporary political conditions, the city administration is under the control of the major opposition party, Partido Demócrata Cristiano (PDC) which means that, not only has the *alcalde* been elected by one of the largest voting blocs in the nation, but he also holds the highest post available to an opposition politician. Thus, the *alcalde* of San Salvador is, *ipso facto*, not only among the two or three leaders of his party, but also its major presidential candidate.

The formal powers of his office, his wide discretionary powers, and his strategic political position all work together to make the *alcalde* the commanding figure in local decision-making. It is not only assumed that he is the initiator of policy proposals, but also the focal point for the articulation of interests on the part of both the great and the insignificant, the powerful and the weak. When you want something done in San Salvador, the man to see is Don Napoleón.

The Síndico. The *Síndico* is the municipality's chief legal officer. Required by custom to be a lawyer, he represents the municipality in all legal proceedings, contract negotiations, and sales of property. He examines and certifies municipal accounts and investigates improper expenditures and oversees the conduct of public employees and reports malpractices to the council. Finally, he is responsible for seeing to it that the municipal government complies with the Ley del Ramo Municipal and has the power to report infractions to the governor of the department.

Administrative Organization. As a result of the efforts of the incumbent Christian Democratic Party to streamline municipal administration, its departmental organization is similar to comparable bodies the world over. The only officer not totally under the control of the council is the secretary who must be certified by the Minister of the Interior. At one time the second most powerful person in municipal government, many of his former functions have been transferred to the office of the *alcalde*. He is responsible, however, for keeping minutes of all council sessions and records of agreements and transactions between the *alcalde* and groups or agencies having business with him.

Administratively, the municipal government is composed of twelve departments under the general supervision of an office of administrative management (*Gerencia Administrativa*), namely, the departments of the Treasury, Accounting, Engineering, Current Accounts, Civil Registry, Cadastre, Sanitation, Police, Livestock, Markets, Cemeteries, and Community Action. Above the Gerencia Administrativa in the administrative hierarchy are three *Organismos Directivos*, staff offices which, to borrow North American terminology, constitute the "office of the alcalde." These are the Planning Office, the Public Relations Department and the Legal office.

Each of the department is under a chief (*jefe*) and is subdivided into operating units, usually called *secciones*. Municipal employees are protected by the national civil service law which regulates grievance procedures. Under this system, each municipality has a commission composed of a representative of the council, a representative of the National Tribunal and a representative of the municipal employees which is empowered to take up disputes involving individual workers. Decisions can be appealed to the National Tribunal.

The constitution guarantees to municipal employees the right to form professional associations and trade unions (Article 191) and the right to strike (Article 192). Most clerical and lesser administrative personnel are members of the Unión Sindical de Trabajadores de la Alcaldía Municipal, while workers in municipally-run industries (slaughterhouse workers, garbage workers, and others) have their own trade unions. Labor contracts are negotiated directly between the municipality and the union.

THE POLITICAL STRUCTURE

The formal structure of government is only the organizational framework within which political power is generated and decisions made. It is out of the interaction of individuals and groups within the formal structure that policy decisions flow. It is precisely the patterned or structured relationships between politicized individuals and groups that constitutes the political structure. More specifically, the political structure is composed of the political parties, interest groups, political classes and sub-cultures of the community under study. For purposes of this essay, two types of political structure need to be identified: (1) A *horizontal* political structure, characterized by a multiplicity of political parties segmented along political class and sub-cultural lines and by the tendency to forge horizontal, inclusivist links with interest groups and (2) A *vertical* political structure, in which political parties tend to cut across class and sub-cultural lines and be composed of coalitions of interest groups. Both of these structural types can be classified further as to the nature of the parties to be found in each political structure: personalist, programmatic, electoral, combat, and so on.

El Salvador, as a whole, appears to be moving from a personalist-horizontal political structure to a more ideological-vertical one. This can be demonstrated by simply counting the number of parties participating in electoral contests and noting their relative strength. It is clear from Table 3 that, due to a combination of factors such as a new proportional representation law, an easing up of military control and the emergence of the Christian Democrats as a major political force, the number of parties in the system has declined steadily since 1956, the strength of the opposition has increased and the number of parties appearing and disappearing has declined. El Salvador seems to be evolving something of a four party system dominated by two fairly competitive ideological parties: the PDC and the Partido de Conciliación Nacional (PCN), representing the center-left and the center-right, with two somewhat more extremist parties to the left (Partido de Acción Revolucionaria, now the MNR), and to the right (Partido Popular Salvadoreño).

Table 3. Development of the Salvadoran Party System, 1950–1968

Year	No. of Parties	Seats held by Majority Party in National Assembly (*percent*)	Municipal Seats held by Majority Party Throughout Country (*percent*)	Parties from Previous Election (*percent*)
1950	2	100	100	—
1954	2	100	100	100
1956	8	100	99	25
1958	3	100	98	100
1960	8	100	90	37
1961	6	100	n.d.	55
1964	4	61	86	75
1966	5	65	66 (est.)	80
1968	4	52	60 (est.)	100

SOURCES: *El Salvador Election Factbook* (1967) and *Prensa Gráfica*, (1968).

Since 1961, when PAR captured the city government, the City of San Salvador has been the center of political opposition to the military-business coalition that has run the nation under the banners of PRUD and the PCN.[7] Although not a precise measure, the growth of this opposition is reflected in the percentage of votes for the National Assembly in the department of San Salvador as shown in Table 4.

The congressional and municipal "off-year" contests in San Salvador are now considered to be the major test of the political opposition nationally. The party that controls the municipality is recognized as the major opposition party and the man who sits in the *alcaldía* its probable candidate. At the moment, this position is held by the Christian Democrats.

While not wishing to term it a municipal party, the PDC can accurately be said to have achieved its national political position by virtue of its success in San Salvador. Directing its appeal to the urban middle sectors,

Table 4. Vote for the National Assembly in the Department of San Salvador, 1961–1968

Year	PCN	PDC	PAR-MNR	PPS
1961	61.0	19.0	19.0	—
1964	37.9	38.5	23.6	—
1966	31.2	55.5	7.5	1.2
1968	33.8	59.3	5.8	1.1

SOURCES: *El Salvador Election Factbook* (1967) and *Prensa Gráfica* (1964, 1966, 1968).

the party fought its first successful campaign—the municipal elections of 1964—on the grounds that it would attempt to apply Christian Democratic political philosophy—a philosophy which places great stress on the importance of the community in the nation state—to the administration of the City of San Salvador.[8] It built its campaign around a two-pronged appeal. First, it sought to win the support of the city's middle sectors, particularly professionals and small businessmen, by promising administrative reform and improved municipal services.[9] Second, to the urban poor and the lower middle class it promised to create institutions to facilitate their participation in the life and governance of the city through neighborhood action programs.[10]

Since 1964, the Christian Democrats have been reelected on two successive occasions on the strength of their fulfillment of this platform, their major accomplishments being a modernized street lighting system, the negotiation of a BID loan to renovate the rundown municipal markets, the establishment of a community-action program and the installation of modern office equipment to expedite municipal business. The major opposition to the Duarte administration is found among the larger businessmen and industrialists who have successfully opposed his attempt to change the municipal tax structure.

Continued political success in San Salvador is crucial to the anticipated attempt of Alcalde Duarte to challenge the official party in the presidential elections of 1972. With approximately 42 percent of its nationwide voting strength coming from the Department of San Salvador, the importance of its record of accomplishment in municipal government becomes apparent.

Interest Groups. Although the major motive force behind the current municipal régime is the ideology and national political ambitions of the party, the *alcaldía* is constantly confronted with the demands of a multitude of interest groups. Although they do not all play this role, interest groups can be considered to be the "opposition" in the municipal political structure. Competing political parties cease to function in municipal politics after an election, preferring to concentrate their attention on the national level. Of course, the nationally dominant party, the PCN, always constitutes a potential opposition when matters concerning the municipality require the approval of the national government.

Three types of interest groups identified by George Blanksten (1965) are active in municipal politics. First there are the assocational groups such as Lions and Rotary which, along with the Amigos de la Tierra, the Comité de Señoras Voluntarias and the Comité pro Ornato y Limpieza, plant trees, build athletic fields, construct schools, and decorate the city at Christmastime. These groups, because their service orientation actually constitutes them as an arm of the administration, are highly successful in achieving goals of low political sensitivity. The Comité por Ornato, for example, led a successful campaign to get trash receptacles placed in the downtown area.

While not numerous, trade unions representing municipal workers are quite powerful. Both the workers in the slaughter houses (a municipal operation) and the garbage collectors have successfully defended their interests through the use of the strike.[11] Other unions, which rarely seek access to the municipality directly but, because they provide services to urban dwellers, involve the municipality in their labor disputes with private industry and the national government.

The most powerful associational groups in San Salvador are the business and industrial organizations. These organizations, although concentrated in the capital city, are made up of member firms and commercial enterprises located throughout the nation. Because of this and their tacit alliance with the PCN, whose fundamental objective is to achieve the industrial development of the country, these organizations can bring enormous pressure to bear upon any issue requiring decision-making by national governmental agencies. The peak organizations of this complex is the Asociación Nacional de Empresas Privadas (ANEP) which is composed of eleven other major business associations such as the Chamber of Commerce and Industry, the Association of Coffee Producers and Exporters, and the Union of Textile Industries.[12] Each of the constituent associations is in turn composed of individual firms. For example, the Chamber of Commerce and Industry, the city's most politically active pressure group, is made up of 400 business, industrial and banking establishments. There is, furthermore, substantial overlapping in membership among the various business groups, the larger enterprises often belonging to as many as three or four organizations (Campbell, 1968: 2–4). These organizations are guaranteed two seats on the National Council of Economic Planning and Coordination, a national governmental agency made up of the ministers of Economy, Finance, Education, Agriculture, Labor and Health, the president of the Central Reserve Bank, and the President of the Republic (Campbell, 1968: 8). This body must give its approval to many municipal projects, particularly those requiring massive internal or external financing.

Non-associational, *ad hoc* groups are probably the most numerous and active of the city's interest groups. Most common are the neighborhood associations and delegations that lobby on all levels for such things as the construction of connecting streets, the elimination of noisy nightclubs, better bus service land for parks and schools. For example, the civic improvement association of colonia "Centro América" built a park with funds from the Ministry of Public Works, water pipes furnished by the residents and landscaping provided by the Club de Jardinería negotiated by the municipality.

Since the municipal law requires that the city "promote the development of public elementary instruction," (Article 50), many ad hoc organizations are formed to petition for such assistance. For example, the Madres Oblatas de Divino Salvador petitioned for a municipally owned lot upon which to build a school. The petition was granted after approval was received from the Ministry of the Interior. Similarly, the Asociación de Señoras Rotarias received a grant of $5,000 for a school to be built on a municipal lot in Cantón el Carmen. Other non-associational groups of substantial power in the city are the sidewalk vendors and the market women, groups which are considered an important element in the Christian Democratic coalition.[13]

The most important institutional interest group in the city is the press. The three major dailies, all of which are headquartered in San Salvador, give significant attention in both their news and editorial columns to city affairs. Their most important role, however, is that of providing a mechanism through which the city's other groups can articulate their interests. Because these newspapers do not retain a large professional staff of reporters, they welcome letters and petitions addressed to governmental agencies for publication. As a result, the non-associational groups find this medium to be an inexpensive way to achieve visibility for their demands.

The many governmental agencies involved in the provision or financing of urban services constitute a weighty assortment of institutional interest groups which are constantly negotiating and bargaining with one another. The church, of course, has a strong moral impact upon the members of the PDC, but it does not appear to play an active or direct role in municipal affairs.

The process of interest articulation by interest groups is generally conducted with the municipal executive, the city council receiving relatively little direct pressure. This is due to a number of factors. The *alcalde,* by virtue of the historic pattern of *caudillismo* in the Latin American political culture, his position as leader of the party (both nationally and locally) and the full-time nature of his position, is the *patrón* of the city. The *regidores,* on the other hand, as businessmen, professionals and industrial workers, spend relatively little time in city hall and are politically relatively anonymous. But everyone in the country knows of "Don Napo."

Furthermore, as executor of council decisions, he is in contact with the many national agencies that are making decisions that affect the city. This makes him a focal point of political access.

An equal number of demands are funnelled into the municipal political system through national governmental agencies. Often, a group will petition the *alcaldía* and other relevant agencies at the same time, thereby hoping to find at least one receptive point of access. At other times, a group will be forced by the structure of the allocative system to petition a number of agencies merely to acquire the needed resources for a given project. As a result, the *alcalde* is constantly involved in negotiations with interest groups, members of the national bureaucracy and deputies of the National Assembly to resolve the problems brought before him.

In summary, the political structure of San Salvador can be conceived as a four-layer cake cut into a number of slices. The top layer represents the national party system, the second layer the municipal party system, the third layer its interest group allies and the bottom layer the many unaffiliated interest groups. More specifically, it is composed of (1) the Christian Democratic Party which controls the city with its allies in the National Assembly and its interest group allies (particularly the community associations which are tied into its Department of Community Action and certain other groups like the market women); (2) the PCN, which controls the national executive branch (Poder Ejecutivo) and the National Assembly with its allies, a weak municipal party organization and a number of powerful city based business and industrial organizations; (3) the PARMNR with its small legislative faction, weak party organization and intellectual and trade union allies; (4) the PPS with its four-man legislative faction, weak party organization and allies among the so-called "fourteen families." The party (PDC) is quite cohesive, held together by its ideology, its national political ambitions and the strength of the opposition. Fragmentation or divisiveness would cause it to be helpless before the official governing coalition. It also depends upon its national legislative faction of nineteen members to provide it with the necessary symbolic support on the many local issues that involve national decision making. The point here is that there is a sense in which the entire political system bears down upon municipal decision-making. For example, it will be shown that when the municipal administration of San Salvador attempted to reform the municipal tax structure, the issue became a struggle between the two national political forces in the nation and, as such, transcended the more narrow question of how to find a more just and adequate financial base for municipal services.

THE POLITICAL CULTURE

Although it is beyond the scope of this essay to describe in detail the Salvadoran political culture (defined by Almond and Verba [1963: Chap-

ter 13] as "the particular distribution of patterns of orientation toward political objects among the members of a nation") as it impinges upon the
city's system, a few generalizations may be of some utility. First, there
does not seem to exist in the city what might be called a "civic élite" oriented toward the development or improvement of the city as a whole.
This is due in large part to the fact that the city's élite is primarily a national
élite whose major interest is the nation and whose mobility aspirations are
achieved through the national economic and/or political system. This class
is concerned, first, with the nation, next with the international community,
and with the city last of all.

One group which is of course concerned about the city is the business
community, the downtown merchants and entrepreneurs who are primarily concerned about city services such as street lighting, parking, garbage collection, and so forth. In no sense can they called a civic élite,
however. The only element that in any way resembles a civic élite—and
this stretches the term somewhat—are the politicians and bureaucrats who
make a career out of solving urban problems. They are probably the only
ones who are concerned about the entire ecological unit.

Lacking a civic élite, the primary focus of attention on the part of
almost all social strata in the city is the neighborhood—the *barrio* for
the lower class and the *colonia* for the middle and upper classes. What
is good for the neighborhood is of primary concern. In this context, although the disintegration and fragmentation we associate with suburbia is
not yet a governmental problem (since urban expansion takes place within
the city limits) as a cultural and/or psychological phenomenon, it is probably every bit as pronounced as it is in North American cities.

The patterns just described have two primary effects. First, if a city-
wide issue does not directly affect the individual or his neighborhood, he
remains apathetic. Civic pride is not a Latin trait. Second, San Salvador's
community leadership, in addition to being highly fragmented, tends to
manifest what can be termed a "political" rather than a "civic" orientation to community affairs. By this I mean that solutions to community
problems—whether they be the repairing of a street or the building of a
school—will be assessed in terms of narrow personal or political advantage. And when it comes to building a library or a theatre—that is the
responsibility of the national government.

TWO CASES IN MUNICIPAL DECISION-MAKING

As a means of describing in greater detail the dynamics of the decision-making process in San Salvador, two cases are presented which
attempt to show not only the interactions between decisional organs and
the political structure, but also the way in which the national and local
governments are inextricably linked together in the municipal political
system. The first case involves the thus far unsuccessful struggle for

municipal tax reform. The second describes the campaign to install a modern system of street lights throughout the city.

The Struggle for Municipal Tax Reform

For the past four years the Christian Democratic administration of San Salvador has attempted to revise the out-dated municipal tax structure, a process that constitutionally requires the approval of the National Assembly.[14] This legislation, pending since March, 1965, has involved some of the most powerful interest groups in the country, the major political parties and a great number of the society's governmental agencies. It is illustrative of the way in which El Salvador's major city is caught between the nation's political forces.

The Problems of Taxation in San Salvador. San Salvador's revenue problems are hardly unique. Like major cities the world over, the municipality faces the problem of providing services for an expanding urban population with a declining tax base. Thus, the city which contains over 10 percent of the nation's population is forced to operate on revenues which amount to about 3 percent of those of the national government. The enormity of San Salvador's fiscal problems can be better understood when it is noted that its population has been growing at close to 6 percent per year, the bulk of this population being made up of persons pouring into the *barrios pobres* who are unable to contribute a sufficient amount in taxes to pay for the services they consume.

San Salvador's declining tax base is due to a number of factors, not the least of which are the incompatibilities between the policy goals of the national and city governments. In attempting to foster the development of the nation, the national government has both preempted certain revenue sources and has also taken over certain service areas that previously produced a profit to the city. For example, in order to promote El Salvador as an attractive location for industrial investment, it not only tries to keep taxes on industry low, but also its Ley de Fomento Industrial absolves new industrial concerns from paying municipal taxes for a ten-year period.

Under the Tarifa de Arbitrios Municipales, in force since 1947, the city derives its revenues from the following sources: (1) capital investment tax on businesses operating in the city; (2) taxes on economic activities carried on in public places, particularly by street vendors; (3) taxes on public entertainment, raffles and lotteries; (4) construction taxes; (5) charges for municipal services such as garbage collection; (6) taxes on the use of market stalls; (7) fees from the sale of licenses, permits and registrations; (8) fines. The Tarifa, however, is so unorganized (it consists simply of an uncoordinated list of impositions; the only ordination is alphabetical) that the contributor is seldom able to determine which of the various taxes he is paying and collection procedures are so out of date that knowledgeable taxpayers can go for years without paying (Campbell, 1968: 15).

Of particular difficulty is the lack of an adequate system of graduated impositions. That is, taxes on commercial enterprises are imperfectly related to their size, location, or capital investment. As a result, most businesses pay the same tax regardless of size or wealth. In fact, a business representing a capital investment of 100,000 colones will pay a capital investment tax equal to that paid by a business with a capital investment of 15 million colones. The few businesses with less than 100,000 colones in investment pay reduced municipal taxes. In relation to its ability to pay, the large business is least affected by municipal taxes (Campbell, 1968: 15–16). A final problem is the fact that the national governmental agencies, a major industry in the city, are not obligated to contribute to the coffers of the city even though they utilize its services.

Objectives of the Tax Reform Proposal. When the Christian Democratic Party came to power in San Salvador in 1964, it saw municipal tax reform as one of its major objectives for a variety of reasons—programmatic, political and ideological. From a political point of view, since the Christian Democrats quickly realized that a successful city administration was the *sine qua non* for achieving further political gains, they felt that they would have to increase municipal revenues if they were to govern the city successfully. Furthermore, if this could be done by shifting the tax load from the small entrepreneur, middle-class professional, and industrial worker—the core of their support—to the large businesses and industries, they would have achieved a political coup.

From a programmatic point of view, the city administration saw in tax reform an answer to the problem of rural-urban migration. Since nearly all of the nation's industry is concentrated in the capital city, large numbers of *campesinos* have migrated to San Salvador seeking better economic opportunities. The result has been the creation of *barrios pobres* which not only are characterized by lack of adequate housing, potable water, electric power and sanitary facilities, but also are without sufficient financial resources to pay for them. The inability of industry to absorb this migratory population has also resulted in the creation of an army of ambulatory peddlers who swarm through the streets of the city hawking toothpaste, pocket combs, and physical culture magazines. Since it is assumed that, under current conditions, the flow of migrants into the marginal areas of the city will continue at a more rapid rate than the increase in industrial employment and that this population will constitute an ever increasing drain upon the resources of the city, the Christian Democrats see increased taxation upon large industry as a means of inducing new industries to locate in other areas.

Ideologically, the Christian Democratic administration hoped to implement its Plan Moralizador by levying heavy taxes on nightclubs, bars, movie theaters, go-go clubs, and pool halls and to enhance the autonomy of the municipality, which it views as an intermediary social organism, by making the city less dependent upon the national government.

Recognizing that the brunt of the new *tarifa* would fall most heavily on the large enterprises, Duarte and members of the city council met with the leadership of the Cámara de Comercio e Industria de El Salvador in October, 1964 to discuss the proposed legislation. At that meeting, the Cámara expressed itself as recognizing the need for a municipal tax law and stated that it would not oppose any measure that did not unjustly burden the already heavily taxed private sectors (Campbell, 1968: 18). In March, 1965, without having consulted further with the Cámara, the mayor delivered copies of the proposed new law to members of the National Assembly's Committee of the Interior and Public Works. He announced that although the new schedule would raise municipal taxes by over 50 percent, the actual tax load on small business had been reduced.

Upon learning of the contents of the new tax schedule, the Cámara reacted immediately by setting up a study commission composed of members of the *juntas directivas* of the Cámara, the Asociación Salvadoreña de Industriales, la Unión de Industrias Textiles, the Sociedad de Comerciantes e Industriales Salvadoreños and the Comité de Bancos, Seguros y Financieras. Under the leadership of the Cámara, this group determined to move against the municipality on three fronts. First, a propaganda campaign was launched in the press. It was argued that since the larger businesses were already among the most heavily taxed enterprises in Latin America, an increased municipal levy would be ruinous. The only way to offset such a tax load would be to shift it back onto the consumer, a measure which, they contended, would greatly hamper the economic growth of the nation. Furthermore, arguing that what was needed was greater efficiency in collection procedures rather than heavier taxes, they stated that all the municipality was doing was increasing the burden on those sectors from which the city had the technical capacity to collect. They chided the Christian Democrats for their slogan, "Pagar más él que tiene más, y menos él que tiene menos," by contending that it should be: "Quien paga con puntualidad está capacitado para tributar el doble." Finally, it attacked the moral objective of the Tarifa, strongly questioning the utility of employing a fiscal instrument to achieve such ends.

Second, the Cámara and its allies determined upon a strategy designed to keep the measure bottled up in the National Assembly as long as possible. Requesting permission to appear before the committee with their study, the four organizations put forward a list of seven items of information which they said would have to be presented by the municipality before they could adequately react to the measure. This the municipality would be unable to provide due to the imprecise character of the current tax law.[15] Duarte responded by inviting the four organizations to meet with him, at which time he stated he would provide them with the information they sought. The Cámara and its allies refused, stating that once the data were supplied to the National Assembly, they would then respond to it. In the end, the municipality refused to reply before the Assembly because of the difficulty in securing hard data on a chaotic fiscal system; and the Cámara refused to discuss the question under any other set of circumstances.

The third area of attack was directed to the National Executive where business interests have two seats on the National Council of Economic Planning and Coordination. Here they argued that the new municipal law threatened the carefully orchestrated program of economic development, the policy around which the PCN has built its governing coalition[16] and for whose success the government is ultimately dependent upon the private economic sectors.

In spite of the objective need for tax reform, the municipal administration found its hands tied. It faced a partisan majority in the National Assembly for whom the successful passage of the new *tarifa* would constitute a major victory for its major political competitors. They certainly did not wish to make "Don Napo" a more formidable presidential aspirant than he already was. At the level of the national executive, the municipality was faced with the fact that the very survival of the governing coalition—a somewhat uncertain alliance of the traditional military and planter aristocracy in tandem with younger, reformist officers, middle-sector economic modernizers, and professionals[17] rested to no small degree on its maintaining economic growth and adequate profit margins. At the local level itself, the municipality, which might have tried to mount a counterattack by mobilizing the small businessmen to fight for the new *tarifa*, hesitated to do so because of other civic projects—most notably a new street lighting system and a BID loan for new municipal markets—for which it needed the support of the Cámara and its allies.

Lighting the Streets of San Salvador

While the particular constellation of political forces described above served to frustrate the Christian Democratic administration of San Salvador in its attempt to secure municipal tax reform, many of these same forces combined to produce a successful resolution of a problem that had long plagued the community. Since the accession to power in 1949 of a modernizing coalition dedicated to rapid industrialization, San Salvador had been growing very rapidly. New middle-class suburbs on the western side of the city and public housing projects in working-class neighborhoods had sprung up very rapidly without adequate utilities such as potable water and electric lighting. For years, the press had been complaining about the vast areas of the city which were shrouded in darkness and called upon the city to do something about it. A major impediment, however, to any forseeable extension or improvement in the city's street lighting system was the fact that the municipality had been running a deficit in its payments to the Canadian-owned Compañía de Alumbrado Eléctrico de San Salvador (CAESS) of over 1.5 million colones. The problem was that, due to the anachronistic municipal tax system, the taxes (*arbitrios*) for street lighting were too low to cover costs. In fact, the deficit would have been greater had it not been possible for many years to make up a portion of the difference from charges for water. However, with the transfer of water services to an autonomous institution (Administración Nacional de Acueductos y Alcantarillados or ANDA) in 1961 this source of revenue was lost.

Capitalizing upon the failure of previous administrations to solve the problem, the Christian Democrats made the issue of *alumbrado público* a major plank in its platform in the 1964 municipal campaign. In addition to its obvious necessity as a public service, the Christian Democrats saw this as necessary to the moral improvement of the community, particularly as an aid in the fight against crime.

Upon taking office, the city administration began negotiations with two foreign firms to install a new system of street lighting. Each of these companies agreed to do the work and provide credit for the equipment if the Central Reserve Bank (BCR) agreed to guarantee the loans. The bank expressed its interest in the project, but asked for a feasibility study from the municipal government.

In its study, the municipality proposed three ways by which the major obstacle in the way of obtaining a BCR guarantee—the deficit owed to CAESS—could be eliminated: (1) by increasing the *arbitrios* covering street lighting; (2) by reducing the rate charged by the electric power company; (3) by shifting monies from other restricted municipal funds to the street lighting fund.[18] Each of these approaches, however, presented clear obstacles to the municipal government. Increasing the *arbitrios* for street lighting involved the approval of the National Assembly, a body clearly not receptive to municipal tax reform for the reasons given earlier.

The second required agreement by the foreign-owned electric company which was already a creditor to the city and claimed that its revenues were steadily declining. The third—pooling of restricted funds—not only required approval by the National Assembly but also the postponement of renovations to the city hall and the reduction of support for public education.

Because of the difficulties involved in pursuing any of these avenues, Alcalde Duarte hoped that the BCR would indicate its preference and then use its influence to secure agreement from the other parties involved. This the bank refused to do however. To attempt to untangle the snarled threads resulting from the conflicting interests of the agencies involved, an ad hoc committee composed of a representative of the BCR, the Ministry of the Interior and the municipality was established. This committee, in response to the urging of Duarte and the Salvadoran press, worked for legislation abolishing the restrictive Fondos Específicos. After negotiations with the members of the committees of Interior, Treasury, and Constitutional Questions of the National Assembly, the needed legislation was passed (Decreto Legislativo No. 294, 1965). With substantial funds now available, all that was needed was to work out a satisfactory bargain with the electric company.

This was undertaken largely through the instrumentality of the tripartite commission established to secure the abolition of earmarked funds. In the end an agreement was worked out directly with CAESS. Under its terms, the municipality would pay one-third of its 1.5 million colón debt to the company and the rest in seven years. In turn, the company agreed to finance installation of the new lighting system. The municipality agreed to pay more for electric power, the increase to be financed by an increase in the *tarifa de arbitrios* for street lighting. The council determined to replace all existing sub-standard light fixtures with the new equipment. Areas of the city where street lighting did not exist were to form *comités pro-alumbrado* to petition the city to install equipment in their areas. By the summer of 1967, the campaign to illuminate the city had been successfully completed.

CONCLUSIONS

This study of decision-making in San Salvador was based on an investigation of sixteen issues or problems confronting that city's municipal government between 1964 and 1967, two of which were described in some detail. It is possible on the basis of these cases to make the following generalizations about this process.

First, fundamental to all other generalizations about decision-making in San Salvador is the very real weakness of city government. Due to the extensive participation of the national government in so many of its service areas, the city has a very narrow range of responsibilities and a limited number of services over which it has direct control. In fact, in a great many such areas, distinctively municipal interests can be vetoed by the national government. This weak position is further compounded by the limitations placed upon its budget-making powers and taxing authority.

Second, because of its institutional position, the city must be conceived of as operating within what Sherwood calls a "national municipal system" (Sherwood, 1967: 57–61) which, in this case, has three fundamental characteristics: (1) a system of political competition not limited to the political forces and groups within the city itself but also embracing national governmental institutions and the political élite controlling them. In this situation, political contests are likely to be between coalitions of political groups and governmental agencies, often embracing both the national and the local levels; (2) a multiple-access system whereby interest groups may utilize decisional points at either the national or local levels either to thwart or implement demands for municipal services and/or other actions; (3) a tie-in with the international political system—particularly the international banking community—due to the fact that municipal improvements are sometimes financed by international loans.

Third, in a situation such as this where the municipal government (or régime) is so inextricably related to the national power balance, there emerge a set of political conditions which have to be carefully assessed if it is to achieve its policy objectives. (1) The municipality requires the support of a fairly wide political coalition if it is to achieve success. Such a coalition will likely be composed of a substantial number of the following elements: local and national interest groups, national governmental agencies, the press, and a national political party. (2) The municipality will probably have to limit its policy objectives to politically non-sensitive areas whenever the national government is controlled by an opposition party unless it has the overwhelming support of major national interest groups which constitute a part of that party's political coalition. (3) When the municipal administration is in the hands of a political party in opposition to the national régime, it must recognize the threat it poses to the national majority party. Under these circumstances it must decide whether in using the municipality as a political "launching pad" for its own political ambitions, the interests of the city will thereby be forfeited.

Fourth, at the municipal level the *alcalde* stands at the center of the political process. This is due in part to his position as *patrón* of the city and in part to the fact that he is the leader of a politically homogeneous council. The council, because of its homogeneity, receives very little direct pressure and is not particularly susceptible to factionalization. In this sense it is weak. It provides few alternative channels for the articulation of divergent interests or political proposals. This is compounded, of course, by the fact that both the *alcalde* and the council are often by-passed in the interest articulation process due to the importance of extra-local agencies in the municipal decision-making process.

Fifth, interest articulation at the municipal level is specific, most demands being directed to immediately tangible ends. There is relatively little demand for community-wide "civic projects" although occasionally, as in the case of the street lighting campaign, the press or the municipal administration itself may seek to initiate such a project.

Finally, the position of a major urban area within a "national municipal system" such as has been described provides certain insights into the recurring controversy in Latin America over municipal autonomy. It can be said that the city of San Salvador is characterized by substantial "political" autonomy without the corresponding "governmental" autonomy it needs if it is to develop a capacity to solve its problems by the mobilization of its own human and material resources. In fact, given the dual conditions of institutional dependency coupled with the minority party status of its régime, the city will never be much more than a political step-child.

In fact, it does not appear that in reality it is much better off than it would be if it had the status of a federal district.

In spite of the fact that the degree of municipal autonomy that does exist has provided a political base for the development of a viable opposition party in El Salvador—without doubt a hopeful development for the nation—it has not resulted in a substantially increased capacity by the city to solve its own problems. By the same token, a governmentally autonomous system in the hands of the national majority would not materially change this situation. This suggests that in addition to political and governmental autonomy, a third condition must be present if the people of a major Latin American urban area such as this are to have meaningful control over their affairs, namely, political competition and diversity. That is, there must be a sufficient pluralism of representation on the council to provide channels for the communication of the multiplicity of demands and proposals generated in a community of this size and complexity. In short, to use Professor Sherwood's terminology again, municipal autonomy in El Salvador involves converting a competitive "national municipal system" into a competitive "community municipal" one (Sherwood, 1967).

NOTES

1. For a discussion of local units of government as political systems see Sherwood (1967).

2. The sixteen issues can be enumerated as follows: (1) controls on neon signs for private businesses; (2) controls on the operations of certain night clubs; (3) changes for certain bus routes and bus stops; (4) the lack of water in certain neighborhoods; (5) controlling parking in the downtown area; (6) the problem of air pollution by exhaust fumes; (7) a project for new markets; (8) a garbage strike; (9) a bus strike; (10) the building of covered bus stands; (11) the building of a new cemetery; (12) the problem of illegal slaughtering; (13) the control of street vendors; (14) the new zoning ordinance; (15) the municipal tax reform; (16) the street lighting project.

3. See Constitution of the Republic of El Salvador, 1962 (1966).

4. Articles 88–91.

5. Article 87.

6. Councilmen are prohibited by law from taking part in either the discussion of or vote on matters involving themselves or their relatives to the fourth degree of consanguinity.

7. In 1962–1963, however, the PCN controlled the municipality when all opposition parties withdrew from the elections of 1962.

8. This approach was particularly appropriate for the party since its philosophy is based on the concept of the state as an organic entity composed of a series of intermediary organisms (family, *municipio*, trade union, corporation, and cooperative) which exist between it and the individual. The democratic state can only be achieved when each of these intermediary organisms is healthy and strong and permitted to carry out its natural functions. Thus, democratic government can only be achieved when people learn to participate in the governing of their communities and seek to solve its problems. Nationalism is found "in germ" in the community. Without political entities (i.e., municipal corporations) that can foment this spirit

of participation, this sense of being an actor rather than a subject, the larger society cannot operate effectively. See Chávez Mena (1966: 27–32).

9. Among the many proposals in its Plan de Gobierno were the creation of more rational building codes, tax reform, improved sanitation in the market and in restaurants, better garbage collection, new street lighting, and the employment of modern business procedures at city hall.

10. Specifically, it promised to create in city government a Department of Community Action which would establish neighborhood centers to provide medical assistance at lower cost, adult education courses, and recreation for juveniles.

11. Sindicato de Trabajadores de la Carne and the Sindicato de Trabajadores de Empresa de Aseo. Another union of importance is the Sindicato Unión de Trabajadores de la Alcaldía.

12. The others are: the Salvadoran Association of Industrialists, the Salvadoran Association of Publicity Agencies, the Chamber of Commercial Representatives of El Salvador, the Salvadoran Association of Graphic Industries, the Salvadoran Chamber of Construction Industries, the Salvadoran Association of Insurance Companies, the Association of Automobile Distributors, and the Salvadoran Association of Means of Publication. The Society of Salvadoran Merchants and Industrialists, an Association of small merchants, recently dropped out of ANEP and is now operating independently. See Campbell (1968: 3).

13. Although the Madres Oblatas and Señoras Rotarias are technically associational groups, the sporadic nature of their demands make them closer in character to non-associational groups.

14. Article 105 states that municipal councils "shall prepare their schedules of local taxes, to be submitted to the Legislative Assembly for enactment as laws, and that body may make any changes deemed necessary."

15. Requested were (1) a detailed breakdown of revenues received by category of tax; (2) detailed data on expenditures by category of service, distinguishing between expenditures for the service and for administration; (3) detailed data on the causes of the municipal deficits; (4) specific estimates of new revenues by category of tax; (5) a detailed plan for investment of projected new revenues; (6) detailed data on uncollected taxes; (7) projected plans for administrative reform of the municipal government.

16. See, for example, Anderson (1964).

17. See Ashton (1967), chap. 2.

18. Until June 1, 1965, municipal tax revenues were assigned to two funds: the Fondo Común Municipal and a series of Fondos Específicos Municipales. The former was used to fund everyday running expenses and was under the direct control of the city government; the latter, drawing its revenue from *arbitrios* earmarked for specific projects, such as roads, cemeteries, public instruction, water and street lighting, were controlled by the Tesorería General de Fondos Específicos Municipales. These could not be used for other than their legally stated purposes without an act of the National Assembly. See Chávez Mena (1966: 113–116).

REFERENCES

ALMOND, GABRIEL and SIDNEY VERBA (1963) *The Civic Culture*. Princeton: Princeton University Press.

ANDERSON, CHARLES W. (1969) "El Salvador: the army as reformer." In Martin C. Needler (ed.) *Political Systems of Latin America*. Princeton: D. Van Nostrand.

ASHTON, RAYMOND (1967) El Salvador and the Controlled Revolution: An

Analysis of Salvadorean Development, 1948–1965. Unpublished Master's Thesis, Dept. of Political Science, Tulane University.

BLANKSTEN, GEORGE (1965) "Political Groups in Latin America." Pp. 185–197 in John D. Martz (ed.) *The Dynamics of Change in Latin American Politics.* Englewood Cliffs: Prentice-Hall.

CAMPBELL, JANE (1968) "The Chamber of Commerce and Industry of El Salvador: Functioning of a Latin American Interest Group." Paper prepared for the Interdisciplinary Seminar, Latin American Studies Program, Tulane University (December 17).

CHÁVEZ MENA, FIDEL (1966) *Organización Municipal.* San Salvador: Facultad de Jurisprudencia y Ciencias Sociales, Universidad de El Salvadore.

Constitution of the Republic of El Salvador, 1962 (1966). Washington, D.C.: Pan American Union, Title VI.

Decreto Legislative No. 294, May 27, 1965. *Diario Oficial,* 207: 6174–6175.

El Salvador Election Factbook (1967). Washington, D.C.: ICSPS.

Prensa Gráfica (1964) March.

———— (1966) March.

———— (1968) March.

SHERWOOD, FRANK P. (1967) *Institutionalizing the Grass Roots in Brazil.* San Francisco: Chandler.

PART IV

POLICY

PROBLEMS: THE

CONSEQUENCES

OF

URBANIZATION

Chapter 9

URBAN-REGIONAL POLICIES FOR NATIONAL DEVELOPMENT IN CHILE

JOHN FRIEDMANN

URBANIZATION AND NATIONAL DEVELOPMENT IN CHILE

Chile has ceased to be a predominantly rural nation. Of her nine million people, approximately half are living today in cities with more than 20,000 inhabitants.[1] The 1960 census counted 9 cities with a population of between 20,000 and 50,000; 12 cities between 50,000 and 100,000, 2 cities between 100,000 and 500,000; and finally the metropolis of Santiago which then had a population of about 2.5 million.[2] Each of these cities was in turn the center of a region to which it extended limited services. The National Planning Office, after a thorough study of the economic characteristics of different sections of the nation, finally recommended a division into ten development regions in addition to the metropolitan zone of Santiago. These regions are diverse, not only in their economic interests, but also in the characteristics of their population. Some of the relevant information is brought together in Table 1.

If we compare Chile's urbanization to other countries, especially to those in Europe, some distinctive features become immediately apparent. In their extreme dependency on the national government, Chilean cities seem more like temporary settlements than permanent communities with a full political expression of their own. This debility is reflected not only in their physical appearance but also in municipal budgets that vary but little and generally run to less than $10 per capita. Despite the fact that each has an individual economic profile, the regions of Chile exhibit only small cultural variations. By and large, Chileans are a fairly homogeneous

AUTHOR'S NOTE: The research supporting this chapter was done while the author served as head of the Ford Foundation's Urban and Regional Development Advisory Program in Chile.

Table 1. Some Characteristics of Development Regions in Chile, 1965

Region	Popula-tion (thou-sands)	Per-cent	Regional Product (million escudos 1965)	Per-cent	Per capita Regional Product (escudos)
I. Tarapacá	137.2	1.6	394	2.4	2,872
II. Antofagasta	251.2	2.9	1,232	7.3	4,904
III. Atacama-Coquimbo	512.0	5.8	1,114	6.6	2,176
IV. Aconcagua-Valparaíso	883.2	10.1	1,755	10.4	1,987
Metropolitan Zone	3,036.1	34.5	6,277	37.4	2,067
V. O'Higgins-Colchagua	472.4	5.4	1,105	6.6	2,339
VI. Curicó-Linares	664.8	7.6	772	4.6	1,612
VII. Nuble-Malleco	1,490.2	16.9	2,246	13.4	1,507
VIII. Cautín-Osorno	897.9	10.2	1,122	6.7	1,250
IX. Llanquihue-Aysén	350.4	4.0	472	2.8	1,353
X. Magallanes	90.6	1.0	312	1.8	3,444
CHILE	8,786.0	100.0	16,803	100.0	1,912

SOURCE: ODEPLAN, *Kardex de Estadísticas Regionales.* Percentages may not add to 100.00 due to rounding.

people and their attachments to soil and place are weak. The nation's regions are therefore economic artifacts more than organic historico-cultural entities and have no political expression at all. Provinces, the units out of which they are composed, are ordinary administrative subdivisions patterned after the model of the French prefectorial system.

The apparent internal unity of Chile as a nation seems impressive, but it is a unity achieved primarily through the overwhelming power of a national government which, from its seat in Santiago, presides over a poorly articulated and dependent periphery—an agglomeration of urban settlements and regional economies—whose orientation is predominantly towards the seat of national power. The survival of secondary centers in the periphery derives more from their ability to focus the attention of the national government upon themselves than from an autonomous, political will to manage their own resources in the interest of local populations.

National unity dates back to the colonial period. It was preserved through independence and subsequent cycles of economic growth that gradually converted a poor agrarian country subsisting primarily on mineral exports into one of the most industrialized of the American States. Chile's process of transition to industrialism which has been underway for generations is not yet complete (Muñoz, 1969). Accompanying the growth of total population estimated at about two percent over the last three decades and an increase in the national product at less than four percent in real terms, a major internal rearrangement occurred in the distribution of its population: the rural sector declined to less than one-third of the total, as the urban sector increased proportionately to over two-thirds of the nation's population.[3]

The rapid, continuous urbanization of Chile generated a series of consequences that were far-reaching in their implications for national development. For the rural areas, it signified, not only an absolute loss of population, but also a marked decline in the agricultural economy which was progressively unable to meet the growing demands for food products and agricultural raw materials in the urban markets.[4] At the same time, but especially during recent years, the city began to penetrate the countryside in various ways, and gradually convert the traditional peasant into a person who is literate, organized, and politically active.

In the cities themselves, urbanization processes contributed to a fragmentation of the inherited social order as new professional, white collar, and working groups claimed for themselves an increasing share of economic, social, and political power.[5] But migration to the cities was in excess of the economic system's ability to integrate successfully the new arrivals at full and productive levels of employment. As a result, a growing proportion of the population in the cities was unable to rise out of a condition of nearly total economic dependency and came to constitute a large and relatively unorganized mass of humanity, the urban sub-proletariat, *los marginados.*[6]

The numerical importance of this sub-proletariat was such, however, that it eventually gained some recognition as different political parties began to compete for its votes. In recent years, the concept of "marginality" has been extended also to the rural sub-proletariat which had always existed but had been politically invisible.[7] In simple terms, the economic dependency of the marginal population manifested itself in an extreme form of poverty, high rates of unemployment (or relatively unproductive employment), deprivation of public services, and impotence to do anything that might substantially transform the economic and social situation of a large portion of the Chilean people, whatever their residence.

Chile came thus to be characterized by a double condition of internal dependency that extended to large numbers of the population living in both cities and rural areas—*los marginados*—and also to cities and regions conceived as spatial subsystems of the national economy. Paradoxical as it may seem a measure of dependency characterized the very groups who, *outside the regional and urban matrix,* were organized to defend their own interests with vigor. It may therefore be claimed that the apparent unity of the nation was achieved through the domination of periphery, urban, and rural sub-proletariats by those who wielded effective economic and political power in the center.

Yet another consequence of the subtle interplay of forces generated by urbanization processes in Chile was the appearance of a high and sustained rate of monetary inflation.[8] Inflation became especially serious with the push for accelerated industrialization that began in 1940. But in a milder form, inflation had existed as an economic problem even before then. The intensified industrialization program during the nineteen forties and fifties was successful in that it significantly altered the composition of employment and production in Chile from a traditional agrarian structure to one in which manufacturing industry finally accounted for about one quarter of total production compared to less than 10 percent for agricultural activities (1967). But industrialization did not appreciably accelerate Chile's overall rate of economic growth which in certain years (1942, 1947, 1949, 1951, 1956, and 1959) was actually negative. Whatever the original causes of inflation, the latter had a double effect on the economy with far-reaching results beyond what is normally considered the realm of economics. Specifically, it tended to change the balance of income distribution in favor of the better organized sectors of the population, most of whom belonged to the rising middle class, *at the expense of* the marginated sub-proletariat, especially in the countryside. More generally, the terms of trade between the periphery and the center changed in favor of the urban population.[9]

At the same time, inflation tended to discourage domestic savings[10] and channel the energies of the more organized groups in the direction of the annual readjustment "game" whereby the Congress, through appropriate legislation, would set the rates at which incomes would have to be readjusted for different salary and wage groups in order to approximately maintain their purchasing power. The "game" was played so that each group would try, through its special connections and bargaining power, to achieve a slight relative gain over other groups in the distribution of an income that was relatively constant on a per capita basis. The resulting "politics of readjustment" were accompanied by an "economics of stagnation." The pay-offs for selected population groups were evidently greater if they followed the political route to economic success compared to the more austere path of enterprise and savings.

But the politics of readjustment eventually led into a dead-end. As inflation fluctuated violently from year to year, the players in the game became increasingly aware that there were mainly losers and few winners, thus turning long-range planning into a bitter joke and making the outcomes of politics so uncertain that it no longer afforded a viable path to a better life.[11] Not only *los marginados* felt themselves to be excluded from economic benefits, but nearly everyone else in Chile as well.

In response to this new situation—which I have elsewhere called the "crisis of inclusion" (Friedmann and Lackington, 1966) a new configuration of political forces took shape that advocated dramatic changes in the life of the nation and advanced new national objectives. It may be worthwhile to restate these objectives. They are very widely held, even if somewhat abstractly, and undoubtedly will continue to be relevant to the situation as it evolves during the next few years. They include:

—increasing the rate of economic growth of to approximately double its traditional rate of 1 or 2 percent per capita;
—significantly reducing the rate of inflation to bring it within more tolerable limits;
—achieving the full integration of Chileans into modern society by a more equitable distribution of income and public services, an increase of employment opportunities especially in the more productive jobs, and a reduction in the dependency levels of all social groups—especially of *los marginados*—through more effective participation or involvement in planning, programming, and production.

The attainment of these goals, however worthwhile they may be in themselves, is contingent upon the existence of a broad consensus with respect to the means to be employed and a thorough-going mobilization of the population around the objectives of national development. Yet, neither consensus nor mobilization is likely to materialize so long as the nation is internally divided, with rural areas set off against the city and, within their own communities, the urban sub-proletariat against the organized working- and middle-class groups. A unifying framework for policy and program was therefore sought that would establish the basis for both consensus and mobilization in the society, be more responsive to the new demands, and permit the linkage of local energies to national power. This unifying framework we may call the urban-regional frame for national development.

In recent years, the urban-regional frame became a new basis for policy and program coordination. It took the aggregate of settlements seriously as communities; where they did not exist, they might come into being as a result of collaborative effort and a new sense of local identity. It emphasized differences of economic structure and need among regions, at the same time as it strove to relate these spatially separate structures into a single organized system.

This, as it turned out, was not altogether a utopian dream, but was lent credence by the gradual disappearance of what might be called the "urban frontier." By the late 1960s, the huge shift of rural populations to the cities had been largely accomplished: considerably less than a third of the Chilean people continued to reside in the countryside, and even fewer were actually engaged in agricultural production. The movement to Santiago—grown to the size of a metropolis with its nearly three million inhabitants—had substantially slowed. The new migration, such as it occurred, was mainly of an urban origin: inter-urban had replaced rural-urban migration.[12] Unemployment in the cities was high, less so in Santiago than elsewhere, but even there this tended to check further in-migration. In general, it can be said—though this is purely speculative—that the people of a given locality increasingly reached an awareness that their economic future had to be found, not in distant cities or pioneering regions, but in the places where they lived; there was nowhere else to go. This new belief tended to give to the proposed urban-regional frame a sense of reality which, in a more fluent environment—and in the absence of strong civic or regional traditions—it might not have had.

City and region therefore became the new units for analysis and action by the central Government, and the hope was that local citizens might be organized to collaborate more meaningfully with the central Government in building up their own communities (Ley de Juntas de Vecinos). But the widespread adoption of the urban-regional frame was not simply a formal and relatively neutral innovation; it also added new dimensions to national policy. Each city and region would project its own set of developmental objectives; it would seek to become a full-fledged community. Since local resources were practically non-existent, given the structure of taxation in Chile, the central Government would have to channel development capital towards the periphery in accordance with certain national priorities. Demands for greater autonomy would begin to be made to make the responses of Government to public needs more agile, to the point, and flexible. Whereas settlement is simply a passive object at the mercy of dominant power, a community will wish to become transformed into an active subject, acting out its own history. All this would foreshadow big changes in the traditional pattern of politics and administration. The urban-regional frame would also pose the challenge of integration in a new form, no longer by authority and hierarchy, but by task-oriented, horizontal, communitarian lines of relationship.

In short, the urban-regional frame as applied to Chile was an attempted reply to what I have called the double condition of internal dependency: on the one hand, it was intended to wipe out the stigma of marginality which marked a large number of the Chilean people; on the other hand, it sought to overcome the gap which separated the rural from the urban condition of life.

From the point of view of the central government, the urban-regional frame threw into high relief a series of quite specific policy questions. Without trying to discuss these in detail, I shall simply list them.

(1) *Regional economic policy:* to guide the location of new economic activities.

(2) *Migration and settlement policy:* to guide the migration process, with respect to its volume, direction, and eventual absorption into new settlement areas.

(3) *Urban development policy:* to guide the evolution of the internal structure of urban and metropolitan communities to the extent to which these act as living environments or eco-systems.

(4) *Housing policy:* to guide the provision of shelter and public services of a local character and the building of community environments to facilitate basic social processes, such as family formation, upbringing of children, acculturation, social mobility, and community organizations.

(5) *Urban land policy:* to guide the growth pattern of cities through controls over the use of land and the pattern of occupancy densities.

(6) *Administrative and political development policy:* to guide the processes by which administrative services might be decentralized and powers devolved to local governments.

(7) *Social development policy:* to guide the processes by which the active participation of all social sectors can be secured in affairs that are vital to their interests and welfare.

Adoption of the urban-regional frame therefore implied a far-reaching reorganization of the processes by which policies would be formulated, programs designed, and projects implemented. It involved nothing less than a major overhaul of the public guidance system in the nation.

PLANNING FOR URBAN AND REGIONAL
DEVELOPMENT: 1964–1969

During the past several years, substantial progress has been made in virtually all of the designated policy areas. One ventures to say that the urban-regional frame had been successfully applied in Chile, though the first stage in the effort has barely been completed, and much remains yet to be done.

Regional development planning has become an irreversible fact. The system of regional planning offices throughout Chile, administratively coordinated and backed with research and policy guidance by the National Planning Office, has made possible, not only a much more thorough knowledge of the economic diversity of Chile's regions and their opportunities for growth, but also the institutionalization of a programming process that is leading to a system of regional budgeting parallel to, but obeying different criteria, from the traditional sectoral capital budget of the nation. In a number of areas, a new regional consciousness and loyalty to place has been created as the result of the new image of the region as a meaningful subsystem of the economy, private groups have been encouraged to intensify their developmental efforts in partnership with government, national investments have been channelled to the regions according to a schedule that gave priority to certain growth centers and frontier areas, and greater coordination in the implementation of programs has been achieved.

The flow of migrants to Santiago appears to have been somewhat reduced. Industrial investments have been diverted from the metropolitan area of the capital to more decentralized locations, and developments in the periphery were accelerated at the same time. Of special importance here was the extension of public services to rural areas, especially in education, and the growing adherence of rural populations to organizations such as labor unions, cooperatives, and peasant associations, serving their immediate needs.

The more important cities outside the metropolitan areas became identified as relevant units for programming investments in housing and urban facilities. On the basis of agreements between the municipalities and the Ministry of Housing and Urbanism, programming offices were established for over 80 cities and a process was initiated in which the initiative for the selection of projects and the ordering of priorities among them came to rest with the local community. The active participation of city officials has been obtained, and the next step is towards more directly involving the local *juntas de vecinos* in the planning and programming process.

In housing policy, a savings principle was introduced as a condition for obtaining government housing loans, and at the same time, the bulk of the housing effort was shifted to favor the poorer sectors of the population. This was made possible by introducing the idea of "urbanization by stages" and the substitution of what has been called "housing solutions" for the construction of a completed dwelling unit. The process of urbanization by stages starts from the basic insight that the needs of poor people are first for security of land ownership and access to basic social services (education, light, water, transportation). The physical "shell" can be initially quite primitive as long as these other conditions are present. The improvement of the shell into a house follows to the extent permitted by the economic means of the family, aided by government loans.

Housing policy has been materially aided by the creation of a mechanism for central land acquisition by the government and the adoption of new expropriation procedures. Some attempts were made to heighten intown densities through multi-story redevelopment projects in the center of Santiago. In the provinces, old-fashioned master planning for land uses has given way to a more modern approach of developmental programming through the new offices mentioned earlier.

In the administrative aspect of development, there has been a notable shift to a more decentralized structure. This is not unconnected to the rising levels of technical expertise available in the regions and cities of Chile. The Housing Ministry is now undertaking a far-reaching decentralization of all its operations through its Delegaciones Zonales. The Development Corporation (CORFO) is also strengthening its regional offices and, in some instances, giving them a significantly greater autonomy of decision. Special development corporations have been created for the far south and the northern regions. The agricultural development institutions— INDAP and CORA—have both gone a good way in decentralizing their operations. And other ministries are following suit.

Social development has moved ahead with the unionization of farm labor, the legalization of *juntas de vecinos,* the creation of many new cooperative establishments, the formation of peasant associations, and the extension of government assistance to many of these new organizations during their initial period. New ways of public-private collaboration have been explored, and the principle of sharing responsibilities for economic development has been widely applied.

With all of these positive gains, however, it would be excessively optimistic to claim that the double condition of internal dependency has been overcome by a new pattern of local and individual autonomy organically welded into a dynamic national force. Perhaps it is still too soon for such transcendent results to occur. Both national and communal consensus are still distant goals. So is effective mobilization of the latent energies of the nation for the tasks of national development. These are the major tasks of the next decade.

POLICY ISSUES FOR CHILE IN THE NEXT DECADE

The preceding discussion suggests the need for accelerating certain processes of change that are already underway and for formulating policy measures capable of meeting the challenges of the next decade. Among the more significant issues that face the next generation of policy planners in Chile, the following appear to deserve their special attention:

—Planning for metropolitan growth
—Reducing the rural-urban gap
—Decentralizing and the sharing of powers
—Integrating of migrants with urban life
—Finding new directions for housing policy
—Promoting regional development
—Perfecting of programming and budget systems
—Instituting programs for research.

Brief comments, outlining the nature of each problem, follow below.

Planning for Metropolitan Growth

The problem of metropolitan expansion has until now been largely ignored in Chile. The emphasis was put instead on encouraging the economic growth of peripheral regions and on the immediately pressing needs for providing hundreds of thousands of Chilean families with physical shelter. But metropolitan expansion can no longer be pushed aside as an issue having subordinate priority. Within the next ten years, the *Macro-región Central,* including the provinces of Santiago, Valparaíso, Aconcagua, O'Higgins, and Colchagua will have increased to 5.7 million people, accounting for 46.5 percent of Chile's total population. The Concepción metropolitan region will have grown to within approximately one million. The sheer physical size of these regions will command the attention of government planners. Whatever the success of regional developments in the periphery, population and economic activity will continue to concentrate in the large metropolitan areas. At the same time, industries will be pushed out of the central cities into the metropolitan field of influence, pulling population with them. The result will be a dispersal of activities throughout the metropolitan field which will not only continue to be linked with the central city through rapid transport, but will also become increasingly joined to each other in a spatially dispersed urban-industrial complex. The critical problem, under these conditions, is how to assure the orderly growth and maintenance of this complex pattern in a new spatial setting.

This can be broken down into a number of distinct sub-problems that have yet to be thought about seriously, especially as they refer to the Santiago-Valparaíso region (Macro-región Central).

a. What should be the physical form of this emerging region? How are population and activities to be distributed in space, and what should be the character of the supporting network of transportation? Specifically, what use can be made of existing railroad facilities for commuting? What should be the nature of the interstitial (local to local) patterns of access routes? What changes in airport and port facilities are necessary to serve the expanded region?

b. How should conflicts in use between urban and agricultural land be resolved? What is the relative economic importance of each? How will the several ways in which these conflicts can be resolved affect the urban settlement pattern? What changes do they imply for the system of agricultural production? How can an urban region of nearly six million be efficiently supplied with fresh agricultural produce?

c. What are the implications of metropolitan expansion for water supply? Are present sources sufficient even under conditions of extended drought? How can ground and surface water resources be combined to maximum benefit for both urban and agricultural uses? Should a single water supply system be provided for the entire region, or is it better to deal with the problem incrementally? Faced with the threat of growing pollution, what measures are necessary to assure adequate control over the quality of the water supply?

d. How should the development of recreational and touristic resources be guided in the region so as to satisfy a rapidly growing demand for space and facilities by low-income groups, the well-to-do, and international tourists? What are the different recreational needs of these population groups, and how can they be properly articulated in space? What kinds of physical facilities need to be provided, and where? Which areas should be protected against urban invasion? What are the implications of the tourist-recreational pattern for the location of transportation routes in the region?

e. What improvements in the communication system are desirable to achieve greater regional coherence and permit greater flows of information to the periphery and to higher-order centers in Latin America and the rest of the world?

f. What system of public administration will best serve the emerging region? How can decisions and action programs be better coordinated? How can planning for the region be made effective?

Reducing the Rural-Urban Gap

One of the least noted events in recent decades has been the gradual penetration of urban forms of behavior, thinking, and organization into the rural population. This process, which is slowly but steadily reducing the traditional polarization of the Chilean population into two antagonistic groups, one rural and the other urban, has been notably accelerated during the past few years. Without attempting to establish their order of importance, since serious studies of the subject are not available, the following "events" have in the past been instrumental in producing the changes referred to:

—construction of rural roads and installation of regular bus services to the major cities of Chile

—extension of public services to rural areas such as postal and telegraph service, production credit (INDAP), technical assistance, electric energy, health services, and others

—participation in the market economy of a large number of "marginal" and subsistence farmers and landless laborers

—increasing incorporation of the mass of the rural population into local organizations, labor unions, cooperatives, and peasant associations

—increasing literacy of rural populations and access to at least primary schools

—growing political participation (voting and direct action)

—increasing use of mass media by rural populations: radio and newspapers.

—small but growing access of rural people to preuniversity and university education through extension of secondary schools in smaller cities and creation of university centers in the provinces.

In spite of the fact that these forces have been operating for some time, the progress made has been uneven. Only a fraction of the rural population has been touched, and then only by some, not all, of the forces enumerated. Complete transition to urbanism has not occurred.

One reason for this spotty record is the low degree of influence wielded by the one third of the nation's population living in rural areas. While large landowners have traditionally had access to power at the highest levels of government and banking, the mass of the rural population has not been mobilized effectively for political ends. There has never been a broadly-based agrarian party in Chile. Urban interests have predominated since the 1920s and, except for the large landed interests who were able to take care of their own, the needs of the rural population have almost always been postponed. One of the results of this policy emphasis has been steadily worsening terms of trade for agricultural products relative to industrial commodities. Another has been the extreme slowness by which urbanizing forces have taken hold within the countryside.

The cultures of rural and urban life continue to be divided in Chile, with the former subsisting in its condition of internal dependency upon the latter. If a reduction in dependency is accepted as one of the major social objectives for Chile—as has been suggested—looking towards its replacement with a greater degree of inter-dependency, a major problem for the next decade would appear to be how to accelerate the urbanization processes operating in rural areas.

Beyond a general relative increase in the resources devoted to rural development—including, not only those for raising production, but also those for improving and intensifying public services—an acceleration of urbanization processes could be achieved by concentrating new resource increments in a number of selected rural development areas. This would greatly facilitate the direction of social and economic change in these areas and would be likely to have a major impact on the transition to urbanism. Coordination of rural-action programs in micro-regions would be in some senses similar to what ODEPLAN has attempted to do for larger regional units composed of one or more provinces, and is related to MINVU's concept of ciudad-proyecto and the programming process based on this concept. It would go beyond these by greater emphasis on actions promising short-term results.

In rural micro-regions, physical and production improvements would be joined. Small towns would be included in the planning effort as potential service centers. Consideration might be given to the regrouping of rural populations into villages that would help to focus the urbanizing forces. New forms of community participation in coordinated area development could be explored. The entire rural development effort might eventually be channelled through local area organizations and in this way call forth a larger volume of local financial and labor resources to supplement the public investment.

Here and there, some beginnings already exist for this kind of an experiment. Techniques have been worked out to a substantial degree. Experience with rural regional planning has been accumulating in other countries, especially in Israel. The approach deserves to be closely studied as an alternative to the uncoordinated, dispersed methods presently in use (Weitz and Rokach, 1968).

Decentralization and the Sharing of Powers

Responsible opinion in Chile has for a long time been strongly critical of what are believed to be the negative effects of the extreme degree of centralization in decision-making and resource management that is characteristic of the nation. All-powerful central ministries and autonomous corporations are affecting the lives of individual families directly and almost without the mediation of intervening organizations. Business, professional, and some working-class groups have been able to organize themselves and to exert some influences at the national levels of government over programs of immediate interest to them, but the majority of the population has been unable to defend its interests in the same way. Nor have the cities and regions of Chile done much better; they have remained largely administrative entities for the convenience of national bureaucrats.

There are some certain ideas about the future of development in Chile: the demand for varied governmental services will multiply at a rate far greater than population or even income, the complexity of governmental operations will increase, even minority interests—though small in relative terms—will acquire political importance in absolute numbers, the volume of work to be accomplished by public agencies will rise astronomically, and technical competence and sophistication will steadily reduce purely political considerations in the administration of governmental programs. At the same time, and this will almost certainly be true regardless of the shape of political events, the demand for participation in public decisions will grow, if only to adapt national programs to local conditions and needs.

The normal consequence of these trends is a progressive overloading of communication channels that will induce greater arbitrariness of decision, standardization of programs, delay in response times, and increasing frustration on the part of the clients of governmental service who not only will fail to receive the services they need but be subjected to humiliating bureaucratic management.[13] Since this course of events, projected for another decade, is likely to reach intolerable proportions, pressures will grow for a more amenable pattern of decentralization in the administration of public services.

The major policy problem appears to be a double one: how, on the one hand, to make governmental action more responsive to local needs, more efficient in the use of resources, and more agile in program execution and, on the other hand, how to stimulate local motivations, self-help, and latent energies for the multiple tasks of national development.

This problem is by no means new, and in recent years notable progress has been made in some areas to decentralize government operations and to obtain wider participation of local interest groups in decisions and program implementation. The formation of *juntas de vecinos,* the establishment of municipal programming offices, the incorporation of peasant associations and cooperatives into agrarian reform programs, the renewed emphasis on self-help construction of housing and communities facilities, and other measures are partial answers to the challenge posed by over-centralization.

It should be recognized, however, that these measures represent only a useful start and that the circumstances of national development, described above, will in the coming years require even more radical solutions.

The basic weakness of popular organizations is that many of them have very little to do that is of truly vital concern to their members. Sport clubs are organized to play football; mothers' centers are started to receive classes in cooking and sewing; neighborhood organizations present their "needs" to the authorities in a respectful maner; labor unions are established on a shop basis to engage in collective bargaining, but their effective bargaining strength is exceedingly weak. There is at present no way by which these several collective activities can be joined to matters that are related to the life of the larger "community." The street, the neighborhood, perhaps the *barrio* command a measure of popular loyalty beyond the family, and are capable of being acted upon by them, but not the city, the region, or the nation.

The capacity for self-help and endogenous development is extremely weak. Everywhere in Chile the bureaucratic model of organization still appears to be dominant, characterized by traditional forms of hierarchy and authority-dependency relations. Only the élites are capable of effective participation, but they, for the most part, continue to act out of a narrowly conceived self-interest. They think that what is good for them is also good for the larger "community" of fellow citizens. Unfortunately, this coincidence of interests is rare in actuality. More often, what is good for the élites is of no special benefit to the nation and may actually be of disservice.

There is a need, therefore, to rethink the meaning of popular participation and the structure and roles of popular organizations with a view to directly involving the Chilean people in activities that really matter: production, city building, education. To involve in this case means to make them co-responsible for the success of these activities. In terms of urban-regional policy, three practical lines of action may be suggested. The first has to do with administrative decentralization of the services of central government and their coordination on a city-wide and regional basis. The second concerns an increased sharing of powers between the central government and local governmental and other representative units in the formulation and administration of national programs. The third, most radical step of all, points in the direction of an outright devolution of certain powers to local governments, particularly in those functional areas where the effects of developmental actions can be effectively internalized at the local level. (To mention an obvious candidate for the last-named line of action: the maintenance of local streets and sidewalks involves no overriding national objectives and should be a matter of primarily local concern.)

A decisive movement in the directions indicated would imply a substantial reorganization of the administrative and even the political system in Chile. Some of the changes may be suggested in quite general terms. They are functional requirements for a successful implementation of decentralization policies.

Political parties will have to become more accountable to local and regional interests. To the extent that political parties serve to aggregate dispersed interests, this requirement will cut across present class and social status alignments and may give rise to new political affiliations. The central ministries will have to give up some of their current powers over detailed program decisions, concentrating on the formulation of policy guidelines, the setting of performance standards, information gathering and dissemination, research and coordination. At the regional level, administrative councils will need to be activated, *intendentes* will have to be given wider authority for coordination of governmental programs as well as a more broadly defined role in the resolution of interest conflicts, and the Regional Planning Offices of ODEPLAN will need to be assigned a key role in the preparation of technical planning and programming documents to guide decentralized development. The municipalities, long neglected and antiquated in their methods of administration, will have to strive for greater technical and administrative competence as their functions multiply. New instruments of financing local and regional development will have to be devised, among them, new forms of local taxation, municipal loan programs, systems of grants-in-aid, and loans for regional development.

None of this will be easy, and most of the necessary adjustments will meet with the bitter resistance of entrenched interests.

Integration of Migrants Into Urban Life

The exodus of population from the rural areas and small towns of Chile that has been such a marked characteristic of national development in the past will undoubtedly continue for some time to come. The percentage contribution of migrants to urban growth may decline as cities grow larger and the available reservoir of rural population slowly dries up. But in absolute numbers, migration to cities may well maintain its present level and may actually show a slight increase. At the same time, however, a reordering of urban populations is likely to occur, as the streams of migrants move from city to city and, more specifically, from smaller cities to the three large metropolitan concentrations in Chile. These trends are for the most part irreversible, at least over the short span of a single decade. The forces operating in favor of the metropolis compared to the countryside or the small town will continue to operate in the foreseeable future: the relatively higher growth of opportunities for social and economic advancement in metro-areas, the continuing urbanization of the countryside acting on aspirations and facilitating movement, the greater political weight of the large city. These forces are too powerful, and countervailing forces too weak to substantially reduce the rate of net migration to the "urban fields" of Santiago, Valparaíso, and Concepción. The spatial structure of development in Chile has acquired a degree of stability that makes any major change over the period of a single decade extremely unlikely.

The persistence of large-scale rural migration to metropolitan areas poses as important policy questions the incorporation of migrants into urban life, specifically into the urban economy, and their increased access to public services and other means for improving their social condition.

In this connection, it is well to remember that the migrant's principal point of contact with the metropolis is the *población* where he lives. It is in the *población* where political parties compete for his vote, where he comes into contact with government service agencies, where he listens to the radio, attends meetings and organizes, from where he sets out on his trips across the city and to which he returns in the evenings. It is through the *población*, whether it be a *callampa* or one of the numerous housing projects on the edge of the city, that he can gain access to what the city has to offer him. A *población* may function at a high or at a low level of efficiency in providing such access, but most of them are operating at a level that is not nearly high enough. It is for this reason that a very large proportion of the urban population continues to be part of a more or less non-differentiated sub-proletariat, marginal to the urban processes that are available to more fortunate but less numerous groups.

The problem of "access" involves a whole series of factors only some of which can be mentioned here. First in order are the *informational services* that are at the disposal of the *poblador* which tell him where he can seek assistance, find a job, or apply for a loan. These services can be public or private and can be rendered locally through a special office or series of such offices as well as through radio, television, and newspapers. *Transportation* is another means of access, this time to dispersed metropolitan resources that may be useful to the *poblador* in his desire to integrate himself more completely with the city. Another means of access is to put certain *general services* at his disposal in the local community, especially where distance would act as a serious obstacle to their effective utilization. Examples would be job training and counselling centers, psychiatric help, pediatric help, day-time nurseries, home management technical services, legal counsel, popular savings banks, youth centers, and adult educaton centers (popular universities). A fourth means of access is through the location of *basic communication services* in the *población*, specifically, telephone centers and a post office.

Most of these services, it will be noted, are non-specialized in the sense that they attend to the needs of new migrants (and indeed of certain older residents of the city) to *relate* themselves to their new environment. This is certainly true of information, transportation, and communication services), and it is also true of the set of general services that, although in an indirect manner, enhance the capacity of the individual or of the family group to enter into larger networks of relationships. Some of them would release time from essential chores at home for remunerated work or political action (e.g., nurseries for small children); others would increase personal capabilities for autonomous action (e.g., psychiatric help, popular savings banks, job training and counselling centers, popular universities); still others would advise the *poblador* of his legal rights and help him avoid being crushed by litigation (legal counselling centers); another category of "access" services would serve primarily as a means for socialization to the city (e.g., youth centers); finally, there would be services whose purpose is to bring elements of urban culture to the home, being directed there primarily at the female members of the family (e.g., pediatric help; home management).

In the provision of access services to the metropolis, certain rules might be considered that would have a beneficial influence on their degree of utilization: the participation of the community in these services (at least through token payment for services received, but going all the way through actual control over their management); an adequate physical setting for the complex of services in the form of multiple-purpose neighborhood centers, and finally, the training of community workers whose special function would be to act as mediators between the governmental bureaucracy and the family of the *poblador*. In these several ways, the efficiency of a *población* in providing generalized access to the metropolis can be considerably increased.

New Directions for Housing Policy

Modern housing policy has moved beyond the simple provision of physical shelter: it has become a tool for community and national development. Chile has been one of the pioneers in applying the latest thinking to the solution of the so-called housing problem. The cynical slogan, *casa CORVI, casa gratis* has lost some of its sting. What is being offered now is a whole series of related but separable housing *services* of which the physical shell is one, but not necessarily the most important element. Methods have been worked out whereby many of the persons receiving these services are also paying for them.

Housing services include land, drinking water, sewage disposal, electric light, roads, transportation to other parts of the city, schools, community halls, shops, sports fields, health clinics, nursery schools, and police and fire stations. They also include a suitable dwelling unit, of course, but the quality of the shelter will depend on the ability of the family to save, and can range all the way from a simple shed to a middle-class home or apartment. What may be called the urban *module* includes all of these elements; an aggregation of modules, in turn, constitutes a housing estate (or *población*), and a cluster of housing estates make up a new urban district or *barrio*. At the *barrio* level work place and certain higher order services are added as additional elements to the original housing module. In this way, the city is built up.

The close relation between the provision of housing services and urban expansion has been receiving special attention in Chile. It is easy to extend the logical relationships even further: from *barrio* units, cities, metropolitan areas, and regions are built up.

Housing policy may be seen as a key element in the realization of the urban-regional frame for national development. It deals, not with shelter essentially, but with a range of services, the design of urban districts, the pattern of the metropolis, the creation and geographical distribution of jobs, and the management of the whole for the benefit of the entire population—communal, urban, regional, and national. Only functional specialization and administrative convenience explain the narrowing of housing policy to the problem of the module itself and the various ways in which it can be provided with an economy of resources.

One of the least recognized aspects of housing policy is its relationship to local and national economic development. Economic planners continue to think of housing as a program with basically social (or welfare) objectives. But current knowledge, based on research, does not bear them out. The principal conclusions may be mentioned here:

   (a) People are willing to save for housing services and the artifacts that go to make up a home. While housing in the upper-income brackets may be considered to a large degree one of the consumption goods, housing for the poor is a means for the production of labor services.
   (b) Housing improvements have been demonstrated to have a positive effect on labor productivity under certain conditions. This effect is probably achieved through the beneficial effects such improvements tend to have on the mental health of the worker.
   (c) Housing, in the narrower sense of shelter, not only protects personal property against the natural elements and theft (and thus makes accumulation possible) but also provides certain services—in conjunction with labor—which even though they may not show up in the national accounts are of extreme importance to an economy. They include the preparation of meals, child care, home education—services that must be paid for in the market place unless they are provided at home. In addition, certain industrial or commercial operations may be conducted in the home.
   (d) People receiving housing services are generally willing to pay for them either in the form of rent or mortgages or, indirectly, through their taxes. Most public investments in the urban module can be recovered

in this way over a period of 15 to 25 years. But to achieve this effect, efficient administrative devices must be arranged for the necessary financial transactions.

(e) Provision of the physical facilities for housing services make up the bulk of construction work in most countries, and the construction industry depends on it to a very large extent. Because of the high degree of interconnectedness between construction and other industrial sectors in a country such as Chile, any change in the level of construction activity may affect an urban economy in much the same way, though the multiplier effect there would tend to be less than for the nation. Construction can therefore have stabilizing or destabilizing effects on the national economy; under certain conditions, it can even act as a propulsive force.

A review of national housing policies from an economic perspective, bearing in mind the developmental character of housing, would appear to be one of the important tasks for the next several years. Some of the questions to be considered would be these:

—how can popular savings be mobilized more effectively in the provision of housing services?

—how can the system of housing finance be improved so as to reduce the government's annual contribution or subsidy to housing?

—how can the construction industry (traditionally the most volatile sector in Chilean economy) be stabilized?

—how can the spectacular rate of increase in the costs of construction, now rising much more rapidly than the consumer index, be reduced?

—how can the time necessary for the execution of the annual housing plan be reduced from the current 4-year span to one or two years at the most so that more houses can be built?

—how can the local multiplier effect of housing construction activity be increased (e.g., through a system of local rather than centralized bidding)?

Promoting Regional Development

Chile has today one of the most advanced systems of regional development planning in the world. This is especially remarkable when the nation's unitary political structure and high centralism in government and administration is recalled. The planning system has reached maturity quickly. Its nerve center is in Santiago in one of the two principal sub-directorates of the National Planning Office which stands under the direct authority of the President of the Republic. Dependent on this center are a series of regional technical offices (ORPLAN) which might best be described as the eyes and ears of ODEPLAN in the regions. In addition, there are a number of other arrangements to complete the picture. In the far south of Chile, a special development corporation has been created for the province (region) of Magallanes to which the local ORPLAN serves as the technical staff. In the far north, at Africa, a special development junta has been in existence for a number of years to decide on the use of investment funds obtained from the Arica casino. As of 1968, ODEPLAN was supplying technical planning services to this junta through a local office.

In general, the activities of this ambitious and well-organized planning system may be said to consist basically of (1) the preparation of planning strategies for each development region; (2) an attempt to guide national investment policies in accordance with specific criteria for location; (3) the preparation of a regionalized investment budget for the nation (which is not submitted to the National Congress for approval); (4) the evaluation of government investment policy in the regions according to the yardstick set up in the development strategy of the area; (5) an attempt to achieve improved coordination of government programs in the regions; and (6) the promotion of local development by the private sector. These activities are backed by careful study of regional resources and economic activities throughout the nation.

The entire operation is a highly imaginative effort to descend from the abstractions of highly aggregative "global" economic planning for the nation, to begin to make sense on the ground of the heretofore uncoordinated sectoral investment programs of the dozen or so ministries operating at the national level, to introduce explicitly a geographical dimension into the system of national objectives for development, and specifically, to counterbalance what is regarded as an excessive growth for the national capital region by accelerating economic development in selected provincial centers (or "growth poles").

If the actual achievements of Chile's regional planning system are compared to the broad purposes stated above, it can be concluded that it has been most successful where either a certain amount of total resources available were managed locally (as in Magallanes and Arica) or where local development was rapid, intense, and complex (as in the Concepción region). As yet, no decentralized planning office exists for the national capital region (macro-región central).

In other respects, ODEPLAN's influence has been relatively weak. The regionalized budget is having only minimal influence over the direction of the actual investment effort of the nation; national policy for regional development exists primarily as a document and has not been effectively "internalized" by the action agencies of the government; relations with sectoral ministries are with one or two notable exceptions relatively weak; and the promotional activities of the ORPLANs have met with little response in the absence of a dynamic private enterprise sector outside of Santiago and Concepción. ODEPLAN's work is becoming increasingly routine and the limits of its internal possibilities will soon be exhausted unless major structural changes in Chile's territorial organization of power are introduced.

Chile's system of development regions has so far not yielded effective decentralization of decision-making and political accountability. The OR-

PLANs in the regions serve little more than a decorative purpose with the exception of the three areas noted above where some degree of financial decentralization has already occurred or where the tasks of development make some form of local coordination indispensable. The regions of Chile are today weak administrative units with no political life of their own, and the provincial *intendentes* are scarcely more than police chiefs subordinate to the Ministry of the Interior. The constitutional provision for the establishment of provincial assemblies has not been acted upon, nor has enabling legislation for the creation of regional development banks. Without passing judgment on the wisdom of these two latent possibilities for more effective decentralization, it would appear to be worthwhile to consider seriously the activation of the existing set of development regions so that each region might acquire control over at least secondary development decisions and the means for their implementation. This would relieve central government ministries of much routine work and of the very real problem of communications overload; at the same time it would allow a much more active participation of vital forces in the regions and local areas in the national development process.

The possibility for actually achieving financial and political decentralization at the regional level are today no longer as remote as they appeared four or five years ago. The Ministry of Housing and Urbanism is seriously considering a radical financial decentralization of its operations in the regional level; CORFO has already passed greater decision authority to its regional offices; and the agricultural development organizations—especially CORA—are already operating with a good deal of autonomy in local areas. The existence of ORPLANs in the regions has removed one of the principal obstacles to the decentralization of development administration—the lack of adequately prepared technical personnel at regional levels. And the present consideration by the Congress of far-reaching constitutional reforms opens the way to the possibility of introducing provisions—similar to those currently operating in Italy and about to be voted by popular referendum in France—that would considerably fortify the economic role of the regions.

All of this would still be within the context of an economic system of State capitalism which appears to be evolving in Chile. It could be strengthened considerably were Chile to consider in the urban sector what it has already introduced—although still on a relatively small scale—in the agricultural sector, the active participation of workers in the management of enterprise. Worker management is clearly not a magic solution to the absence of a powerful dynamism in private entrepreneurship but the possibilities inherent in this institutional reform—widely practiced in Yugoslavia—have not even been seriously considered, much less explored specifically. If worker management of industries were to be introduced to Chile, it is quite likely that the promotional and guiding efforts of the regional ORPLANs would encounter much greater receptivity than is due today. Worker management councils would also find it much easier to participate in a decentralized regional system of development administration than do the representatives of individual private industries or the organized Chambers of Commerce and Industry that are active in the regions today but whose primary interest lies in the defense of their own interests rather than in the development of regional and urban-metropolitan economies.

What is being proposed here would have far-reaching effects on the entire framework of the economy and polity of Chile. Yet considering the groundwork that has already been prepared, it is an alternative that should be seriously considered if Chile is to break out of its traditional institutional deadlock into a new kind of national democracy—dynamic, participatory, and dedicated to social justice. It would provide an adequate context for many of the reforms at the local level that have been suggested in preceding sections of this essay.

Perfection of Programming and Budget Systems

At the present time, it would be fair to say that Chile has only a rudimentary system of programming and budgeting for development in her cities and regions. The system is anchored in two institutions: for co-ordinated urban development it is working through the Ministry of Housing, and for regional development through the National Planning Office. It is a new system and, in many ways, still an experimental one. Even so, it has already permitted a wider involvement of local officials in proposing priorities for governmental action and, through the improved coordination of investments on the ground, better information, and more precise controls, has begun to raise the level of efficiency in the management of available resources. But a great deal remains to be done in moving towards a truly sophisticated system of programming for coordinative area development on a national scale.

What are some of the tasks that lie ahead? By 1970, it is likely that the Housing Ministry will have successfully established about 40 communal programming offices on the basis of formal agreements with individual municipalities. But these offices must be staffed with competent technicians and must be strongly backed by institutions capable of providing assistance, certain information services, and policy guidelines. At the same time, ministries that are still excluded from the system—for instance, Public Works and Transportation, Education, and Health—must gradually be involved to make the concept of *ciudad-proyecto* a reality. All this implies a close collaboration between government, university, and private institutions such as the Institute for Communal Development (IDEC) currently being organized.

Further problems arise from the need to extend the programming process to metropolitan areas. For this purpose, it will probably be necessary to create some form of intermediate-level planning organization with the participation of metropolitan municipalities. The programming and budget process will also be affected by the present move of the Ministry of Housing to decentralize its operations to Zonal Offices. While both of these initiatives should facilitate coordination with regional programming through ODEPLAN, they will impose exacting requirements for technical performance, inter-sectoral coordination, and timing. And if this were not enough, there is now also an increasingly strong desire for the newly created communal federations of *juntas de vecinos* to take part in the programming process and make a local influence felt.

Neither in urban nor in regional programming is the budget yet an accurate reflection of the physical programs drawn up; consequently, it cannot be used as a management device in monitoring and controlling the progress of public works. No system has been established whereby changes in budgetary allocations, for instance, bring about a corresponding reordering of program priorities. Nor is the present timing adequate; the lead time is not nearly long enough to permit necessary adjustments to be made, and the time period over which both programs and budgets are projected should be doubled or tripled to provide a reasonable perspective for evaluating alternative programs.

Turning to regional programming proper, we find that little coordination exists as yet between the regional programs prepared by ODEPLAN (in collaboration with its decentralized regional offices) and the programs of the Housing Ministry which have the city as their focus. In contrast to urban programming, regional planners have not yet evolved a normalized pattern of local participation, not even on the restricted "official" level. Consequently, the regional program largely reflects the thinking of central government technicians, only occasionally an agreement of regional representatives from the central ministries, and hardly ever the emphasis that private organized interests would wish to give to governmental action. Also, the National Planning Office does not directly control investment resources of its own. Its programming is only indicative for action agencies of the government, while the generally poor communications that exist between national and sectoral planning suggest that the amount of "indication" is not very large. None of the ministries feel themselves bound to follow the suggestions of ODEPLAN for regional investment allocations. Although some advances have been made, there does not yet exist an operational model whereby differing sectoral and regional allocations could be reconciled within the framework of a national plan.

Finally, there is missing from the architecture of Chile's programming and budget system the basic information component. This would eventually have to be an all-purpose national computer system which could be used on a time-sharing basis (and by means of telephone or telex) by the growing network of decentralized and centralized programming and planning offices throughout the nation. Elements of such a system are beginning to appear, but most of its development remains for the future.

A staggering amount of coordination will be needed for successfully guiding the processes of area development. This is likely to call for major reforms in administrative arrangements, above all in the direction of further decentralization. Without the return of a substantial amount of "minor" decisions to local units of government, as was suggested earlier, the ambitious programming system Chile has initiated is likely to come to grief on the simple grounds of communications overload. For the kind of programming that has been discussed is a voracious consumer of data, and existing bureaucratic structures are not prepared to cope with this demand.

The Need for Research

Until recently, research for coordinated area development has not been necessary for Chile. Decisions used to be made on the basis of intuition, political judgment, and rules of thumb. But clearly this method is no longer adequate as problems become more complex and the penalties for faulty decisions more severe.

During the last few years, some knowledge relevant to area development has become available: the dimensions of the problem are now known, descriptive data have become more abundant, and certain conceptual and analytical tools have been evolved and found useful. The National Planning Office has done a good deal of practical research on questions of regional development and is now moving to coordinate its activities with the National Institute for Natural Resources. The Interdisciplinary Center for Urban Studies (CIDU) at the Catholic University of Chile has likewise contributed to the general knowledge, but the full needs for problem-focussed and basic research are still far from being met.

Even a partial listing of the existing lacunae may be instructive. It is not meant to suggest an ordering of relative importance, nor is it a topic outline of proposed research. But an account of current information needs will at least help to identify some of the more important areas where additional knowledge must become available.

Much of the area planning done in Chile is still based on anachronistic and frequently misleading information; often there is no information at all. At the regional level, for instance, product has been estimated, but not income; output/ capital coefficients have not been calculated on a current or projected basis; the pattern of interregional commodity and capital flows is practically unknown; regional resources surveys have yet to be conducted with a view to possible economic use.

At the city level, the so-called "pre-investment" studies correspond to the regional development strategies prepared by ODEPLAN during its first few years of activity. But these studies are growing quickly out-of-date and frequently do not contain the information needed for middle-range programming, nor have they been extended to metropolitan areas as yet. No methods exist at present for evaluating the effects of alternative plans and investment programs, and cost information on a comparative area basis is not available.

In connection with more problem-focussed research, next to nothing is known about the attitudes of people towards housing services, their use of these services, and the processes by which they ensure themselves of an essential supply. The occurrences in the "zone of transaction" where citizens meet face-to-face with representatives of their government have not been studied. We do not know the frustrations that arise in the course of certain types of transaction, nor the distortions of law and policy that occur as messages are passed down along an extended series of hierarchical steps in the government bureaucracy and across to potential clients. Little research has been done on problems of municipal financing and administration. It is quite simply assumed that municipalities are hopelessly inefficient, corrupt, and incapable of constructive action on their own behalf.

Passing on to more fundamental research questions, a step or two removed from the urgencies of problem-solving, the student of urban and regional development ventures into almost totally unexplored territory. There is ignorance from basic urbanization processes to studies in the economics of housing and systems of indicators for the evaluation of urban "performance." One would like to know something of the process of migration *within* the larger cities and their effects on housing availabilities. One would also like to know how ecological sub-units of urban society are organized and in what relationship they stand to each other. One hopes some day to better know the effects of different types of housing situation on family savings and social integration. One would like to explore the effects of different decentralization patterns on political behavior.

To move with reasonable speed towards greater knowledge and insight of these and other questions, the government will have to evolve an explicit research policy that will include, not only the organization of small research units within action and planning agencies such as the Ministry of Housing, but also the expansion of the system of contracted research with universities and private consultants, and a major effort to upgrade available skills for research within this particular area of study. There is still a notable reluctance on the part of certain government functionaries, not to mention professional politicians, to promote research as one of the methods for accelerating the pace of national development. But these prejudices will have to be discarded over the next decade. Intuition, unaided by the instruments of scientific research, is no longer an adequate basis for government decision and policy design.

CONCLUSION

There can be little doubt that Chile is today leading the rest of Latin America in her ability to formulate and carry out public policies within a coordinated framework of urban and regional planning. Programs are centrally guided, but are worked out, and frequently implemented, with the steadily-growing participation of local people from the cities and regions of the nation. If during the next few years, Chile continues to make progress in subnational area development, it is similarly clear that her position on the continent as a leader in planning will be consolidated. And there is every reason to hope that this progress will be noted, not only in the adoption of formal procedures, but also in a revitalized periphery, greater national integration, and a new sense of community.

The next decade should see the emergence of planning for metropolitan growth, especially in the Santiago region, further reductions in the economic and social gap separating rural from urban populations, an increasing sharing of powers between central and local governments, the more complete economic and cultural integration of urban migrants with life in the cities, new departures in housing policy that will stress to an even greater extent the role of housing as a tool for community and regional economic development, the perfection of planning and budgeting systems for coordinated area development, and an increasingly influential role of scientific and technological research in the formulation of subnational policies. If this prognosis is correct, many of the current problems of urban and regional development will have been brought close to a solution.

Nevertheless, it would be foolish to think that the need for further innovation will gradually disappear as these accomplishments pass into history. The future will reveal new problems, requiring a new response; there are no definite, once-and-for-all solutions.

This is the lesson learned, for instance, in programming for housing. It used to be thought that the physical deficit for housing units is a constant quantity. By intensifying the effort in the construction of new housing units, it was hoped that substantial gains might be made on the housing problem, that the deficit could be reduced and eventually, perhaps, even eliminated. This simplistic view has given way now to a more sophisticated understanding of the operation of housing markets. The needs for housing change with economic conditions and family aspirations. What is an acceptable solution in one period, becomes substandard in another. A family satisfied with a 2-room dwelling in 1969, may demand (and be able to afford) a 4-room house a decade later. The physical concept of housing "shortage" is therefore no longer useful for planning purposes. It has to be replaced with an economic concept.

As population increases and industrialization proceeds, as urbanization reaches deeper into the countryside, as experience is gained with new patterns of participatory democracy, the complexity of policy issues will increase at a speed far greater than any of these, and the demands on government for processing information and for anticipatory planning will pose entirely new problems that will require high ingenuity for resolution. Government will have to respond with greater agility and more flexibility and, above all, with even greater relevance to local conditions. The need for technical judgment will rise as purely political responses will no longer be adequate to meet the new demands. As the requirements of national growth press against available resources, the question of efficiency in their use will also be put forth with greater insistence than now. All this implies that the guiding institutions of Chile's development will more than ever before have to resort to planning to improve the allocation of existing resources, and to undertake certain structural reforms in the character of the guiding system itself which will permit a more adequate level of performance by the "concert" of Chile's cities and regions. Not only allocative planning but continuing planning for institutionalizing innovations will impose itself as an unavoidable necessity.

NOTES

1. According to the 1960 census, 48.7 percent of the population lived in cities with 20,000 or more inhabitants and 68.2 percent in cities over 5,000. In the succeeding nine years, it is highly probable that these percentages of Chile's urban population have risen still higher.

2. The actual census data were modified by counting metropolitan areas and other "intercommunal" urban concentrations, such as La Serena-Coquimbo and Quillota-Calera as single units.

3. The following cumulative annual growth rates for population are reported by the Dirección de Estadística y Censos:

	1940–52	1952–60	1940–1960
Chile total	1.8	2.4	2.0
Urban	3.8	4.4	0.1
Rural	−0.1	−0.0	−0.1

Between 1950 and 1960, the economically active population engaged in agriculture declined from 31.1 to 26.4 percent of the total.

4. Chile's increasing dependence on external food supplies can be gleaned from the following table:

FOREIGN TRADE OF AGRICULTURAL AND
LIVESTOCK COMMODITIES
(MILLIONS OF DOLLARS)

Year	Exports	Imports	Balance
1950	36.5	69.2	− 32.7
1955	36.1	112.7	− 76.6
1960	30.3	117.1	− 86.8
1965	n.a.	n.a.	−120.2

SOURCE: CIDA (1965).

5. The following analysis is in the main based on John Friedmann and Thomas Lackington (1966).

6. The measurement of the "marginal" urban sub-proletariat will, of course, depend on the definition used. If unemployment is taken as an index, 6–7 percent of Santiago's labor force and 8–10 percent for larger provincial cities could be classified as "marginal." These figures rise rapidly to about 20 percent if underemployment and low-productivity employment are added. The figures cited for unemployment correspond roughly to the illiterate populations of the provinces of Santiago (7.1 percent), Valparaíso (6.0), Antofagasta (6.4) and Concepción (11.4) for 1960. According to a complex index of marginality, constructed by Armand

Mattelard (1968), the 5 lowest-ranking *comunas* in Santiago accounted for slightly more than 20 percent of the total metropolitan population. But, of course, not everyone living in these *comunas* could be classified as belonging to the sub-proletariat. (For instance, persons with completed secondary education accounted for between 16 and 29 percent of the adult male populations of these 5 *comunas,* while housing in poor condition accounted for 16 to 32 percent.) These data suggest that, at least for Santiago, the sub-proletariat in recent years probably accounted for between 6 and 20 percent of total population. The figures for provincial cities are probably somewhat higher. However, about half the urban working population in Chile had an estimated average annual income of between 30 to 40 percent of that for white collar workers and therefore represent the most disadvantaged sector of the population (1964). See Gavan, table I (1968). These different figures suggest that the phenomenon of marginality must be understood in terms of a continuum of values through a range of vectors, rather than in absolute terms.

7. The degree of economic marginality in rural areas can be measured more accurately than in the urban areas. Thus, in 1955, 46.5 percent of all agricultural families worked no land of their own and 25.2 percent farmed lands that were insufficient to provide a basic living standard to the family according to local standards. These data are illustrative of the scale of the phenomenon; they could, however, be considerable refined; see CIDA (1966: 42).

8. Annual Percent Rates of Increase in Cost of Living Index

Year	Percent	Year	Percent	Year	Percent
1930	−5	1943	8	1956	38
1931	−4	1944	15	1957	17
1932	26	1945	8	1958	33
1933	5	1946	30	1959	33
1934	9	1947	23	1960	5
1935	−1	1948	17	1961	10
1936	12	1949	21	1962	28
1937	10	1950	10	1963	45
1938	2	1951	23	1964	38
1939	7	1952	12	1965	26
1940	10	1953	56	1966	17
1941	23	1954	71	1967	22
1942	26	1955	84	1968	28

Sources: Hirschman (1963: 160) and *Boletín del Banco Central de Chile* (1969).

9. Data to prove this hypothesis are hard to come by and inconclusive. The wholesale industrial price index published by the Central Bank of Chile is not very adequate for the purpose of rural-urban price comparisons since no data exist on the major industrial product components of rural consumption and investment. But to the extent they can be accepted, the data show, relative to industrial prices, significant long-term price declines for farm products, other than livestock, since at least 1947. The livestock sector has generally fared better, maintaining price parity, but the number of farmers engaged in animal production on a commercial basis is only a fraction of the total number of farm families. It is also quite likely that the adverse terms of trade affected small, inefficient farmers more sharply than large farming enterprises. Since most farm family consumption takes place outside normal market channels, however, the real test would be a comparison of farm output with input prices for agricultural production. I have been unable to locate any studies dealing with this phenomenon, but the impression among Chilean economists is that, at least during the last decade, input prices have been rising more rapidly than prices for output.

10. Chile's gross investment rate has traditionally been among the lowest in

Latin America. Between 1940 and 1959, it was only 10.4 percent. Since then it has risen significantly, approaching 14 to 16 percent in recent years. (Universidad de Chile, 1963: Vol. II, Table 9, and *Fourth Presidential Message, 1968*: 18.)

11. For example, note the fluctuations in the "sueldo vital" from year to year in the following table. Even more striking is the gradual decline of the "vital" from 1952 to 1966. Since about half of the urban workers in Chile get paid at or near the "sueldo vital," these data suggest a gradual decline in the real income of the urban worker.

"SUELDO VITAL" IN SANTIAGO
(IN 1964 ESCUDOS)

1950	218.3	1956	165.8	1962	162.8
1951	217.7	1957	184.0	1963	143.0
1952	252.4	1958	166.6	1964	150.2
1953	201.1	1959	172.1	1965	161.4
1954	170.5	1960[a]		1966	165.4
1955	155.8	1961	198.2		

a. None established in 1960.

SOURCE: Sergio Undurraga S. (1967) "Key Factors in Chilean Economic Development," *Economic Development Issues: Latin America*. CED Supplementary Paper Nu. 21 (August).

12. According to census computations, 60 percent of the resident migrant population in Santiago in 1960 was born in cities which in 1952 had 10,000 or more population. Of the remaining 40 percent, one-fifth were foreigners, also presumably of urban origin.

13. The effect of communications overload on institutional behavior has been analyzed extensively by Richard L. Meier of the University of California at Berkeley. According to Professor Meier (1962: 75–87), an institution adopts successively the following measures as the pressure of communication increases: (1) Queuing inputs at peak periods; (2) Setting priorities in queue; (3) Destroying lowest priorities; (4) Adapting to redundancy with active files; (5) Creating branch facilities; (6) Encouraging middlemen; (7) Creating a mobile reserve; (8) Evolving explicit performance standards; (9) Reducing standards of performance; (10) Searching for the "Magic formula"; (11) Developing customer self-service; (12) Escaping; (13) Working to rule; (14) Salvaging of component units.

For those who have watched the Chilean Housing Ministry at close range over a number of years, Meier's predictions seem well confirmed by experience.

REFERENCES

Boletín del Banco Central de Chile (1969) 492 (February).

Comité Interamericano de Desarrollo Agrícola (CIDA) (1966). *Chile: Tenencia de la tierra y desarrollo socio-económico del sector agrícola.* Santiago.

——— (1965) *Chile: Tenencia de la Tierra y desarrollo socio-económico del sector agrícola.*

Fourth Presidential Message to the Congress (1968) (May 21).

FRIEDMANN, JOHN and TOMÁS LACKINGTON (1966) *La hiperurbanización y el desarrollo nacional en Chile: Algunas hipótesis.* Santiago: Centro Interdisciplinario de Desarrollo Urbano y Regional, Universidad Católica de Chile. Revised in English: "Hyperurbanization and national development in Chile: some hypotheses." *Urban Affairs Quarterly* 2, No. 4 (June): 3–29.

GAVAN, JAMES D. (1968) "Sobre le distribución funcional del ingreso en Chile." *Cuadernos de Economía* 5, No. 15 (August).

HIRSCHMAN, ALBERT O. (1963) *Journeys Toward Progress*. New York: The Twentieth Century Fund.

MATTELARD, ARMAND (1968) "La Morfología Social de una Capital Latinoamericana: Santiago de Chile." *Cuadernos de Economía* No. 11.

MEIER, RICHARD L. (1962) *A Communications Theory of Urban Growth*. Cambridge: M.I.T. Press.

MUÑOZ, OSCAR (1969) *Crecimiento Industrial de Chile, 1914–1965*. Santiago: Universidad de Chile, Instituto de Economía y Planificación.

UNDURRAGA S., SERGIO (1967) "Key Factors in Chilean Economic Development." In *Economic Development Issues: Latin America*. CED Supplementary Paper No. 21 (August).

Universidad de Chile, Instituto de Economía (1963) *La Economía de Chile en el Período 1950–1963*. Santiago.

WEITZ, RAANAN and AUSHALOM ROKACH (1968) *Agricultural Development*. Dordrecht, Holland: D. Reidel.

Chapter 10

THE PROCESS OF URBANIZATION IN MEXICO: DISTRIBUTION AND GROWTH OF URBAN POPULATION

LUIS UNIKEL

The process of urbanization and the accelerated growth of total population constitute, without doubt, two world-wide phenomena of major importance in the development of human society and the environment in which it unfolds.[1]

Urbanization is a complex process which is manifested in two outstanding phenomena: the first and most evident is that of the increasing concentration of urban populations through the growth of existing urban localities and the rise of new urban sites (Dorselaer and Gregory, 1962: I, 11; Eldridge, 1963; Hatt and Reiss, 1957: 79). The second phenomenon, more difficult to define, consists of the evolution of a population's culture pattern from a so-called traditional-rural type to a modern-urban one (Dorselaer and Gregory, 1962: I, 12; Hauser, 1965: 8–9).

The aspects of the process of urbanization studied in this essay are concerned with manifestations of the first phenomenon mentioned and are exclusively *demographic-spatial* in nature.[2] Accordingly, this study has as

AUTHOR'S NOTE: This chapter is translated from an article published in *Demografía y Economía* (1968) 2, No. 2: 139–182. It is a revised and slightly expanded version of a paper prepared for publication in a book entitled "La Urbanización Como Campo de Investigación en las Ciencias Sociales" (Buenos Aires: Centro Editor de América Latina). The author is grateful for the cooperation of both El Colegio de México (publishers of the journal) and Centro Editor de América Latina in granting permission for this reprint, in translation.

The author gratefully acknowledges the close collaboration in the preparation of this study of Julio Boltvinik, Andrés Necochea, Agustín Porras, Federico Torres, and Edmundo Victoria, and the suggestions of Raúl Benítez, Gustavo Cabrera, Susana Lerner, and Eliseo Mendoza, who revised the original draft. English translation by Felicity M. Trueblood.

Table 1. Mexico and Other Countries: Relative Position of Level and Pace of Urbanization, 1940–1960

| | COUNTRIES IN DECREASING ORDER OF DEGREE OF URBANIZATION | | | COUNTRIES IN DECREASING ORDER OF RATE OF URBANIZATION | |
| | *1940* | | *1960* | | *1940–1960* | |
Rank	Countries	"Degree"	Rank	Countries	"Degree"	Rank	Countries	Rate*
1	England and Wales	67.9[a]	1	England and Wales	70.4	1	Venezuela	4.46
2	United States	42.5[b]	2	Chile	54.7	2	Peru	3.41
3	Chile	36.4	3	Venezuela	47.2	3	*Mexico*	3.07
4	Spain	35.9	4	United States	46.9[b]	4	Brazil	2.95
5	Hungary	35.4	5	Spain	45.4	5	India	2.48
6	Canada	34.2	6	Canada	39.4	6	Egypt	2.36
7	USSR	23.7	7	Hungary	37.5	7	Turkey	2.28
8	Egypt	22.5	8	Egypt	36.4	8	Chile	2.01
9	Finland	20.9	9	USSR	35.6	9	USSR	2.00
10	*Mexico*	18.4	10	*Mexico*	34.7	10	Finland	1.77
11	Venezuela[c]	18.1	11	Finland	29.9	11	Spain	1.16
12	Brazil	15.3	12	Peru[e]	28.9	12	Canada	0.71
13	Peru	14.2	13	Brazil	28.1	13	United States	0.49
14	Turkey	13.7	14	Turkey	21.8	14	Hungary	0.28
15	India[d]	8.2	15	India	13.6	15	England and Wales	0.18
	World Average	18.2[f]		*World Average*	24.0		*World Average*	1.37

a. Lineal interpolation of 1931 and 1951 data.

b. Approximate calculation based on the study of Durand and Peláez, below. However, according to Breese (1966), table 6, these figures are more likely to correspond to Northern America than to the United States. In any case, the difference is not considered to be significant.

c. 1941.

d. Includes Pakistan.

e. 1961.

f. Because of the lack of data, this estimate was based on the supposition that the percentage of urban population grew at the same rate between 1940 and 1950 as it did between 1950 and 1960. See Breese (1966).

* The rate of urbanization equals the annual mean increment in the degree of urbanization. Its numerical expression is as follows: $2(G_1 - G_0)/(G_1 + G_0) \cdot 1/n \cdot k$; in which G_1 and G_0 are the proportions of the total population residing in localities of 20,000 or more inhabitants; n is the number of years; k equals 100.

SOURCES: John Durand and César Peláez, "Características de la urbanización en América Latina." In Clyde Kyser, ed., *Componentes de los cambios demográficos en América Latina,* Milbank Memorial Fund. Vol. 43 (4), Part II, 1965; United Nations, "La urbanización y los cambios económicos y sociales," urbanization seminar, University of Pittsburgh, 1966; United Nations, *Demographic Yearbook,* 1960, 1962, 1963; and Breese (1966), tables 2, 6, 7.

its objective the description of the process of urbanization in Mexico in the 1940–1960 period in terms of the level and rapidity attained by this phenomenon and also of certain characteristics of the structure of urban localities.

This study is composed of three parts: in the first, an attempt is made to locate Mexico's position in the context of the world-wide process of urbanization with respect to the level and pace of urbanization, and also to identify the structure of Mexico's cities according to size. This structure is compared to that of countries which consider themselves to be representative of "type" systems.[3] In the second part, the three previously mentioned aspects of the "process" in Mexico are studied in greater detail: included are level and rate, as well as the structure of localities. Finally, in the third part, these manifestations of the process of urbanization are analyzed on a regional scale.

MEXICO IN THE CONTEXT OF THE WORLD-WIDE PROCESS OF URBANIZATION

As may be observed in Table 1,[4] Mexico in 1940 had a level of urbanization similar to the world average, and by 1960, had amply surpassed that average. Of the countries appearing in the table, only Venezuela and Peru achieved a pace of urbanization higher than that of Mexico. Another outstanding fact is that normally the rate of urbanization of the underdeveloped countries is greater than that of the industrialized nations, some of which have achieved such high levels of urbanization that their degree of urbanization can only increase slowly. Such is the case with England and Wales.

According to Breese's study (1966: esp. tables 6, 7) it may be affirmed that Mexico's level of urbanization (18.4 percent)[5] in 1940 was already greater than that of the underdeveloped countries as a whole. In this work, Breese classified Mexico with the group of countries having a "medium high" level of urbanization. On the other hand, Mexico's level of urbanization in 1950 and 1960 was 26.4 and 34.7 percent, respectively, while the average estimated by Breese for the developed countries of the world in those years was 38.0 and 41.0 percent, which indicates that Mexico is rapidly approaching the level of urbanization achieved by the developed countries as a whole. If the tendencies of this period continue until 1970, it may be supposed that Mexico's level of urbanization will reach the average level of the developed countries.

Similarly, according to calculations by H. Browning (1962), Mexico and Venezuela have doubled their urban populations in localities of 20,000 or more inhabitants in half the time that England and the United States required in the last century, proceeding from identical levels of urbanization, and in less than half that time if one refers to localities of more than 100,000 inhabitants.

Comparative analysis of Tables 1 and 2 clearly corroborates that the countries with the most rapid urbanization are those which have begun this process most recently (Davis and Golden, 1957: 126), among which Mexico occupies one of the first ranks.

Table 2. Mexico and Other Countries: Rapidity of the Process of Urbanization

Countries	LOCALITIES OF 20,000 OR MORE INHABITANTS			LOCALITIES OF 100,000 OR MORE INHABITANTS		
	Year	*A**	*B*	*Year*	*A*	*B*
England and Wales	1802	17	46	1802	10	42
United States	1873	16	38	1866	10	36
Japan	1898	16	24	1907	10	26
Argentina	1874	16	37	1875	10	22
Mexico	1933	16	26	1936	10	16
Venezuela	1934	16	19	1931	10	14

* A–Percentage of total population; B–Number of years necessary to double A.
SOURCE: Browning (1962), table II-5, p. 40.

Concerning urban structure,[6] Mexico may be classified within the group of countries having a "primate" city system, according to which one or more large cities dominate the rest, not only in population but also in all or almost all aspects of the socio-economic, cultural, and political life of the country.

Figure 1 represents the urban structure of the principal cities of Mexico and their evolution from 1940 to 1960,[7] as well as the urban structure of two countries which are considered at a given moment (1950) to be representative of the two systems of prototype cities: the United States, with respect to the system known as rank-size rule,[8] and Guatemala in relation to the primate city system.

Mexico's system of cities may also be studied through the "index of primacy"[9] (Table 3), according to which Mexico in 1950 occupied an intermediate position in Latin America and one slightly higher than the world average.

According to Figure 1 and the behavior of the index of primacy, Mexico has a basically primate urban structure but one which tends toward an intermediate type.[10]

In the world context, Mexico enjoys a relatively advanced level of urbanization which is rapidly approaching that of the highly urbanized countries; her accelerated process of urbanization is surpassed only by a

Table 3. Mexico and Other Countries and Regions: Index of Primacy of Four Cities, 1950[a]

Regions	Index	Latin-America	Index	Other Countries	Index
World	2.01	Uruguay	5.67	France	3.25
Latin America	2.94	Guatemala	5.27	Denmark	3.21
North America and Oceania	0.75	Peru	4.60	United Kingdom	1.48
Europe, including USSR	1.84	Argentina	3.88	USSR	1.28
Asia Minor and North Africa	1.50	*Mexico*	2.87	Japan	1.16
Central Africa and		Chile	2.38	United States	0.95
South Africa	1.26	Venezuela	1.64	India	0.76
Asia, without Asia Minor	2.35	Brazil	0.85	Canada	0.60

a. $I_p (4) = P_1/(P_2 + P_3 + P_4)$ in which P_1, P_2, P_3, and P_4 are the populations of the cities which in that year occupied the first, second, third, and fourth ranks.

SOURCE: Kingsley Davis (1962) "Las causas y efectos del fenómeno de primacía urbana con referencia especial a América Latina." *Estudios Sociológicos del Congreso de Sociología del Desarrollo* (Mexico: Instituto de investigaciones Sociales) Vol. I: 376, table 3.

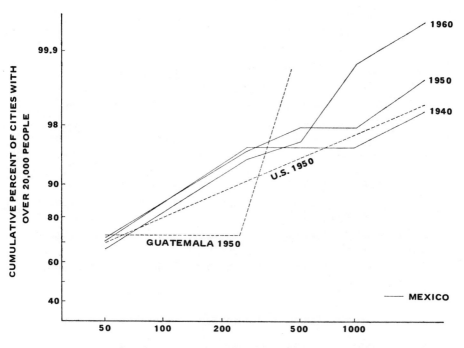

Figure 1. Mexico and Other Countries: Urban Structure.

SOURCE: Distribution of cities in the United States and Guatemala from Berry (1965: 140, 142); that of Mexico based on data from the present study.

few countries. This has been accompanied by changes in the structure of Mexico's cities, changes manifested in a decrease in the system's index of primacy and changes which are indicative of the formation of urban centers of regional importance.

Based upon the foregoing, the hypothesis may be advanced that the urban structure of Mexico is "maturing"— in Friedmann's term—that is, that urban centers are arising that can satisfy regionally the necessities of their growing populations and of important peripheral zones, better their socio-economic, cultural, and political situation, and prove themselves to be external economies of some scale. This presumably permits them to compete with the primate city in population and economic activities (Berry, 1965; Browning, 1962: chap. VI; Friedmann, 1956; Neutze, 1965).

THE PROCESS OF URBANIZATION IN MEXICO
ON A NATIONAL SCALE

Level and Pace of Urbanization

In order to express the level of urbanization achieved by a country or region, the degree of urbanization is generally used. Nevertheless, if one departs from the premise that a city is the more urban the larger its population is (Davis and Golden, 1957: 121), "degree" is not sufficiently representative of the level of urbanization, due to the fact that it does not distinguish the distinct urban structures that the city may implicitly contain. According to this reasoning, of two regions which have the same proportion of urban population, the more highly urbanized region is that whose urban population resides in cities of greater size. Thus, Mexico's level of urbanization was measured by means of a numerical expression given the name "index of urbanization."[11]

The level of urbanization in Mexico in the 1940–1960 period almost doubled, as may be observed in Table 4.

Table 4. Mexico: Level of Urbanization, 1940–1960

Indicators*	1940	1950	1960
Index of urbanization (percent)	16.16	23.59	31.69
Degree of urbanization (percent)	19.99	27.92	36.50
E factor	0.81	0.84	0.87

* For further details see note 11.

The rapid urbanization of the country in the period studied—measured through changes in the "level"—was owed principally to the important increase experienced by the "degree."[12] At the same time, it is noteworthy that during the 1950–1960 decade both of the "levels'" indicators rose with decreasing rapidity, which may signal the beginning of an important change in the future tendency of the process of urbanization in Mexico, an assumption that is reinforced by results presented later in this study.

The level of urbanization achieved by Mexico in both decades is explained, as may be observed in Table 5, by the elevated participation in the "degree" of the large cities of the country—the 17 urban areas of 100,000 or more inhabitants in 1960—and most especially the urban area of Mexico City.[13]

The deceleration occurring in the level of urbanization during 1950–1960 may also be explained in large part by the slower growth of these cities, and in particular Mexico City. Nevertheless, Mexico City maintained its national predominance.

Table 5. Mexico: Population and Participation in Degree of Urbanization of the 17 Largest Cities, 1940–1960

Population and percentage participation in the "degree"	*1940*	*1950*	*1960*
Urban population[a] (inhabitants)	3,927,694	7,209,528	12,746,685
Population of the 17 urban areas of 100,000 or more inhabitants in 1960[b] (inhabitants)	3,005,214	5,256,804	8,968,591
Population of the urban area of Mexico City[b] (inhabitants)	1,559,782	2,872,334	4,909,961
Participation in the "degree" by the 17 urban areas[c] (percent)	76.51	72.91	70.36
Participation in the "degree" by the urban area of Mexico City[c] (percent)	39.71	39.84	38.51

a. See Table 13.

b. General population censuses and calculations realized for the delimitation of urban areas of principal cities of the country. For greater detail, see note 13.

c. Participation in the "degree" is equivalent to the percentage relation between the corresponding urban population and the total for the country.

In order to study in depth factors which influence the level of urbanization, "degree" and the E factor will be analyzed below; the former is studied through growth in total population and by classes of localities,[14] and the latter as a part of the analysis of urban structure.

Growth of Total Population and by Classes of Localities. The pace of Mexico's total population growth has been rising constantly from 2.7 percent annually in 1940–1950 to 3.1 percent in 1950–1960, and, according to recent estimates, to 3.5 percent during the 1962–1967 period (Secretaría de Industria y Comercio, 1965). Nevertheless, the urban, mixed, and rural localities which make up the total population registered very different rates of growth (Table 6); the increase in rates of growth of urban localities is noteworthy, more than triple that of rural localities.

The rates of annual growth previously mentioned stimulated an increase in the participation of urban population in total population from 20.0 to 36.5 percent between 1940 and 1960—which is nothing more than the increase in degree of urbanization to which reference was previously made—and a decline in the participation of rural population from 72.4 to 55.6 percent. The group of mixed localities, in spite of demonstrating an erratic behavior during the 1940–1960 period, maintains its participation (see Table 13) in total population. The rate of growth of urban localities decreased between the 1940–1950 and 1950–1960 decades, while that of non-urban localities rose.

To examine more closely the dynamics of the changes in level of urbanization, total growth of urban population will be studied here in the following three ways: first, through growth of already existing urban localities, as well as through reclassification of localities from the non-urban group to the urban; second, from the point of view of growth in population caused by physical expansion of the cities; and finally, through the urban population's growth, both natural and social (by migration).

Growth of Urban Population; Existing and Reclassified Cities. The growth of urban population is composed of the increase in the number of inhabitants of cities existing at the beginning of the period of study (1940),

Table 6. Mexico: Absolute and Relative Increase in Total Urban and Non-Urban Population, 1940–1960

	POPULATION INCREASE 1940-1950		POPULATION INCREASE 1950-1960	
	Absolute	*Mean Annual increase (percent)*[a]	*Absolute*	*Mean Annual increase (percent)*[a]
Total	6,130,092	2.70	9,143,875	3.01
Urban[b]	3,281,834	5.89	5,537,157	5.54
Mixed	521,444	2.97	743,201	3.12
Rural	2,326,814	1.51	2,863,517	1.59
Urban[b]	3,281,834	5.89	5,537,157	5.54
At beginning of decade	2,654,016	5.05	4,791,703	4.98
Reclassified localities	627,818	6.13	745,454	4.79
Urban[c]	2,987,419	4.90	4,883,146	4.78
Natural	1,262,649	2.06	3,122,203	3.06
Social	1,724,770	2.84	1,760,943	1.72

a. The mean annual increase was calculated by means of the following: $2(P_1 - P_0)/(P_1 + P_0) \cdot 1/n \cdot 100$; P_1 and P_0 are population at the end and beginning of the period, respectively, and n the number of years.

b. Gross increase in urban population is obtained from the difference between urban population at the end and the beginning of the period (the figures come from Table 13).

c. Increase in population, 1940–1950, and 1950–1960, of urban localities in 1960. Regarding cities with "urban areas," the population in 1940 and 1950 of all localities which formed part of these "urban areas" in 1950 was considered; in the following decade, the population in 1950 of all localities which formed part of these "urban areas" in 1960 was considered.

and of those localities which, although not urban in 1940, became so between 1940 and 1960. These are known as localities reclassified as urban. In the case of Mexico, growth of urban population, as demonstrated in Table 6, was due basically to the demographic increase experienced by cities existing in 1940: 80.8 percent in the first decade and 86.2 in the second. Nevertheless, it is significant that 19.2 and 13.4 percent of the gross increase in urban population in 1940–1950 and 1950–1960, respectively, is a result of the incorporation of new urban nuclei. In the first decade studied, 30 non-urban localities were reclassified, localities whose mean annual increase was 6.1 percent. In the succeeding ten years, 40 centers of population, whose mean annual increase was 5.0 percent, became urban.

Growth of Urban Population by Physical Integration. The growth of urban population by physical expansion of the cities is a recent phenomenon in Mexico. This process in which localities near the city are integrated into the urban area is produced by the movement of population from the center toward the periphery in the large cities of Mexico and by the growth of certain peripheral localities themselves. The cases of Mexico City, Monterrey, Cuernavaca, and others clearly illustrate this phenomenon.

The increase in urban population by means of the physical integration of non-urban localities into the cities of Mexico was estimated in 1940–1950, at 214 localities having a total population of 418,074 inhabitants. From 1950 to 1960, the integrated localities numbered 249, with a total population of 457,588 inhabitants.[15]

The participation of this demographic increase in total growth of urban population represented 12.7 percent in the 1940–1950 decade and 8.3 percent in the following period. The urban area of Mexico City alone contributed 10.2 and 5.2 percent, respectively, to that growth; the remaining small percentage corresponded to other areas such as Guadalajara, Monterrey, and Puebla. Nevertheless, it is significant that this process was accentuated in relative terms from 1950 to 1960 in these three cities, as well as in others of less importance. It is probable, therefore, that this phenomenon, characteristic of developed and highly urbanized countries, is beginning to acquire importance in Mexico and is increasing in magnitude as regional centers multiply.

In synthesis, the growth of urban population through reclassification and physical integration, if one considers both as "new urban population," constituted 31.0 percent from 1940 to 1950, and 21.7 percent from 1950 to 1960. Consequently, it may be seen that the rapidity of incorporation of new urban population in Mexico from 1940 to 1960 lost its relative importance within overall urban growth from the first to the second decade, a factor which has influenced the deceleration of that growth. It is probable that reclassification of non-urban localities and integration by physical expansion will achieve greater absolute levels in the future.

Table 7. México: Total, Natural, and Social Growth of Urban Population, and the Principal Cities of Attraction, 1940–1950[a]

Cities[b]	TOTAL GROWTH		NATURAL GROWTH		SOCIAL GROWTH	
	Absolute	Percent	Absolute	Percent	Absolute	Percent
Urban total	2,987,419	100.00	1,262,649	100.00	1,724,770	100.00
Ciudad de México	1,228,610	41.13	381,413	30.21	847,197	49.12
Guadalajara, Jal.	158,602	5.31	60,956	4.83	97,646	5.66
Monterrey, N.L.	161,853	5.42	64,812	5.13	97,041	5.63
Puebla, Pue.	82,723	2.77	16,278	1.29	66,445	3.85
Ciudad Juárez, Chih.	73,685	2.47	16,136	1.28	57,549	3.34
Mexicali, B.C.	46,739	1.56	11,653	0.92	35,086	2.03
Tijuana, B.C.	43,466	1.45	8,894	0.70	34,572	2.00
Torreón, Coah.	77,500	2.59	46,393	3.67	31,107	1.80
San Luis Potosí, S.L.P.	51,790	1.73	23,840	1.89	27,950	1.63
Mérida, Yuc.	46,006	1.54	22,911	1.82	23,095	1.34
Total	1,970,974	65.97	653,286	51.74	1,317,688	76.40
Other urban localities	1,016,445	34.03	609,363	48.26	407,082	23.60
León, Gto.	48,571	1.63	29,050	2.30	19,521	1.13
Veracruz, Ver.	29,516	0.99	10,050	0.80	19,466	1.13
Hermosillo, Son.	24,918	0.83	9,227	0.73	15,691	0.91
Chihuahua, Chih.	30,195	1.01	15,965	1.26	14,230	0.83

a. Localities of attraction are those whose net migration is positive. The analysis used the ten principal cities of attraction, as well as the four—which appear at the end of the table—that are among the ten principal cities of attraction in the following decade.

b. Corresponds to localities which were urban in 1960. Regarding cities with "urban area," the population in 1940 and 1950 of all localities which formed part of these "urban areas" in 1950 was considered.

SOURCE: Dirección General de Estadística, Oficina de Estadísticas Demográficas, and general population censuses.

Table 8. Mexico: Total, Natural, and Social Growth of Urban Population and of the Principal Cities of Attraction, 1950–1960[a]

Cities[b]	TOTAL GROWTH		NATURAL GROWTH		SOCIAL GROWTH	
	Absolute	Percent	Absolute	Percent	Absolute	Percent
Urban total	4,883,146	100.00	3,122,203	100.00	1,760,943	100.00
Ciudad de México	1,930,933	39.54	1,191,880	38.18	739,053	41.97
Guadalajara, Jal.	395,398	8.10	167,492	5.36	227,906	12.94
Monterrey, N.L.	336,519	6.89	164,226	5.26	172,293	9.78
Ciudad Juárez, Chih.	139,553	2.86	54,398	1.74	85,155	4.84
Mexicali, B.C.	112,160	2.30	51,381	1.65	60,779	3.45
Tijuana, B.C.	92,309	1.89	41,649	1.33	50,660	2.88
León, Gto.	89,439	1.83	52,117	1.67	37,322	2.12
Chihuahua, Chih.	69,890	1.43	35,524	1.14	34,366	1.95
Veracruz, Ver.	46,019	0.94	19,462	0.62	26,557	1.51
Hermosillo, Son.	52,250	1.07	26,842	0.86	25,408	1.44
Total	3,264,470	66.85	1,804,971	57.81	1,459,499	82.88
Other urban localities[c]	1,618,676	33.15	1,317,232	42.19	301,444	17.12
Puebla, Pue.	69,954	1.43	49,209	1.58	20,745	1.18
Torreón, Coah.	72,152	1.48	79,246	2.54	-7,094	-0.40
Mérida, Yuc.	28,091	0.58	38,666	1.24	-10,575	-0.60
San Luis Potosí, S.L.P.	36,208	0.74	49,851	1.60	-13,643	-0.77

a. See footnote a, Table 7.

b. Corresponds to localities which were urban in 1960. Regarding cities with "urban area," the population in 1950 of all localities which formed part of these "urban areas" in 1960 was considered.

c. The four cities additionally studied appeared among the ten principal cities of attraction in the previous decade.

SOURCE: Dirección General de Estadística, Oficina de Estadísticas Demográficas, and general population censuses.

Their relative importance to urban growth will continue to diminish, however, and growth of existing cities will predominate.

Natural and Social Growth of Urban Population.[16] Between 1940 and 1950, urban population increased by 2,987,419 inhabitants (Table 6), of which 57.7 percent was social growth. In the following decade, urban population rose by 4,883,146 inhabitants (Table 6); that is, it increased 63.4 percent over the preceding decade; however, only 36.1 percent was due to migration. This pronounced change in the importance of the components of growth—natural and social—from one decade to the other, was due as much to diminution in rates of social growth in the majority of urban localities (Tables 9 and 20) as to the considerable increase in rates of growth.[17] These changes in the rates caused urban social growth in 1950–1960 to be slightly higher in absolute numbers than in the preceding period, and natural growth of the population of urban localities as a whole almost to triple (see Tables 7 and 8).

It is probable that this change has been maintained or accentuated from 1960 to date, since the volume of migrants—even though it has increased in absolute numbers—will have less relative importance in the face of the great volume of urban natural growth.[18] This makes one believe it improbable that the pace of urbanization of the country, from 1960 to 1980, will achieve the rate experienced from 1940 to 1950; rather, two alternatives are more feasible: that the 1950–1960 rate will be maintained or that it will decrease, following the 1940–1960 tendency. The latter is considered the more likely.

On analyzing the behavior of the rates of natural and social growth according to different sizes of cities (Table 9), it may be observed that the rates of the first-rank cities diminish as their population grows in size (more clearly in 1940–1950). Similarly, the increase in rates of natural growth of all groups of localities in the 1950–1960 period is outstanding.

Social growth of urban population in both decades was due, as may be seen in Tables 7 and 8, to the attraction exercised by a few cities of the country. In 1940–1950, ten localities absorbed 76.4 percent of net urban in-migration, and in the 1950–1960 decade ten localities again absorbed 82.9 percent. Less than half of these ten localities in both periods were important urban centers of more than 100,000 inhabitants at the beginning of the corresponding period. Outstanding for their importance as centers of attraction are Mexico City, in both decades, and Guadalajara and Monterrey, above all in the second decade. Mexico City absorbed 49.1 percent of net urban migrants in 1940–1950—even though its rate of social growth was not one of the highest—and 42.0 percent in 1950–1960. Guadalajara and Monterrey increased their participation substantially and were converted into Mexico's most important regional centers—one of the principal factors of the change observed in the urban structure of Mexico.

In Tables 7 and 8 it may be seen that the ten principal cities of attraction in both decades also contributed a substantial part of total growth

Table 9. Mexico: Total, Natural, and Social Mean Annual Increase in Urban Population, by Size of Locality, 1940–1960[a] in Percentages

Size of Locality[b]	1940–1950[a]			1950–1960		
	Total	*Natural*[c]	*Social*[d]	*Total*	*Natural*[c]	*Social*[d]
5,000 or less	9.6	2.5	7.1	13.7	4.5	9.2
5,000–10,000	6.2	2.7	3.5	6.8	3.2	3.6
10,000–15,000	3.6	2.5	1.1	3.9	3.4	0.5
15,000–20,000	5.8	2.4	3.4	4.2	3.3	0.9
20,000–50,000	3.9	2.3	1.6	4.6	3.4	1.2
50,000–100,000	3.3	2.1	1.2	4.7	3.1	1.6
100,000–200,000	4.8	2.1	2.7	3.8	2.9	0.9
200,000–500,000	4.9	1.9	3.0	5.7	2.7	3.0
500,000 or more	5.4	1.7	3.7	4.9	3.0	1.9
Total	4.9	2.1	2.8	4.8	3.1	1.7

a. The localities for both decades are *only* those that became urban in 1960. Therefore, consider the data as for *all* localities of 5,000 or less, 5,000–10,000, etc.— but, repeating, only those which were urban in 1960. Oaxaca's two urban localities were excluded because of lack of necessary vital statistics.

b. Size of the localities' population at the beginning of each period.

c. This mean annual increase was calculated in the following way: $2(CN)/(P_0 + P_1) \cdot 1/n \cdot 100$, in which CN is natural increase in absolute terms in each interval of population, and P_0 and P_1 are the populations at the beginning and end of the period.

d. This mean annual increase was calculated using the expression: $2(CS)/(P_0 + P_1) \cdot 1/n \cdot 100$, in which CS is social growth in absolute terms in each interval of population and P_0 and P_1 are the populations at the beginning and end of the period.

of urban population: 66.0 and 66.9 percent in each period and more than half the natural growth, 51.7 and 57.8 percent. Of course, these participations are less than those relating to social growth.

Natural and Social Growth of Urban Localities. One of the notable characteristics of urbanization in Mexico in the period studied, and particularly in the 1940–1950 decade, is the considerable number of urban localities which experienced exceedingly rapid population growth, without precedent in the demographic development of the country. As mentioned earlier, the migration from countryside to city and from city to city had the greatest influence upon this phenomenon during 1940–1950, while in the following decade natural growth of population exercised greater weight. (See Tables 6 and 9.)

The relative decrease in social growth of urban population is also reflected in changes in the number of urban localities grouped according to annual net migration. In Table 10, one notes, in the first place, the diminution between the first and second decades in the number of localities of attraction (from 95 to 82), and the increase in the number of centers of rejection (from 30 to 39); in the second place, the notable

Table 10. Mexico: Number of Urban Localities of Attraction and Rejection, 1940–1960

Classification according to rate of social growth[a]	1940–1950			1950–1960		
	Absolute	Percent	Percent	Absolute	Percent	Percent
Localities of attraction[b]	95	76.00	100.00	82	67.77	100.00
Moderate attraction (0 to 1 percent)	12	9.60	12.64	25	20.66	30.49
High attraction (1 to 4 percent)	53	42.40	55.78	46	38.02	56.10
Very high attraction (4 percent or more)	30	24.00	31.58	11	9.09	13.41
Localities of rejection[c]	30	24.00	100.00	39	32.23	100.00
Moderate rejection (0 to −1 percent)	11	8.80	36.67	27	22.31	69.24
High rejection (−1 to −2 percent)	12	9.60	40.00	3	2.48	7.69
Very high rejection (−2 percent and less)	7	5.60	23.33	9	7.44	23.07
Total	125[d]	100.00	—	121[e]	100.00	100.00

a. The limits established are points of reference arbitrarily selected and based upon the mean annual social increase of the localities studied.
b. Those whose net migration is positive.
c. Those whose net migration is negative.
d. Of these localities, 4 were integrated into different urban areas in the following decade and do not appear in Table 20. In addition, Juchitán and Oaxaca are not included because of the lack of necessary data.
e. Does not include Juchitán and Oaxaca.

diminution in the number of localities of "very high attraction." Localities of "high attraction" are now concentrated in the categories of "attraction" and "moderate rejection." Similarly, in Table 20, a clear decrease may be observed in the positive annual net migration of cities of "very high attraction" from the second to the first decade. In general, the localities' total and social rates of growth are less in 1950–1960, with the exception of those of centers which were incorporated into urban localities, and which for obvious reasons tend to be high. A possible explanation for this phenomenon is that a city, as its population increases, and especially when it attains important size, finds it difficult to maintain elevated rates of growth.

Notwithstanding, it is unquestionable that a considerable number of Mexico's largest cities grow at rates which may be considered quite high. The cases of Guadalajara and Monterrey are clearly evident, as well as that of Mexico City.[19]

The predominance of localities in the border states of the north in the "attraction" and especially the "very high attraction" groups should be noted.[20] In the localities of rejection, one observes the predominance, although not in clear form, of localities in the center of the Republic, and the presence, in both periods of the majority of the traditional mining cities of the country. The ten most important urban centers of "rejection" contribute a substantial part of the total of negative net migration of urban localities of rejection (see Tables 11 and 12). It may be observed that

Table 11. Mexico: Most Important Urban Localities of Rejection, 1940–1950

	NEGATIVE NET MIGRATION	
Cities*	*Absolute*	*Percent*
Total of urban localities	86,600	100.00
Aguascalientes, Ags.	11,505	13.29
Pachuca, Hgo.	9,518	10.99
Matehuala, S.L.P.	6,285	7.26
Guanajuato, Gto.	4,922	5.68
La Barca, Jal.	3,995	4.62
Atlixco, Pue.	3,803	4.39
Lagos de Moreno, Jal.	3,646	4.21
Zacatecas, Zac.	3,205	3.70
San Pedro de las Colonias, Coah.	3,024	3.49
Nueva Rosita, Coah.	3,023	3.49
Total	52,926	61.12
Other urban localities	33,674	38.88

* Corresponds to only those which were urban in 1960. Regarding cities with "urban area," the calculation was made by taking into consideration localities which formed part of such "urban areas" in 1950.

Table 12. Mexico: Most Important Urban Localities of Rejection, 1950–1960

	NEGATIVE NET MIGRATION	
*Cities**	*Absolute*	*Percent*
Total of urban localities	131,482	100.00
Pachuca, Hgo.	14,068	10.70
San Luis Potosí, S.L.P.	13,643	10.38
Mérida, Yuc.	10,575	8.04
Fresnillo, Zac.	7,310	5.56
Torreón, Coah.	7,094	5.40
Nueva Rosita, Coah.	6,224	4.73
Acámbaro, Gto.	5,668	4.31
Ciudad Mante, Tamps.	5,173	3.93
Tampico, Tamps.	5,068	3.86
Parras de la Fuente, Coah.	4,946	3.76
Total	79,769	60.67
Other urban localities	51,713	39.33

* Corresponds to localities which were urban in 1960. Regarding cities with "urban areas," the calculation takes into consideration the localities which formed part of such urban areas in 1960.

this type of locality manifests changes of greater importance than the ten principal centers of attraction. Only two cities, Pachuca and Nueva Rosita—mining centers—appear in both periods, as distinct from six cities of attraction: Mexico City, Guadalajara, Monterrey, Ciudad Juárez, Mexicali, and Tijuana, which together absorbed 67.8 and 75.9 percent of the social growth of the country in the 1940–1950 and 1950–1960 decades, respectively (see Tables 7 and 8). Consequently, the latter—the capital of the Republic, the two regional centers, and the three most important border cities—constituted the principal poles of Mexico's demographic growth in the period studied. The map of Mexico (Figure 2) presents the localities of attraction and rejection by entities and population size in the 1950–1960 period. It clearly captures the diffusion of the urban phenomenon in Mexico to 1960, especially if one compares it to a similar map of localities which were urban in 1940.

Structure of Urban Localities in Mexico

The distribution of population and of urban localities in Mexico in the census years studied, as well as changes operative in that structure, may be observed in Table 13. Outstanding is the great increase in the number of urban localities—more than double between 1940 and 1960—an increase which was greater in relative terms in cities of larger size. This explains, in part, changes in urban structure manifested through increase

Table 13. Mexico: Distribution of Population by Size of Localities, 1940 to 1960

Size of Localities	1940			1950			1960		
	Number of localities	Population	Percent of total population	Number of localities	Population	Percent of total population	Number of localities	Population	Percent of total population
Total for Mexico	105,508[h]	19,649,162[i]	100.00	98,325[h]	25,779,254[i]	100.00	89,005[h]	34,923,129	100.00
Urban	55	3,927,694[k]	20.00	84	7,209,528[k]	27.96	123	12,746,685[k]	36.50
1,000,000 or more[a]	1	1,559,782	7.94	1	2,872,334	11.14	1	4,909,961	14.06
500,000–1,000,000[b]	—	—	—	—	—	—	2	1,511,092	4.33
100,000–500,000[c]	5	781,244	3.98	10	1,926,776	7.47	14	2,547,538	7.29
50,000–100,000[d]	8	589,106	3.00	12	808,381	3.14	20	1,532,628	4.39
15,000–50,000[e]	41	997,562	5.08	61	1,602,037	6.21	86	2,245,466	6.43
Non-urban	105,453	15,721,468	80.00	98,241	18,569,726[j]	72.04	88,882	22,176,444	63.50
Mixed	195	1,492,170	7.59	253	2,013,614	7.81	342	2,756,815	7.89
10,000–15,000[f]	35	430,738	2.19	57	676,756	2.62	72	880,501	2.52
5,000–10,000[g]	160	1,061,432	5.40	196	1,336,858	5.19	270	1,876,314	5.37
Rural	105,258	14,229,298	72.41	97,988	16,556,112	64.23	88,540	19,419,629	55.61
1,000–5,000	2,390	4,448,811	22.64	3,098	5,666,020	21.97	3,950	7,292,285	20.88
100–1,000	28,546	7,775,830	39.57	29,829	9,119,066	35.38	33,083	10,571,237	30.27
Less than 100	76,322	2,004,657	10.20	65,061	1,771,026	6.87	51,507	1,556,107	4.46

a–g. The different sizes of cities have been named, for better identification, in the following way: [a]Metropolis; [b]regional centers; [c]large cities; [d]medium cities; [e]small cities; [f]mixed urban; [g]mixed rural.

h. Does not include localities "enumerated with others" or uninhabited ones.

i. This datum differs in less than 4,390 inhabitants from the figure in the VI Population Census. There were three errata in state volumes of this census: 2,000 inhabitants in the city of Mérida, 2,345 inhabitants in the state of Durango, and 45 inhabitants in the state of Oaxaca.

j. This population differs from that given in the VII Population Census by 11,763 inhabitants whom the census classifies as complementary and as not attributable to any population size or any state.

k. This population differs from that obtained from census information for localities of 15,000 or more inhabitants, because it includes principal urban areas of the country: 6 in 1940, 21 in 1950, and 28 in 1960. SOURCES: VI, VII, and VIII general population censuses.

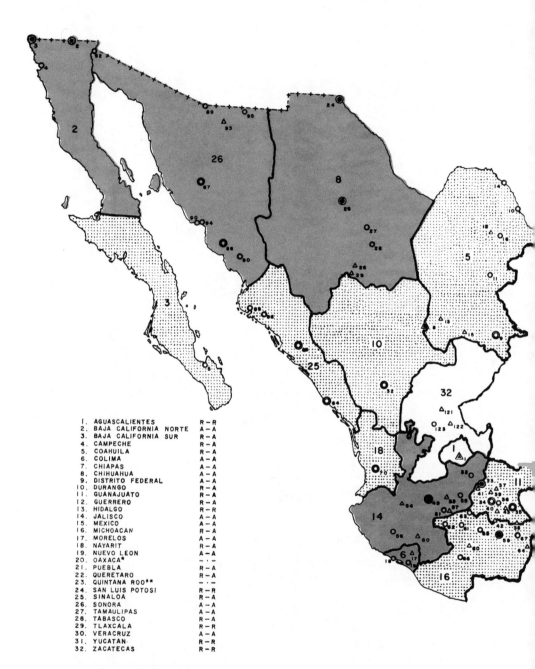

1.	AGUASCALIENTES	R – R
2.	BAJA CALIFORNIA NORTE	A – A
3.	BAJA CALIFORNIA SUR	R – A
4.	CAMPECHE	R – A
5.	COAHUILA	R – A
6.	COLIMA	A – A
7.	CHIAPAS	A – A
8.	CHIHUAHUA	A – A
9.	DISTRITO FEDERAL	A – A
10.	DURANGO	R – A
11.	GUANAJUATO	R – A
12.	GUERRERO	R – A
13.	HIDALGO	R – R
14.	JALISCO	A – A
15.	MEXICO	A – A
16.	MICHOACAN	R – A
17.	MORELOS	A – A
18.	NAYARIT	R – A
19.	NUEVO LEON	A – A
20.	OAXACA*	– · –
21.	PUEBLA	R – A
22.	QUERETARO	R – A
23.	QUINTANA ROO**	– · –
24.	SAN LUIS POTOSI	R – R
25.	SINALOA	R – A
26.	SONORA	A – A
27.	TAMAULIPAS	A – A
28.	TABASCO	R – A
29.	TLAXCALA	R – R
30.	VERACRUZ	A – A
31.	YUCATAN	R – R
32.	ZACATECAS	R – R

KEY

▨ A – A State of attraction with urban population of attraction.

▨ R – A State of repulsion with urban population of attraction.

▢ R – R State of repulsion with urban population of repulsion.

Figure 2. Mexico: Urban Localities According to Population in 1960 and According to Net Migratory Balance during the 1950–1960 period.

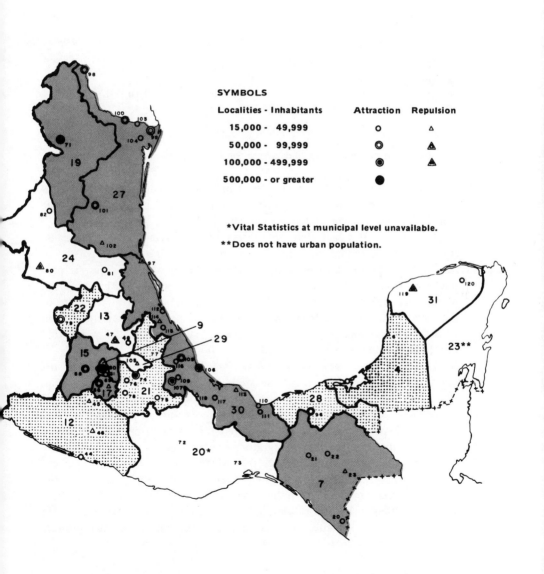

SYMBOLS

Localities - Inhabitants	Attraction	Repulsion
15,000 - 49,999	○	△
50,000 - 99,999	◎	▲
100,000 - 499,999	◉	▲
500,000 - or greater	●	

*Vital Statistics at municipal level unavailable.

**Does not have urban population.

in the *E* factor which have influenced the level of urbanization. (See Table 4.)

Formation of regional centers and large cities has played an important role in this phenomenon, a fact which has led to the gradual change of Mexico's urban structure to one of an "intermediate" nature, as compared to the primate structure it enjoyed in 1940.

What becomes evident with the manipulation of the number of cities is confirmed by analysis of the sums of population of principal cities by means of the "index of primacy." In Table 14 it may be noted that the

Table 14. Mexico: Index of Primacy, 2 to 10 Cities, 1900, 1940, 1950, 1960

Index of primacy of:	1900	1940	1950	1960
2 cities	4.40	6.48	7.16	6.05
4 cities	1.70	2.74	2.92	2.70
6 cities	1.20	1.99	2.19	2.09
8 cities	0.94	1.62	1.82	1.79
10 cities	0.82	1.40	1.57	1.59

* For determination of the "index," see footnote a, Table 3.

first four "indexes" (from 2 to 8 cities) increase systematically from 1900 to 1950, and decrease from 1950 to 1960, the latter phenomenon due principally to the accelerated growth of Guadalajara and Monterrey.

In spite of the fact that both ways of identifying the phenomenon signal the same tendency, it may be seen that the movement away from the primate system, measured by means of the number of cities, is produced in 1940–1950, while the decrease in the indexes of primacy is not manifested until the following decade in which the change in structure of the cites is accentuated. It is not unduly unreasonable to conjecture, even with the reservations imposed by a period of study of only 20 years, that this tendency has been maintained from 1960 to date.

Distribution of Non-Urban Localities. Study of the process of urbanization demands knowledge, as well, of certain aspects of non-urban localities. Thus, for example, in the migratory phenomenon, it is of capital importance to determine in what numbers the non-urban population of the nation is dispersed, since it is considered that such dispersion influences the magnitude of country-city migratory movements.[21]

Table 13 clearly demonstrates that Mexico is a country with an exceedingly dispersed rural population. Even in 1960, 34.7 percent of the national population, or 12.1 million people, lived in localities of less than 1,000 inhabitants. Incorporation of this population into the central system of cities becomes difficult, since it remains marginal to the evolution of cultural patterns experienced by the rest of the country.

The composition of Mexico's rural population manifests changes in only one sense, and then of little magnitude: the R factor of the "rural level index"[22] fell slowly during the entire period, which indicates that distribution of rural population moved toward groups of higher magnitude (see Table 13). This decrease may imply a lesser number of localities of under 100 inhabitants or an increase in the average size of rural localities. Nothing definite may be concluded due to the fact that the diminution in relative and absolute terms of localities of under 100 inhabitants could not be quantified exactly because of the problem of comparison of census data.[23]

If the greater part of localities "enumerated with others" pertains to the group of less than 100 inhabitants, and if, as may be supposed, they were grouped with localities of larger size, the census would tend to underestimate the population in the smallest group and overestimate the population in the rest. In any case, even though the former localities were "enumerated with others" of the same size, this would diminish the number of such localities, though not their population.[24]

Rate of Urbanization

The rate of urbanization was defined as the mean annual increase in the index of urbanization.[25] For this reason, its development on a national level has been left until the end of this section, since in a certain sense such treatment is a summary and a corollary of what has previously been discussed regarding level and pace of urbanization.

Mexico's rate of urbanization is among the highest in the world.[26] Nevertheless, it decreased substantially between the 1940–1950 decade and the following one: from 3.7 percent anually to 2.9. This change in rate reflects changes in the factors determining level of urbanization, which may be summarized in the following way:

(a) The mean annual increase in total population was larger, between the first and second decades studies, than that of urban population. This brought as a result an increase in degree of urbanization from 1950 to 1960 of 30.7 percent, while the increase in the previous decade had been 39.6 percent. Influencing this relative diminution were the loss of importance of the multiplication of urban localities through reclassification, and the decrease in the annual rates of urban localities' net migratory balances.

(b) Modification of the structure of localities also influenced the rate of urbanization; participation of the higher intervals of urban population continued growing, although with less intensity than in 1940–1950.

Marginally, an hypothesis which has been presented to explain the decrease in rate of urbanization may be mentioned. The fact that the indexes of urbanization have a fixed limit of 100, according to this hypothesis, implies that a rapid pace of urbanization cannot be maintained for long periods. Based on this reasoning, Browning (1965) suggested that

Table 15. Mexico: Index of Urbanization of States, Participation of State Index in National Total, and Rank of States According to Their Participation, 1940, 1950, 1960

States	1940			1950			1960		
	Index	Percent Participation	Rank	Index	Percent Participation	Rank	Index	Percent Participation	Rank
National Total	16.16	100.00	—	23.59	100.00	—	31.69	100.00	—
Aguascalientes	38.14	1.94	12	37.23	1.15	15	52.03	1.15	18
Baja California Norte	11.17	.28	24	43.53	1.62	12	67.92	3.19	8
Baja California Sur	—	—	—	—	—	—	14.86	.11	30
Campeche	12.86	.37	22	12.80	.26	28	19.33	.29	29
Coahuila	19.26	3.34	7	31.12	3.69	7	38.66	3.17	9
Colima	14.34	.35	23	14.52	.27	27	20.02	.30	28
Chiapas	1.14	.24	25	3.69	.55	20	4.70	.51	22
Chihuahua	12.68	2.50	9	24.62	3.42	9	38.30	4.24	4
Distrito Federal	88.75	49.10	1	94.29	47.28	1	96.33	42.40	1
Durango	6.12	.93	15	14.18	1.47	13	17.68	1.22	17
Guanajuato	9.50	3.13	8	15.90	3.47	8	23.58	3.70	7
Guerrero	—	—	—	2.08	.31	25	3.58	.38	24
Hidalgo	5.18	1.26	13	5.72	.80	18	6.39	.57	20
Jalisco	17.76	7.93	2	24.10	6.93	2	35.76	7.90	2
México	1.90	.69	18	2.88	.66	19	15.80	2.71	11
Michoacán	3.07	1.14	14	6.02	1.41	14	10.98	1.84	12
Morelos	—	—	—	12.11	.54	21	19.52	.68	19
Nayarit	2.02	.14	27	4.24	.20	29	10.40	.37	26
Nuevo León	35.13	5.98	3	47.84	5.82	3	64.82	6.32	3

Oaxaca	1.23	.46	20	1.64	.38	24	3.55	.55	21
Puebla	11.34	4.62	4	14.90	3.99	6	17.49	3.12	10
Querétaro	6.87	.53	19	8.64	.41	23	14.59	.47	23
Quintana Roo	—	—	—	—	—	—	—	—	—
San Luis Potosí	9.14	1.95	11	15.39	2.17	11	18.05	1.71	14
Sinaloa	5.50	.85	16	8.83	.92	17	17.29	1.31	16
Sonora	1.28	.15	26	12.34	1.04	16	25.82	1.83	13
Tabasco	4.40	.39	21	4.88	.29	26	8.36	.37	25
Tamaulipas	29.15	4.22	6	34.14	4.04	5	41.82	3.87	5
Tlaxcala	—	—	—	—	—	—	1.13	.04	31
Veracruz	8.66	4.42	5	12.31	4.13	4	15.23	3.75	6
Yucatán	17.45	2.29	10	27.64	2.34	10	28.68	1.59	15
Zacatecas	4.11	.73	17	4.07	.45	22	4.57	.34	27

NOTE: The percentage participation of the state index in the national total was calculated on the basis of the following expression: State participation $= (P_t/P) \times (I_t/I) \times 100\%$, in which P_t and P are the population of the state and the total population of the country, respectively. I_t and I are the indexes of state and national urbanization, respectively.

the 1940–1950 period contains the point of inflection in the urbanization curve in Mexico. This conclusion has proved to be valid in the light of the present study's results. It may be said, in general terms, that all manifestations of urbanization, structure of cities, rates of social and natural growth, etc.—demonstrate a change in tendency between the two periods of study.

In addition, this conclusion allows for the thought that, given the maintenance of the tendency in the process of urbanization in the 1950–1960 period, Mexico's urban structure will change definitively toward a system of non-primate cities, in which the urban area of Mexico City would have a demographic and possibly socio-economic predominance inferior to the present, and a parallel network of cities of growing interdependence would be formed. This signifies that Mexico would pass from a process of urbanization which Sovani called "primary" to another of "mature" characteristics which is found with greater frequency in the developed countries.[27]

THE PROCESS OF URBANIZATION
IN MEXICO ON A REGIONAL LEVEL

Level of Urbanization

In order to complement the description of Mexico's process of urbanization, the phenomenon's manifestations in states are studied in this section, based upon determination of similar patterns of behavior according to level and pace of urbanization. (NOTE: The territories of Baja California Sur, Quintana Roo, and the Federal District, are treated as states.)

In 1940, Mexico's level of urbanization was fundamentally determined, as indicated in Table 15, by the Federal District (49.1 percent) and another five states which as a total contributed 76.3 percent of the national index of urbanization. In 1960, 75.4 percent of Mexico's level of urbanization corresponded to the Federal District (42.4 percent) and seven additional states.[28]

From the foregoing it may be inferred that Mexico's level of urbanization continues to depend in great measure upon the Federal District—even though to a lesser degree in the second decade studied—and upon a reduced number of states, while the rest continue to demonstrate predominantly rural characteristics. Similarly, it is important to point out that although all of Mexico's states increased their level of urbanization, regional inequalities in urbanization were accentuated during the period.[29]

The level of urbanization of Mexico's states are classified in five categories, as indicated in Table 16. In the same table, the constant diminution in the number of states of very low "level" may be observed. These states are distributed among the groups of high, medium, and low urbanization, a clear reflection of the fact that the process of urbanization is being diffused throughout the national territory.

Table 16. Mexico: Categories of States According to Level of Urbanization and Participation in the "Level" of the Country, 1940, 1950, 1960

States according to level of urbanization	1940		1950		1960	
	A*	B	A	B	A	B
Very high (more than 70 percent)	1	49.11	1	47.28	1	42.40
High (40 to 70 percent)	0	—	2	7.44	4	14.53
Medium (20 to 40 percent)	3	12.15	6	21.57	7	22.73
Low (10 to 20 percent)	8	21.71	9	17.34	12	17.58
Very low (less than 10 percent)	20	17.03	14	6.37	8	2.76
Total for country	32	100.00	32	100.00	32	100.00

* A–Number of states; B–Participation in index of urbanization (percent).
SOURCE: Table 15.

It may be said, in general terms, that the states which have remained at the lowest levels of urbanization in 1960 are those of limited socio-economic development. Less clearly, the most urbanized states of Mexico correspond, in general, to those having a greater level of development.[30]

Pace of Urbanization

To determine which type of states urbanized most rapidly in the 1940–1960 period, the index and rate of urbanization were examined comparatively. In Table 7 it is clearly noticeable that states of a higher level of urbanization (Table 15) were those which urbanized more slowly,[31] and as they descend in the "level" their rate of urbanization grows. From 1950 to 1960, the latter phenomenon was accentuated. These results are congruent with the previously presented hypothesis on a national level, i.e., that as level of urbanization rises, the rapidity of the "process" tends to diminish. Similarly, on a regional level, a turning point is also manifested in the urbanization of states of greater weight in the "level" of the country between both decades.

The pace of urbanization of the country's states in the period studied was owed as much to growth of cities existing at the beginning of each decade as to reclassification of new urban localities. The latter process showed in certain states, such as may be observed in Table 18, greater relative importance than the former phenomenon, given cases like Guer-

Table 17. Mexico: States According to Pace of Urbanization, 1940–1960

RATE OF URBANIZATION[a]

| | *1940–1950*[b] | | *1950–1960*[c] | |
States	*Greater than the national*	*Less than the national*	*Greater than the national*	*Less than the national*
Aguascalientes	—	−0.24	3.32	—
Baja California Norte	11.83	—	4.38	—
Baja California Sur	—	—	20.00[d]	—
Campeche	—	−0.04	4.06	—
Coahuila	4.70	—	—	2.16
Colima	—	0.12	3.18	—
Chiapas	10.56	—	4.41	—
Chihuahua	6.40	—	4.35	—
Distrito Federal		0.60	—	0.21
Durango	7.94	—	—	2.20
Guanajuato	5.04	—	3.89	—
Guerrero	20.00[d]	—	5.30	—
Hidalgo	—	0.99	—	1.10
Jalisco	—	3.03	3.90	—
México	4.10	—	13.83	—
Michoacán	6.49	—	5.83	—
Morelos	20.00[d]	—	4.68	—
Nayarit	7.09	—	8.41	—
Nuevo León	—	3.06	3.01	—
Oaxaca	—	2.86	7.36	—
Puebla	—	2.71	—	1.59
Querétaro	—	2.28	5.12	—
Quintana Roo	—	—	—	—
San Luis Potosí	5.09	—	—	1.56
Sinaloa	4.64	—	6.48	—
Sonora	16.24	—	7.06	—
Tabasco	—	1.03	5.25	—
Tamaulipas	—	1.57	—	2.02
Tlaxcala	—	—	20.00[d]	—
Veracruz	—	3.48	—	2.10
Yucatán	4.52	—	—	0.37
Zacatecas	—	−0.10	—	1.16

a. The rate of urbanization was calculated by means of the expression:

$$2 \frac{I_1 - I_0}{(I_1 + I_0)} \cdot \frac{1}{n} \cdot 100,$$

in which I_1 and I_0 are the indexes of urbanization at the end and the beginning of the period; n is the number of years.

b. The rate of urbanization of the country in 1940–1950 was 3.73 percent.

c. The rate of urbanization of the country in 1950–1960 was 2.93 percent.

d. This is maximum value of rate of urbanization when I_0 has a value of zero.

rero and Morelos in 1940–1950, and Baja California Sur and Tlaxcala in the following decade, in which gross increase in urban population resulted exclusively from reclassification of non-urban localities. On the other hand, many localities (such as Nayarit, Nuevo Léon, and five others) did not undergo any reclassification at all between 1940 and 1960, indicative either of the limited amount of mixed population or of the very slow growth of these communities.

Analysis of the reclassification of non-urban localities indicates that a pattern of regional behavior does not exist.[32] Nevertheless, the number of states in which reclassification shared in urban growth rose from 15 to 21 between 1940–1950 and 1950–1960. Similarly, the multiplication of small cities signals the formation of actual or potential elements of regional systems of cities, which may be supposed to have significant socio-economic implications in the development of the regional and national domestic market, in the distribution of income, and, in general, in a greater flow of goods and ideas, as well as in greater diffusion of the urban way of life throughout the whole nation.

Growth by physical expansion of Mexico's principal cities also contributed to regional urbanization. This phenomenon took place in a more dispersed form, geographically speaking, from 1950 to 1960 than in the previous decade. The number of states—and therefore of cities—in which it occurred increased from 15 to 20. On the one hand, the Federal District-State of Mexico area,[33] in spite of maintaining its great predominance in the country's total of urban integrated population during the entire period—because of the significant physical expansion of Mexico City—lost relative importance, from 79.7 to 63.5 percent, from the first to the second decades. At the same time, other states increased their relative importance, outstanding among which in both periods were: Morelos (Cuernavaca and Cuautla), Coahuila-Durango (Torreón-Gómez Palacio-Lerdo), Puebla (Puebla), Nuevo León (Monterrey), and Jalisco (Guadalajara), which as a whole attained 15.6 percent of total integrated population in the first decade, as against 26.4 percent in the second.

Similarly, physical expansion of certain of the country's important cities contributed to the gross increase in urban population of its respective states. Noteworthy among these were those states previously mentioned, as well as Chihuahua (Chihuahua), Guanajuato (León), and San Luis Potosí (San Luis Potosí). In this respect, it is worth mentioning that the Federal District and the State of Mexico area experienced a decrease from 24.5 to 14.5 percent from the first to the second decade. On the other hand, Nuevo León and Jalisco sustained considerable increases (4.6 to 13.9 percent and 1.8 to 6.0 percent, respectively) due to accelerated physical expansion of the peripheries of Monterrey and Guadalajara. This signals the appearance in both cities of an ecological center-periphery process, characteristic of metropolises, such as that which began in Mexico City in 1940.

Table 18. Mexico: Participation of Localities Reclassified as Urban in Gross Increase in Urban Population, 1940–1960

	1940–1950			1950–1960		
	Gross increase urban population	Percent of increase due to reclassification with respect to:[a]		Gross increase urban population	Percent of increase due to reclassification with respect to:[a]	
		state[b]	nation[c]		state[b]	nation[c]
National Total	3,270,666[d]	19.2	100.0	5,548,325[d]	13.4	100.0
Aguascalientes	11,124	—	—	33,259	—	—
Baja California Norte	108,590	16.7	2.9	230,722	—	—
Baja California Sur	—	—	—	24,253	100.0	3.2
Campeche	7,995	—	—	33,766	62.7	2.8
Coahuila	115,165	16.6	3.0	173,883	20.8	4.7
Colima	10,018	—	—	51,260	70.5	4.7
Chiapas	44,636	39.2	2.8	45,868	33.6	2.0
Chihuahua	130,002	14.1	2.9	276,779	12.6	4.6
Distrito Federal	1,340,209	2.9	6.2	1,807,162	—	—
Durango	60,131	—	—	60,263	30.4	2.4
Guanajuato	155,410	46.9	11.6	222,836	16.1	4.7
Guerrero	47,934	100.0	7.6	46,082	39.1	2.4
Hidalgo	23,833	77.8	3.0	16,535	—	—
Jalisco	193,899	16.5	5.1	522,816	17.5	12.0
México	10,052	—	—	268,754	—	—
Michoacán	77,248	48.9	6.0	161,398	52.4	11.1
Morelos	66,070	100.0	10.5	45,941	—	—

Nayarit	7,048	—	—	29,474	—	—
Nuevo León	163,986	—	—	345,149	—	—
Oaxaca	17,326	—	—	48,361	40.9	2.6
Puebla	93,674	—	—	136,495	24.9	4.4
Querétaro	15,811	—	—	19,618	—	—
Quintana Roo	—	—	—	—	—	—
San Luis Potosí	38,006	—	—	84,367	51.9	5.7
Sinaloa	58,100	37.1	3.4	105,473	16.6	2.3
Sonora	134,514	81.5	17.5	196,473	32.0	8.2
Tlaxcala	10,304	—	—	19,942	—	—
Tabasco	151,492	36.6	8.8	216,116	15.4	4.4
Tamaulipas	—	—	—	15,705	100.0	2.1
Veracruz	124,350	43.8	8.7	236,449	38.1	11.8
Yucatán	46,006	—	—	45,020	34.9	2.1
Zacatecas	7,733	—	—	28,106	53.4	2.0

a. The gross increase in urban population was considered to be composed of two elements: growth of urban localities existing at the beginning of each period, and population of localities reclassified during the period from mixed to urban.

b. This percentage expresses the importance of the phenomenon of reclassification within each state. The difference with respect to 100 percent expresses the relative participation of existing cities in the gross increase in urban population in each state.

c. In this case, the percentage expresses the relative importance of reclassification in each state with respect to the national urban increase due to reclassification of urban localities.

d. Presents a difference of 11,168 inhabitants with respect to calculations made with national figures. This was due to the decision to consider statistically, in 1950, as mixed-urban—between 10 and 15,000 inhabitants—a locality in the state of Mexico integrated that year into the "urban area" of Mexico City.

Structure of Localities

The structure of localities at the state level was studied by means of distribution of the number of localities by population size, and percentage participation in the population of each state, of rural, mixed, and urban groups. (NOTE: Tables 21 to 23 appear at the end of this work.) In 1940, distribution of localities by population size was characterized by an elevated percentage of population in small cities. In nearly half the states, the urban population in small cities represented 100 percent of the state urban population. Similarly, it is important to point out that the majority of states lacked medium and large-sized cities. On the other hand, the number of urban localities within the states was very small; only seven states in that year had three or more. From 1940 to 1960, an increase in the number of urban centers in the majority of states may be observed, and, at the same time, a decrease in the relative importance of small cities as a consequence of the expansion of the larger urban centers.

With the formation of a wider system of cities and a probable decrease in dispersal of the population, an increase in Mexico's demographic concentration has been experienced. In a recent study, it was determined that the concentration of Mexico's population has been increasing from 1930 to 1960, the phenomenon most clearly evident from 1940–1950.[34] These results, added to those previously expressed regarding the structure of cities, demonstrate a growing territorial concentration of the Mexican population, and are principally explained by an accelerated intra-regional concentration—in spite of the fact that inter-regional differences continue to be greater. This reflects the formation of poles of demographic growth additional to that of Mexico City.

Social Growth of Total and Urban Population

Just as on a national level growth of urban population is explained by the transfer of population from rural and mixed groups to urban, so, too, at the state level this phenomenon is due to intra- and inter-state migratory flows, as much from countryside to city, as from city to city. This gives rise to two types of states: those of attraction and those of rejection.[35] Based upon these categories and the positive or negative net migration of the urban population of the states, the following groups of states were formed:

Group I: States of attraction with urban population of attraction (A – A)
Group II: States of rejection with urban population of attraction (R – A)
Group III: States of rejection with urban population of rejection (R – R)

Mexico's states were then classified according to this typology, as may be seen in Table 19.

The grouping of states and group changes present interesting characteristics. It may be observed, in the first place, that states which predominate in Group I (A – A) are of a high level of urbanization and—according to diverse studies of Mexico's regional development (Contla, 1967; Huerta Maldonado, 1960; Yates, 1960)—of advanced socio-economic development. Such is the case of those states along the northern border with the exception of Coahuila, and the Federal District. On the opposite side states in Group III are of a low level of development and, in general, with the exception of Aguascalientes, of limited urbanization. From the foregoing it may be deduced that states which rise in group rank have probably bettered their level of development. Jalisco and Mexico—states which have ascended to Group I—are two cases which appear to confirm the foregoing. The contrary may not be said with equal security of states which descend in group rank.

Another type of comparative analysis of this grouping of states, relating to other demographic factors previously studied on a national level, presents certain interesting results. Based upon Tables 19, 21, 22, and 23, states having the greatest proportion of rural population are, in the majority, ones of rejection; that is, they correspond to Group III (R – R).

Variations in the proportions of mixed population demonstrate reasonably well-defined patterns. On a national level, this proportion of population did not show any significant variation (see Tables 21 and 23); on

Table 19. Mexico: States Classified According to Net Migratory Balance in Urban and Total Population, 1940–1960

States	Net migration state–urban 1940–50	Net migration state–urban 1950–60	States	Net migration state–urban 1940–50	Net migration state–urban 1950–60
Aguascalientes	R – R	R – R	Michoacán	R – A	R – A
Baja California			Morelos	A – A	A – A
Norte	A – A	A – A	Nayarit	A – A	R – A
Baja California			Nuevo León	A – A	A – A
Sur	R – R	R – A	Oaxaca[a]	—	—
Campeche	A – A	R – A	Puebla	A – A	R – A
Colima	A – A	A – A	Querétaro	R – A	R – A
Coahuila	R – A	R – A	Quintana Roo[b]	—	—
Chiapas	A – A	A – A	San Luis Potosí	R – A	R – R
Chihuahua	A – A	A – A	Sinaloa	R – A	R – A
Distrito Federal	A – A	A – A	Sonora	A – A	A – A
Durango	R – A	R – A	Tabasco	R – A	R – A
Guanajuato	R – A	R – A	Tamaulipas	A – A	A – A
Guerrero	R – A	R – A	Tlaxcala	R – A	R – R
Hidalgo	R – R	R – R	Veracruz	A – A	A – A
Jalisco	R – A	A – A	Yucatán	R – A	R – R
México	R – A	A – A	Zacatecas	R – R	R – R

a. Vital statistics data were not available at the municipal level.
b. Did not have urban population.

the other hand, among R – R states there were clearly identifiable variations. In 1940, the proportion of mixed population in these states was much below the national average, while in 1960 its relative value increased substantially, exceeding the national average in almost all states. Similarly, variations in the number of mixed localities in each state confirm this situation even more, since R – R states experienced an increase three times larger than the national (246 and 75.4 percent, respectively). The foregoing expresses that R – R states, generally of limited and immature (high index of primacy) urban structure, demonstrate the possibility of reinforcing their urban system through small cities. This phenomenon is not produced with the same regularity in R – A and A – A states, since on comparing their values with the national average substantial variations in one sense or another may be observed.

A certain relationship between the aforementioned grouping of states and population total has also been observed. A – A states (1940–1960) contained 43 percent of the 12 states which in 1960 exceeded one million inhabitants (see Tables 19 and 23). This proportion decreases to 21.4 and 7.1 percent in R – A and R – R groups, respectively. Hence, it may be stated, albeit with weak evidence, that the most heavily populated states are those of greatest attraction, as much at the state level as at the urban.

From the analysis, it may be deduced that the behavior of A – A and R – R states (the two extremes of the scale) is more stable than that demonstrated by those classified as R – A, or those which change groups. Nevertheless, they do not display clearly defined regional patterns of behavior, except as concerns the demographic and economic developmental relationship.

The results of this study will be complemented and analyzed correlatively in projects of subsequent stages of the research program. We shall then be able to test in a more categorical manner the assumptions and hypotheses presented herein, to the extent that the studies programmed in addition to this demographic-spatial analysis contribute greater and more detailed criteria regarding this complex process of social change.

GENERAL CONCLUSIONS

(1) The level of urbanization of Mexico in 1960 approaches that observed in the developed countries as a whole.

(2) Mexico's rate of total population growth and rate of urbanization are among the highest in the world, which explains why it has attained this "level" in a shorter period of time than that required by the developed countries.

(3) The country's level of urbanization almost doubled from 1940 to 1960. This was due to the elevated growth of urban population with respect to the total, outstanding among which was the growth of the 17 urban areas of 100,000 or more inhabitants in 1960, and in particular the urban area of Mexico City.

(4) The large increase in Mexico's urban population was due, in the first decade studied, principally to the high rates of country-city migration; in the second, fundamentally, to the rates of natural growth.

(5) Growth of urban population was due basically to the increase undergone by cities existing at the beginning of the decades analyzed. Nevertheless, a significant characteristic of the process of urbanization in Mexico continues to be that localities which acquired the category of urban by reclassification have participated at the rate of 19.2 and 13.8 percent in the first and second decades, respectively, in the cited gross increase in Mexico's urban population.

(6) Physical expansion of the country's principal cities constitutes another trait of the "process" which must be taken into account, inasmuch as, being a phenomenon characteristic of metropolises in advanced and highly urbanized countries, it is beginning to be manifested and diffused in Mexico. This ecological process has been noteworthy in Mexico City, whose physical expansion accounted for 10.2 and 5.2 percent of the gross increase in the country's urban population.

(7) One of the most notable features of the process of urbanization in Mexico from 1940 to 1960 has been the near doubling of the number of urban localities and the more than tripling of cities of 100,000 or more inhabitants. In spite of this phenomenon, Mexico maintains a structure of exceedingly highly dispersed rural localities, especially those of under 1,000 inhabitants.

(8) Mexico's urban structure is classified as primate, but a tendency toward a system of cities of an "intermediate" nature has been experienced in the period studied, a result of the formation of cities of regional importance.

(9) The process of urbanization in Mexico experienced between both decades important changes in all characteristics analyzed: deceleration in the rate of urbanization, diminution in the rate of increase in urban population, change in weight of the components of urban growth, decrease in relative terms of urban growth by reclassification and integration, and reduction of the relative importance of Mexico City in population growth. All this indicates that in this period a turning point was observed in the process of urbanization.

(10) The process of urbanization is being diffused throughout the nation; however, regional inequalities in the "level" have been accentuated.

(11) States remaining in 1960 at the lowest level of urbanization are those of limited economic development. In less clear form, the most urbanized states correspond to those of a greater level of development. In the first group are generally found states of attraction $(A - A)$, and in the second, those of rejection $(R - R)$.

The notes and references for this chapter appear on the pages following Tables 20 to 23.

Table 20. Mexico: Population and Mean Annual Increase in Urban Localities in 1960 by States, 1940–1960

States and Cities	POPULATION[a]			MEAN ANNUAL INCREASE[b]						Class[c]	
				1940–1950			1950–1960			1940 1950	1950 1960
	1940	1950	1960	Total	Natu-ral	So-cial	Total	Natu-ral	So-cial		
National Total[a]	4,564,359	7,666,041	12,746,685	4.9	2.1	2.8	4.8	3.1	1.7		
Aguascalientes	82,234	93,358	126,617	1.3	2.6	-1.3	3.0	3.4	-0.4		
1. Aguascalientes	82,234	93,358	126,617	1.3	2.6	-1.3	3.0	3.4	-0.4	RE	RM
Baja California Norte	39,877	143,851	374,573	11.3	2.6	8.6	8.8	4.0	4.8		
2. Mexicali	18,775	65,749[e]	179,539[e]	11.0	2.8	8.3	9.1	4.2	4.9	AME	AME
3. Tijuana	16,486	59,952	152,473[e]	11.4	2.3	9.1	8.7	3.9	4.8	AME	AME
4. Ensenada	4,616	18,150	42,561	11.9	3.3	8.6	8.0	3.5	4.5	AME	AME
Baja California Sur	10,401	13,071	24,253	2.3	3.2	-0.9	6.0	3.8	2.2		
5. La Paz	10,401	13,071	24,253	2.3	3.2	-0.9	6.0	3.8	2.2	RM	AE
Campeche	30,964	42,875	65,038	3.2	2.9	0.3	4.1	3.7	0.5		
6. Campeche	23,277	31,272	43,874	2.9	3.0	-0.1	3.4	3.6	-0.2	RM	RM
7. Ciudad del Carmen	7,687	11,603	21,164	4.1	2.6	1.5	5.8	3.9	1.9	AE	AE
Coahuila[g]	217,321	335,494	486,756	4.3	3.2	1.1	3.6	3.4	0.2		
8. Torreón[f]	101,354	188,203	263,564	5.2	3.1	2.1	3.2	3.5	-0.3	AE	RM
9. Saltillo	49,430	69,842	98,839	3.4	3.7	-0.3	3.4	3.3	0.1	RM	AM
10. Piedras Negras	15,663	27,581	44,992	5.5	2.7	2.8	4.8	3.1	1.7	AE	AE
11. Monclova	7,181	19,049	43,077	9.0	3.2	5.8	7.7	3.6	4.1	AME	AME
12. Nueva Rosita	25,551	29,625	34,302	1.5	2.6	-1.1	1.5	3.4	-1.9	RE	RE
13. San Pedro de las Colonias	15,713	19,258	26,018	2.0	3.8	-1.7	3.0	3.6	-0.6	RE	RM
14. Villa Acuña	5,607	11,372	20,048	6.8	2.8	4.0	5.5	3.2	2.3	AE	AE
15. Parras de la Puente	15,555	18,547	19,768	1.8	3.4	-1.6	0.6	3.2	-2.6	RE	RME

16. Sabinas	6,825	11,249	16,076	4.9	3.0	1.9	3.5	3.4	0.1	AE	AM
Colima	*32,727*	*52,842*	*83,879*	*4.1*	*2.2*	*1.9*	*4.6*	*4.2*	*0.4*		
17. Colima	22,601	32,619[e]	47,767[e]	2.8	2.4	0.4	3.9	5.0	−1.1	AM	RE
18. Manzanillo	6,831	13,006	19,950	6.2	2.0	4.2	4.2	3.2	1.0	AME	AM
19. Tecomán	3,295	7,217	16,162	7.5	1.8	5.7	7.7	3.2	4.5	AE	AME
Chiapas	*51,521*	*87,459*	*121,574*	*5.2*	*1.7*	*3.4*	*3.3*	*2.8*	*0.5*		
20. Tapachula	15,187	29,990	41,578	6.6	1.5	5.1	3.2	2.6	0.6	AME	AM
21. Tuxtla Gutiérrez	15,883	28,243	41,244	5.6	2.6	3.0	3.7	3.0	0.7	AE	AM
22. San Cristóbal de las Casas	11,768	17,473	23,343	3.9	0.7	3.2	2.9	2.8	0.1	AE	AM
23. Cumitán de Domínguez	8,683	11,753	15,409	3.0	2.1	0.9	2.7	2.8	−0.1	AM	RM
Chihuahua	*157,544*	*286,672*	*536,698*	*5.8*	*2.2*	*3.6*	*6.0*	*3.0*	*3.0*		
24. Ciudad Juárez	48,881	122,566	262,119	8.6	1.9	6.7	7.3	2.8	4.4	AME	AME
25. Chihuahua	56,805	87,000	158,389[e]	4.2	2.2	2.0	5.7	2.9	2.8	AE	AE
26. Hidalgo del Parral	24,231	32,063	41,474	2.8	2.2	0.6	2.6	3.5	−0.9	AM	RM
27. Delicias	6,020	18,290	30,919	10.1	3.3	6.8	7.4	3.1	4.3	AME	AME
28. Ciudad Camargo	7,705	11,945	18,951	4.3	3.1	1.2	4.5	3.4	1.1	AE	AE
29. Santa Bárbara	13,902	14,808	15,846	0.6	2.4	−1.8	0.7	3.5	−2.8	RE	RME
Distrito Federal[e]	*1,584,588*	*2,899,991*	*4,707,153*	*5.4*	*1.7*	*3.7*	*4.6*	*3.1*	*1.5*		
30. Ciudad de Mexico[f]	1,559,782	2,872,334	4,909,961	5.4	1.7	3.7	4.9	3.0	1.9	AE	AE
31. Xochimilco	14,370	20,685	30,031	3.6	0.9	2.7	3.7	2.5	1.2	AE	AE
Tlalpan[h]	10,436	18,140	—	5.4	2.2	3.2	—	—	—		
Durango[g]	*68,319*	*119,101*	*179,364*	*5.4*	*2.8*	*2.6*	*3.8*	*3.4*	*0.4*		
32. Durango	33,412	59,869[e]	99,436[e]	5.6	2.5	3.1	4.7	3.3	1.4	AE	AM
Guanajuato	*240,082*	*351,812*	*548,708*	*3.8*	*2.9*	*0.9*	*4.3*	*3.1*	*1.1*		
33. León	74,155	122,726	216,246[e]	4.9	2.9	2.0	5.2	3.0	2.2	AE	AE
34. Irapuato	32,377	49,445	83,768	4.2	3.0	1.2	5.1	3.4	1.7	AE	AE
35. Celaya	22,766	34,424	58,851	4.1	2.9	1.2	5.2	2.2	3.0	AE	AE
36. Salamanca	11,985	20,610	32,663	5.3	2.7	2.6	4.5	3.5	1.0	AE	AM
37. Guanajuato	23,521	23,379	28,212	−0.1	2.0	−2.1	1.9	1.9	0.0	RME	RM

Table 20. (Continued)

States and Cities	POPULATION[a]			MEAN ANNUAL INCREASE[b]						Class[c]	
				1940–1950			1950–1960				
	1940	1950	1960	Total	Natu-ral	So-cial	Total	Natu-ral	So-cial	1940 1950	1950 1960
38. Acámbaro	17,643	23,004	26,187	2.6	3.0	−0.4	1.3	3.6	−2.3	RM	RME
39. Silao	13,880	18,463	24,229	2.8	2.6	0.2	2.7	3.3	−0.6	AM	RM
40. Valle de Santiago	12,278	15,628	21,795	2.4	3.0	−0.6	3.3	4.1	−0.8	RM	RM
41. San Francisco del Rincón	12,015	18,193	20,878	4.1	3.0	1.1	1.4	3.7	−2.3	AE	RME
42. Moroleón	10,418	13,801	17,954	2.8	2.8	0.0	2.6	3.2	−0.6	AM	RM
43. Cortázar	9,044	12,139	17,925	2.9	3.2	−0.3	3.8	4.2	−0.4	RM	RM
Guerrero	*31,583*	*60,607*	*94,016*	*6.3*	*2.7*	*3.6*	*4.3*	*4.3*	*0.0*		
44. Acapulco de Juárez	9,993	28,512	49,149	9.6	3.4	6.2	5.3	5.0	0.3	AME	AM
45. Iguala	12,756	19,422	26,845	4.1	2.5	1.6	3.2	3.3	−0.1	AE	RM
46. Chilpancingo de Bravo	8,834	12,673	18,022	3.6	1.7	1.9	3.5	3.9	−0.4	AE	RM
Hidalgo	*65,906*	*77,187*	*93,722*	*1.6*	*2.5*	*−0.1*	*1.7*	*3.1*	*−1.4*		
47. Pachuca	53,354	58,658	66,883[e]	1.0	2.7	−1.7	1.1	3.3	−2.2	RE	RME
48. Tulancingo	12,552	18,529	26,839	3.8	2.1	1.7	3.7	2.8	0.9	AE	AM
Jalisco	*343,163*	*518,117*	*979,606*	*4.0*	*2.1*	*1.9*	*5.9*	*2.9*	*3.0*		
49. Guadalajara[f]	240,721	401,283	811,829	4.9	1.9	3.0	6.4	2.7	3.7	AE	AE
50. Ciudad Guzmán	22,170	23,630	30,941	0.6	1.7	−1.1	2.7	2.8	−0.1	RE	RM
51. Ocotlán	14,289	16,824	25,416	1.6	3.0	−1.4	4.1	3.6	0.5	RE	AM
52. Lagos de Moreno	12,490	13,190	23,636	0.6	3.4	−2.8	5.7	3.9	1.8	RME	AE
53. Tepatitlán de Morelos	8,894	15,053	19,835	5.1	3.3	1.8	2.8	3.7	−1.0	AE	RM
54. Ameca	13,003	13,589	17,588	0.4	2.4	−2.0	2.6	3.2	−0.6	RE	RM
55. Arandas	7,254	9,335	17,071	2.5	3.6	−1.1	5.9	3.3	2.6	RE	AE

56. Autlán	10,915	11,345	17,017	0.4	2.9	-2.5	4.0	3.4	0.6	RME	AM
57. La Barca	13,427	13,868	16,273	0.3	3.2	-2.9	1.6	3.7	-2.1	RME	RME
Mexico	52,021	64,649	322,235	3.6	2.4	1.2	9.6	2.0	7.6		
58. Toluca^g	43,429	53,481^e	89,396^e	2.0	2.4	-0.4	4.1	3.0	1.1	RM	AE
Michoacán	130,445	202,725	318,980	4.3	2.3	2.0	4.4	3.4	1.0		
59. Morelia	44,304	64,979^e	106,077^e	3.6	1.6	2.0	4.7	3.0	1.7	AE	AE
60. Uruapan	20,583	31,420	45,727	4.2	2.5	1.7	3.7	3.9	-0.2	AE	RM
61. Zamora	15,447	23,397	34,372	4.1	3.0	1.1	3.8	3.7	0.1	AE	AM
62. Sahuayo	10,465	12,511	25,611	1.8	4.1	-2.3	6.9	4.6	2.3	RME	AE
63. La Piedad	12,369	17,843	24,337	3.6	1.4	2.2	3.1	2.1	1.0	AE	AM
64. Zitácuaro	11,434	19,943	23,883	5.4	2.2	3.2	1.8	3.6	-1.8	AE	RE
65. Zacapu	6,169	14,346	22,200	8.0	3.3	4.7	4.3	4.1	0.2	AME	AM
66. Apatzingán	2,080	8,358	19,568	12.0	1.1	10.9	8.0	2.7	5.3	AME	AME
67. Hidalgo	7,594	9,928	17,155	2.7	3.0	-0.3	5.3	3.5	1.8	RM	AE
Morelos	20,767	66,070	112,011	7.0	1.7	5.3	3.7	2.7	1.0		
68. Cuernavaca	14,336	43,309^e	77,484^e	8.1	1.9	6.2	4.0	2.3	1.7	AME	AE
69. Cuautla	6,431	22,761^e	34,527^e	5.1	1.3	3.8	2.9	3.5	-0.6	AE	RM
Nayarit	17,547	24,595	54,069	3.3	2.6	0.7	7.5	3.3	4.2		
70. Tepic	17,547	24,595	54,069	3.3	2.6	0.7	7.5	3.3	4.2	AM	AME
Nuevo León	190,128	354,114	699,263	6.0	2.4	3.6	6.3	3.1	3.2		
71. Monterrey^f	190,128	354,114	699,263	6.0	2.4	3.6	6.3	3.1	3.2	AE	AE
Oaxaca^i	43,856	60,451	94,993	—	—	—	—	—	—		
72. Oaxaca	29,306	46,632	75,196^g	—	—	—	—	—	—	AM	
73. Juchitán	14,550	13,819	19,797	—	—	—	—	—	—		
Puebla	187,254	289,610	401,972	4.0	1.0	3.1	3.0	2.0	1.0		
74. Puebla	138,491	226,646^e	305,469^e	4.5	0.9	3.6	2.6	1.8	0.8	AE	AM
75. Tehuacán	16,278	23,209	31,897	3.5	0.9	2.6	3.2	2.1	1.1	AE	AE
76. Atlixco	17,034	15,622	30,650	-0.9	1.5	-2.4	6.5	2.7	3.8	RME	AE
77. Teziutlán	8,386	13,536	17,400	4.7	1.6	3.1	2.5	2.7	-0.2	AE	RM

Table 20. (Continued)

| | POPULATION[a] | | | MEAN ANNUAL INCREASE[b] | | | | | | Class[c] | |
| | | | | 1940–1950 | | | 1950–1960 | | | | |
States and Cities	1940	1950	1960	Total	Natu-ral	So-cial	Total	Natu-ral	So-cial	1940 1950	1950 1960
78. Izúcar de Matamoros	7,065	10,597	16,556	4.0	1.0	3.0	4.4	2.1	2.3	AE	AE
Querétaro	*33,629*	*49,440*	*69,058*	*3.8*	*2.1*	*1.7*	*3.1*	*2.7*	*0.4*	*AE*	*AE*
79. Querétaro	33,629	49,440e	69,058e	3.8	2.1	1.7	3.1	2.7	0.4	AE	AM
San Luis Potosí	*100,949*	*160,260*	*216,082*	*4.3*	*2.3*	*2.0*	*2.7*	*3.2*	*-0.5*		
80. San Luis Potosí	77,161	131,715e	172,332e	4.9	2.3	2.6	2.3	3.2	-0.9	AE	RM
81. Ciudad Valles	7,240	14,382	23,823	6.6	2.8	3.8	4.9	3.4	1.5	AE	AE
82. Matehuala	16,548	14,163	19,927	-1.6	2.5	-4.1	3.4	2.5	0.9	RME	AM
Sinaloa	*67,079*	*120,748*	*217,715*	*5.1*	*2.6*	*2.5*	*5.7*	*3.4*	*2.3*		
83. Culiacán	22,025	48,936	85,024	7.6	2.6	5.0	5.4	3.9	1.5	AME	AE
84. Mazatlán	32,117	41,754	76,874e	2.6	2.1	0.5	5.8	2.8	3.0	AM	AE
85. Los Mochis	12,937	21,552	38,307	5.0	3.3	1.7	5.6	3.7	1.9	AE	AE
86. Guasave	4,997	8,506	17,510	5.2	3.6	1.6	6.9	3.3	3.6	AE	AE
Sonora	*85,142*	*178,044*	*349,588*	*7.1*	*3.1*	*4.0*	*6.5*	*3.9*	*2.6*		
87. Hermosillo	18,601	43,519	96,019e	8.0	3.0	5.0	7.5	3.8	3.7	AME	AE
88. Ciudad Obregón	12,497	30,991	67,956	8.5	3.4	5.1	7.5	4.3	3.2	AME	AE
89. Nogales	13,866	24,478	37,657	5.5	2.5	3.0	4.2	3.4	0.8	AE	AM
90. Guaymas	8,796	18,890	34,865	7.3	2.8	4.5	5.9	4.1	1.8	AME	AE
91. Navojoa	11,009	17,345	30,560	4.5	3.2	1.3	5.5	3.8	1.7	AE	AE
92. San Luis Río Colorado	558	4,079	28,545	15.2	1.7	13.5	15.0	4.8	10.2	AME	AME
93. Cananea	11,006	17,892	19,683	4.8	4.1	0.7	1.0	3.4	-2.4	AM	RME
94. Empalme	4,703	10,379	18,964	7.5	2.8	4.7	5.8	4.1	1.7	AME	AE

95. Agua Prieta	4,106	10,471	15,339	8.7	2.5	6.2	3.8	3.5	0.3	AME	AM
Tabasco	*25,114*	*35,418*	*55,360*	*3.2*	*1.9*	*1.3*	*4.4*	*2.8*	*1.6*	*AE*	*AE*
96. Villahermosa	25,114	35,418[e]	55,360[e]	3.2	1.9	1.3	4.4	2.8	1.6	AE	RM
Tamaulipas	*193,685*	*337,761*	*542,242*	*5.4*	*2.2*	*3.2*	*4.6*	*3.3*	*1.3*		
97. Tampico[f]	110,550	135,419	176,163	2.0	2.0	0.0	2.6	2.9	−0.3	AM	RM
98. Nuevo Laredo	28,872	57,668	92,627	6.6	2.0	4.6	4.6	3.0	1.6	AME	AE
99. Matamoros	15,699	45,846	92,327	9.8	2.4	7.4	6.7	3.9	2.8	AME	AE
100. Reynosa	9,412	34,087	74,140	11.3	2.5	8.8	7.4	3.9	3.5	AME	AE
101. Ciudad Victoria	19,513	31,815	50,797	4.8	2.9	1.9	4.6	3.2	1.4	AE	AE
102. Ciudad Mante	8,616	21,291	22,919	8.5	2.8	5.7	0.7	3.1	−2.4	AME	RME
103. Río Bravo	936	4,610	17,500	13.2	2.5	10.7	11.7	3.9	7.8	AME	AME
104. Valle Hermoso	87	7,025	15,769	19.5	2.4	17.1	7.7	3.9	3.8	AME	AE
Tlaxcala	*6,768*	*12,710*	*15,705*	*6.1*	*2.9*	*3.2*	*2.1*	*2.9*	*−0.8*		
105. Apizaco	6,768	12,710	15,705	6.1	2.9	3.2	2.1	2.9	−0.8	AE	RM
Veracruz	*294,971*	*409,729*	*585,278*	*3.2*	*1.5*	*1.6*	*3.5*	*2.3*	*1.2*		
106. Veracruz	71,720	101,246[e]	147,501[e]	3.4	1.2	2.2	3.7	1.6	2.1	AE	AE
107. Orizaba[f]	76,825	86,656	108,894	1.2	1.5	−0.3	2.3	2.2	0.1	RM	AM
108. Jalapa	39,530	51,169	68,524[e]	2.7	1.2	1.5	2.5	2.2	0.3	AE	AM
109. Córdoba	17,865	32,888	47,448[e]	5.9	0.9	5.0	3.6	2.6	1.0	AME	AM
110. Coatzacoalcos	13,740	20,850[e]	40,406[e]	3.7	1.4	2.3	6.4	2.8	3.6	AE	AE
111. Minatitlán	18,539	22,455	35,350	1.9	1.8	0.1	4.5	2.8	1.7	AM	AE
112. Tuxpan	13,381	18,415[e]	26,948[e]	1.7	2.7	−1.0	3.8	2.6	1.2	RM	AE
113. San Andrés Tuxtla	10,154	15,150	20,256	3.9	3.6	0.3	2.9	3.1	−0.2	AM	RM
114. Poza Rica	4,119	14,901	19,564	11.3	2.0	9.3	2.7	3.6	−0.9	AME	RM
115. Papantla	6,644	11,359	18,865	5.2	1.6	3.6	5.0	1.6	3.4	AE	AE
116. Coatepec	11,459	13,747	18,022	1.8	1.2	0.6	2.7	2.7	0.0	AM	AM
117. Cosamaloapan	3,740	8,881	16,944	8.2	2.7	5.5	6.2	2.5	3.7	AME	AE
118. Tierra Blanca	7,255	12,012	16,556	4.9	2.7	2.2	3.2	3.8	−0.6	AE	RM
Yucatán	*103,539*	*153,507*	*187,878*	*3.9*	*2.0*	*1.9*	*1.9*	*2.5*	*−0.6*		

Table 20. (Continued)

| | POPULATION[a] | | | MEAN ANNUAL INCREASE[b] | | | | | | Class[c] | |
| | | | | 1940–1950 | | | 1950–1960 | | | | |
States and Cities	1940	1950	1960	Total	Natu-ral	So-cial	Total	Natu-ral	So-cial	1940 1950	1950 1960
119. Mérida	96,852	142,858	172,155[e]	3.8	1.9	1.9	1.8	2.5	-0.7	AE	RM
120. Tizimín	6,687	10,649	15,723	4.6	2.5	2.1	3.9	3.7	0.2	AE	AM
Zacatecas	55,235	64,609	82,299	1.6	2.8	-1.2	2.4	3.7	-1.3		
121. Fresnillo	24,614	29,936	35,582	1.9	2.9	-1.0	1.7	3.9	-2.2	RM	RME
122. Zacatecas	21,846	24,257	31,701	1.0	2.4	-1.4	2.7	3.4	-0.7	RE	RM
123. Jerez de García Salinas	8,775	10,416	15,016	1.7	3.2	-1.5	3.6	3.5	0.1	RE	AM

a. The population in 1940 and 1950 corresponds to that of localities which were urban in those years (see Table 13) plus the population of those localities reclassified as urban during the 1940–1960 period. In 1960, the population is the urban population in that year (Table 13). This clearly explains the difference between the figures for the country's urban population in the years studied appearing in Tables 13 and 18.

b. The mean annual increase was obtained by means of the following expressions:

$$\text{Total} = 2(P_1 - P_0)/(P_1 + P_0) \cdot 1/n \cdot 100;$$
$$\text{Natural} = 2(CN)/(P_1 + P_0) \cdot 1/n \cdot 100;$$
$$\text{Social} = 2(CS)/(P_1 + P_0) \cdot 1/n \cdot 100;$$

in which P_0 and P_1 are the populations at the beginning and the end of the period; CN is natural growth; CS is social growth, and n is the number of years of the jeriod. The calculation was made for the 1940–1950 and 1950–1960 periods, with the urban areas of 1950 and 1960, respectively, taken at the beginning of the period. For this reason, in the case of certain urban areas, there are small differences between real population and that used to calculate the mean annual increase and therefore in that of other states having urban areas (only in the case of the state of Mexico is the difference important because of changes in the area corresponding to the urban area of Mexico City).

c. The classification of localities into cities of "attraction" and "rejection"—"very high," "high," and "moderate"—is based on the mean annual social growth. The letter abbreviations presented have the following significance:

AME–Very high attraction	AM–Moderate attraction	RE–High rejection
AE–High attraction	RME–Very high rejection	RM–Moderate rejection

For more detail regarding the numerical limits of each group, see Table 10.

d. In the calculation of the country's mean annual increases, the urban population of Oaxaca (Oaxaca and Juchitán) is not included because of the lack of necessary information.

e. The population of these "urban areas" is composed of that tabulated by the Census—called central city—plus peripheral localities which are considered physically integrated into the former on the basis of contiguity and relative accessibility to the central city.

f. These six cities had urban area during the entire period.

g. The urban areas of the cities of Torreón and Mexico City have overflowed the boundaries of the states of Coahuila and the Federal District, respectively, in the direction of the states of Durango and Mexico. For this reason, it has been considered convenient to record the total population of such urban areas in the list of cities of the state in which the central city is located. Regarding the state computation, the population of these two urban areas was counted in accordance with the corresponding political-administrative boundaries.

h. The locality of Tlalpan was recorded in independent form in 1940 and 1950. It was not presented in similar form in 1960 because of being counted as incorporated into the urban area of Mexico City. For this reason, it was not enumerated.

i. Mean annual increases are not included because of the lack of necessary vital statistics.

SOURCES: (1) Information provided by the Oficina de Estadísticas Demográficas, Dirección General de Estadística, Secretaría de Industria y Comercio; (2) Robert Stevens (1966) Internal Migration in Mexico. M.A. thesis, University of Florida. (3) Cartographic and aerial photometric information provided by the Dirección de Planeación y Programación of the Secretaría de Obras Públicas.

Table 21. Mexico: Distribution of Population by State, Classified into Rural, Mixed, and Urban, 1940

| States | Total population | RURAL POPULATION | | | | MIXED POPULATION[b] | | URBAN POPULATION[c] | |
| | | 1–2,500 inhabitants[a] | | 2,501–5,000 inhabitants | | | | | |
		Number of Localities	Percent	Number of Localities	Percent	Number of Localities	Percent	Number of Localities	Percent
Total	19,649,162	104,822	64.9	436	7.5	195	7.6	56	20.0
Aguascalientes	161,693	552	42.6	3	6.5	—	—	1	50.9
Baja California Norte	78,907	709	49.5	1	5.9	—	—	2	44.7
Baja California Sur	51,471	1,208	64.2	1	5.0	2	30.8	—	—
Campeche	90,460	678	50.4	4	15.4	1	8.5	1	25.7
Coahuila	550,717	2,219	49.4	8	4.5	9	10.3	6	35.9
Colima	78,806	373	54.9	2	7.8	1	8.7	1	28.7
Chiapas	679,885	7,806	83.9	8	4.2	7	7.3	2	4.6
Chihuahua	623,944	4,630	63.3	12	6.4	7	9.5	3	20.8
Distrito Federal	1,757,530	235	5.9	10	1.9	7	3.5	1	88.8
Durango	481,484	3,330	75.8	13	8.7	2	3.2	2	12.3
Guanajuato	1,046,490	4,502	64.9	14	4.6	18	14.2	5	16.3
Guerrero	732,910	2,886	85.5	18	7.9	6	6.7	—	—
Hidalgo	771,818	3,151	81.9	15	6.4	4	4.8	1	6.9
Jalisco	1,418,310	9,483	58.8	34	8.4	26	14.2	2	18.5
México	1,146,034	3,190	77.3	48	13.2	11	5.7	1	3.8
Michoacán	1,182,003	5,768	71.1	38	11.0	17	11.1	3	6.8
Morelos	182,711	266	72.1	9	16.5	2	11.4	—	—
Nayarit	216,698	1,220	69.8	5	7.7	4	14.4	1	8.1
Nuevo León	541,147	4,196	55.3	8	4.4	4	5.2	1	35.1

Oaxaca	1,192,749	84.9	32	9.2	5	3.4	1	2.5
Puebla	1,294,620	72.2	36	9.6	9	4.9	3	13.3
Querétaro	244,737	80.7	2	2.8	1	2.7	1	13.7
Quintana Roo	18,752	75.1	1	24.9	—	—	—	—
San Luis Potosí	678,779	74.7	11	5.3	6	6.2	2	13.8
Sinaloa	492,821	78.2	5	4.3	4	6.5	2	11.0
Sonora	364,176	67.3	11	10.3	6	17.2	1	5.1
Tabasco	285,630	82.0	6	6.6	1	2.6	1	8.8
Tamaulipas	458,832	54.5	1	1.0	4	6.4	4	38.1
Tlaxcala	224,063	70.4	11	16.7	4	12.8	—	—
Veracruz	1,619,338	71.2	38	8.3	14	6.7	5	13.9
Yucatán	416,210	51.5	13	10.6	9	14.7	1	23.3
Zacatecas	565,437	75.3	18	12.0	4	4.4	2	8.2

a. This datum has been presented due to the lack of state population subtotals of localities of 1–1,000 inhabitants.

b. Includes mixed rural localities (5–10,000 inhabitants) and mixed urban (10–15,000 inhabitants).

c. Includes localities of 15,000 or more inhabitants.

SOURCE: Calculations based upon the VI General Population Census.

Table 22. Mexico: Distribution of Population by State, Classified into Rural, Mixed, and Urban, 1950

States	Total population	RURAL POPULATION				MIXED POPULATION[a]		URBAN POPULATION[b]	
		1–1,000 inhabitants		1,001–5,000 inhabitants					
		Number of Localities	Percent	Number of Localities	Percent	Number of Localities	Percent	Number of Localities	Percent
Total	25,779,254	94,890	42.3	3,098	22.0	254	7.9	85	27.9
Aguascalientes	188,075	819	35.1	17	15.3	—	—	1	49.6
Baja California Norte	226,965	534	27.3	14	9.3	—	—	3	63.4
Baja California Sur	60,864	2	32.9	—	—	1	9.5	1	25.6
Campeche	122,098	1,251	58.7	3	8.4	8	9.5	7	43.4
Coahuila	720,619	883	32.2	16	32.7	2	18.0	1	29.0
Colima	112,321	2,202	33.0	63	14.1	9	8.0	3	8.4
Chiapas	907,026	541	34.1	10	18.8	9	9.4	4	30.7
Chihuahua	846,414	6,704	64.6	93	19.0	4	1.1	3	95.1
Distrito Federal	3,050,442	5,268	46.4	65	13.5	2	1.8	2	18.9
Durango	629,874	71	0.6	46	3.3	18	11.4	9	24.5
Guanajuato	1,328,712	3,427	55.9	79	23.4	6	5.5	2	5.2
Guerrero	919,386	4,828	51.5	91	12.6	6	5.3	2	9.1
Hidalgo	850,394	2,988	58.9	151	30.0	29	13.7	4	26.2
Jalisco	1,746,777	2,841	63.2	111	22.4	17	8.2	1	3.8
México	1,392,623	9,149	40.0	185	20.2	21	12.0	5	11.1
Michoacán	1,422,717	2,423	39.3	368	48.7	3	8.4	2	24.2
Morelos	272,842	5,867	50.3	199	26.6	7	18.7	1	8.5
Nayarit	290,124	212	27.4	55	40.0	5	5.7	1	47.8
Nuevo León	740,191	1,055	46.3	44	26.6	4,034	35.3	44	11.2

Oaxaca	1,421,313	52.5	295	36.4	15	7.8	1	3.3
Puebla	1,625,830	38.8	351	37.6	15	7.2	3	16.3
Querétaro	286,238	61.5	32	18.6	1	2.6	1	17.3
Quintana Roo	26,967	64.5	1	8.6	1	26.9	—	—
SanLuis Potosí	856,066	57.9	82	17.4	8	9.3	1	15.4
Sinaloa	635,681	58.8	62	15.7	7	7.8	3	17.7
Sonora	510,607	41.9	57	21.3	4	6.8	6	30.0
Tabasco	362,716	59.2	59	28.8	1	2.3	1	9.8
Tamaulipas	718,167	40.3	39	11.0	3	3.3	6	45.4
Tlaxcala	284,551	33.4	69	44.7	8	21.9	—	—
Veracruz	2,040,231	52.4	240	21.9	23	8.6	8	17.1
Yucatán	516,899	27.0	74	28.7	11	16.7	1	27.6
Zacatecas	665,524	61.5	83	22.2	8	8.2	2	8.1

a. Includes mixed-rural localities (5–10,000 inhabitants) and mixed-urban (10–15,000 inhabitants).

b. Includes localities of 15,000 or more inhabitants.

SOURCE: Calculations based upon the VII General Population Census.

Table 23. Mexico: Distribution of Population by State, Classified into Rural, Mixed, and Urban, 1960

States	Total population	RURAL POPULATION				MIXED POPULATION[a]		URBAN POPULATION[b]	
		1–1,000 inhabitants		1,001–5,000 inhabitants					
		Number of Localities	Percent	Number of Localities	Percent	Number of Localities	Percent	Number of Localities	Percent
Total	34,923,129	84,590	34.7	3,950	20.9	342	7.9	125	36.5
Aguascalientes	243,363	736	31.4	16	11.7	2	4.8	1	52.0
Baja California Norte	520,165	399	14.3	32	10.4	3	3.4	3	72.0
Baja California Sur	81,594	1,194	51.4	6	12.3	1	6.6	1	29.7
Campeche	168,219	463	26.6	22	31.4	1	3.3	2	38.7
Coahuila	907,734	2,148	25.1	63	11.9	9	9.3	9	53.6
Colima	164,450	440	27.3	15	21.7	—	—	3	51.0
Chiapas	1,210,870	6,566	61.6	138	21.4	9	7.0	4	10.0
Chihuahua	1,226,793	4,152	33.8	94	13.6	12	8.9	6	43.8
Distrito Federal	4,870,876	57	0.4	39	2.0	7	1.0	2	96.6
Durango	760,836	2,359	48.3	103	24.2	5	4.0	2	23.6
Guanajuato	1,735,490	4,630	44.9	133	13.8	18	9.6	11	31.6
Guerrero	1,186,716	3,020	53.7	205	31.5	11	6.9	3	7.9
Hidalgo	994,598	2,454	58.7	147	24.5	10	7.4	2	9.4
Jalisco	2,443,261	8,375	30.2	219	18.2	33	11.6	9	40.1
México	1,897,851	1,939	29.7	438	44.4	23	8.9	2	17.0
Michoacán	1,851,876	5,242	43.2	262	26.8	30	12.8	9	17.2
Morelos	386,264	200	18.8	71	38.3	6	14.0	2	29.0
Nayarit	389,929	1,333	41.0	58	27.8	7	17.9	1	13.9
Nuevo León	1,078,848	3,004	22.6	41	7.3	6	5.3	1	64.8

Oaxaca	1,727,266	48.3	374	36.9	20	9.2	2	5.5
Puebla	1,973,837	33.3	417	38.5	20	7.8	5	20.4
Querétaro	355,045	59.0	37	16.8	2	4.8	1	19.5
Quintana Roo	50,169	59.0	5	15.4	1	25.6	—	—
San Luis Potosí	1,048,297	54.2	105	18.2	8	7.0	3	20.6
Sinaloa	838,404	46.7	97	19.0	9	8.3	4	26.0
Sonora	783,378	32.9	63	15.7	7	6.8	9	44.6
Tabasco	496,340	47.2	103	34.8	5	6.9	1	11.2
Tamaulipas	1,024,182	33.8	56	11.1	3	2.1	8	52.9
Tlaxcala	346,699	26.0	88	47.9	9	21.6	1	4.5
Veracruz	2,727,899	46.7	305	20.5	40	11.3	13	21.5
Yucatán	614,049	24.5	83	29.0	12	15.9	2	30.6
Zacatecas	817,831	54.8	115	23.9	13	11.3	3	10.1

a. Includes mixed-rural localities (5–10,000 inhabitants) and mixed-urban (10–15,000 inhabitants).

b. Includes localities of 15,000 or more inhabitants.

SOURCE: Calculations based upon the VIII General Population Census.

NOTES

1. The present study is the first of eight projects which make up the program of research concerning the process of urbanization in Mexico being carried out by the Centro de Estudios Económicos y Demográficos of the Colegio de México. The program has as its objective recognition of the factors which have intervened in the present distribution of population and socio-economic activities between urban and rural zones, determination of the most significant effects of the phenomenon of urbanization in Mexico, as well as establishment of the bases for estimating the probable urban structure of Mexico to 1980. At a later stage, based upon results obtained, it will be possible to achieve the normative study of the process of urbanization, from which strategies for the urban development of the country may be derived. For further details see Centro de Estudios Económicos y Demográficos (1967).

The present study constitutes an expanded version of that published by the Centro Editor de América Latina of Buenos Aires, in the book entitled *La urbanización como campo de investigación en ciencias sociales*. It contains additional information and a wider regional analysis, principally in the third section. The adjustment of certain calculations and the modifications introduced augment the study's clarity and its statistical exactitude; nevertheless, these changes do not alter the original conclusions.

2. The demographic-ecological definition is limited; there is no doubt that the phenomenon does not consist, exclusively, of a process of concentration of population at determined geographic points. Nevertheless, in view of the undeniable interdependence of urbanization and other processes of change, such as modernization, secularization, and economic development—all of which, according to Germani, tend to be considered global processes and therefore difficult to define and measure—it has been considered that up to the moment the only concrete formulation of the phenomenon susceptible to being translated into operation is that of the demographic-ecological type. Similarly, this permits analysis with greater clarity of the association of the process of urbanization with the other processes previously mentioned. The limitation of the demographic focus made necessary a definition of "urban" based upon an analysis of the population variable and its relation to other social and economic variables (Unikel, 1968). Finally, it is important to point out that this description of a demographic-spatial nature, although considered fundamental, constitutes a point of departure which will be complemented by analysis of non-demographic variables in subsequent projects of the research program. For greater detail regarding the foregoing, see Germani (1963) and Eldridge (1954).

3. In general, there are two "type" systems of cities, the primate and the rank-size, both of which are represented by Figure 1. The case of Guatemala is used to illustrate the former, and the United States the latter.

4. Figure 1 presents the level and pace of urbanization in sixteen countries in 1940 and 1960. The selection—even though restricted by the availability of data—offers a general panorama of urbanization in countries in diverse states of development and in different regions of the world.

5. Traditionally, the level of urbanization of a territorial unity is measured through "degree of urbanization." This is defined as the proportion of urban population to total population. Commonly, for international comparisons, population is considered urban in localities of 20,000 or more inhabitants, as in the cited case. In the internal analysis of Mexico, the second and third sections of this work, a limit of 15,000 inhabitants is applied. This division is the result of a specific study of the subject. See Unikel (1968).

6. By "urban structure" is understood the hierarchy of a country's urban communities according to population size.

7. It is believed that log-normal presentation of urban structure expresses with greater clarity the "rank-size" and "primate" prototype cases than semi-logarithmic or logarithmic figures are able to do. For more detail, see Berry (1965).

8. In this system, cities are classed according to a distribution in which the population of the largest city is double that of the second, triple that of the third, and has a population n times greater than that of the city of rank n. For greater detail, see Stewart (1960).

9. The index of primacy expresses the degree to which the principal city predominates in population over the following n cities. Its numerical expression is:

$$I_p(n) = \frac{P_1}{P_2 + P_3 + P_4 + \ldots + P_n}$$

in which $I_p(n)$ is the index of primacy of n cities, and $P_1, P_2, P_3, P_4 \ldots P_n$ are populations of the cities corresponding to ranks $1, 2, 3, \ldots, n$.

10. Berry (1965: 143). This author distinguishes three types of urban structure; primate, intermediate, and rank-size rule.

11. The numerical expression of the index of urbanization is the following:

$$I_u = \frac{1}{4} \left(\frac{U_1}{P} + \frac{U_2}{P} + \frac{U_3}{P} + \frac{U_4}{P} \right) 100\%$$

$$= G(0.25 \, p_1 + 0.50 \, p_2 + 0.75 \, p_3 + p_4) \, 100\%$$

$$= (G) \cdot (E \text{ factor}) \, 100\%$$

in which U_1, U_2, U_3, U_4 are population in localities of 15,000 or more, 20,000 or more, 50,000 or more, and 100,000 or more inhabitants, respectively; P is the total population of the country or of the territorial unity studied; G is the degree of urbanization (U_1/P); $p_1, p_2, p_3,$ and p_4 are the participations with respect to the urban population of the population at intervals of 15–20,000, 20–50,000, 50–100,000, and 100,000 or more inhabitants, respectively. The participations considered, as indicated in the numerical expression, constitute what has been called the E factor, an indicator of urban structure. It should be noted that the number of intervals which make up the index is arbitrary; nevertheless, this number was considered more convenient for analysis than the two and six intervals previously tested. Similarly, it is important to note that the "index" only attempts to quantify the different levels of urbanization of one or more territorial unities in the years studied.

12. The change in "degree" explained 86 and 90 percent of the variation in the index of urbanization in the first and second decades, respectively. On the other hand, the weight of the E factor was reduced from 10 to 8 percent, and the combined weight of both also decreased from 4 to 2 percent. These figures were calculated by means of the following expression:

$$I = G \cdot \triangle E + E \cdot \triangle G + \triangle E \cdot \triangle G$$

(See the definition of terms in note 11.) The limited dynamism of the E factor is due, among other things, to the fact that cities larger than 100,000 inhabitants have been losing importance relative to urban centers of lesser size.

13. Much can be said regarding the definitions, applications, and methods used to delimit urban areas. See the diverse studies of J. Gibbs, M. Maçura, G. Goudswaard, O. Boustedt, as well as that of the General Registry Office and of the U.S. Bureau of the Census, in Gibbs (1961: 14–73); the lack in Mexico of data at the local level, however, concerning occupation, density of population and construction, and urban characteristics in general makes extremely difficult the use of relatively complex methods. Considering the necessity of relying on the population figures,

even approximate, of principal urban areas of the country, it was decided—in accordance with information available, i.e., census statistics as well as cartographic and aerial photogrametric material—to apply contiguity and accessibility as basic criteria for determining the localities which compose, together with the central city, urban areas. These two criteria connote the occupational dependency of the peripheral population upon the central city, as well as the continual movement—or the great possibility thereof—of people and goods to and from the central city. This procedure has been recommended by the United Nations (1950: 4) and Elizaga (1961: 11). Greater availability of information permitted obtaining the population of urban areas in more detailed and trustworthy form for 1960, particularly in the case of Mexico City.

14. For the purposes of this study, localities have been divided into four classes: rural (less than 5,000 inhabitants), mixed-rural (from 5,000 to 10,000 inhabitants), mixed-urban (from 10,000 to 15,000 inhabitants), and urban (15,000 or more inhabitants). See Unikel (1968).

15. The measurement of this phenomenon is laborious and difficult to carry out with exactitude due to the scarcity of adequate information available at the time of the censuses. It is considered that the figures obtained constitute an acceptable approximation of the real urban population. Of the 418,074 added in 1940–1950, 29,371 correspond to four localities reclassified as urban; the rest was incorporated into existing cities. From 1950 to 1960, all such integration took place into existing cities.

16. This population corresponds to urban localities in 1960, with the exception of the two in Oaxaca for which data were not available. Calculation of natural and social growth was based on vital statistics of municipalities with urban localities in 1960. To obtain natural growth at the locality level it was supposed that it shared in the growth of the municipality in the same proportion as it shared in the municipality's total population. Social growth was calculated using the vital-statistics method, starting with the compensatory equation:

$$P_1 = P_0 + (B - D) + (I - E)$$

in which P_1 and P_0 are the population in the final and initial years of the period in each locality, $(B - D)$ natural growth, and $(I - E)$ social growth. $(I - E)$ was obtained by subtraction. In spite of the limitations implied by use of this method, tests achieved with vital statistics assured the reliability of results obtained. Nevertheless, in a few cases, the mean annual increase is considered to be considerably above or below what is reasonable to expect and therefore social growth should be taken with the proper reservations.

17. This increase may be explained on the basis of the hypothesis that the strong migratory current of the 1940–1950 decade altered the age structure of the urban population and therefore the rates of natural growth of said population. In addition, a marked fall in the mortality rate was noted in 1950–1960.

18. The basis of the assumption concerning natural growth is grounded upon the significant increase in the rate of natural growth of the country's population from 1960 to 1967 and the probability—according to the studies of Raúl Benítez—that rural-urban differential fertility has been maintained to date.

19. The approximate rates of annual growth, 1930–1960, of the 50 most populated cities of Latin America indicate the following: of the 22 cities with more than 500,000 inhabitants in 1960 (or close to 1960), 12 acknowledged a rate of annual growth higher than the mean rate of the 50 (3.6 percent), among them the three Mexican cities—Mexico City, Guadalajara, and Monterrey. Of the ten cities of more than 1,000,000 inhabitants in 1960, only Caracas, Lima, and Bogotá surpassed Mexico City; notwithstanding, Mexico City grew at greater speed than the 3 remaining cities of more than two million, Rio de Janeiro, São Paulo, and Buenos Aires. See Cole and Twigg (1966: 38, Table 5.1).

20. 63 percent in 1940–1950 and 73 percent in the following decade of localities of very high attraction pertained to the said northern border states, outstanding among which were Sonora and Tamaulipas, entities having a high socio-economic level.

21. Such a consideration is based upon the hypothesis that localities of extremely reduced population, save for exceptions, have a precarious level of living, lack elementary public services, are frequently geographically isolated, and offer limited sources of income, vulnerable to diverse external factors. In synthesis, such localities demonstrate characteristic conditions of economic instability, making their population a potential source of migrants.

22. A "rural level" index, similar to the "index of urbanization" previously explained, was constructed using the following numerical expression:

$$I_r = (1/5) \ (R_{1/P} + R_{2/P} + R_{3/P} + R_{4/P} + R_{5/P}) \ 100\%$$

in which R_1, R_2, R_3, R_4, and R_5, are the population of localities of under 100, 500, 1,000, 2,500, and 5,000 inhabitants, respectively; P is the total population of the unit studied. Similarly, the "rural level" index is equivalent to $I_r = R \times$ (percentage of rural population). The R factor expresses the greatest weight one desires to give to localities of lesser population.

23. Analyzing the cases of uninhabited localities and those "enumerated with others," one arrives at the consideration that such a drastic reduction in the number and population residing in localities of under 100 inhabitants is doubtful. It gives greater possibility of a reduction only in the participation of the total population, which, however, was significant, since it descended from 10.2 to 4.5 percent from 1940 to 1960. (See Table 13.) Regarding localities "enumerated with others," many indications suggest that censuses are not comparable in this aspect. Although the precise reasons for enumerating some localities with others are not known, these reasons appear in any case to change from one year to the next, as the great variations in the data indicate. So far as the number of uninhabited localities is concerned, this figure almost doubled between 1940 and 1960, implying that in this period approximately 10,000 localities were abandoned. This would certainly serve as an element to explain why the number of small localities is diminishing.

24. The 1950 census (by indicating with which locality localities "enumerated with others" were grouped) reveals that in the majority of cases they were enumerated with larger localities.

25. The rate of urbanization was calculated according to the following expression:

$$T_u = 2(I_1 - I_0) \ / \ (I_1 + I_0) \cdot 1/n \cdot 100$$

This is equivalent to the rate of mean annual increase in the index of urbanization, since I_1 and I_0 are the indexes of urbanization at the end and beginning of the period. This expression was formulated in accordance with that presented by the United Nations based on degree of urbanization. See United Nations (1964: 40).

26. This conclusion was noted in the section of the international analysis in which the rate was calculated on the basis of degree of urbanization. The fact that "index" is used instead of "degree" does not alter this conclusion.

27. See the declaration presented by N. V. Sovani as moderator of the A8 meeting of the World Population Conference in Belgrade in United Nations (1966: 169–174).

28. In 1940 (Table 15) the five states additional to the Federal District were: Jalisco, Nuevo León, Puebla, Veracruz, and Tamaulipas. In 1960, the seven entities additional to the Federal District were the same, with the exception of Puebla, and Chihuahua, Guanajuato, and Baja California Norte. If the analysis is extended to the 10 states of greatest participation in the country's level of urbanization, it may be observed that in 1940 they contributed 87.5 and in 1960, 81.7 percent. It is important to point out that of the 10 states, 4 are from the northern border in 1940,

and 5 in 1960. In accordance with their relative participation in the "index," the states of the northern border contributed 16.0 and 20.7 percent, respectively, and therefore their participation together with the Federal District was two-thirds of the country's level of urbanization.

29. The standard deviation of the index of urbanization increased from 17 to 21 in the 1940–1960 period. This movement was due to the fact that the non-weighted average of the index of urbanization rose rapidly in absolute terms, as a result of increases in the "index" of highly-urbanized entities which maintained their elevated participation in the index. The remaining states, even though as a whole they had a more accelerated rate of urbanization, were made up of states of such low levels that increases in absolute terms were less than those recorded in the national average.

30. This inference is based on a preliminary test in which ranks occupied by each state were compared, according to level of urbanization and of development, in 1940 as well as in 1960. The rank correlations, +0.967 in 1940 and +0.977 in 1960, indicate a high degree of correspondence between both hierarchies and, certainly, an elevated association between both phenomena. Information regarding the level of state socio-economic development was obtained from Calixto Rangel Contla (1965), El desarrollo diferencial de México (1940–1960), tesis profesional, Escuela National de Ciencias Políticas y Sociales, Universidad Nacional Autónoma de México, pp. 133–134.

31. The following states: Federal District, Jalisco, Nuevo León, Puebla, Veracruz, and Tamaulipas had annual rates of urbanization, in the 1940–1950 period, of less than the mean national rate, and occupied, in that order, the first six places in the level of urbanization in 1940. From 1950 to 1960, this phenomenon was repeated in the Federal District, Puebla, Veracruz, Tamaulipas, Coahuila, and Durango, which occupied in 1950, respectively, the first, and from the fourth to the eighth places in the country's level of urbanization. Jalisco and Nuevo León were the two principal exceptions; having been second and third in the "level," they urbanized more rapidly than the national mean. The accelerated growth of Guadalajara and Monterrery contributed to this phenomenon.

32. The rank correlation in 1940–1950 and 1950–1960 between the increase in urban population by reclassification and the percentage of mixed population at the end of both decades resulted in +0.03 and +0.12, respectively. Similarly, a significant association is not observed between the first variable and the level of urbanization at the end of the periods, or with net migratory balance by state.

33. In the case of Mexico City's urban area, as in Torreón, calculations were selected using the two contiguous federative states which contain parts of such urban unities.

34. The author of this work applies non-parametric measurements of concentration based upon concepts of the theory of information which permit determining intra- and inter-regional demographic concentration. See Pedro Uribe, Jr. (1967: 151–180).

35. The two categories mentioned are the result of the impact of net migratory balance. Although at this point it was not possible to estimate its amount at the state level, because of limitations presented in attempting to apply the vital-statistics method—which was used in the case of localities—the calculations are considered reliable only to define the impact of net migratory balance.

REFERENCES

Berry, Brian J. L. (1965) "City size distributions and economic development." Pp. 138–152 in John Friedmann and William Alonso (eds.) *Regional Development and Planning.* Cambridge: M.I.T. Press.

BREESE, GERALD (1966) *Urbanization in Newly Developing Countries.* Englewood Cliffs: Prentice-Hall.

BROWNING, HARLEY (1962) Urbanization in Mexico. Unpublished Ph.D. dissertation, University of California, Berkeley.

Centro de Estudios Económicos y Demográficos (1967) *El proceso de urbanización en México: anteproyecto de investigación.* El Colegio de México, April (mimeo.).

COLE, J. P. and TWIGG, B. (1966) "Notes on the towns of Latin America." *Bulletin of Quantitative Data for Geographers* (Nottingham) 4 (June).

CONTLA, CALIXTO RANGEL (1965) El desarrollo diferencial de México (1940–1960). Professional thesis, Escuela National de Ciencias Políticas y Sociales, Universidad Nacional Autónoma de México.

DAVIS, KINGSLEY and HILDA HERTZ GOLDEN (1957) "Urbanization and the development of pre-industrial areas." In P. Hatt and A. J. Reiss, Jr. (eds.) *Cities and Society.* New York: Free Press.

DORSELAER, JAIME and AFONSO GREGORY (1962) *La Urbanización en América Latina.* Bogotá: FERES.

ELDRIDGE, HOPE T. (1963) "The process of urbanization." Pp. 338–343 in Joseph Spengler and Otis Duncan (eds.) *Demographic Analysis.* New York: Free Press.

————— (1954) "Urban theory and concepts in relation to the definition of urban agglomerations. Pp. 581–586 in *Proceedings of the World Population Conference,* meeting 9, Rome.

ELIZAGA, JUAN (1961) *Distribución espacial de las poblaciones.* Santiago: CELADE (mimeo.). Summary of notes for course given by author.

FRIEDMANN, JOHN (1956) "The concept of a planning region." *Land Economics* 32 (February).

GERMANI, GINO (1963) "Urbanización, secularización y desarrollo económico. *Revista Mexicana de Sociología* 25, No. 2: 625–646.

GIBBS, JACK, ed. (1961) *Urban Research Methods.* Princeton: D. Van Nostrand.

HATT, P. and A. J. REISS, JR., eds. (1957) *Cities and Society.* New York: Free Press.

HAUSER, PHILIP (1965) "Urbanization: an overview." In P. Hauser and L. F. Schnore (eds.) *The Study of Urbanization.* New York: John Wiley.

HUERTA MALDONADO, M. (1960) "El nivel de vida en México." *Revista Mexicana de Sociología* 22 No. 2 (May-August): 463–527.

NEUTZE, G. (1965) *Economic Policy and the Size of Cities.* Canberra: The Australian National University.

Secretaría de Industria y Comercio, Dirección General de Estadistica (1965) *Cálculos de la población de las Estados Unidos Mexicanos, al 30 de junio de cada año.* Mexico.

STEWART, CHARLES, JR. (1960) "The size and spacing of cities." Pp. 240–256 in H. Mayer and C. Kohn (eds.) *Readings in Urban Geography.* Chicago: University of Chicago Press.

UNIKEL, LUIS (1968) "Ensayo sobre una nueva clasificación de población rural y urbana en México." *Demografía y Economía* 2, No. 4.

UNITED NATIONS (1950) *Data on Urban and Rural Population in Recent Censuses.* Population Studies No. 8. New York.

—— (1964) *Administrative Problems of Rapid Urban Growth in the Arab States.* New York.

—— (1966) *World Population Conference, 1965.* Vol. I, Summary Report. New York.

URIBE, PEDRO, JR. (1967) 'Concentración demográfica y estructura urbana: un enfoque vía teoría de la información." *Demografía y Economía* 1, No. 2: 151–180.

YATES, P. L. (1960) *Desarrollo regional de México.* Mexico: Banco de México.

APPENDIX

URBAN STUDIES CENTERS IN LATIN AMERICA

EDITORS' NOTE: The following list does not pretend to be exhaustive, and we ask the indulgence of institutions omitted. Official government entities have been excluded. If a center has been omitted, or mistakes made, we should appreciate being informed so that oversights may be corrected in the next volume. For more detailed, though somewhat dated, information, see James H. Street and Guido G. Wiegend, *Urban Planning and Development Centers in Latin America: Report of a Study Tour* (New Brunswick: Rutgers, The State University, 1967).

Argentina

Centro de Estudios Urbanos y Regionales (CEUR)
Instituto Torcuato Di Tella
Virrey del Pino, 3257
Buenos Aires

Secretaría Ejecutiva
Consejo Latinoamericano de Ciencias Sociales (CLACSO)
Florida 142, 4° piso B
Buenos Aires

Bolivia

Secretariado Nacional de Estudios Sociales
Conferencia Episcopal Boliviana
Casilla 2309
La Paz

Brazil

Centro de Estudos de Planejamento Urbano e Regional
Faculdade de Arquitetura
Universidade Federal de Pernambuco
Av. Conde de Bôa Vista, 1424
Recife, Pernambuco

Centro de Estudos Urbanos e Regionales
Instituto Brasileiro de Administração Municipal
Fundação Getúlio Vargas
Rua Miguel Pereira 34
Rio de Janeiro ZC-02

Centro Latinoamericano de Pesquisas em Ciências Sociais
Rua Dona Mariana 138
Botafogo, Rio de Janeiro ZC-02

Centro de Pequisa e Estudos Urbanistícos
Faculdade de Arquitetura e Urbanismo
Universidade de São Paulo
Rua Maranhão 88
São Paulo

Faculdade Cândido Mendes
Praça Quinze Novembro 101
Rio de Janeiro

Instituto Brasileiro de Administração Pública
Fundação Getúlio Vargas
Praia de Botafogo 186
Rio de Janeiro

Chile

Centro Interdisciplinario de Desarrollo Urbano y Regional (CIDU)
Universidad Católica de Chile
Nueva de Lyon 150
(Casilla 16002)
Santiago

Centro para el Desarrollo Económico y Social de América Latina (DESAL)
Av. Miguel Claro 127
Santiago

Economic Commission for Latin America (ECLA–CEPAL)
Providencia 871
Santiago

Facultad Latinoamericana de Ciencias Sociales (FLACSO)
Av. J.P. Alessandri 832
Santiago

Sociedad Chilena de Planificación y Desarrollo (PLANDES)
Moneda 973
Santiago

Colombia

Asociación Colombiana de Facultades de Medicina
Estudios Socio-demográficos
Calle 45A No. 12-79
Bogotá

Centro Interamericano de Vivienda y Planeamiento
Organización de los Estados Americanos
Apartado Aéreo 6209
Bogotá

Centro de Investigaciones para el Desarrollo (CID)
Universidad Nacional de Colombia
Bogotá

Oficina de Investigación
Federación Internacional de los Institutos Católicos de Investigaciones
    Sociales y Socio-religiosas (FERES)
Bogotá

Mexico

Centro de Estudios Económicos y Demográficos
El Colegio de México
Guanajuato 125
México, D.F.

Peru

Instituto de Estudios Peruanos (IEP)
Horacio Urteaga 694
Lima

Instituto de Planificación de Lima (IPL)
Universidad Nacional de Ingeniería del Perú
Lima

Puerto Rico

Secretaría General
Sociedad Interamericana de Planificación
Apartado 1729
San Juan 00903

Venezuela

Centro de Estudios del Desarrollo (CENDES)
Universidad Central de Venezuela
Edificio Azovac
Av. Neverí, Colinas de Bellomonte (Apartado 6622)
Caracas

Instituto de Urbanismo
Facultad de Arquitectura
Universidad Central de Venezuela
Caracas

Other

Inter-American Municipal Organization
International Trade Mart
2 Canal Street
New Orleans, Louisiana, USA

Secretariado Iberoamericano de Municipios
Instituto de Estudios de Administración Local
Joaquín García Morato, 7
Madrid 10, Spain

ABOUT THE EDITORS

FRANCINE F. RABINOVITZ is Assistant Professor of Political Science at the University of California at Los Angeles. She has served as a consultant on metropolitan politics to the Assistant Secretary of Metropolitan Development of the Department of Housing and Urban Development and consultant to the International Urbanization project of the Institute of Public Administration. She is a former member of the research staffs of the Center for Latin American Studies at the University of Florida, the Rutgers Urban Studies Center, and the Harvard-MIT Joint Center for Urban Studies. She is the author of two books which systematically compare the politics of cities: *City Politics and Planning* (an analysis of six American cities), and *Urban Government for Greater Stockholm* (co-authored with Hans Kalmfors and Daniel Alesch).

FELICITY M. TRUEBLOOD is Assistant Professor of Comprehensive English and a member of the Latin American Faculty of the University of Florida. She is Editor of the *Southeastern Latin Americanist,* the quarterly bulletin of the Southeastern Conference on Latin American Studies, and previously served for five years as Assistant Editor of the *Journal of Inter-American Studies.* She has been a consultant and translator to various university presses specializing in Latin American publications, and has published translations of Spanish language fiction and non-fiction.

The authors have previously collaborated in the preparation of *Latin American Political Systems in an Urban Setting: A Preliminary Bibliography* (Center for Latin American Studies, University of Florida, 1967), with Charles J. Savio.

ABOUT THE AUTHORS

HARLEY L. BROWNING is Associate Professor of Sociology and Director of the Population Research Center at the University of Texas at Austin. His Ph.D. is from the University of California at Berkeley. His research interests over the past decade have been concentrated on Latin America, specifically Mexico. Urbanization, internal migration, and the transformation of the labor force in the process of economic development are his particular concerns. Currently he is in the process of finishing a book, along with his co-authors Jorge Balan and Elizabeth Jelin, on the Monterrey Mobility Project.

WAYNE A. CORNELIUS, JR. is a Ph.D. candidate at the Department of Political Science, Stanford University. He is currently in Mexico under a National Science Foundation dissertation grant, conducting a comparative survey study of migrant political attitudes and behavior. He was previously the recipient of Danforth and Woodrow Wilson fellowships. He is the author of "Urbanization as an Agent in Latin American Political Instability: The Case of Mexico" (published in the *American Political Science Review*), "Crisis, Political Entrepreneurship, and Problem-solving in the Mexican Revolution," forthcoming in Gabriel A. Almond, ed., *Historical Crises and Political Development,* and (with Richard Fagen) was co-editor (and co-author) of *Political Power in Latin America: Seven Confrontations* (1969).

ROLAND H. EBEL is Associate Professor of Political Science, Tulane University. He received a Social Science Research Council grant for Latin American Studies (1965–1966) and a Tulane-Ford Summer Research grant in 1967. His publications include several articles (in English and in Spanish) on Guatemalan politics, and a research study published in

1969, *The Process of Political Modernization in Three Guatemalan Communities.*

WALTRAUT FEINDT has had extensive experience in survey research in Germany, was awarded his M.A. degree in Sociology from the University of California at Berkeley, and is Special Researcher at the Population Research Center at the University of Texas at Austin.

WILLIAM L. FLINN, Assistant Professor of Rural Sociology and Chairman of the Department of Sociology Extension at the University of Wisconsin (Madison), has conducted several studies on the migration process in Colombia. He was a Fulbright Professor in the Faculty of Sociology at National University in Bogotá, Colombia, in 1964–65 and holds a Ph.D. from the Ohio State University. With A. Eugene Havens, Flinn co-authored *Internal Colonialism and Structural Change in Colombia.*

JOHN FRIEDMANN is Professor and Chairman of the Urban Planning Program in the School of Architecture and Urban Planning of the University of California at Los Angeles. He was formerly Director of the Ford Foundation's Urban and Regional Development Advisory Program in Chile, and a Visiting Professor at the Interdisciplinary Center for Urban Development (CIDU) of the Catholic University of Chile. Prior to his stay in Chile, Dr. Friedmann was on the faculty of MIT—where he was actively involved in the planning of the Guayana region of Venezuela. In addition to numerous articles and chapters in books, Dr. Friedmann is the author of *Venezuela: From Doctrine to Dialogue* (1965), *Regional Development Policy* (1966), and *Urban and Regional Development in Chile* (1969). He edited a special issue of the *Journal of the American Institute of Planners* on "Regional Development and Planning," and co-edited (with William Alonso) *Regional Development and Planning: A Reader* (1964).

BRUCE H. HERRICK is Assistant Professor of Economics, University of California at Los Angeles, and a consulting economist. His recent field work includes extensive experience in Chile—where he served as Consultant to the Chilean Ministry of Public Health (under an AID grant); he had previously served as a Visiting Professor in the Escuela de Ciencias Económicas and Research Associate of the Instituto de Economía y Planificación, both at the University of Chile. In addition to several articles and book reviews in both English and Spanish journals, Dr. Herrick is the author of *Urban Migration and Economic Development in Chile.* He is also the contributing editor in economics to the *Handbook of Latin American Studies* (Hispanic Foundation, Library of Congress) for the countries of Chile, Peru, Bolivia, Paraguay and Uruguay.

RICHARD M. MORSE is Professor of History and Chairman of the Council on Latin American Studies at Yale University. He is the author of *From Community to Metropolis: A Biography of São Paulo, Brazil* and *The Bandeirantes: The Historical Role of the Brazilian Pathfinders*, as well as numerous articles—including "Latin American Cities: Aspects of Function and Structure" (which originally appeared in *Comparative Studies in Society and History*) and "Recent Research on Latin American Urbanization" (originally published in the *Latin American Research Review*). Dr. Morse has been the recipient of a Guggenheim Fellowship, and a Social Science Research Council grant; and is currently spending a year at the Center for Advanced Study in the Behavioral Sciences.

CHARLES J. SAVIO is currently doing field work in Venezuela under a Fulbright-Hays Fellowship. He had previously lived in a barrio in Caracas, while in the Peace Corps from 1964 to 1966. Mr. Savio received a B.S. in Chemical Engineering from Stanford in 1958, and was awarded his M.A. in Political Science-Latin American Studies from the University of Florida in 1969. His publications include a master's thesis on "The Electoral Politics of Metropolitan Caracas: The 1958 and 1963 Presidential Elections" and (with Francine F. Rabinovitz and Felicity M. Trueblood) *Latin American Political Systems in an Urban Setting: A Preliminary Bibliography*.

LUIS UNIKEL is currently in charge of the research program on "Urban Development in Mexico" at the Center for Economic and Demographic Studies of El Colegio de México. He is also a professor for the master's degree course on urban and regional planning of the Universidad Nacional Autónoma de México (UNAM). He received his civil engineering degree from UNAM, and his master's degree (MCP) in city planning from MIT (1958). Since then, he has worked for the Puerto Rico Industrial Development Company (1958–60), the Planning Department of the Ministry of the Presidency, the Hydraulic Commission of the Valley of Mexico (1960–1965), as well as for other government and private agencies. Ing. Unikel has taught courses on urban development at the School of Social and Political Studies, UNAM, at the Universidad Iberoamericana, and at the School for Municipal Engineers. His published works include: "El tamaño óptimo de las ciudades" (1962); "La urbanización y la zona metropolitana de la ciudad de México" (1966); "Ensayo sobre una nueva clasificación de población rural y urbana en México," "El proceso de urbanización en México: Distribución y crecimiento de la población urbana" y "La urbanización y la planificación urbana en México" (1968).